CICERO: ON FATE (De Fato)
BOETHIUS: THE CONSOLATION OF PHILOS

But yit I can not bult it to the bren,
As can the holy doctor Augustyn,
Or **Boece**, or the bisshop Bradwardyn,
Whether that Goddes worthy forwetyng
Streigneth me needely for to do a thing,
(Needely clepe I simple necesité),
Or elles if fre choys be graunted me
To do that same thing, or to do it nought,
though God forwot it, er that it was wrought;
Or if his wityng streigneth never a deel,
But by necessité condicionel ...

(Chaucer, *The Canterbury Tales*)

ARIS & PHILLIPS CLASSICAL TEXTS

CICERO

On Fate

& Boethius: The Consolation of Philosophy
IV.5-7, V

Edited with an introduction, translation and commentary by

R. W. Sharples

Aris & Phillips is an imprint of Oxbow Books

First published in the United Kingdom in 1991. Reprinted 2015 by
OXBOW BOOKS
10 Hythe Bridge Street, Oxford OX1 2EW

and in the United States by
OXBOW BOOKS
908 Darby Road, Havertown, PA 19083

Paperback Edition: ISBN 978-0-85668-476-0

A CIP record for this book is available from the British Library

For a complete list of Aris & Phillips titles, please contact:

UNITED KINGDOM
Oxbow Books
Telephone (01865) 241249
Fax (01865) 794449
Email: oxbow@oxbowbooks.com
www.oxbowbooks.com

UNITED STATES OF AMERICA
Oxbow Books
Telephone (800) 791-9354
Fax (610) 853-9146
Email: queries@casemateacademic.com
www.casemateacademic.com/oxbow

Oxbow Books is part of the Casemate Group

Printed and bound by CPI Group (UK) Ltd, Croydon, CR0 4YY

CONTENTS

PREFACE

The two texts considered here are linked by more than one common feature. They are examples of the writings of the two men who did more to communicate Greek philosophy to the Latin-speaking West than anyone else in antiquity, with the possible exceptions of Augustine and (in one particular field) Lucretius. They are works which reflect two very different branches of the tradition that goes back to Plato, or to Plato's Socrates. Cicero writes as a follower of the sceptical New Academy, which derived its readiness to challenge dogmatic positions from Socrates even if its belief that certainty is impossible was not one he would have shared; Boethius' *Consolation* is in the tradition of the revived dogmatic Platonism of the Imperial period, a Platonism that welcomed, and made use of, ideas from Aristotle as well as from Plato. They are works of philosophy written by two men each of whom played a part in the public life of their times – and paid with their own lives for doing so; though there is the difference that Boethius' *Consolation of Philosophy* was written when its author was already under sentence of death, while Cicero's *On Fate* was written in haste as its author was planning the return to the political arena that was ultimately to be his downfall. Above all, however – and this is the justification for uniting the two texts, or rather one fragmentary text and one partial extract, in this single volume – they represent two stages in a story, the story of man's attempt to understand whether he is or is not in control of his own destiny; this story in one guise or another pervades the literature of antiquity, and is not finished yet.

That said, there are also great differences between the two texts. Cicero's treatise *On Fate* survives in fragmentary form only; we may have about two-thirds of the whole text, but it lacks its beginning and its end, and there are major gaps which seriously affect our interpretation of the whole. Questions concerning the literary form and structure of the treatise as originally composed, of Cicero's sources and of philosophical interpretation are here all closely intertwined with one another, giving this work a particular fascination over and above that of the subject-matter itself; but, while it has been extensively quarried for technical discussions, and extensive extracts have been included in source-books, English readers have been poorly served until now as far as the availability in a single volume of a reliable continuous text *and* translation is concerned.

The situation with Boethius' *Consolation* could hardly be more different. It is one of the major works of world literature; the work that – along perhaps with Augustine's *City of God* – marks the boundary between ancient and medieval thought; a work which profoundly influenced the thought of the Middle Ages; a work translated into English by, among others, Alfred the Great, Chaucer, and Elizabeth the First. It is a daunting prospect to write about such a work, a work moreover that can be approached from many different perspectives: its relation to earlier Latin literature both in prose and in poetry, its relation to Boethius' philosophical interests on the one hand and his Christian beliefs on the other, its influence on later thought and literature. In a book of the present size it would scarcely be possible to do justice to all these perspectives; given the reason for including Cicero and Boethius together in this book in the first place, I hope that my comments may at least be helpful for those who wish to consider the part of the *Consolation* here included as a stage in a particular philosophical debate.

That, too, must be the justification for violating Boethius' design by including only a part of the whole, even though it is the final part and culmination. I can only hope that those who read the end of the work here will want to go on and read what precedes. Boethius does mark a new stage in the discussion by Philosophy's observation that "You summon me to a matter which involves the greatest enquiry of all"; the reason for including the end of book 4 as well as book 5 is that it introduces the question of how fortune and freedom are to be reconciled with the divine providence which has formed the topic of the discussion since 3.12.

- - - -

It may be desirable to comment briefly on what the present book is, and on what it is not, attempting to do. The Latin *texts* presented here are based on published texts and published reports of the MSS (for details, cf. Introduction §14). No attempt has been made to construct a new text by going back to the original MSS, which according to some criteria would alone justify description as an "edition". My aim has rather been, where Cicero is concerned, to make a better Latin text than heretofore available to those who want more than a plain text and whose first language is English; and in the case of Boethius, to provide text and translation on a similar basis as a supplement to the Cicero. (There is little need to point out that my translations of Boethius' poems make no pretence to being poetry themselves.) The *commentary*, too, is offered not so much as an exhaustive treatment of all the philosophical issues raised by the texts, but rather as an aid to understanding for the readers, not exclusively specialists in the relevant fields, at whom this series is aimed – though it is hoped that specialists too may find something of value here. My indebtedness on many points to the commentaries of Yon and Bayer on Cicero, and of Gruber and O'Donnell on Boethius, will be apparent to the reader, and I hope general acknowledgement here may help to avoid repeated acknowledgements on particular points which would distract the reader. Not every variant reading recorded in the apparatus has been discussed in the Commentary; readers who are interested in textual matters will be able to consult the critical apparatus, and to discuss every such issue in the Commentary could be distracting for others. The *bibliography* reflects the aims of the book as a whole; I have not attempted to give equal coverage to all aspects of the study of Boethius, but have concentrated on literature that is particularly relevant to the interpretation of the section here included as a contribution to a philosophical debate. The bibliography, and still more the citations in Introduction and Commentary, are selective; I have attempted not to give detailed references to every discussion in the secondary literature of each particular issue, but rather to give prominence to those discussions which will be most useful and accessible to the readers for whom the book is intended.

My interest in Cicero's treatise and Boethius' arguments began while I was studying the issues of freewill and determinism for what became a Cambridge Ph.D. thesis (1977) on another treatise *On Fate,* that of Alexander of Aphrodisias. My thanks are due to the successive supervisors of that thesis, the late Professor W.K.C. Guthrie and Professor J.D.G. Evans and G.E.R. Lloyd; to Professor Richard Sorabji for much discussion on these and related topics over the years; to Professor Malcolm Willcock both for suggesting the present book in the first place and to him and to Alan Griffiths for reading through the whole before publication. Thanks are also due to the students with whom I discussed Cicero's treatise and my text and translation of it during the year 1989-90; Jim Evans of King's College London and Fedja Dalagija, Padraic Daly and Christianne van der Lee of University College London; and to many others with whom I have talked and corresponded about these topics at various times, especially Pier Luigi Donini, Alan Douglas, Woldemar Görler, Hans Gottschalk, Alan Griffiths, Mario Mignucci, Letitia Panizza, David Sedley, Anne Sheppard and Malcolm Willcock. My thanks are especially due to David Sedley for showing me a draft of Sedley [1993] and allowing me to refer to some of the points made in it before its publication, and also for showing me some of his notes on Cicero's treatise. The responsibility for the use I have made of the advice others have given me, and for remaining errors and infelicities is of course my own. Above all my thanks are due as ever to my wife Grace and daughter Elizabeth for their unfailing encouragement and support.

University College London
August 1991

This second impression is substantially unchanged in content, but the opportunity has been taken to correct an error in the apparatus on p.144 and to note some additions to the bibliography.

University College London
July 1996

NOTE ON ABBREVIATIONS AND CITATIONS

Modern works that have a general relevance to the topics of this book have been listed in the Bibliography and are generally referred to in the body of the book by author's name and, where required, date of publication. With the readers for whom this book is primarily intended in mind, the titles of ancient works have been given in English wherever there is any reasonable and readily identifiable English equivalent for the original title. It may be helpful to note some frequently used abbreviations here:

CCSL	*Corpus Christianorum, Series Latina* (Turnhout).
DG	H. Diels (ed.), *Doxographi Graeci,* Berlin 1879.
DK	H. Diels and W. Kranz (eds.), *Fragmente der Vorsokratiker,* ^{7}Berlin 1954
EK	L. Edelstein and I.G. Kidd (eds.), *Posidonius, vol. 1, The Fragments* (second edition) and I.G. Kidd, *Posidonius, vol.2, The Commentary,* Cambridge 1989.
KRS	G.S. Kirk, J.E. Raven and M. Schofield, *The Presocratic Philosophers,* Cambridge ^{2}1983.
LS	A.A. Long and D.N. Sedley, *The Hellenistic Philosophers,* Cambridge 1987.
PG	J.-P. Migne (ed.), *Patrologiae cursus, series Graeca.*
PL	J.-P. Migne (ed.), *Patrologiae cursus, series Latina.*
SVF	H. von Arnim, *Stoicorum Veterum Fragmenta,* Leipzig 1903–5.
Boethius	*On* On Interpretation^1, *On* On Interpretation^2 = Boethius' *first* and *second commentary* on Aristotle's *On Interpretation:* cited according to the Teubner edition by C. Meiser, Leipzig 1880.

References to Cicero's works are given by section, rather than by chapter numbers; thus the end of *On Fate* itself, for example, will be referred to as §48 rather than as chapter XX. (Similarly for Pliny the Elder.) Boethius' *Consolation* is cited thus: V.1.2 = book V, prose 1, section 2: V m.1.2 = book V, *metrum* 1, line 2. The marginal line numbers for the text of Cicero are arranged according to the pages of this book, but those for Boethius are arranged in accordance with the prose and verse sections; this is to avoid the situation where line 2 of a poem, say, becomes line 37 because that happens to be its position on the page. Proclus' *Timaeus* commentary is cited by volume, page and line number in Diehl's Teubner edition; his *Parmenides* commentary by column and line number in the edition by V. Cousin (Paris 1864, reprinted Hildesheim 1961); and his three *opuscula (Ten Problems concerning Providence, On Providence* and *On the Existence of Evils)* by the section number *(only)* in the edition by H. Boese, Berlin 1960 (so that "*Ten Problems* 8" = <Problem 2>, section 8).

1. Cicero and the Latin reception of Greek philosophy.

1.1. It is with Cicero (and, for the Epicurean school, Lucretius) that the transfer of Greek philosophy into a Latin guise essentially begins; those Romans who had concerned themselves with Greek philosophy had previously done so in the original language, and there had in Latin only been a few Epicurean prose treatises of little stylistic merit.[1] Cicero himself justifies his work of putting Greek philosophy into Latin as a service to his country when political circumstances prevent him from serving it more directly;[2] the possession of Greek philosophical literature will bring glory to the Roman people,[3] and he argues at length against those who despise Latin literature in comparison with Greek.[4] Although in one notorious passage[5] he appears to describe his work as merely one of translation, we should not take this at face value, or assume that he follows his sources in an unoriginal way; even if not himself a philosopher of the first rank, he had studied the subject since his youth, and was certainly not unskilled in the techniques of rhetorical and forensic argument whose affinity with philosophical argument he himself emphasised.[6]

1.2. Cicero's own philosophical position was that of the New Academy.[7] Plato's earliest successors as head of the school he founded continued

---

1. Cf. Cicero, *Tusculan Disputations* 1.6, 4.6, *Letters to his Friends (ad Familiares)* 15.19.2.

2. *On Ends* 1.10, *Tusc. Disp.* 1.5, *On the Nature of the Gods* 1.7, *On Divination* 2.1, 2.4-7.

3. *On the Nature of the Gods* 1.7, *On Divination* 2.5-6.

4. *On Ends* 1.4ff.; cf. ⟨*Posterior*⟩ *Academics* 1.10.

5. *Letters to Atticus* 12.52.3: "They are copies *(apographa)*; they are done with less effort (that way); I just supply the words, of which I have a great supply." But contrast *On Ends* 1.7, and cf. Douglas [1964] 138-9 and Barnes (1985,1) 230-2. Douglas indeed argues that in technical works like *On Fate* Cicero 'had nothing of substance to add(*sc.* to the arguments), "only the words"'; but that is not the same as claiming that he was only translating. The boundary between arguments and their expression is hard to draw; it is not the same as that between a translation and an – admittedly derivative – original work.

6. See below, Commentary on §2. Nor was an interest in technical arguments concerning necessity and possibility something new for Cicero; in 46 B.C. he had opened a letter to Varro *(Letters to his Friends* 9.4) with a joke relating to Diodorus' view of possibility (see below, Introduction §3.2.4).

7. This is true, at any rate, for the period of the treatise *On Fate,* even though in his middle years he was more inclined to favour the dogmatic approach of Antiochus. Cf. J. Glucker, 'Cicero's philosophical affiliations', in J.M. Dillon and A.A. Long (eds.), *The Question of Eclecticism,* Berkeley 1987, 34-69.

the dogmatic tendencies of Plato's own later philosophy;[1] but from Arcesilaus (316-242 B.C.) onwards the Academy rather emphasised the sceptical tendencies that could also be seen in Plato's own Socratic dialogues, challenging the arguments of others rather than developing dogmatic claims of their own.[2] Particularly influential in this regard was Carneades (214-129 B.C.), the founder of the Third or New Academy, who scandalised the elder Cato by coming to Rome on an embassy in 155 B.C. and arguing for and against justice on successive days.[3] Cicero himself had studied under Antiochus of Ascalon,[4] who reacted against Academic scepticism to such an extent that he was described as almost a Stoic.[5]

1.3. Greek philosophy, especially in the Hellenistic period, had developed an elaborate technical jargon. In order to reproduce this in Latin both Cicero and Lucretius had to give existing Latin words new meanings, often using in an abstract sense words which had previously only had a concrete one.[6] Sometimes Cicero will use several words to make his

---

1. This dogmatic period was later labelled the "Old" Academy, by contrast with the "Middle" of Arcesilaus and the "New" of Carneades.

2. Cf. Cicero, *On Divination* 2.150, where Cicero says that he will follow the practice of the Academy, which consists in saying what there is to be said on each side of the question and *not* stating any judgement on one's own authority, but leaving one's audience free to decide the matter for themselves. This does not however preclude an inclination on Cicero's part for one view rather than another; see below §2.1, and Douglas [1964] 143-4. At *Tusculan Disputations* 2.9 Cicero says that the Academic approach gives the best practice in oratory (see below, Commentary on *On Fate* §3. The advocate's job, after all, is to argue a case – not just to argue for what he personally believes in.) But he *also* emphasises that presenting arguments for both sides of a question is the only way in which the *probable* truth *(veri simile)* can be discovered; so too at *Tusculan Disputations* 1.8. Both there and at *On the Nature of the Gods* 1.11 he explicitly draws the parallel with the practice of Socrates. (I am grateful to David Sedley for drawing *Tusculans* 1.8 to my attention.)

3. Lactantius, *Divine Institutes* 5.14.3-5 = LS 68M. However Schofield 61 n.27 suggests that Cicero's Academic scepticism allows him to incline to one side of the argument rather than the other, without committing himself definitely, and connects this with the changes introduced into Academic scepticism by Philo of Larisa. Plato's Socrates does after all in some dialogues combine pretty positive assertions with a continued commitment to investigating further what has been asserted; cf. *Gorgias* 509a, *Phaedo* 107b. On Philo see further H. Tarrant, *Scepticism or Platonism? The philosophy of the fourth Academy,* Cambridge 1985.

4. c.130-120 – c.68 B.C. Cicero attended his lectures in Athens in 79-78 B.C.; *De finibus* 5.1.

5. Cicero, *Lucullus* (= ⟨Prior⟩ *Academics,* 2) 132. On the question of Antiochus' possible influence on the particular treatise *On Fate,* see below Introduction §4.2.1-2.

6. For example, *comprehensio* applied to mental rather than physical grasping, *Lucullus* 2.31. Cf. below, commentary on §42, on *visum.*

meaning clear,[1] or use a periphrasis.[2] He also on occasion coined new words of his own, some of which have passed on from Latin to other western European languages and are today taken for granted; it is to Cicero that we owe our words "quality"[3] and - at least according to Seneca - "essence".[4]

1.4. Boethius too, five and a half centuries later, had consciously undertaken a programme of making Greek philosophy accessible in a Latin form; it had been his intention to translate Aristotle's works into Latin and provide commentaries on them. In the event he did not get beyond Aristotle's logical works, the *Organon;* but those translations and commentaries, obscure though their Latin sometimes is through the difficulty of rendering Aristotle's highly idiomatic and compressed Greek,[5] played a major part in determining the shape of philosophical study in the West until the renewal of acquaintance with other Aristotelian texts, first in Latin translations from Arabic and then in versions from the original Greek, in the thirteenth century. His contribution to Latin philosophical language, too, was no less than Cicero's.[6] And Boethius' work on the commentaries forms part of the foundation for the *Consolation,* even though it has the literary qualities which they lack.

2. The place of *On Fate* among Cicero's philosophical works.

2.1. The treatise *On Fate* is part of the second group of Cicero's philosophical writings, those dating from the period of Julius Caesar's ascendancy at the end of the Civil War and the period immediately after his assassination. Most of these works are on ethical topics (the *Tuscu-*

---

1. Cf. e.g. *Tusc. Disp.* 2.46, where Cicero explains that he is deliberately using several similar terms to get across a single idea.

2. Cf. *On Ends* 1.12, where *peri telôn* is rendered by *de finibus bonorum et malorum;* ibid. 3.16, where the Greek term *telika* applied to good things is rendered by *ad illud ultimum pertinentia.* Here again Cicero comments explicitly on the device he is adopting.

3. Cf. *Academics* 1.24–5, where *qualitas* is explicitly coined on the model of the Greek *poiotês* - itself coined by Plato at *Theaetetus* 182a.

4. Cf. Seneca, *Moral Letters* 58.6, citing Cicero as authority for the word *essentia.* However Quintilian (*Education of the Orator* 2.14.2, 3.6.23, 8.3.33) assigns it rather to Sergius Plautus, a Stoic of the first century A.D. On the whole issue of the rendering of Greek technical terms see also below, *On fate* §1. In the preceding paragraph I am heavily indebted to lectures by Professor F.H. Sandbach. See also, on the whole question, M. Puelma, 'Die Rezeption der Fachsprache der griechische Philosophie im Lateinischen', *Freiburger Zeitschrift für Philosophie und Theologie* 33 (1986) 45–69 (*essentia* being discussed at 61–2).

5. See further below, Introduction §10.3.

6. "It was finally Boethius who established the vocabulary of abstraction with which the schoolmen of later generations could do their work", Liebeschütz 540.

lans, On Ends and *On Duties*) or on the theory of knowledge that must underlie ethical assertions (the *Academics);* but a connected group of three treatises, *On the Nature of the Gods, On Divination* and *On Fate,* consider the relation of the gods to human affairs and problems that arise therefrom. In *On the Nature of the Gods* the Epicurean view, denying the concern of the gods with human affairs, and the Stoic view that the world is the product of divine providence, are successively stated and subjected to attack from the viewpoint of Academic scepticism; Cicero himself appears as narrator but not as a speaker, and at the end of the fictitious conversation states that the Epicurean spokesman Velleius sided with the Academic Cotta (who has been attacking the Stoic view more recently than the Epicurean), while he himself thought the Stoic Balbus had the better of the argument. Presumably this is an indication that Cicero inclines to the view that the world is providentially ordered, even if as a follower of the Academy he will not commit himself to this view without question.

2.2. In the second book of *On Divination,* however, Cicero presents himself as arguing against the Stoics on one particular issue, the reliability of divination; doing away with superstition does not mean doing away with religion.[1] And, since the Stoics based their theory of divination on their claim that everything that happens is predetermined,[2] this topic naturally leads on to discussion of determinism generally and its relation to human freedom, in the treatise *On Fate.*[3] Here too Cicero rejects the extreme Stoic position; the natural connection between different occurrences that the Stoics spoke of as "sympathy" may have *some* influence on human behaviour, but not in such a way as to remove our freedom of action altogether.[4] And while the Epicureans were right in insisting on freedom of the will, Cicero is characteristically scornful of the arguments by which they defended it, favouring the view of Carneades that free will could be defended against the Stoics

---

1. *On Divination* 2.148. But a distinction needs to be drawn, as Schofield points out, between Cicero the spokesman in book 2 of the dialogue, whose emphases in any case vary from passage to passage (Schofield 59) and Cicero the author whose concern is in part to present us with a demonstration of the Academic method of considering arguments on both sides of the question.

2. See below, Introduction §3.1.6.

3. *On Divination* 2.3: "When these things (Cicero has just referred to his *Hortensius, Academica,* and *Tusculan Disputations)* had been published three books *On the Nature of the Gods* were completed, in which the whole investigation of that topic is contained. When this had been altogether and copiously completed, we began to write *On Divination* in the present books; and if we add *On Fate* to these, as we have in mind (to do), this whole investigation will have been dealt with adequately and abundantly." Cf. also *On the Nature of the Gods* 3.19, and, on the relation between the three treatises, Schofield 48-51.

4. Cf. *On Fate* 7-11; and, on the question how favourable to the Stoics the eventual position indicated in the treatise is, below, Introduction §4.2.5.

without recourse to such arguments.[1]

2.3. The treatises *On the Nature of the Gods* and *On Divination* are in the characteristic form of the Ciceronian dialogue, a series of speeches for opposing points of view; in *On Fate* §1 Cicero explains this as enabling each person more easily to recommend his own view.[2] In the case of *On Fate* itself, however, Cicero informs us that he was prevented by circumstances from giving the work this form, and although it is set in the form of a discussion between himself and Aulus Hirtius, the consul-designate for 43 B.C., it would seem, according to what Cicero himself says and what we can judge from the fragmentary text of the treatise, that it was basically cast in the form of an exposition by Cicero to Hirtius rather than of a dialogue between them.[3]

2.4. The dramatic date of the conversation is not far removed from the date of actual composition. Cicero was at Pozzuoli or in the vicinity from 17th April 44 to 23rd May 44 B.C., and Hirtius, whom he was trying to win over to the senatorial party, came to hear him declaim.[4] As for the date of actual composition, it is most probably to be placed in this period or in the next few weeks, when Cicero was at Tusculum. Cicero left there after the 17th of July, intending to join the conspirators in Greece; he changed his mind and returned, reaching Pompeii on the 19th of August, but was then preoccupied with writing the first and second *Philippics* (the first being delivered on the 2nd of September, the second being completed by the end of October[5] though never delivered) and *On Duties*. From December onwards he was fully engaged in political activity in Rome. It therefore seems probable that *On Fate* was written before Cicero's abortive departure for Greece in July 44. The lost treatise *On Glory* is perhaps mentioned in a letter of the 26th

---

1. *On Fate* 23-5; below, Introduction §3.1.8.

2. See above, Introduction §1.2.

3. The reference to the work as a *dialogue* by Macrobius in the context of fr.5 below need not be regarded as a serious difficulty for this view. On the plan of the treatise see further below, Introduction §4. Büchner [1964] 415 suggests that the claim that circumstances prevented Cicero from writing the treatise in the form of opposing speeches is simply a literary device to enable Cicero to expound his own views; this raises the question of how far he as a sceptic is committed to the views set forth (see below, Introduction §4.2.6). But it could be that both explanations are true; Cicero *was* prevented from giving the treatise a more elaborate form, but would not have wanted to anyway. In the *Tusculans* too the form of an exposition by one person is adopted; Lerer 40-5 interprets this as an exploration by Cicero of the problem of reconciling discussion and authority.

4. cf. *Letters to Atticus* 14.12.2 and *On Fate* 2-4; Yon, p.iii.

5. *Letters to Atticus* 15.13.

or 27th June,[1] and Cicero sent it to Atticus on 11th July and in a revised version on 17th July.[2] Yon, on whom the foregoing discussion is heavily dependent, suggests that Cicero wrote the treatise *On Fate* in late May or early June before proceeding to the composition of *On Glory*. The treatise *On Divination* seems to have been substantially complete before the assassination of Julius Caesar on 15th March 44.[3]

3. The freewill problem before Cicero.

3.1.1. This is not the place, nor do I have the space, to give a comprehensive treatment of the debate in antiquity over freedom of the will and related issues. All I can hope to do, here and in Introduction §§7-9 below, is to outline some of the major contributions and developments in so far as they are important for our understanding of the texts of Cicero and Boethius included here.

3.1.2. Discussion of freedom of the will in antiquity can be divided into two main areas; that concerned with physical causation, and that concerned with questions of logic. The issue does indeed relate very closely also to the third main division of Hellenistic philosophy, ethics, but as will be seen it will be convenient to treat ethics and physics closely together.

3.1.3. By "physical determinism" I shall mean the thesis upheld by the Stoics, and subsequently by Laplace,[4] that all that happens in the physical world (the only one they recognised) is the inevitable consequence of antecedent causes and circumstances; that in a given situation one and only one outcome can follow; and that, given the state of the world at any one time, it would at least in principle be possible for a superhuman intelligence to deduce its state at any subsequent time. The position of Aristotle on this question, and on whether or not human actions come within its scope, is unclear;[5] most probably, he did not see the universe in terms that would give rise to the question at all,[6]

---

1. *Letters to Atticus* 15.14.4; Yon, iv n.3. Cicero simply refers to "compositions" or "treatises" *(suntaxeis)*; Shackleton Bailey vol.6 p.273 suggests the reference is to *On Glory* and to other works. In the letter, as in *On Fate* 1-2, Cicero refers to distractions from his writing.

2. *Letters to Atticus* 16.2.6, 16.3.1. In 16.6.4 (July 25th) he apologises to Atticus for having used the same opening for *On Glory* and for book 3 of the *Academics,* explaining that he keeps a stock of such openings and forgot that he had already used the one in question.

3. Yon, p.ii n.4; cf. A.S. Pease, *M. Tulli Ciceronis De divinatione,* Urbana 1920-23, 13-15.

4. Laplace, *Philosophical Essay,* p.4; R. Harré in P. Edwards (ed.), *Encyclopedia of Philosophy,* New York 1967, vol.4 p.392.

5. See below on Cicero, *On Fate* §39.

6. Cf. D.M. Balme, 'Greek science and mechanism. I, Aristotle on nature and chance', *Class. Quart.* 33 (1939) 129-138; Sharples [1983,1] 4-6.

and assumed that our responsibility for our actions involved freedom to choose between alternatives without finding it necessary to consider the physical, as opposed to psychological, basis of that freedom.[1] Nor does it seem that anyone before Aristotle considered the question in the terms in which it came to be posed later; Plato raises questions about our responsibility for the course of our lives, not least in the Myth of Er in *Republic* 10, and prophecy of the future plays a part in the plots of many Greek tragedies, but this is not the same as discussion of universal physical determinism.

3.1.4. That discussion starts with Epicurus. He saw the physical system of the earlier atomist Democritus as incompatible with free-will,[2] and sought to preserve freedom of the will by claiming that atoms could swerve very slightly from the trajectories that their weight and the impact of other atoms would otherwise cause them to follow.[3] That this abolishes physical determinism is clear; what is less clear is how it can establish the freedom of our will to make responsible choices. For the random nature of the swerve would seem to rule out *responsible* choice just as much as determinism rules out *free* choice.[4]

3.1.5. David Sedley has argued convincingly that Epicurus should not, either in this or in other contexts, be interpreted in terms of an eliminative reductionism.[5] Human beings, and everything else there is, may be *made up of* atoms, but that does not mean that all meaningful talk about them can be *reduced to* talk about atoms; and in particular, what

---

1. Cf. Sharples [1983] 4-7. A different interpretation in Fine and in Stephen Everson, 'Aristotle's Compatibilism in the *Nicomachean Ethics*', *Ancient Philosophy* 10 (1990) 81-104. Englert 112ff. stresses that Aristotle did consider problems in reconciling responsibility with the analysis of human choice and motivation, notably in *Nicomachean Ethics* 3.5, but grants that a new emphasis on *efficient* causes in the Hellenistic period changed the terms of the question.

2. Epicurus, *Letter to Menoeceus* 134 (= 20A LS); *On Nature* 34.30 (= 20C LS); cf. Diogenes of Oenoanda 32.1.14ff. (= 20G LS). Democritus is not explicitly named in the two texts from Epicurus, and indeed Sedley argues that Epicurus' argument was directed not so much against Democritus himself as against those, perhaps including some in Epicurus' own school, who subsequently interpreted his theory in a deterministic sense. The important point is that both chronology and expression show that it was not *Stoic* determinism that Epicurus was historically opposing, for the development of Stoic determinism as a causal theory was due to Chrysippus. (This does not, of course, make it inappropriate to discuss the Stoic and Epicurean positions as rival *philosophical* positions.) Cf. Sedley (1983) 29-36 and LS vol.1 pp.107-8.

3. Lucretius 2.251ff. (= LS 20F); Diogenes of Oenoanda, cited in the preceding note. The swerve is not explicitly mentioned in extant texts from Epicurus himself, but it is clear, not least from §§21-2 of our treatise where Cicero refers to Epicurus' formulation of the theory, that it was Epicurus' own. See Englert 9-11; Asmis 277-8.

4. See Mitsis 154-160.

5. Sedley [1983] and [1989]: LS vol.1 pp.109-112.

appears only as random swerving on the level of individual atoms may be free but rational choice on the level of whole human organisms.[1] What is less clear, however, is exactly how rational choice and the swerve are related to one another; Sedley indeed suggests that it might have been better if Epicurus had not introduced the swerve at all,[2] and also suggests that choice actually *causes* the swerves of certain atoms, which seems questionable.[3] The alternative is to suppose that what appears as a particular decision on the human level is an alternative description of what is a swerve (or swerves) on the atomic level, and that if this is caused at all on either level it is "self-caused", without Epicurus having any clear explanation of *why* it is random on one level and not on the other.[4]

3.1.6. For the Stoics, as already indicated, everything that happens is an inevitable result of what has preceded; the chain of causes that constitutes fate is identified with providence and with God,[5] and everything that happens does so for the best. It is impossible for different outcomes to arise from exactly similar situations; where this seems to happen, there must in fact be some difference in the situation which causes the difference in outcome. Otherwise something would have occurred without a cause; and this, Chrysippus held, was impossible.[6] Most Stoics believed in divination, which they explained by the universal network of causes and used as an argument for determinism;[7] the state of the liver of the sacrificial victim does not *cause* the army's defeat in battle, but is linked to it in that both are part of the deter-

---

1. This much had already been asserted – but in the context of an interpretation of Epicurus' materialism that undermines the insight – by Cyril Bailey (*The Greek Atomists and Epicurus,* Oxford 1928, 435-6; cf. Sedley (1989) 326-7.

2. See below, Introduction §3.1.8, and *On Fate* §23, Commentary.

3. See below, commentary on *On Fate* §22.

4. Cf. Gulley, especially 46-51; Mitsis 163-6. I hope to discuss these matters in more detail elsewhere.

5. Or said to derive from providence; but for the Stoics God *is* the world, or rather the active principle that is present in everything in the world and gives it its being. So the more radical formulation *identifying* fate and providence seems the more appropriate one. This is the orthodox Stoic position; Cleanthes apparently argued differently. See below, Introduction §8.1-3.

6. Plutarch, *On Stoic Self-Contradictions* 23 1045C = SVF 2.973; not in LS. Cf. also Cicero *On divination* 1.126 = SVF 2.921 = LS 55L; there is nothing that is going to be that does not have natural causes. Uncaused motion would destroy the unity of the universe; Alexander *On Fate* 22 192.11ff. = SVF 2.945 = LS 55N. It was Chrysippus, the third head of the school, who in effect codified Stoic doctrine in his extensive writings; in what follows, when "Stoic" doctrine is referred to it will generally be that of Chrysippus, unless otherwise indicated.

7. Cicero *On Divination* 1.127 = SVF 2.944 = LS 55O; Diogenianus ap. Eusebius *Preparation for the Gospel* 4.3.1 = SVF 2.939 = LS 55P.

minist nexus, linked as the Stoics put it by "sympathy",[1] so that those who are expert can observe their regular correlation and infer one from the other.[2]

3.1.7 In spite of this uncompromising determinism, the Stoics insisted that men are responsible for their actions and can be justly praised or blamed for them.[3] Chrysippus argued this essentially by insisting that our decisions, though predetermined, still have a crucial role to play in the causal nexus. Different people react in different ways to similar situations, and even though it is predetermined in each case how a given person will react, it is still *that person's* reaction, in a sense that was strong enough to satisfy Chrysippus even if not all his critics, just as the fact that a cylinder and a cone roll, and roll in different ways, when pushed depends on their shape and not just on their being pushed.[4] Nor does determinism imply that we cannot influence the course of events; on the contrary, certain future events can only come about as a result of our acting in certain ways,[5] and that is not altered by the fact that whether we do act in these ways or not is itself predetermined. All human beings are *responsible* for their predetermined actions, but only the wise are *free*, for only they recognise which things they have the power to affect (in a predetermined way) and which things they cannot alter; it is futile to struggle against fate (though if certain people do struggle against fate, as they do, that is itself predetermined),[6] especially as what is fated is ordained by providence for the best. The wise man will make the most reasonable choices he can, given the state of his knowledge, but will always act "with reservation", ready to accept that if things seem to go against him it is

---

1. Cf. *On Fate* §7, and *On Divination* 2.34 = SVF 2.1211 = Posidonius F106EK; 2.124, 142, 143; Sextus Empiricus *adv. math.* 9.79 = SVF 2.1013; Cleomedes in SVF 2.534, 546; and compare Plotinus, 3.3 6.23ff. The important point is that sympathy connects even things which are apparently far removed from one another. See Talanga 87-90.

2. Cicero *On Divination* 1.118 = SVF 2.1210 = LS 42E; also 1.25.

3. A distinction is to be drawn here between "soft" determinists like Chrysippus, who believe that determinism does not exclude people's responsibility for their actions, and "hard" determinists (like Manilius, *Astronom.* 4.107-116) who argue that people should be punished even if they are not responsible for their actions, in order to protect society. Cf. Sharples [1983,1] 10 n.53 and references there.

4. Cf. Cicero *On Fate* 41-5; Gellius *Attic Nights* 7.2 (Appendix (C) below).

5. Cf. Cicero *On Fate* 28-30 and commentary; Origen, *Against Celsus* 2.20 = Appendix (A) below; also Diogenianus in SVF 2.998 = LS 62F, [Plutarch] *On Fate* 574e, and Stobaeus *Ecl.* 2.8.25 (vol.2 p.158.15-159.7 Wachsmuth) = Plutarch *Moralia* fr.22 Sandbach.

6. Cf. on this Alexander of Aphrodisias *Quaest.* 1.4 = SVF 2.962, and more generally Sharples [1986] 274ff.

well that they should.[1]

3.1.8. Carneades rejected Stoic determinism, but argued that Epicurus need not have introduced the swerve, with its attendant problems; human choice is free but not uncaused, just because it is the nature of human choice to be free; *that* is the cause or explanation of our free choices.[2] Carneades has justly been claimed as a precursor by modern advocates of an "agent causation" theory, who reject a deterministic account of responsibility, but argue that the dilemma of determinism or random indeterminism on the physical level is irrelevant to the analysis of human choice.[3] To the present writer, and perhaps to many readers also, this seems inadequate as an answer; our actions have, it appears, some effect in the physical world, and little seems to be achieved by claiming that our actions are free as actions if it is still the case that what happens in the physical world can be inferred, with no real alternatives, from the situation as long beforehand as one likes.[4] It also has to be admitted that Carneades does not treat human agency as a special case, the sole exception to determinism, in the way that this interpretation might suggest.[5] This could be because he is not, or not only, advocating action theory, but also rejecting the whole Stoic approach to causation that gives rise to the dilemma of determinism or uncaused motion.

3.1.9. There is also a question whether Carneades, as a sceptic, was actually concerned to uphold free will, or whether he simply wished to

---

1. Thus Chrysippus said that one's foot, if it had understanding, would be glad to be covered with mud (Epictetus *Diss.* 2.6.9f. = SV 3.191 = LS 58J). For "reservation" cf. also Seneca, *On Good Deeds* 4.34, *Letters* 54.7, 61,3; Stobaeus, *Selections* 2.115 Wachsmuth = SVF 3.564 = LS 65W. This is the point of Cleanthes' prayer (cited by Epictetus, *Manual* 53 = SVF 1.527 = LS 62A), "Lead me, Zeus, and you too, Fate, to the place for which I am appointed by you; for I shall follow without hesitating. But if I am unwilling, becoming bad, I shall follow none the less", and of the analogy of the dog tied to the chariot (Hippolytus, *Refutation* 1.21 = SVF 2.975 = LS 62A): "if a dog is tied, as it were, to a chariot, then if the dog wishes to follow it will both be pulled and follow, acting by its own choice together with the necessity; but if it does not wish to follow, it will in any case be compelled."

2. Cf. Cicero, *On Fate* 23-5 and commentary.

3. So R. Taylor, art. 'Determinism', in P. Edwards (ed.), *Encyclopedia of Philosophy*, New York 1967, vol.2 p.369; N. White at *Philos. Review* 94 (1985) 127. Cf. Sharples [1987,2] 215 and nn.

4. Cf. O'Connor 105-9, and Mitsis 165, presenting this as one reason why Epicurus might not accept Carneades' and Sedley's argument that it would be better to dispense with the swerve altogether (above, Introduction §3.1.5.) Hamelin 30 argues that Epicurus at least understood the "negative" conditions for freedom – that is, that the swerve was necessary though not sufficient – and "showed himself a better philosopher than Carneades on this point".

5. He fails to distinguish clearly between choice and chance. See commentary on §§19, 27 and 28; Donini [1989] 134-6.

point to what he saw as shortcomings in the Stoic and Epicurean positions. The latter seems more in accord with his position as a sceptic.
Long indeed has argued that Carneades could assert positively that we
have free will, because this claim ultimately depends on introspection,
rather than involving claims about the external world.[1] But this seems a
questionable interpretation. It is true that the most telling arguments
against a belief in universal determinism are those that start from our
subjective experience of freedom.[2] But it is not clear that a committed
sceptic has any right to argue that this experience is not illusory.
Alexander of Aphrodisias can argue that it would be odd if divine
providence had led us to think that we have free will if in fact we do
not;[3] but that argument depends on a belief in divine government of
the universe, effective *ad homines* against the Stoics, but not clearly
one of which a sceptic could make use.

3.2.1. While the relation of Aristotle to the debate about physical determinism is unclear, his contribution to discussion of logical determinism
was a fundamental one. In chapter 9 of his treatise *On Interpretation*
he states a problem that arises if we suppose that all propositions with
definite subjects, even those relating to the future, are either true or
false. For if it is true that a sea-battle will happen tomorrow, it does
not seem that a sea-battle can fail to happen; if it is false, it does not
seem that it can happen; and either way any freedom of choice about
the matter seems to be excluded.

3.2.2. How Aristotle himself thought the paradox should be resolved is
unclear; we shall have occasion later to return to the standard interpretation of his solution in late antiquity.[4] What is clear is that the

---

1. Long [1974] 103-4. A different view is taken by LS vol.1 p.465.

2. Cf. Alexander *On Fate* 12 180.24ff.; Sharples [1983, 1] 142, Henry 32-
42.

3. Alexander, *On Fate* 11 179.23-8.

4. Below, Introduction §7. The modern literature both on the paradox
itself and on Aristotle's view of it is immense; there is a convenient
bibliography in D. Frede [1985] 84-7. Interest was aroused especially by
Łukasiewicz' observation that regarding propositions relating to future
contingents as neither true nor false, by introducing a third intermediate "truth"-value, gives an interpretation to at least the simplest case
of a logical system operating with more than two truth-values, multi-
valued logical systems being objects of theoretical interest in their own
right - though whether it really is a third *truth*-value that is involved
here is debatable. G. Fine, 'Truth and Necessity in Aristotle *De inter-
pretatione* 9', *History of Philosophy Quarterly* 1 (1984) 41 n.2, sees
Aristotle himself as adopting a position not unlike that of Carneades.
What is certain is that Cicero at any rate associates the discussion of
future contingents with Epicurus and Carneades, *not* with Aristotle,
whose school-treatises were relatively unknown until the edition by
Andronicus. This may or may not have appeared in Cicero's own life-
time, but there is no evidence for interest on Cicero's part in the
school-treatises in general or in *On Interpretation* in particular. Cf.
Donini [1989] 127 nn.9-10.

Epicureans and Stoics took up the paradox, and stated positions on it which were in a way opposite to one another but in a way similar. Both schools agreed that, if statements referring to future events are either true or false, those future events cannot be contingent, able either to happen or not. Epicurus, denying physical determinism, also insisted that some future events are contingent, and so denied that all future-tense propositions are true or false; his followers, much to Cicero's scorn, modified this to the claim that neither "x will happen" nor "x will not happen" is true even though "either x will happen or x will not happen" is true. The Stoics, committed to the view that all events are predetermined, pointed out that on their view the problem of the truth of future contingents did not arise, and used this as an argument to support their belief in determinism.[1]

3.2.3. Once again, as with the dilemma of determinism or uncaused motion, Carneades rejected the shared assumption of both schools, arguing that the truth of a future-tense statement had nothing to do with the necessity of the event predicted, but only with its occurrence. Here too the essentials of Carneades' position have been asserted by modern philosophers, notably by Gilbert Ryle, whose discussion of the question in ch.2 of his *Dilemmas* should be read by every student of Cicero's treatise. To many now – though not apparently in antiquity, Cicero apart – Carneades' solution will seem to settle the question of the truth of future contingents adequately; though the question of whether the contingency of future events is compatible with divine *foreknowledge* of them is less easily settled than that of whether it is compatible with the truth or falsity of future-tense statements.[2]

3.2.4. Discussion of logical determinism was not however confined to the problem of the truth of future contingents. Important too was the debate that centred on the Master Argument of Diodorus Cronus, an older contemporary of Epicurus and of Zeno the founder of the Stoic

---

1. The main source for the Epicurean and the Stoic positions and for Carneades' criticisms is our treatise itself; see §§17-21, 26-8, 37-8 and the Commentary there. It should be emphasised that the argument here attributed to the Stoics is *not* the same as an argument that the truth of the future contingent itself *causes* the event to be necessary; cf., for a comparable point in the context of divine *foreknowledge,* Introduction §7.4 and the Commentary on Boethius, *Consolation,* Book 5 prose 3 §7.

2. See below, Introduction §7. On Carneades' (and Cicero's) position and its relation to modern views see further White 193-203, with interesting suggestions which cannot be further pursued here on the difference between our view of time and that of the ancients (197) as a reason for *our* finding the Carneadean approach the natural one. Not all modern critics have approved of Carneades' solution, and especially not those who find it lacking in metaphysical depth; cf. Hamelin 30, and A. Magris, *L'idea di destino nel pensiero antico,* vol.2, Udine 1985, 569-70. Hamelin 76 even argues that Carneades, far from distinguishing real necessity from the logical necessity that relates the truth of a proposition and the occurrence of the event, *confuses* them by claiming future truth in the absence of real necessity to justify it.

school.[1] Diodorus held that only that which either was or would be true was possible.[2] This claim he supported by means of the Master Argument, which claimed that the three propositions (1) all that is past and true is necessary,(2) nothing impossible follows from what is possible,[3] and (3) what neither is nor will be the case is possible, were incompatible. Diodorus himself asserted the truth of the first two propositions and used it to deny that of the third.[4] On what grounds he claimed that the three propositions were incompatible is unclear; perhaps he argued that, if a future event was possible but would not actually occur, it must always have been true, and therefore necessary, that it would not in fact occur, and thus impossible for it to have been going to occur; but from its future occurrence it would follow that it had already been going to occur, and since the latter is impossible, so is the former.[5] What does not seem likely is that Diodorus himself introduced any element of physical, causal determinism into the argument.[6]

3.2.5. However, an analogous argument could be and was used against the Stoics by their critics;[7] if a future event is not in fact going to occur, then, since all is predetermined, there must already in the past have been a state of affairs that would eventually lead to the non-occurrence of the hypothetical future event; but that state of affairs, being past, is necessary; and so the occurrence of the event would

---

1. On Diodorus' date cf. D.N. Sedley, 'Diodorus Cronus and Hellenistic Philosophy', in *Proc. Camb. Phil. Soc.* n.s. 23 (1977) 74-120, at 78-80.

2. Perhaps a modification of an earlier Megarian position which restricted the possible to what was actually the case at any given time, thus rendering the notion of the possible redundant. Cf. Aristotle, *Metaph.* Θ 1046b29ff.

3. Aristotle's definition of possibility; *Prior Analytics* 1.13 32a19.

4. The Master Argument is reported by Epictetus, *Diss.* 2.19.1-5 = LS 38A.

5. This is essentially the interpretation of A.N. Prior, 'Diodorean Modalities', *Philos. Quart.* 5 (1955) 205-213, and *Past, Present and Future*, Oxford 1967, 32-4. It turns on three assumptions: (a) that statements about future events are true before the event, (b) that the claim that all that is past and true is necessary extends not just to statements about past events but to those about the past truth of future events, and (c) that the first premiss is to be taken as referring to what follows from the supposition that what is possible *actually occurs*, and not just from the *supposition that it is possible*. Hintikka's interpretation replaces (a) and (b) by the assumption that we can consider a time after p, assumed to be possible, has failed to occur, so that it will *then* be impossible for it to have occurred. Again, the bibliography on the Master Argument is immense; cf. Hintikka 179-80 and nn., LS vol.2 499, and the surveys of views in Sorabji [1980,2] 107-9 and White 79-86.

6. See below on §17, and further on Diodorus, White ch.3 especially pp.78-9, 88-9.

7. Cf. Plutarch *On Stoic Self-Contradictions* 46 1055d = SVF 2.202; Alexander of Aphrodisias, *On Fate* 10 176.14-177.6 = SVF 2.959 = LS 38H; and, without explicit reference to causal necessity, Boethius *On On Interpretation*[2] 235.9ff. Hintikka, 201-5; White 86-90.

imply that the state of affairs in the past was otherwise than it necessarily was; but if the actual state of affairs was necessary, any other state of affairs was impossible. Or else, as in Cicero's treatise,[1] the argument could turn on the claimed truth of divination; if the future can be inferred from some past prophecy, or from some past event with which the future is linked by observed correlations if not by direct causation (Cicero's example being "if someone was born with the Dog-star rising, he will not die at sea), then the past prophecy or event is necessary, and its being otherwise, as a different future would require, is impossible.

3.2.6. It may seem that the claim that what will not in fact happen is impossible is one that the Stoics, as determinists, would naturally accept. In fact, though, both Cleanthes, the second head of the Stoic school, and Chrysippus the third head argued otherwise, claiming that there were things that would not in fact happen but were none the less possible.[2] To argue this they had either to reject the Master Argument as a whole or else deny one or other of the first two premisses; and in fact Cleanthes denied the first, claiming that not all that was past was *ipso facto* necessary, while Chrysippus denied the second, claiming that what was impossible could in fact follow from what was possible.[3] Of course, denying a premiss of the Master Argument could not be the whole story, for there still seems a need to explain *how* something that would not in fact happen in the future could be possible, given that for the Stoics it would follow from its not happening that it was predetermined that it would not happen. The Stoics defined the possible as what was not prevented;[4] it may be that they regarded some things that would not in fact occur in the future as possible because the factors by which their non-occurrence was predetermined were not

---

1. Cicero, *On Fate* 13-16.

2. This is attested not only by Cicero *On Fate* 13 but also by Plutarch, Alexander and Boethius cited above. And cf. the next note. Admittedly, while these passages clearly commit Chrysippus to a distinction between fate and necessity - all things are fated, but not everything that happens is necessary or its opposite impossible -, there are others which attribute an identification of fate and necessity to him. These cannot all be easily dismissed as the distortions of hostile critics; the explanation may be in terms of a divine and human point of view (cf. Long [1971] 176; Sharples [1981] 87-88).

3. That these were the reactions of Cleanthes and Chrysippus is asserted by Epictetus, loc. cit. in §3.2.4 above. For Chrysippus' argument see Commentary on Cicero, *On Fate* §14. Cleanthes' approach may seem more logical than Chrysippus', for it amounts to saying that what is possible but will not happen in the future can, once it has failed to occur, still be described in the past as something that was possible but did not happen; in other words, that the distinction between impossibility and mere non-occurrence is the same regardless of the temporal relation of events to us.

4. Alexander, loc. cit.; Diogenes Laertius 7.75 = SVF 2.201 = LS 38D; Boethius, op. cit. 234.27ff.= SVF 2.201. For this interpretation of the Stoic definition cf. M. Frede [1974] 107ff.; White 100-102.

known, so that possibility would be a reflection of our ignorance only; it may also be that they supposed that certain things were not prevented *yet*, even though it was predetermined that they would be, because no preventing factors sufficiently closely linked with the actual outcome had yet emerged. In particular, future outcomes might be regarded as possible when there was nothing to prevent them coming about except the fact that it was already predetermined that we would choose not to do them.[1]

3.2.7. Libertarian critics both ancient and modern have tended to suppose that Chrysippus was trying to smuggle possibility into a deterministic system where it did not in their view belong, in order to mitigate or disguise the implications of that system for responsible human action; not surprisingly, they have found his treatment unsatisfactory. It is not clear how a predetermined outcome can be any more in my control, in a libertarian sense, just because I do not *know* how it is predetermined that it will turn out, or just because its opposite is not prevented yet; though it can be argued that our ignorance of what is predetermined to happen is at any rate necessary if we are to have a sense of things being under our control.[2] However, Chrysippus may well have seen a link between possibility and human responsibility as *he* conceived it, not in libertarian terms; even in a deterministic system there is a place for a distinction between cases where I have an opportunity to influence events (in a pre-determined way) and those where I do not. A determinist, like anyone else, will not accept that I should be praised or blamed for what was necessitated by the nature of the thing involved or by factors beyond my control; and if I recognise that an outcome is necessary in this way, I should not waste effort trying in vain to alter it.[3]

---

1. I owe this last suggestion to David Sedley. *Chance* was certainly defined as "a cause obscure to human reasoning"; cf. SVF 2.965-6, 970-1. Simplicius *On the* Categories 196.2-4 refers, in stating a view of possibility which appears to correspond to the Stoic one, to the absence of *obvious* impediment; this might at first sight be taken as evidence for an epistemic view, but it could also be taken as evidence for an objective rather than a subjective one – "obviousness" not being relative to particular observers. (Cf. Denyer cited by LS vol.2 p.237.) Admittedly Carneades in §26 of Cicero *On Fate* attributes to the Stoics the view that everything that will happen in the future already has *causes* now; one would have to suppose that this does not however mean that the opposites of the things that will happen are already *prevented*. The literature on the Stoic doctrine of possibility is considerable; see for example Sharples [1983] 134-5, 285, and LS vol.1 p.235, vol.2 p.489. Boethius *On* On Interpretation[2] makes chance for the Stoics depend on our ignorance, 194.23ff., but possibility on our power, 197.13ff.

2. Cf. Spinoza, *Ethics* pars I, Appendix, cited by Donini [1974-5] 228 n.1; also Gould [1970] 152 n.1.

3. Cf. LS vol.1 235. That the Stoics regarded what depends on us as what is not hindered by external factors is suggested by Origen and Nemesius in SVF 2.990 and 991.

4. Cicero's treatise *On Fate:* plan and sources.

4.1.1. Cicero's treatise *On Fate* survives only in a mutilated form. There are four gaps in the text, which I will label (A)–(D) for convenience. At this point it may be useful to give a summary of the whole:

	<lacuna A>
1-4	Introduction
	<lacuna B>
5-11	Criticism of Posidonius and Chrysippus on universal causal sympathy.
11-16	Chrysippus as a determinist must accept Diodorus' view that only what actually happens is possible.
17-20	The truth of future-tense statements does not involve the predicted events' being predetermined.
20-28	Denial of determinism does not require the uncaused motion of the Epicurean atomic swerve, or the denial of the truth of future-tense statements.
28-33	Chrysippus' answer to the fatalism of the Lazy Argument is insufficiently radical; there are events which are not predetermined in advance, and even the gods cannot foreknow these.
34-38	Not everything that precedes an event is correctly described as a cause of it, even if it is a necessary condition.
39-45	Chrysippus' position, regarding sense-impressions as necessary initiating causes of action but not as determining it, is less removed from that of the libertarians than one might suppose.
	<lacuna C>
46-48	The Epicurean atomic swerve is unacceptable because it is uncaused.
	<lacuna D>

4.1.2. Calculations of the possible length of the lacunae were carried out by Yon, based on Clark's theory[1] that the extant MSS containing *On Fate* along with other works of Cicero derived from a lost MS (Q) which had 27 lines of the 1878 Teubner edition of Müller to a page, in two columns, and 54 Teubner lines (about 1½ pages of the present text) to a two-sided leaf, and on what can be inferred about the content of that archetype. These calculations are highly speculative, but I will summarise them for what they are worth.

4.1.3. Our text opens in the middle of an introduction by Cicero himself speaking in his own person. This is characteristic of the openings of Cicero's philosophical dialogues. Where a dialogue consists of more than one book, Cicero will sometimes provide an introduction of this sort to

---

1. Clark 328, 336.

books other than the first;[1] but §§1-4 are clearly an introduction to the whole work. Though it has sometimes been supposed that Cicero's *On Fate* consisted of more than one book, there is no evidence to suggest this, and indeed Cicero in *On Divination* 2.3 at least suggests that it did not.[2] It therefore seems that the opening of our text comes from the opening of the dialogue as a whole, and that not all that much has been lost before the opening words.

4.1.4. Yon, lviii-lix, points out that sections 1-4 of *On Fate* amount to exactly one of the leaves of Q. Moreover, *On Fate* is preceded in MSS A and V by *On the Nature of the Gods, On Divination*, and Cicero's translation of Plato's *Timaeus*. Much of the last-mentioned has been lost, but its probable length can be estimated from that of the Platonic original; and on that basis Clark calculated that the three works together might have amounted to 191 leaves of Q.[3] One more leaf would be needed to make up 24 gatherings of eight leaves (there is a misprint on p.lix of Yon, where the number is given as 34; Philippson 1032-3 n.2). Yon therefore suggests that our §§1-4 of *On Fate* come from the last leaf of the last of these gatherings, which somehow survived when the rest did not; and the implication would be that very little has been lost from before the extant sections 1-4. But Clark rightly did not claim precision for his calculations of the length of the lost part of the *Timaeus*,[4] and with sections 1-4 both preceded and followed by lacunae, there can be no certainty that they do not represent, for example, the first leaf of the 25th gathering in Q rather than the last leaf of the 24th – in which case an amount equivalent to our sections 1-4 would have been lost from before them.

4.1.5. Lacuna B follows section 4. Yon (lix) argues that, on the basis of Clark's figures, the contents of the postulated MS Q from *On Fate* 5 onwards (allowing for the loss of a page after §48; see below) amounted to 122 leaves of Q. If Q was formed of gatherings of eight leaves, and *On Fate* 1-4 was the last leaf of its gathering, there should be six extra leaves after *On Fate* 4 to bring 122 up to the required multiple of eight; those six leaves would amount to just under a third of the amount of *On Fate* that has survived.

4.1.6. It is true that this supposition gives Q as a whole the convenient round number of 40 gatherings or 320 leaves; but it is difficult to see how one can exclude the supposition that there were originally even more. Indeed Clark 340 commented, more cautiously, "in all probability Q contained not less than 40 quaternions ... *very possibly more*" (my ital-

---

1. He does so in the case of *all* the books of the *Tusculan Disputations* (but these are in effect separate treatises); in the *Lucullus;* in *On Divination* 2; and in *On Ends* 3 and 5 (book 2 of that treatise being a reply to 1, and 4 to 3).

2. Cf. Yon ix-x, citing also the form of citation in our fr.1.

3. This is Yon's summary of the calculations at Clark 339.

4. This is pointed out, against Yon, by Eisenberger 154 n.2.

ics).[1] On the other hand, not as much of the lost material may have been in lacuna B as Yon supposes; see below, §4.1.9.

4.1.7. What came in lacuna B? Hirtius must clearly have propounded the thesis against which Cicero is to argue; presumably that was the Stoic doctrine of fate. [2] Rackham argues, from the words *prima oratione* in §40, that Cicero made *two* speeches in the dialogue; but the words can as well be rendered by "in the first part of my speech" as by "in my first speech", and Cicero's words in §1 suggest that the structure of the treatise was relatively simple. §40 does show that assent to sense-impressions was one topic discussed in the lacuna. The cylinder argument too may have been referred to[3]; and it is clear that there was discussion both of Chrysippus' claim that human characters were determined by natural causes (cf. §§7-11)[4] and of examples of divination given by Posidonius (cf. §§5-6).[5] Explicit mention was probably made of the Stoic explanation of divination in terms of the observation of regular correlations reflecting the underlying causal nexus, and of the Stoic objection to the introduction of uncaused events (above, §3.1.6).[6] And Amand suggests that Cicero reproduced the arguments of Carneades concerning the moral implications of determinism which are reflected,

---

1. Philippson 1032 and n.1 comments that the treatise as Yon reconstructs it would be very short in comparison with even a single book of *On Divination,* for example. Hamelin 11, writing before Clark's researches, had suggested that *over half* the treatise was lost between §§4 and 5.

2. One might suppose that Hirtius' thesis was more complex, for instance the claim that neither the Stoic position nor the Epicurean was acceptable. But one wonders whether Hirtius was philosophically sophisticated enough to be a plausible proponent of such a position. Turnebus, cited by Bayer 121, suggests that Hirtius might rather have related the Stoic doctrine of fate to the recent political history of Rome, but Eisenberger 159 rightly finds this implausible after the contrast between philosophical and political issues in the preface.

3. See Commentary on §42. It is however difficult to see how the cylinder argument could have been referred to in a way that would not unduly anticipate the account of Chrysippus' attempt to reconcile fate and freedom in §§41ff.; it is not I think likely that this attempt was not mentioned at all until §41 (see Commentary on fr.1, after §4 below), but equally it should not be anticipated in all its detail. Philippson 1033 suggests that at this point there was only a statement of Chrysippus' position, not criticism of it.

4. Donini [1989] 133 suggests that the influence of external factors on assent was discussed before §5 as it was also, in his view, in the lacuna after §45 (see Introduction §4.2.2 below); and he further suggests, speculatively, that there might have been discussion in this regard of the "old philosophers" including Aristotle who reappear in §39.

5. On the claim that some of this discussion may be reconstructed from Augustine, *City of God* 5, see the commentary on Fragment 4 (between §4 and §5).

6. Cf. Philippson 1037; Eisenberger, 163-4. See below on §11.

for example, in Alexander, *On Fate* chs. 16-20.[1]

4.1.8. We have five probable ancient citations of *On Fate* which do not appear in our extant text. Editors have normally placed some or all of these fragments together at the end of their editions of the treatise. But it is possible, though only as a matter of conjecture, to argue that they all belong in the lacuna between §4 and §5, and to say something about their probable order within it; and they have been so arranged in this text.[2] I have retained the earlier editors' numbers for the fragments, though it is not for the conventional order that I shall be arguing. One of the fragments relates to a point put forward by Posidonius and challenged by Cicero soon after the text resumes in §5; it is clear that the other points challenged in sections §§5-6 had also been asserted towards the end of the lacuna.

4.1.9. Lacuna C follows §45. Some scholars have argued that relatively little material has been lost at this point; indeed Yon p.xxxii n.3 cites Lörcher with approval for the view that the argument of the treatise is substantially complete in §45 (§§46-8 on any view adding relatively little to the argument). Others however have rightly pointed out that the discussion of Chrysippus' views announced in §39 is *not* complete by the end of §45, and that a substantial amount of material has therefore been lost after that point; see below, §4.2.2.

4.1.10. Lacuna D follows the end of the preserved text in §48. In MS B the first 27 lines of Cicero's *Topics*, which follows *On Fate* in the MSS, are copied on one side of a separate leaf, and in A they are omitted altogether. Clark 336 suggested that in the archetype too the lost conclusion of *On Fate* was on the first side of the leaf which had the opening of the *Topics* on its reverse side, and that the corrector of B recopied the latter but not the former. This would suggest that not more than a page has been lost from the end of the treatise.

4.1.11. Another problem, which also has a bearing on the contents of lacuna B, is the arrangement of topics in the treatise as a whole. It has been suggested (cf. Yon xxxviii-xl) that it might have followed the standard Hellenistic division of philosophy into physics, ethics and logic; references to ethics and logic appear in §1, and a reference to physics might have been lost beforehand. §§5-11 are concerned with the effects of natural causes. §§11-38 are broadly concerned with questions relating to the truth of predictions of future events. A case can therefore be made for saying that §§11-38 represent a "logical" section, preceded by the remains of the "ethical" section; the "physical" section, if there was one, will then have disappeared into the lacuna before §5.

---

1. Amand, 80. The reconstruction of these arguments is the theme of Amand's book.

2. Others have placed some of the fragments in lacunae A or C. See the Commentary.

4.1.12 Yon however argues (p.xxxv, following Hamelin 12) that the treatise included only an ethical and a logical section; he points out that at §40 Cicero refers to an earlier treatment of assent (above, Introduction §4.1.7), and suggests that this was in the context of ethics. He also points out (p.xxxvi) that the list of topics in the debate on determinism at pseudo-Plutarch *On Fate* 11 574DF refers successively to causation, universal sympathy, divination and the truth of future contingents; the last three topics appear in the same order in the extant text of Cicero's treatise, and so Yon suggests that the topic of causation was discussed in connection with assent in the lacuna before §5.[1] But causation generally would be more at home in physics than in ethics.

4.1.13. There are also more general difficulties with either of these reconstructions of the plan of Cicero's work. First, it is necessary, with Yon, to regard both §§39-45 and §§46-8 as in some sense appendices to the general scheme. That §§46-8 form a rhetorical peroration is not disputed, but Yon's view (xxxiv) that §§39-45 are also part of a conclusion, reconciling views earlier presented as conflicting, is highly questionable (below, Introduction §4.2.2). Second, §§5-6 have little obviously to do with ethics; they are linked to §§7-11 rather by a *physical* concern with the effects of natural causes, and in particular of universal "sympathy" (see Introduction, §3.1.6).[2] But §§7-11 could hardly constitute a whole ethical section. And, while §§11-38 do have a common thread in concern with the truth of predictions, they also involve points relating to causation in general and to the causation of human action in particular. It therefore seems likely that the structure of Cicero's discussion was less formal than these reconstructions would suggest, and that while physics, ethics and logic all played a part in it, he is not in §1 giving us a programme of a treatise divided into separate sections.[3]

4.2.1. A major part of the surviving text is devoted to reporting the views of Carneades; Carneades himself wrote nothing, but his views were recorded by his disciple Clitomachus. In §§39-45, however, a view is put forward which is more favourable to Chrysippus than what has preceded and suggests (wrongly) that the difference between his position and that of those who uphold freedom of the will is a purely verbal one. Since assimilation of the views of different schools[4] and the suggestion that differences are purely verbal[5] are characteristic of Cicero's teacher Antiochus of Ascalon, it has been suggested, first that §§39-45 represent his views, and secondly that a work of his may have

---

1. So Turnebus ap. Bayer 123.

2. This objection was already made against Yon by Philippson 1032.

3. So Eisenberger, 158.

4. Cf. Cicero, *Academics* 1.18 and 1.24. A general survey of what is known for certain about Antiochus in J. Barnes, 'Antiochus of Ascalon', in M. Griffin and J. Barnes (eds.), *Philosophia Togata*, Oxford 1989, 51-96.

5. Cicero *On the Nature of the Gods* 1.16.

been the intermediary through which the views of Carneades as well reached Cicero, from which it is only a small step to suggesting that he is the substantial source of the whole of Cicero's treatise,[1] though the specifically Roman illustrations, the preface and the concluding attack on Epicureanism seem likely to be Cicero's own.

4.2.2. However, it would be odd for Antiochus, if he wanted to assimilate Chrysippus' view to his own, to devote so much space to recording Carneades' attacks on Chrysippus without apparently answering them; for the account in §§39-45 does not so much modify the aspects of Chrysippus' position that prompted Carneades' criticisms, as ignore them.[2] And the mere fact that differences are said to be purely verbal is hardly conclusive evidence that Antiochus and no-one else must be the source[3]. Moreover, Cicero in §39 says that Chrysippus *attempted* to accommodate free will but failed to do so[4]; in §§41-5 we have the statement of how he attempted this, but we do not have the explanation of how he failed. It therefore follows that the argument is *not* complete at §45 and that further criticism of Chrysippus was to follow,[5] whether the argument of §§41-5 was itself explicitly found wanting (as Eisenberger seems to suggest) or whether Cicero returned to considerations of

---

1. This was the view of Gercke 693 and of Lörcher (Donini [1989] 126 n.7; it is favoured by Yon xlvi, Amand 66 n.2, J.M. Dillon, *The Middle Platonists,* London 1977, 85-7, and Talanga 139; and for the claim that §§39-45 come from Antiochus cf. Bayer 113 and Donini [1974-5] 196 n.1 (but now rejected, Donini [1989] 139 n.47). If Cicero was confronted with two separate sources, one giving the views of Carneades and one those of Antiochus, it would have been *easier* for him to write *On Fate* in the form of two opposing speeches rather than in the form in which we have it (cf. Yon, xliii). On the other hand, if Antiochus were the source of the *whole* treatise it would become harder to justify the sort of awkwardnesses of organisation that might be expected if §§39-45 came from him but what precedes did not; see §4.2.2 below.

2. See Commentary on section §39.

3. Similar observations are also attributed to Carneades (Philippson, 1038); cf. Cicero *On Ends* 3.41. And at ibid. 4.2 and 4.5 they form part of a sceptical Academic argument against the Stoics. Cf. Donini (1989) 141 n.52.

4. Cf. also fr.1 below; Schröder 148.

5. Schmekel (1892) 178-9, (1938) 270-1; Philippson 1035-6; Weische 33-4; Eisenberger 167f.; Donini [1989] 141; Schröder 146-152). Hamelin initially doubted that the whole work derived from Antiochus, because of the attacks on the Stoic position (Hamelin, 4); but subsequently he was persuaded by Gercke's view, and rejected as arbitrary Schmekel's claim that criticism of Chrysippus had been lost after §45 (Hamelin, 6-7). Amand 67 n.3, though regarding Antiochus as the source, takes §§41-3 as showing (on the basis of §39) that Carneades *rejected* Chrysippus' alleged attempt to combine fate and freedom.

the influence of circumstances on character, as Donini supposes.[1] The suggestion will then be that Carneades, or rather Clitomachus, is the primary source.[2]

4.2.3. However, Clitomachus' report of Carneades cannot be the only source. The discussion of Posidonius' views on interconnections between events in §§5-6 must come from a later source than Carneades,[3] even if thematic links between the discussion of Chrysippus' views in §§7-11 and the issues raised in §§39-45 and in the lacuna thereafter may suggest that the discussion of Chrysippus in §§7-11 comes from Carneades.

4.2.4. Moreover, as Jonathan Barnes has pointed out, the report of the Lazy Argument and of Chrysippus' response to it at §§28-30 is closely parallelled in Origen, *Against Celsus* 2.20.[4] It is unlikely that Origen would have drawn on a Latin source; and Barnes therefore argues that the common source of Cicero and Origen must be Chrysippus' own text. He further argues, from the closeness of the wording in the two texts and on grounds of economy, that both authors are using Chrysippus directly. The way in which Cicero continues his discussion in §31 may suggest that Carneades has not been his source for what precedes.[5]

4.2.5. Clearly the attitude adopted towards Epicurus in Cicero's treatise was characteristically critical; it is argued both in §23 and in §46 that Carneades was right to claim that there is no need to have recourse to Epicurus' stratagems, the atomic swerve and the denial of the truth of future contingents, in order to reply to Chrysippus' arguments for

---

1. For Donini, §§39-45 are but the first part of a two-pronged argument advanced by Carneades against Chrysippus; here Carneades attempts to state Chrysippus' position in the form that is most acceptable to a libertarian, but in the following, missing discussion Carneades would have pointed out that Chrysippus' position is unacceptable *even* when construed in this favourable way. See below, Commentary on §45.

2. So Schmekel (1892) 180, Philippson 1038, and Eisenberger. Schmekel (1892) 181-4 further supported his argument that the §§39ff. derived from the same source as what precedes them by claiming that the arrangement of topics in Cicero's treatise is similar to that in the much more compressed treatment in Plutarch *On Stoic Self-Contradictions* 46-7, and that both derived from the same source. J. Mansfeld, 'Diaphonia: the argument of Alexander *De fato* chs. 1-2', *Phronesis* 33 (1988) 181-207, at 194 n.41 suggests an Academic sceptical source.

3. Philippson 1038; Donini (1989) 132 n.27 and 144-5. Philippson suggests that the *criticisms* of Posidonius in §§5-6 are Cicero's own.

4. Barnes [1985,1]. Below, Appendix (A).

5. Barnes [1985,1] 239 n.36. Against the possibility that Cicero is using an intermediate source, Barnes 239 n.37 cites as evidence for Cicero's direct knowledge of Chrysippus' works the reference at On Ends 4.7 (though that is to a *rhetorical* treatise). Donini [1988] 29-30 n.18 however points out that it is more economical to suppose that, if Cicero is not using Chrysippus directly in §§39-45, as the one-sided presentation of his views there would suggest, he is not doing so here either.

determinism. It is likely that Chrysippus' attempt to preserve freedom was rejected in discussion after §45, now lost. Cicero thus concludes that neither Epicurus nor Chrysippus gave an acceptable account of freedom. This much Carneades too had asserted. Carneades may or may not have gone further and actually claimed that human free will *did* exist (see above, Introduction §3.1.9); but whether he did so or not, it seems likely that Cicero does want to make such a claim. Human freedom does exist, we are responsible for our actions, and Carneades' way of resolving the apparent problems of something happening without a cause and of the truth of future contingents should be accepted.[1]

5. An evaluation of Cicero's treatise.

5.1. Even in its present fragmentary state, and with all the problems of interpretation which this involves, the importance of Cicero's treatise *On Fate* can scarcely be over-stated. It is a major source both for the debate on physical determinism and for that on logical determinism, and is the earliest extant text to draw a distinction between the two. Thanks to the Academic technique of presenting and discussing several different views, it gives us perhaps a clearer sense of the interactions between them than any other ancient text - and this in spite of the real difficulties, then as now, for the proponents of one view in giving a fair account of another. A treatise *On Fate* like that of Alexander of Aphrodisias, in the early years of the third century A.D., may do much to develop the philosophical debate and the criticisms of arguments; but Alexander does not name his opponents, and for those with a historical, as opposed to purely philosophical, interest in the arguments the relation of the determinism he attacks to that actually advanced by the Stoics has to be judged with the help of other sources, of which Cicero's treatise is one.

5.2. Cicero's text is not merely of interest in the reconstruction of the views of Epicurus, Diodorus and the Stoics; it is our main source for Carneades' own contributions to the discussion of the free-will problem[2] and while opinions may differ as to the validity of Carneades' contributions,[3] their importance can scarcely be questioned. Indeed, the interest

---

1. That Cicero makes the existence of free will a postulate is the theme of Henry's article; she associates this with a practical Roman approach (especially 32, 39-42). Cf. above, Introduction §3.1.9, and commentary on §32.

2. A partial exception should be made here for Carneades' contribution to the criticism of determinism for its ethical implications, and also for his contribution to specifically anti-astrological argument; Amand reconstructs both of these on the basis of other texts. But the ethical arguments, in particular, did not start with Carneades (see commentary on §40); and it is in connection with the causation of human action and the problem of future truth that Carneades makes his philosophically most significant contributions.

3. See Introduction §§3.1.8 and 3.2.3.

of the philosophical arguments in the treatise as a whole can scarcely be overstated.[1]

5.3. It must be admitted that Duhot, in particular, takes a very different view of the merits of Cicero's treatise (193-210, especially 203-210); but while admitting that some of the real difficulties in interpretation may be the result of hasty composition, it must be pointed out that there is nothing unphilosophical - if anything the reverse - in Cicero's presentation of his argument in §§39-45 in terms of a debate between opponents some of whom are spokesmen for artificially constructed positions rather than actual historical antagonists. Thus, when Duhot says (206) that "Cicero shares with the doxographers the illusion that all philosophers are replying to the same perpetual questions the formulation of which can be found in scholarly manuals", one may reply that philosophical problems *are* in a sense perpetual, and that it is not unreasonable to characterise a philosopher's position in terms of its implications in relation to the views of others, whether these were realised by the original proponent or not - which is not to say that one should not *also* be constantly aware of the possibility that an ancient thinker's preoccupations may not be the same as our own. The classification of views on a particular issue may be a mark of scholarly preoccupations, but it may also be undertaken in the context of philosophical debate; it was characteristic of Carneades,[2] and the connections between doxography and sceptical dialectic are currently being explored in a series of papers by Jaap Mansfeld.[3]

6. The influence of Cicero's treatise.

6.1. The influence in antiquity of Cicero's treatise *On Fate* is limited but significant. Aulus Gellius cites it in his discussion of Chrysippus (see below on fragment 1), but only refers in passing to Cicero, preferring to go back to Chrysippus' own text (see Appendix (C)). Apart from Gellius and Augustine (below), the other ancient citations of the treatise are by Macrobius (fragment 4) and, apparently, in Servius' commentary on the *Aeneid* (fragment 2); but the latter cites Cicero for what is very much a standard definition of a central term, not showing any particular knowledge of our treatise. It was also used as a source for Diodorus' and Chrysippus' definitions of possibility by Jerome.[4]

---

1. Schofield comments (50): "*(On Fate)* conveys the interplay of ingenious minds arguing and putting fresh and unexpected lines of thought to each other better than any of Cicero's other philosophical writings, even though it is formally presented not as dialogue but as the continuous discourse of a single speaker. It is the Ciceronian treatise philosophers most enjoy reading."

2. Cf. the "Carneadea divisio" of Cicero, *On Ends* 5.16. I am grateful to David Sedley for drawing this point to my attention.

3. Cf. Mansfeld [1988], [1990] 3173, and id. 'Phusikai doxai from Aristotle to Aëtius and beyond', forthcoming in *Rutgers University Studies in Classical Humanities* volume 5.

4. *Dialogues against the Pelagians* 1.9; Courcelle [1969] 66 n.67.

6.2. However Augustine, who draws extensively on the treatise in his discussion of divine foreknowledge in *City of God* 5.9,[1] ensured future awareness - one is tempted to say, notoriety - of Cicero as an opponent of determinism. Admittedly it is *On Divination* rather than *On Fate* that he cites by name,[2] though his discussion draws on both treatises. His discussion is an attack on Cicero for denying divine foreknowledge because of his inability to reconcile it with human freedom. As Hagendahl (526-534) points out, Augustine is here reading Cicero in the light of his, Augustine's, own priorities; Cicero does not himself see the denial of determinism primarily in terms of the denial of divine foreknowledge, though the very fact that he wrote *On Fate* as a sequel to *On Divination* helps to justify Augustine's approach, and Augustine did have access to more of *On Fate* than we do. But in any case the issue of divine foreknowledge *is* raised, in §§32-3, where Cicero cites Carneades as saying that what is not predetermined cannot be foreknown even by the gods; so Augustine's presentation of Cicero's argument involves at most a selective emphasis, of the sort that philosophers have always practised in reading their predecessors for what they can glean from them in the context of their own preoccupations. Augustine's presentation of Cicero did however lead him to present Cicero primarily as an irreligious opponent of divine knowledge and power (while recognising Cicero's motive as concern with morality);[3] and, in reaction to this, it was in these terms that Renaissance writers saw him as an opponent of Augustine.[4]

6.3. For Boethius, like Augustine, it is the question of divine foreknowledge that is central; and for Boethius too it is Cicero's *On Divination* rather than his *On Fate* that is the important work (see below on Boethius, *Consolation* book 5 prose 4 ad init.). Before we come to Boethius, however, it will be appropriate to say something about developments in the discussion of divine foreknowledge, providence and evil between Cicero's time and his.

7. Divine Foreknowledge from Cicero to Boethius.

7.1. Divine foreknowledge had been used by the Stoics as an argument for universal determinism; the gods can only know what will happen in the future if there are already causes that determine what will eventu-

---

1. And to some extent earlier in the book; but the extent to which he did so is disputed. See below on Fragment 4 (between §4 and §5). For Augustine's dependence on Cicero cf. also Donini [1974-5] 206 and n.2.

2. Cf. Yon xxxix n.1.

3. *City of God* 5.9; Henry, 33.

4. I am grateful to Dr Letitia Panizza for drawing this point to my attention. Henry 35 presents Cicero as in effect a Pelagian, supporting human responsibility in contrast to Augustine's doctrine of divine grace.

ally come about.[1] Carneades, as reported in Cicero's *On Fate* §§32-3, shares the view that the gods can only foreknow what is predetermined; *if* he wished to assert positively that there are some things – free human actions, for example – that are *not* predetermined, it would follow that there are some things that the gods cannot know about the future. This was certainly the position, later, of the Aristotelian commentator Alexander of Aphrodisias; he points out that the argument from divine foreknowledge to universal determinism turns on a limitation of the gods' power, since they can only know what is predetermined, and argues that in the light of this it would be more appropriate first to establish whether things are predetermined or not and then deduce the extent of the divine knowledge, rather than postulating that the gods must know everything and inferring the way in which things happen from that.[2] After all, presumably even the gods do not know the exact ratio between the diagonal of a square and its side.[3] Porphyry, the follower and editor of Plotinus, adopted a similar view to Alexander;[4] so too does Calcidius, the Latin commentator on the *Timaeus*.[5]

7.2. A change however came with the Neoplatonist Iamblichus, who argued that the nature of knowledge depended on that of the knower rather than on that of the thing known – a principle which will be important in our analysis of Boethius' argument in *Consolation of Philosophy* 5.[6] Proclus adopts the same view.[7] The gods thus have necessary and definite foreknowledge of what is in itself contingent and

---

1. Calcidius, *On the Timaeus* 160 193.17ff. Waszink = SVF 2.943; cf. Cicero *On Divination* 1.127 = SVF 2.944 = LS 55O, and Nemesius *On the Nature of Man* 36 p.106.22 Morani.

2. Alexander, *On Fate* 30. Alexander's point is essentially a negative one against the Stoics; it is not clear how far he himself wishes to assert that the divine has knowledge of contingent possibilities. What is at any rate certain is that there cannot be divine foreknowledge of the *outcomes* in such cases. Cf. Huber 13-14, Sharples [1983,1] 28 and 164-6, Mignucci [1985] 225-234.

3. A similar example in modern terms might be; does an omniscient God know the decimal expansion of the quantity π ?

4. For Porphyry's view cf. Proclus, *in Tim.* 1.352.12; cf. Huber 18-19, 42 n.18. Mignucci [1985] 234-7 attributes a similar view to Plotinus; cf. Sorabji [1983] 264.

5. Calcidius, *On the Timaeus* 162 p.195.1-17 Waszink. Cf. Klingner [1921] 98-9; den Boeft 53ff.; Huber 18-19. On Calcidius' philosophical affinities and date cf. J.M. Dillon, *The Middle Platonists*, London 1977, 401-5.

6. Iamblichus cited by Ammonius *On On Interpretation* 135.14ff. and by Stephanus *On On Interpretation* 35.19ff. Huber 40ff., Gruber 398-9, Sorabji [1980,2] 124 and [1983] 255.

7. Proclus *Elements of Theology* 124 (cf.93), *Ten Problems* 7-8, *On Providence* 63-5, *On the Timaeus* 1.352.11-16, *On the Parmenides* 957.14ff. Cousin, *Platonic Theology* 1.21. Klingner [1921] 107-8; Patch [1935,1]; Obertello [1974] 515-20, 703; Huber 26-30, 40-42; Mignucci [1985] 237-246; Talanga 155.

indefinite – a view which Proclus explicitly contrasts both with the Stoic position and with that of the Peripatetics.[1] The same position is found in the Neoplatonists Ammonius and Stephanus, commenting on Aristotle *On Interpretation* 9,[2] and in the Christian writer Origen.[3]

7.3. Proclus and Iamblichus' concern is not generally with how future contingent events can be contingent although foreknown by the gods, but with the more general question of how unchanging and determinate divinities can have knowledge of the changing and indeterminate world of sense.[4] As a solution to the foreknowledge problem Iamblichus' position is incomplete; it is all very well to be told *that* the gods can have definite knowledge of an indefinite and undetermined future, but that does not tell us *how* the future outcome can be indefinite if the gods foresee it now.[5] It is Boethius, in the *Consolation,* who provides the further stage of the argument, by adding the claim that to God all time is as the present, and that thus God's knowledge of what I will do in the future no more removes my freedom to do otherwise than someone's knowledge now of what I am doing now removes the fact that I could have chosen to do otherwise.[6]

7.4. It is common ground between both sides in this debate that divine foreknowledge must be foreknowledge of the contingent *as contingent;* that is, God must not suppose that what is in fact contingent is necessary, for if he did he would not *know* it. But this formulation is ambiguous; it may mean either that the divine knows that "p will happen" and that "p will not happen" are possible, *and nothing more,* or that the divine knows that p will in fact happen, while also knowing that either p or not p is possible. Those who side with Alexander and

---

1. Proclus *On Providence* 63.4–8; Hager, 175–7, Huber 22. One may compare Carneades' challenging, both on the question of uncaused motion and on that of future truth, the shared assumptions of Stoics and Epicureans.

2. See above, and Ammonius *On* On Interpretation 137.1, 13ff.; Stephanus *On* On Interpretation 36.32–4. Courcelle [1967] 213–14, [1969] 309; Merlan 199–200; Obertello [1974] 704; Huber 40–42; Talanga 143; Sorabji [1983] 262. On the status of the divine beings that have such foreknowledge, in Proclus on the one hand and Ammonius on the other, see Verrycken 213.

3. Origen *On Prayer,* PG 11.437B; Klingner [1921] 98–9. Cf. also Appendix (A) to Cicero *On Fate,* above.

4. Cf. Sorabji [1980,2] 125, and below §12.2.4. Exceptions are Proclus *On Providence* 63 and *Ten Problems* 8 at lines 18–19 Boese; Patch [1935,1] 399. Philo Judaeus, *That God is Unchanging* 6.29 and 32, already has the notion that God can foreknow individual future events because to him the future is as the present (Sorabji [1983] 256 and 264), but he does not there connect the point with the problem of human freedom.

5. Cf. Huber 54, on Ammonius.

6. See below, Introduction §12.2.4.

Porphyry naturally intend the former,[1] those who side with Iamblichus and Proclus the latter.[2] Secondly, it is also common ground that for God to foreknow the future is not the same as for him to cause it[3]; but as Boethius points out,[4] to say that God does not *cause* my future actions is not on its own sufficient to answer the problem apparently posed for free will by the fact that it must be what God foresees that eventually happens.

7.5. Boethius himself touches briefly on the question of divine foreknowledge in his second commentary on Aristotle's *On Interpretation* (224.27-226.25). It is a sign of the ambiguities indicated in the preceding paragraph that a number of scholars seem to have interpreted his position there in terms of his adopting the same view as Alexander and Porphyry.[5] But this is not so; God knows what is contingent *as being contingent,*[6] but Boethius' words at 226.9-13 make it clear that here as well as in the *Consolation* he agrees with Iamblichus and Proclus that divine foreknowledge of the contingent does involve knowledge of what the outcome will be: "God knows future things not as coming about of necessity, but as doing so contingently, in such a way that he is not unaware that something else too could happen, *but what comes about he knows on the basis of the human beings themselves and their actions*".[7] The clause in italics serves, in its context, to emphasise that our actions depend on our choices and are not controlled or caused by God;

---

1. Cf. Alexander *On Fate* 30 201.13-18; Calcidius *in Tim.* 160 195.4-7 Waszink. Cf. Hager 176-7 on Alexander; and cf. Boethius' remarks about Tiresias' prophecy at V.3.25.

2. Cf. Proclus *Ten Problems* 8, and §5 below on Boethius.

3. Cf. Alexander *On Fate* 30 201.14; Origen *On Prayer,* PG 11.436D and id. cited by Eusebius, *Preparation for the Gospel* 6.11.36; Ammonius *On On Interpretation* 136.25. This is so even though supporters of the view that the gods have determinate knowledge use the claim that they cause things to argue that they must have knowledge of them (cf. Cicero *On Divination* 1.82; Philo, *That God is unchanging* 6.30; Epictetus *Dissertationes* 1.14.6; Proclus, *On the* Parmenides 957.25, 964.7, *Ten Problems* 8 and *On Providence* 63; Ammonius *On* On Interpretation 134.3, 136.4, 132.14, 135.30; Simplicius *On Epictetus'* Manual 102.31f.); for that is not the same as to say that the fact of foreknowledge *itself* causes what is foreknown to happen (though Proclus *On the* Timaeus 1.352.8 and *On the* Parmenides 957.25 does suggest that the very acts of knowing and causing are identical where the gods are concerned). For Boethius cf. Commentary on V.3.15 and V.6.42 below. Obertello [1974] 703-4.

4. *Consolation* V.3.9-13.

5. So Gegenschatz [1966] 529, Huber 18 n.45, and Chadwick 159, attributing the same view to Boethius here and to Alexander.

6. *On* On Interpretation[2] 226.1-12. Cf. 212.8ff., 213.12ff., and *Consolation* V.3.23; V.6.24.

7. Or "what comes about on the basis of the human beings themselves and their actions he knows". The point is unaffected.

but it also indicates that God does know what the outcome will be.[1] As to how Boethius' account in the *second commentary* differs from that in the *Consolation*, see below, Introduction §12.2.4.

7.6. The standard solution in late antiquity, adopted by Boethius, to the problem of *future truth*, and the standard interpretation of Aristotle's position, is distinct both from the position of Epicurus and from that of Carneades (above, Introduction §§3.2.2-3). It is to claim that, while of the affirmation and the denial one is true and the other false, neither is true or false "definitely", in such a way that one can assert the truth of one and the falsity of the other[2] - this reflecting, it must be emphasised, not just the limitations of human understanding, but the truly undetermined nature of the outcome.[3]

8. Fate and Providence

8.1. For Chrysippus providence and fate were identical; God is present in the universe as the active principle which, combined with inert, passive matter, causes each thing to be what it is; the sequence of things in the world is thus in a sense identical with God, and God, the sequence of causes which is fate, and providence are all identified[4]. Cleanthes, we are told, had regarded providence as narrower in its scope than fate[5]; but the general Stoic view was the Chrysippean one

---

1. So, rightly, Courcelle [1967] 213-14, [1969] 309, pointing out that Boethius here *rejects* Alexander's view.

2. Indeed one might well adopt the proposal of White 60 and translate the Greek term *aphorismenôs* not as "definitely" but as "separately".

3. The position, though not with the terminology of 'determinately' and 'indeterminately', can be seen as implied in Aristotle *On Interpretation* 9 19a36-8. Cf. Ammonius, *On On Interpretation* 131.2-4, 138.16f., 139.14f., etc.; Simplicius, *On the Categories* 406.6ff.; Boethius, *On On Interpretation*[1] 106.30, 115.5 etc., *On On Interpretation*[2] 191.5, 208.11f., 215.21ff., 245.9, 246.12, 249.29. For further references cf. D. Frede [1985] 42-5, 76-7; Sorabji [1980,2] 93-4; Chadwick 157-163; Talanga 144-6; on the philosophical merits of the view cf. Kretzmann, and White 196.

4. All three are identified by Arius Didymus ap. Eusebius, *Preparation for the Gospel* 15.15.6 = SVF 2.528 (providence and fate being names of God); Plutarch *On Stoic Self-contradictions* 34 1050a = SVF 2.937. Fate and God are identified in reports relating to Stoic views by Philodemus *On Piety* 11 = SVF 2.1076; Cicero *On the Nature of the Gods* 1.40= SVF 2.1077 = LS 54B; Diogenes Laertius 7.135 = SVF 1.102 and 2.580 = LS 46B; Alexander, *On fate* 22 192.25ff. = SVF 2.945 = LS 55N; scholium on Homer, *Iliad* 8.69 = SVF 2.931; fate and the mind of Zeus by Proclus, *On Hesiod's Works and Days* 105 = SVF 2.929; fate and providence by "Aëtius" 1.27.5 = SVF 1.176.

5. Calcidius *in Timaeum* 144 = SVF 2.933 = LS 54U. M. Dragona-Monachou ('Providence and Fate in Stoicism and prae-Neoplatonism', ΦΙΛΟΣΟ-ΦΙΑ (Athens) 3 (1973) 262-300, at 289ff.) has convincingly argued that this is interpretation rather than reporting, resulting from a combination of Cleanthes' explicit statement that the actions of evil men are not the results of divine purpose even though it can turn them to its own ends (Cleanthes, *Hymn to Zeus* 17ff. = SVF 1.537 = LS 54I), combined with Calcidius' desire to find a contrary to his own Plato-

that everything that happens is the result both of fate and of divine providence.[1]

8.2. Even while this was asserted, however, there was a natural tendency to distinguish between fate and God even while asserting the total dependence of the former on the latter, to regard fate as proceeding from God[2] or to treat God as the first cause[3]. Some of these statements may relate to God as the temporally prior cause that begins each new world-cycle; but they can also be seen in the context of a tendency towards an increasingly hierarchical view of the organisation of the universe, which will reach its culmination in late Neoplatonism.[4]

8.3. This tendency develops further in those Middle Platonists who distinguish a hierarchy of three levels of providence based on Plato's *Timaeus;* the primary providence of the highest god, concerned with the heavens and with rational souls, the secondary providence of the secondary or planetary gods concerned with the orderly coming-to-be of perishable things and the preservation of natural kinds, and the tertiary providence of *daemones* concerned with the detailed events of

---

...Continued...

nist view that fate is wider than providence (see below, Introduction §8.3).

1. The Stoics regard the traditional Greek gods as aspects of a the single divine active principle: LS 54A. Boethius' view of the relation of fate and providence is contrasted with that of the Stoics by Courcelle [1967] 204, [1969] 305 n.68, citing Fortescue.

2. Chrysippus spoke of fate as identical with Zeus' reasoning, rationale or plan *(logos;* cited by Plutarch, *On Stoic Self-Contradictions* 47 1056c = SVF 2.997 = LS 55R); but he also referred to fate as the rationale of the things arranged in the world by providence (Chrysippus cited by Stobaeus 1 p.79.6-7 Wachsmuth = SVF 2.913 = LS 55M). According to Calcidius *On the* Timaeus 144 = SVF 2.933 the series of causes is both providence (as being God's will) and fate (as being the sequence of causes); den Boeft 14 argues that this is a later development. The Stoics are said to *attribute* the sequence of causes to God's will by Augustine *City of God* 5.8 = SVF 2.932. Posidonius distinguished god, nature and fate (Aëtius 1.28.5 = Posidonius F103 E-K, Cicero *On Divination* 1.125 = Posidonius F107 E-K); but Kidd argues that this was for explanatory purposes in discussing divination, and not an attempt to introduce a metaphysical hierarchy (EK vol.2 pp.414-8, 426-8).

3. Seneca, *On Good Deeds* 4.7.2 = SVF 2.1024 identifies fate and God by arguing that God is the first cause; at *Questions on Nature* 2.45 God is identified with fate and providence, as being the cause of causes. Cf. Marcus Aurelius 4.40, 9.39. Plotinus contrasts a view according to which fate is an interweaving of causes with their source in a single (world-)soul (3.1.4) and one according to which it is the chain of causes (3.1.7). Cf. Theiler [1946] 55-7.

4. On the issues discussed in this section cf. also Scheible, 184-7.

individuals' lives.[1] These writers identify fate with the world-soul.[2] Pseudo-Plutarch *On Fate* explicitly raises the question of whether fate, linked with the movement of the heavens presumably for astrological reasons, is on the same level as secondary providence or subordinate to it;[3] whatever view is taken on that, however, it is clear that fate is subordinate to the highest level of providence.[4] And the Neoplatonists continue this theme, linking providence with the timeless unity of intellect and fate with the nature of the physical universe extended in time and governed by soul,[5] and speaking of the individual soul rising above the level of fate.[6] Both these themes are important for Boethius' *Consolation;* the former is central to the argument of IV.6,[7] and the latter underlies the whole structure of the work.[8]

9. The problem of evil.

9.1. A full discussion of ancient solutions to the problem of evil would not be appropriate in the present context. But since the question is prominent, in different ways, both in the part of book IV of Boethius' *Consolation* that precedes that here printed and in the concluding chapters of book IV, some comment at least may be in place.

9.2. The Stoic answer to the problem of evil is twofold. Firstly, for the Stoic nothing is good except virtue and nothing bad except wickedness, so that from this point of view the problem of evil reduces to that of explaining why, in a providentially ordered world, most people - indeed for the Stoics *all* people except for the wise man who is as rare as the phoenix - should fall short of perfect moral goodness and thus, for the

---

1. Apuleius, *De Platone* 1.12 96.2ff. Thomas; [Plutarch], *On Fate* 9 572F-573A; Nemesius of Emesa, *On the Nature of Man* 43 125.21-126.12 Morani. The account in the text above is that of pseudo-Plutarch; for the details of the various accounts cf. Sharples [1983,2] 142 and nn.

2. [Plutarch] *On Fate* 568E; Calcidius *On the Timaeus* 144 p.182.16 Waszink; Nemesius *On the Nature of Man* 38 p.109.11 Morani. On the origin of these doctrines cf. J.M. Dillon, *The Middle Platonists,* London 1977, 295-8, 320-38, 406-7.

3. [Plutarch] *On Fate* 10 574CD.

4. A contrast between providence and fate is also found in Calcidius (above, §8.1; and cf. id. 145 p.183.18-20 Waszink, 151 p.187.1-3 Waszink, 177 p.206.1-2 Waszink), in Nemesius *On the Nature of Man* 38 p.109.16-18 Morani, and in Hierocles ap. Photius 251 461b20ff.; Huber 17 n.40.

5. Plotinus 3.3 5.14-25, Proclus *On Providence* 3-4, 5-9, 14. Patch [1935,1] 64-7; Courcelle [1967] 204 and [1969] 305 n.71; Huber 17 n.40; Gruber 357.

6. Plotinus, 3.1.9-10, cf. 3.2.10, 3.3.4; cf. Calcidius, *On the Timaeus* 186 p.212.4ff. Waszink. Patch [1935,1] 398.

7. See below on IV.6.8-17.

8. See below, Introduction §11.1, on Boethius' return to true understanding; and Commentary on V.5.12.

Stoics, be morally wicked.[1]

9.3. However, the Stoics also felt impelled to explain why what are regarded by most people as misfortunes should occur in a providentially ordered world, even if they are not evils in the Stoic sense of the term. Here they introduced or developed a whole range of arguments which became the stock in trade of subsequent attempts at theodicy, of justifying the ways of God to man; among them the claim that disasters happen for some purpose that is not obvious to us,[2] and the argument that desirable purposes necessarily involve less than desirable concomitants.[3]

9.4. Rather different, though, are two arguments attributed to the Stoics which seem to conflict with the claim that everything that happens is part of a single divine plan. Plutarch quotes Chrysippus – if indeed this is a fair report and not the quoting out of context of a view advanced for the sake of argument – as saying that some (apparent) evils can be explained by certain things being under the charge of inferior *daimones*.[4] And Cicero cites the Stoics as saying that the gods care for great matters, but disregard small ones[5].

9.5. If the latter is a claim that divine providence *consciously* sacrifices lesser interests to greater ones, then it is not in conflict with the original Stoic doctrine of a universal divine providence. If however it is a claim that lesser interests are simply neglected, then it does seem to conflict with the original Stoic position. What is certain is that, in the first two centuries A.D., views developed which sought to reconcile divine providence and the existence of evil by making God remote from the sublunary world or by claiming that divine providence was concerned only with generalities, the preservation of species or the struc-

---

1. Cf. Cicero, *On the Nature of the Gods* 3.79; Plutarch, *On Stoic Self-Contradictions* 1048ef, *Common Notions* 1076b; Philodemus in SVF 2.1183; Alexander, *On Fate* 199.14ff. = SVF 3.658 = LS 61N. The question why moral evil should exist at all can be answered by the claim that it is logically impossible for good to exist without evil; Chrysippus ap. Gellius *Attic Nights* 7.1.1ff. = SVF 2.1169 = LS 54Q; Plutarch *On Stoic Self-Contradictions* 1050F ff. = SVF 2.1181-2 = LS 61R. But this does not explain why virtue is so rare and wickedness so prevalent. The best attempt to answer that question is reported by Calcidius *on the* Timaeus 165-7 = SVF 3.229, who reports the Stoics as attributing the misdirection of our desires to our surroundings and to the false opinions of others; but that simply raises again the question of whether providence could have arranged things better.

2. Plutarch, *On Stoic Self-Contradictions* 1040c (= SVF 2.1175), 1050e (= SVF 2.1176), 1049a (= SVF 2.1177). The true interest of the part is in fact that of the whole: Epictetus *Dissertations* 2.6.9 = SVF 3.191.

3. Gellius *Attic Nights* 7.1.7ff. = SVF 2.1170 = LS 54Q.

4. Plutarch, *On Stoic Self-Contradictions* 1051BC = SVF 2.1178 = LS 54S; cf. D. Babut, *Plutarque et le stoïcisme,* Paris 1969, 291f.

5. Cicero, *On the Nature of the Gods* 2.167. Cf. Sharples [1983,2] 150.

32

ture of the universe, and not with the fortunes of individuals.[1]

9.6. The Platonists, however, insisted on the control of everything by divine providence. The hierarchical theory of three providences developed by some Middle Platonists[2] provided a way of claiming that even the fortunes of sublunary individuals were under the control of providence, even if an inferior version; and other Middle Platonists such as Atticus attacked the Peripatetics for denying divine concern with the sublunary.[3]

9.7. For Plotinus, too, in his reaction against the Gnostic dualism which regarded the physical world as evil, matter and the things composed of it are not a separate principle over and against the good that comes from the One and from Intellect, so much as the last point in the outflowing of goodness; not so much a separate principle of darkness as the point where the light gives out.[4] Plotinus and subsequent Neoplatonists are even less metaphysical dualists than Plato is in the *Timaeus*.[5] And, if there is a predominant theme which emerges in Plotinus' complex discussion of providence and human responsibility in *Enneads* 3.2 and 3.3, it is that evil is a by-product, the result of interference between the expressions in space and time of principles which were compatible on the formal level[6]. The notion that evil is essentially not-being is adopted by Augustine, who argues that to ask the cause of evil is like asking to see darkness or hear silence.[7]

9.8. The theme that evil is essentially negative, the absence of power rather than its expression[8] is taken up by Boethius in IV.2. But even while claiming that no true evil can befall the good man, he also feels the need to argue that even the apparent misfortunes of the virtuous and the apparent prosperity of the wicked have some providential rationale. To argue this he claims, essentially, that we are in no position to criticise divine providence, since we cannot see the whole picture; the misfortunes of the righteous may serve to exercise their virtue, and the prosperity of the wicked may either indicate to them

---

1. This was the view of the Peripatetic Alexander of Aphrodisias, on whom see Sharples [1983,1] 25-7, [1987] 1216-1218. Cf. also Epictetus, *Dissertations* 1.12.2; Justin Martyr *Against Trypho* 1.4; Nemesius *On the Nature of Man* 43 128.13 Morani. Cf. Sharples [1983,2] 148-152.

2. Above, Introduction §8.3.

3. Atticus, fr.3 des Places.

4. Plotinus 4.3 9.21ff., cf. 1.8 7.17ff.

5. Cf. Wallis 157 and F.P. Hager, 'Die Materie und das Böse im antiken Platonismus', *Mus. Helv.* 19 (1962) 73-103. (I am grateful to Anne Sheppard for discussion of this issue.)

6. 3.2.2, 3.2.15; cf. 3.3.7.

7. Augustine *City of God* 12.7; cf. 11.9 and *Confessions* 3.7. Chadwick 250.

8. Cf. Plato, *Gorgias* 466b-468e.

how worthless is the worldly fortune which they clearly do not deserve, or else reflect the awareness of providence that adversity might lead them to commit even worse crimes[1].

10. Boethius' life and works

10.1. Anicius Manlius Severinus Boethius was born in the early 480's A.D.[2] into an established senatorial family. Although the last Western emperor had been deposed in 476, and Italy was now ruled by Gothic kings in Ravenna, the Roman senate continued to function in relation to the administration of the city in the way it had done in the last century of the Empire; the emperors had been based at Ravenna too. Boethius was appointed *consul ordinarius,* giving his name to the year, in 510, and, as an exceptional honour, his two sons were appointed joint consuls in 522.[3]

10.2. Boethius set out to make the liberal arts available to the Latin west, writing on arithmetic, on music - linked by Pythagoreans and Neo-Platonists with the structure of the universe[4] - geometry and astronomy.[5] His work may well have formed part of an attempt by his father-in-law Symmachus to establish Greek culture in Rome in the face of traditional Latin opposition, an attempt initially favoured by Theodoric the Gothic king.[6]

10.3. Boethius also endeavoured to make the works of Aristotle accessible in the West, by translating them and writing commentaries on them.[7] In the event he was unable to carry his plan further than the logical works of Aristotle, the *Organon;* though on some of these he produced two commentaries, the second intended for the more advanced reader. His first logical work, completed in 504/5, was a commentary on Porphyry's *Introduction (Eisagoge),* which was regularly studied in the Neoplatonic schools as a preliminary to Aristotle's works.[8] Boethius was not the first to translate the Aristotelian treatises into Latin, and indeed is critical of his predecessor Marius Victorinus. The Latin of the commentaries, by contrast with that of the *Consolation,* is crabbed and

---

1. Cf. below, *Consolation* IV.6 and commentary.

2. Discussion at Chadwick, 1.

3. On the role of the Roman senatorial class in general in this period, and on Boethius' political career in particular, see Matthews.

4. For echoes of this theme in the *Consolation,* cf. Chadwick 101 and Chamberlain.

5. Cf. Courcelle [1969] 275-280; Chadwick 69-107; Reiss 14-27.

6. So Courcelle [1969] 322-330.

7. Cf. Boethius *On* On Interpretation[2] 79.9ff.; Gruber 7 n.56. The comparison with Cicero's activity five and a half centuries earlier is a natural one to make; cf. e.g. Shiel 371, 14-31, Lerer 25-9, and above §1.

8. Gruber 5; cf. 4-7, and references given there, on the general question of the chronology of Boethius' works.

difficult, following Aristotle's Greek idiom - itself idiosyncratic enough - to the extent that it is difficult for anyone not familiar with Aristotelian thought to understand.[1]

10.4. Boethius also produced works on questions of Christian doctrine.[2] His interest and skill in applying techniques of philosophical analysis to theological questions may have played a part in his downfall. The Ostrogothic kings in Ravenna followed the Arian heresy, which denied that Christ and the Father shared a single substance. In 484 there had been a breach between Catholic Christians in Rome and in Constantinople (the Acacian schism); Rome was more opposed to the Monophysite heresy (which claimed that Christ had only one *nature*), while Constantinople was more opposed to Nestorianism (which claimed that Christ had two *persons*, divine and human), and suspected Rome of insufficient opposition to it. Boethius felt that what was needed was better understanding of the issues involved, and he attempted in his theological writings to clarify the issues.[3] But when in 519 the new emperor in Byzantium, Justin, achieved reconciliation between Catholics in Rome and in the East, questions of religious orthodoxy and of attempts by Byzantium to regain control over Italy became linked, in the view of Theodoric at least.[4] Theodoric was further threatened by doubt over his successor[5] and the election in 523 of a pro-Byzantine pope, John I, probably identical with "John the Deacon" to whom Boethius had dedicated several of his theological treatises.

10.5. In 522, Boethius became Theodoric's *Magister officiorum,* a position which gave him considerable power and in which he made enemies. The crisis came in 523 or 524, when Theodoric's secretary Cyprian denounced a senator, Albinus, for treasonable correspondence with associates of the emperor, and Theodoric declared Albinus guilty without trial. It seems possible that letters had indeed been sent, and that the senate, or part of it, was trying to secure its position in advance of anticipated hostility from Theodoric.[6] Boethius claimed that the accusation against Albinus was in fact false, but that if it had been true all the senate would have joined in the action.[7] Supporters of Cyprian accused Boethius himself of treasonable correspondence and of trying to prevent an informer producing evidence; in the *Consolation* he admits

---

1. Others have found similar difficulties in translating Aristotle's logical works; cf. Barnes [1981] 77. In general see Liebeschütz 540-3; Courcelle [1969] 280-295; Chadwick 133-163; Reiss 28-54; Ebbesen.

2. Accounts in Liebeschütz 543-6; Chadwick 174-222; Reiss 58-79.

3. Chadwick, 25.

4. On the whole story of the schisms see Courcelle [1969] 273-5; Chadwick 22-46; Reiss 64-6. Bark 411-423 claimed that Boethius' theological writings were actively used by the supporters of Constantinople.

5. See Chadwick 51-2.

6. So Coster, 65.

7. Anonymus Valesianus 85.

the latter charge, claiming that he was trying to preserve the safety of the Senate, but denies the former.[1] It is clear, at the least, that Boethius' loyalty was to the senate rather than the king, whether or not he was actually guilty of treason.[2] He was also accused of sorcery; not for the first or last time, an interest in the heavens proved dangerous for a philosopher.[3] Boethius and Albinus were arrested; Boethius was taken to Pavia and sentenced to death in his absence by a senatorial court in Rome. But the sentence was not carried out immediately, whether because Theodoric wanted more evidence or because he was using Boethius' life as a bargaining counter to bring pressure on Justin and on the Roman senate.[4] During his imprisonment at Pavia Boethius wrote the *Consolation of Philosophy*.

10.6. In 524-525 Justin began to persecute the Arian heretics in the East, no doubt in order to provoke Theodoric and exacerbate the tensions between him and the Catholics in Italy.[5] In the late autumn of 525 Theodoric sent the pope on an embassy to Constantinople with threats of reprisals against Catholics in Italy if Justin did not cease his persecution of the Arians.[6] On his return the pope was imprisoned and tortured by Theodoric. Whether Boethius was still alive by this point, being kept as a hostage for the success of the papal mission, or whether he had already been executed as a warning, is uncertain.[7] According to the lurid account in the *Anonymus Valesianus* Boethius was tortured by a cord round his head before being clubbed to death; but Morton

---

1. *Consolation* I.4.22, 26.

2. On the question of Boethius' guilt cf. Matthews 35-8. It has been asserted particularly by Bark; more plausible perhaps is Coster's acceptance (62-3) that Boethius had not known of a conspiracy, but would have supported it if he had.

3. *Consolation* I.4.41. Cf. Courcelle [1969] 330; Chadwick, 49-50.

4. Chadwick, 55.

5. Chadwick, 67.

6. The chronological relation between Justin's persecution and the embassy it provoked on the one hand, and Boethius' arrest and execution on the other, is controversial. Coster, 66, placed the arrest after the departure of the embassy; but in a postscript to the reprinted version of his article in his *Late Roman Studies* he reverted (98) to the traditional view, influenced by the *Anonymus Valesianus,* that Boethius was arrested in 523 and executed in 524. Chadwick puts the *arrest* before the persecution, but suggests that the execution may have been later and that, if so, the persecution is evidence that Justin regarded Boethius' life as expendable. Courcelle [1969] 330 puts Boethius' condemnation after the persecution; Obertello [1974] 139-143 says that the sequence of the anti-Arian measures and Boethius' condemnation is unclear, but suggests that the former provoked the latter. Clearly the question of the interval between arrest and execution has considerable implications for the composition of the *Consolation*.

7. Chadwick 62. Coster 70 argued that Boethius' execution was probably after the pope's return in 526; but see above for Coster's change of view.

argues that this account is unreliable and that the early tradition is that Boethius was simply beheaded.[1] Symmachus his father-in-law was also executed.[2] Theodoric issued an edict that on 30th August 526 the Arians would take over the Catholic churches in Ravenna; but on that day he died. His attempt to create harmony between Romans and Goths in Italy had collapsed; and by 554 the generals of Justin's nephew and successor Justinian had reconquered Italy.

11. The *Consolation of Philosophy*.

11.1. The *Consolation* is written in the form of a Menippean satire, an alternation of verse and prose passages.[3] It is presented as a dialogue between Boethius himself and Philosophy, personified as Lady Philosophy. The work opens with Boethius in his prison cell lamenting his plight in elegiac verse: 'I who once flourished writing songs with enthusiasm am now compelled, alas, in my tears to adopt mournful measures ...".[4] Philosophy banishes the Muses as harlots who encourage passion rather than reason, and on hearing Boethius' account of what has happened to him declares that he has been banished not just from his home but from his true self and his true country, that is from philosophical understanding (I.5); a remedy is needed, and her discourse will provide it.[5] She proceeds to indicate the worthlessness of the gifts of fortune conventionally regarded as good (II), the powerlessness of evil and the fact that wickedness is its own punishment and virtue its own reward (III-IV). Boethius, who even at the outset had recognised but not understood that everything is governed by divine providence (I.6), asks why even so external "goods" seem to be allotted unjustly; Philosophy explains this by the inability of human understanding fully to comprehend the dispensations of divine providence (IV.7). In response to Boethius' request, she explains the true nature of chance, which is ultimately traceable to divine providence (V.1); and when Boethius protests that he cannot see how God's providence and foreknowledge can be reconciled with human freedom (V.3), Philosophy resolves the problem by the argument that God in his eternity sees our

---

1. Matthews 38 n.1 also expresses hesitation about following the *Anonymus Valesianus* account.

2. For the whole story cf. Obertello [1974] 85-143; Chadwick, 46-56.

3. The form had been originated by Menippus in the third century B.C., in Greek; notable examples included Varro's *Menippean Satires* (lost except for fragments), Seneca's *Apocolocyntosis,* and Petronius' *Satyricon.* It had been linked with philosophy at its outset; particularly significant for Boethius was Martianus Capella, *Marriage of Philology and Mercury,* on the liberal arts. Cf. Courcelle [1967] 17; Chadwick 21, 223-4; Gruber 17-19.

4. On the Ovidian character of this poem cf. Crabbe 244-51.

5. See also IV.5.2, V.1.4, and Commentary. De Vogel [1973] 357 compares Plotinus' reference (5.1.1) to souls who have forgotten God.

actions not as future but as present (V.4-6).[1]

11.2. The work is described as a "Consolation"; and consolation to the bereaved, or written by the bereaved to console themselves,[2] was an established genre.[3] But Boethius is writing a consolation to himself in the context of his *own* misfortune. And the work is not only a consolation, but a protreptic advocating the study of philosophy; that too was a genre with a long history.[4] The ultimate inspiration of the *Consolation* is Plato's *Phaedo*;[5] there too we have an account, in the context of an impending execution, of the philosopher's concern with higher realities than those of this world, culminating in a complex philosophical argument.[6] Socrates' execution will release him from the distractions of the body, presented as a *guard-house*,[7] and his death is presented as a journey to better gods and a better place.[8] Moreover, Socrates in *his* condemned cell had begun to write poetry.[9]

---

1. For a fuller summary of the work than can be given here see Chadwick, 225-47.

2. Cicero's lost consolation to himself on the death of his daughter Tullia was the first example of the latter (Liebeschütz 547).

3. Cf. Courcelle [1967] 115, Gruber 25-7.

4. Notable examples were Aristotle's *Protrepticus* and Cicero's lost *Hortensius* (the work that inspired Augustine; *Confessions* 3.4); but Boethius' *Consolation* is an appeal not to begin the study of philosophy but to return to it (Gruber 30). It is also a protreptic cast in the form of a revelation; for the use of revelation scholars have compared especially Fulgentius (cf. Klingner [1921] 114-5; Courcelle [1967] 17-20, [1969] 296; Lerer 58-62, 102 n.22). The scenario of a female figure who has features that seem more than human, even if not divine (see on IV.6.38) enlightening a male enquirer has a long history, going back to the goddess who enlightened Parmenides, and to Diotima and Socrates. Moreover, as Rand [1904] 8 points out, the *Consolation* is not just a consolation or a protreptic, but an attempt to justify the ways of God to man. "Satire" - in its broad, original Latin sense - had always involved a medley of themes (Crabbe 238).

5. Chadwick 228-9.

6. There is however nothing in the *Consolation* to correspond to the final myth of the *Phaedo*. Socrates' execution is referred to as a precedent for Boethius' plight by Philosophy in I.3; Crabbe 241-2.

7. On whether this implies that the soul is on guard-duty caring for the body, or that it is itself imprisoned in the body like Boethius in his cell, see J. Burnet, *Plato: Phaedo*, Oxford 1911, ad loc., and J.G. Strachan, 'Who *did* forbid suicide at *Phaedo* 62B?', *Class. Quart.* 20 (1970) 216-20.

8. Cf. Shanzer [1984] 364-6.

9. Curley 366-7. Socrates had been admonished by dreams to "make music" (*Phaedo* 60e), which in Greek includes poetry, and had always supposed that philosophy was the true music; but (as Plato portrays it) had second thoughts and supposed he had better compose some music in the literal sense, to be on the safe side. That is Socratic, or rather Platonic, irony; philosophy is the true music for Plato, and the true poetry for Boethius.

11.3. The elaborate literary structure of the *Consolation,* and especially the thematic connections and responsions between the poems, the use of recurrent images and the way in which the dialogue medium is used, all suggest a careful literary construction. It is at any rate unlikely that the *Consolation* is a sort of common-place book, a record of Boethius' thoughts in his prison cell as and when they occurred (implying that at the start of the work the author had no more idea than the reader how it would end).[1] This being so, a distinction needs to be drawn between Boethius the author and Boethius the character in the dialogue. Lerer, who has perhaps done more than anyone to elucidate the complexities of the *Consolation*'s form, marks this distinction by referring throughout to the character as "the prisoner", reserving "Boethius" for the author. With some hesitation I have decided not to follow him; the *Consolation* is after all presented by Boethius as his philosophical testament, and in a general commentary it seems wrong to obscure that.

11.4. The Muses are banished at the start of the *Consolation,* but the poems continue; and what Boethius gives us is poetry in the service of philosophy, the sort that Plato would be prepared to accept.[2] Verse is a suitable medium for the treatment of an invalid,[3] but - as Orpheus' failure to recover Eurydice in III m.12 shows - it has its limitations.[4] The poems serve to establish the framework within which the discussion moves; in particular, the apparent contrast between the orderliness of the heavens above and the disorder of earthly affairs, symbolised by the cell in which Boethius is confined, a contrast which it is indeed the task of the *Consolation* to resolve.[5] In book I the poems are placed in the mouth of Boethius; but thereafter they are given to Philosophy, until V.3, which shows that Boethius is cured - he too can now write philosophical poetry. Where Book I begins and ends with poetry, book V begins and ends with prose; poetry has played its role.[6]

11.5. Significant, too, is the way in which the dialogue form is used to mark Boethius' recovery of philosophical understanding. Boethius' initial silence, followed by rhetorical self-defence, gives place to debate and questioning, but that in turn gives way, once Boethius' philosophical

---

1. Cf. Reiss 103.

2. Cf. Plato, *Republic* 607a, where Plato accepts hymns to the gods and praise of good men. Boethius' metres are tabulated by Gruber at 16 and discussed by him at 22-3.

3. I.6.21; Curley, 358-9.

4. Curley 361.

5. The poems are certainly *not* just literary embellishments to a philo- sophical exposition in prose. The very form of Menippean satire was, Curley 367 argues, chosen by Boethius in order to play off poetry and prose against each other. The relation of poetry to philosophy had already been examined in Augustine's dialogues (Silk 27-30). Cf. also Reiss 145-7.

6. Curley 361.

understanding has been restored, to exposition by Philosophy,[1] and the work ends with the character Boethius having become silent; in effect he has dropped out of the picture, and Philosophy – i.e. Boethius the *author* – is addressing us, the readers, directly; or putting it another way, Boethius the character has become just another reader, a student of Philosophy's timeless truths, along with the rest of us.[2]

11.6. It may not be out of place to note that there are two, at least, of Plato's dialogues that end in a lengthy exposition by Socrates answered only by silence. In the *Gorgias,* which is a dialogue in dramatic form (with speeches by the characters, but no narrator), Socrates' statement of the myth and final appeal to Callicles provokes no response. Callicles has been only a reluctant participant in the discussion for the last 20 pages or so; he has clearly been unconvinced by Socrates' arguments, and the final silence leaves it open whether he is at all persuaded at the end. Perhaps that shows Plato's honesty in recognising that his arguments may not convince everybody; perhaps it may also suggest that what matters is not whether Callicles, a character in a dialogue, is convinced, but whether we, the readers, are. The *Republic,* which is narrated by Socrates himself, ends again with Socrates' narration of the myth and his concluding statement as to how we can fare well – the theme of the dialogue; he reports no response from the other characters. Here Plato is in effect addressing his readers through Socrates; the other characters in the dialogue have faded out of sight (and, compared to those in the *Gorgias,* did not contribute much anyway).[3] The difference in Boethius' *Consolation* is that here it is the author himself, or rather the character representing him, who fades out of sight at the end of the work; but the author too knew that, as far as this world is concerned, he himself would soon cease to exist.[4] By the end of the *Consolation* the author has in effect become one with his work.

---

1. This is Lerer's analysis. See below on IV.7 and V.3.

2. Lerer, 229–31. Crabbe 274 n.137 compares the way in which personal concerns give way, in V, to the study of a philosophical problem in general terms, with the similar development in books 11 and 12 of Augustine's *Confessions.* Cf. also Shanzer [1984] 364–5.

3. The comparison between the end of the *Republic* and that of the *Consolation* is made by Gruber, 415.

4. Reiss 86–95 has questioned this, arguing that the *Consolation* emphasises ruin and exile rather than imminent death, and that not just Boethius' presentation of his recovery of philosophical understanding, but also his narration in I.4 of the events that led to his condemnation and his presentation of his current situation, are guided by the requirements of the literary work rather than by concern for historical truth. In particular, he suggests, Boethius had access to books since he was not in prison at all (94–5). Against this Shanzer [1984] argues that if Boethius was not under sentence of death the parallel with the *Phaedo* would be unconvincing.

12. The sources and arguments of IV.5-7 and V

12.1.1. With Boethius, as with Cicero, there is a danger that the attempt to identify sources may detract from appreciation of the work as a whole and of what the author has made of the material derived from his predecessors. As Obertello puts it, it is "easy for the learned reader to consider *Cons. Phil.* with eyes overshadowed by the network of refer- ences and citations which is considered an indispensable accompaniment of competence in philology ... losing sight of the originality and inde- pendence of the work." [1]

12.1.2. The problem has been exacerbated by our ignorance of the circumstances in which Boethius wrote. We do not know how many books were available to him in his imprisonment; and this has tempted some, such as Usener, to look for a single written source for each part of the work. It may be that Boethius wrote from memory rather than with many books available.[2] In I.4.3 Boethius laments the loss of his library; but in I.5.6 Philosophy replies that what matters is not books but the ideas they contain; and what is striking in the *Consolation* is the way in which Boethius draws on his own earlier studies, and goes beyond them.[3]

12.1.3. This raises the question of the sources of the commentaries themselves, and particularly of those on Aristotle's *On Interpretation* which chiefly concern us here. This has been and continues to be a matter of some controversy. Courcelle argued that Boethius had studied at Alexandria under the Neoplatonist Aristotelian commentator Ammo- nius,[4] and, from similarities between Boethius' and Ammonius' commen- taries, that Boethius' *On Interpretation* commentaries reflect the teach- ing of Ammonius, deriving in its turn particularly from the commentary on *On Interpretation* by Plotinus' follower Porphyry.[5] Shiel however argued that Boethius' commentaries were based on marginal scholia in his copy of Aristotle, largely derived from Porphyry, and rejected

---

1. Obertello [1974] 448. Cf. also de Vogel [1971] 52-3; Crabbe 239.

2. So Gruber 39, Chadwick 221; the availability of some books is argued by Sulowski [1957] 80 and Courcelle [1967] 333-4.

3. Reiss 99 goes so far as to suggest that the *Consolation* represents work Boethius had already been planning before his fall; above, §§11.3, 11.6. On the history of source-criticism of the *Consolation* in general, and the sources for the whole work, cf. Rand, Courcelle [1967] 113-127, 161-176, and Courcelle [1969] 295-318.

4. Courcelle [1969] 275-295, 316-318. At 316-17 n.129 he speculates that Boethius' father may have been identical with a Boethius who had been the prefect of Egypt. Cf. also De Vogel [1971] 49-54, 65, and Reiss 6-9, both of whom find the theory of an education in Alexandria plausible; and, in general on Boethius' education and intellectual background, Obertello [1981,1] 156ff.

5. Courcelle [1969] 282-3, 291-5.

Courcelle's theory of dependence on Ammonius.[1] Others have found Shiel's theory too extreme and have argued that Boethius used Porphyry directly.[2]

12.1.4. Courcelle further argued that book V of the *Consolation* itself derives from Ammonius' commentaries on Aristotle's *On Interpretation* and *Physics*.[3] But the distinctiveness of Boethius' arguments (below, §12.2.4) makes this implausible.[4] Chadwick suggests that the similarities between Boethius and Ammonius are to be explained by a common use of Porphyry, and, more generally, that whether book V derives from Ammonius or not, it should be seen in the context of a whole Neoplatonic tradition of Aristotelian exegesis.[5]

12.1.5. Also controversial has been the question of Boethius' relation to Augustine. Silk argued that Boethius, in making philosophy replace poetry, was developing themes which Augustine had only hinted at, so that in effect the *Consolation* is a sequel to Augustine's dialogues. This was scarcely the same as suggesting that Augustine was a source for Boethius' specific philosophical doctrines, but nevertheless prompted criticism from Courcelle in particular.[6] Similarities have been seen between Boethius and Augustine on the relation between time and eternity and the doctrine of God's eternal present;[7] and it seems likely that Boethius is influenced by Augustine in his reporting of Cicero's *On Divination* in *Consolation* V.4.1.[8] In earlier works, however, it seems that Boethius shows direct acquaintance with the Ciceronian work, *not*

---

1. Shiel, especially 356-361. Obertello [1974] 522-544, especially 532-3, supports Shiel against Courcelle on the question of dependence on Ammonius.

2. Obertello [1974] 482; Chadwick 129-30; Ebbesen 375-7; cf. also de Vogel [1971] 56-61.

3. Courcelle [1967] 215-229, [1969] 308-16.

4. Gruber 378.

5. Chadwick 53-4, 244. Sulowski ([1957], [1960]) used parallels between the *Consolation* and Calcidius' commentary on the *Timaeus* to argue that Porphyry's *Timaeus* commentary was the common source of both. Against this cf. Courcelle [1967] 8, 230; Courcelle argues that Boethius read the *Timaeus* through Proclus' commentary and not Porphyry's ([1967] 164-7; cf. Obertello [1974] 509-10, and Commentary on V m.2. As Obertello [1974] 489-90 points out, Sulowski's parallels are not close, and may indicate nothing more than a shared interest in topics that had a prominent role in the philosophical tradition of late antiquity.

6. Courcelle [1967] 340 n.1. Cf. Crabbe 251-3; Lerer 46 and nn.

7. See Commentary on V.6.15.

8. See Commentary there.

through Augustine;[1] whether the influence of Augustine in *Consolation* V.4 reflects Boethius' situation when he was writing, and limited access to books, is unclear.

12.1.7. Even though Boethius is heavily dependent upon Neoplatonist writings, he does not refer by name to any writer later than Cicero.[2] Lerer notes an increasing use of Greek quotations at the end of the *Consolation*, in order to indicate Philosophy's *auctoritas*.[3]

12.1.8. The poems in the *Consolation* draw extensively on Seneca's tragedies in particular. Boethius no doubt found Seneca particularly relevant as a philosopher who was also a courtier who fell from favour; he mentions Seneca's fall twice in the *Consolation*.[4]

12.2.1. In IV.6 Philosophy explains the apparent anomalies in the way divine providence allots different fortunes to good and bad men by pointing to the limitations of human understanding and our inability to comprehend the judgements of divine providence. This explanation is prefaced by an account of the difference between providence, which is timeless, and the outworking of providence in time, which is fate; this contrast is relevant to the argument of IV.6, showing that our understanding is only partial and limited by our temporal context, but which will also be important for the argument of V.4-6 (below). Both the contrast between providence and fate, and even more that between time and a timeless eternity, had a long history.[5] Discussion of Boethius' specific sources has concentrated on his use of the image of a circle and its centre to illustrate the relation of fate to providence (IV.6.15-17); Patch traced it to Plotinus, but Courcelle argued forcefully for Proclus. It seems highly probable that elements from both have entered into Boethius' account.[6]

12.2.2. In V.1 Philosophy explains to Boethius the nature of chance in essentially Aristotelian terms. Courcelle attempted to show, from the fact that Boethius like Simplicius incorporates an example from Aristotle's *Metaphysics* into a discussion based on his *Physics,* that Boethius was here dependent on Ammonius; but the example had in fact been a commonplace for centuries. The fact that Boethius implies that it comes

---

1. Courcelle [1967] 210 n.5, [1969] 308 n.86, noting the citation of Ennius from Cicero *On Divination* at Boethius *On* On Interpretation[2] 82.14 and at *On Division*, PL 64 878a. Gruber following Rand notes an echo of Cicero *On Divination* 2.101 in *Consolation* IV.6.7, *tunc velut ab alio orsa principio,* but this seems tenuous.

2. Crouse 77; cf. Courcelle [1969] 297.

3. Lerer 212, 215-6.

4. I.3.9, III.5.10-11. Lerer 245-6, Crabbe 242-3.

5. For the former see above, Introduction §8; for the latter, Commentary on V.6.4.

6. See further below, commentary on the passage.

43

from the *Physics* may suggest that he failed to check his references;[1] this might show that his access to books was limited, but he may simply have thought the point unimportant. His account does however show one feature (the notion of a concurrence of causes) which seems characteristic of Platonist writers in particular within a broadly Aristotelian tradition;[2] and he puts the Aristotelian account of chance in a different perspective from Aristotle's own by presenting it as the working out of a divine providence even though that providence is unclear to us.[3]

12.2.3. Boethius begins his treatment of the problem of reconciling free will and divine foreknowledge in V.3 by rejecting as inadequate the argument that divine foreknowledge does not cause our actions; even if it does not cause them, it still seems to imply logically that they have to happen. His solution, developed by Philosophy in V.4-6, combines three elements: (a) the doctrine that the nature of knowledge depends on that of the knower rather than on that of the object known;[4] (b) the distinction between a thing's being necessary in itself and its being necessary under some condition – in this case, God's foreknowledge of it;[5] and (c) the notion that to God in his eternity all time is as the present. (a) and (c) together show that (d) God's knowledge of our future actions is like our knowledge of what is happening at present; but (b) the necessity of present events happening if we are to be aware of them is purely conditional and in no way implies that the events are other than contingent in themselves. By (d) the same will apply to God's knowledge of our *future* actions.

12.2.4. It is important that all three of (a), (b) and (c) play a part in Boethius' solution. The discussion in V.3 shows that (b) alone would not provide an adequate solution;[6] but neither would (a). (a) and (c) are both to be found in discussions by Neoplatonists like Proclus and Ammonius;[7] and (b) is to be found in commentaries by Boethius and

---

1. Cf. Gruber, 40.

2. See Commentary on V.1.12.

3. See Commentary on V.1.19.

4. See above, Introduction §7.2.

5. See Commentary on V.6.25.

6. That the contrast between absolute and conditional necessity is not enough on its own to solve the problem is pointed out, in effect, by Pike 37-8.

7. For (a) see above, Introduction §7.2, and for (c) see Commentary on V.6.15. Klingner [1921] 106ff. linked (a) with Iamblichus, Proclus and Ammonius; Courcelle [1967] 216-21 and [1969] 310 argued that Boethius derived it specifically from Ammonius. Obertello [1974] 518-21 points rather to parallels with Proclus *Ten Problems* 7-8, arguing that it is impossible to say whether Boethius depends on Proclus or both have a common source. Huber 56-7 points out that in Ammonius and in the Boethius *commentaries* the contrast is related not to the problem of divine foreknowledge but rather to the contrast between permanent unchanging truths and those relating to individual events.

others on Aristotle's *On Interpretation*.[1] But the combination of all three points, and the argument that, because our knowledge of present events does not render them necessary in themselves, God's knowledge of our future actions does not do so either, is a new contribution by Boethius and new with the *Consolation*.[2]

12.2.5. Whether Boethius' solution is a satisfactory one depends largely on whether sense can be made at all of the notion of God, in a timeless eternity, being aware of the actions of human agents in time.[3] In any case, it is notable that Boethius has only attempted to answer the specific problem of divine *foreknowledge;* he gives no clear indication of his views on the relation between divine providential *agency* and human free will,[4] beyond conceding that God may not cause us to act as we do.[5] In this his approach to the problem is very different from that of

---

1. See Commentary on V.6.25. The distinction in the *Consolation* clearly derives from Boethius' commentaries on Aristotle's *On Interpretation;* Klingner [1921] 111, Courcelle [1967] 214-218 and [1969] 310-11. Courcelle derives its appearance there in turn from Ammonius; but a common source remains a possibility.

2. Gegenschatz [1958] 124ff., especially 128; Dronke 126; Scheible 176-7 n.3; Huber 44-58, arguing that Courcelle saw (a),(b),(c) as three separate solutions, but failed to see the significance of the way in which Boethius combines them; Sorabji [1980,2] 124-5 and [1983] 255-6. Klingner [1921] 110-12 had already pointed out that Proclus and Iamblichus emphasised the superiority of divine knowledge, and not, as does Boethius, the point that future things are present to it; Klingner argued that Boethius was here influenced by Augustine (see above, §12.1.6, and commentary on V.6.15), but Sorabji [1983] 256 points out that Augustine does not link the point that for divine knowledge all things are present with the problem of human freedom.

3. Cf. Sorabji [1980,2] 125-6; [1983] 253-67, on this and other problems; also Huber 50 and below, Commentary on V.6.17. In the final chapters Boethius attempts to raise the level of understanding of the character representing him in the dialogue, and hence of the reader, to a level which transcends the limitations of time (see above, §§11.5-6); whether or not one judges the attempt a success, one is reminded of another major work of literature which is structured as an attempt to move away from the purely temporal - Eliot's *Four Quartets. There* indeed the culmination is an affirmation of the *intersection* of time and eternity in Christ's Incarnation; the difference may have a bearing on the question of the Christianity of the *Consolation*. See below.

4. This even though both predestination and divine causation are mentioned in IV.6.4, as Huber 28 points out. *This* problem (rather than that of foreknowledge, as Courcelle [1969] 308-9 implies) was passed over at *On* On Interpretation[2] 232.10.

5. V.3.14. But this may be only for the sake of argument, to show that there is still a problem in divine foreknowledge even if the divine will does not cause our actions. Cf. also V.3.15 and V.6.42 with Commentary. In *Consolation* IV.2 Boethius, following Plato's *Gorgias* 467-8 and 509, argues that the will of all men is directed towards the good; what the wicked lack is not the will for the good but the power to achieve it, and they lack the power to achieve it because they pursue it in the wrong way.

Augustine. It is also different from that of writers like Cicero, who is concerned (in *On Divination*) with the implications of divination and prophecy for human freedom; Boethius' discussion is concerned with specifically philosophical issues of the sort raised by his study of and commentary on Aristotle's logical writings.[1]

13. The *Consolation* and Christianity

13.1. There is no doubt that Boethius was a baptised Christian. His following a career in public administration in the early sixth century presupposes it;[2] and there has been no doubt, since the publication of the *Anecdoton Holderi,* a fragment of writing by Cassiodorus referring to Boethius as the author of theological works, that the treatises on Christian theology attributed to him really are his.

13.2. This being so, surprise and perplexity have been caused since early medieval times by the absence of specifically Christian themes from the *Consolation*.[3] Admittedly, some specifically Christian ideas have been detected; Boethius represents the supreme being not as above intelligence and detached from the world, but as its creator and even as caring for his creatures;[4] and echoes of biblical or liturgical language have been detected.[5] There is also relatively little in the work

---

1. Courcelle [1967] 210-12, [1969] 308-9; cf. Huber 28, Reiss 127.

2. Courcelle [1969] 318; Gruber 14 and n.106.

3. For the medieval debate cf. Courcelle [1969] 275-332 and 335, Obertello [1974] 766-7; for the modern controversy, Courcelle [1969] 318-19, De Vogel [1972] and [1973], Obertello [1974] 767-8 and Starnes 27-9, in addition to the references below.

4. Rand [1904] 19-20, 23; De Vogel [1973] 358; Obertello [1974] 732-4. See below on IV m.6 ad fin. Rand 18-19 and Liebeschütz argue that Boethius in IV.6.13 adapts Neoplatonic doctrine to Christian monotheism and recognises man's freedom to approach God directly, thus emphasising the irrelevance of the Neoplatonic hierarchy of forces intermediating between God and ourselves; such a direct relationship is indeed stressed elsewhere in the *Consolation* (V.3.35) but it is hardly the central point in IV.6.13 itself. On the features that may have made the Alexandrian Neoplatonism, with which in particular Courcelle linked Boethius, more acceptable to Christianity (Liebeschütz 554, Courcelle [1967] 341), cf. A.C. Lloyd in A.H. Armstrong, ed., *The Cambridge History of Later Greek and Early Medieval Philosophy,* Cambridge 1967, 315-316, and Merlan 200-1. Lloyd suspends judgement; even more sceptical is Verrycken.

5. Chadwick 238 notes Biblical allusions but remarks that they are not used to make specifically Christian points. In particular there is an allusion in III.12.22 to the book of *Wisdom* (8.1) in the Apocrypha; Obertello [1974] 772-3 suggests that this may be an *unconscious* reminiscence of words from *Wisdom* included in the Advent Antiphon *O Sapientia,* but De Vogel [1973] 358 and Chadwick 237-8 point out that Boethius explicitly expresses pleasure at the form of words used. (Cf. also Rand [1904] 274 n.111 and Lerer 147-8). On echoes of liturgical language cf. Mohrmann 61; and see below, Commentary on V.3.34 and V.6.47.

that would be positively unacceptable to orthodox Christianity;[1] some pagan elements, such as the Muses (who are in any case banished), are purely literary devices.[2] Some doctrinal aspects are at first sight at odds with Christian teaching; but some of these, such as the world's having always existed rather than having a beginning in time, were not yet excluded from orthodox doctrine at the time when Boethius wrote,[3] and in other cases Boethius takes ideas which some Christian writers had rejected and adapts them in such a way as to make them acceptable.[4] The *Consolation* is in short to a large extent neutral, neither Christian nor pagan[5] in the sense of making assertions that one side would favour and the other find absolutely unacceptable.

13.3. The overall impression is thus of the relatively small part played by Christian ideas in the *Consolation*. Even De Vogel, who stresses the Christian elements in the *Consolation*, points to pagan elements in its general world-view;[6] and Gruber, who regards the work as non-Christian, points out that specifically Christian ideas like forgiveness of sin, the bodily resurrection and the doctrine of the Trinity are all excluded.[7] To say that it is a Consolation of *Philosophy*,[8] concerned with reason rather than with revelation,[9] and to stress that the social class and intellectual background from which Boethius came did not regard the pagan cultural heritage as necessarily in conflict with Chris-

---

1. Obertello [1974] 773.

2. Cf. Mohrmann 54-5. Courcelle [1967] 339-344, [1969] 319-322 notes that the emphasis on philosophy rather than theology excludes Christian and pagan *religious* elements alike.

3. Rand [1904] 28. See Commentary on V.1.9 and V.6.9. However, the pre-existence of souls (see Commentary on V.2.8), though asserted by Origen, had been condemned as heretical.

4. Mauro notes that Boethius keeps the *term* "fate" where Augustine does not; for Augustine, fate is simply our misunderstanding of providence. Cf. the Commentary on V.1.19.

5. So Courcelle [1967] 339-344, [1969] 319-322; Chadwick 247-251.

6. De Vogel [1973] notes the emphasis on the natural world, on cosmic religion and on looking upwards to the heavens, tracing these features to the influence of Seneca (367). See also De Vogel [1971] 52-4; [1972] 31-3.

7. Gruber 14-15, 357. Reiss 96, too, argues that the work as a whole is not Christian.

8. De Vogel [1973] 364-5.

9. Rand [1904] 27-8; Courcelle [1967] 24, 342-4; Obertello [1974] 748; Chadwick 224. The theological treatises too display an interest in theology which is primarily intellectual and philosophical (Courcelle [1967] 339-344, [1969] 319-322; Leibeschütz 543-5 describes Boethius as a layman who applies philosophy to theology but accepts that faith is the final arbiter.) Crouse 81 argues that Boethius relies on reason and not revelation not only in the *Consolation* but also in the theological works, pointing out that Aquinas already noted this (Aquinas, *Commentary on Boethius On the Trinity*, prologue 5 (pp.47-8 Decker).

tianity,[1] is really only to restate the question; why did Boethius, if he was a Christian, seek consolation in the condemned cell from philosophy rather than from faith?

13.4. Various answers to this problem have been suggested: that Boethius had lost his faith in Christianity,[2] or that it had always been an intellectual rather than a devotional matter for him;[3] that the *Consolation* is incomplete,[4] or that, not knowing how imminent his execution was, he did not regard the *Consolation* as his final work[5] and may have intended a second, theological *Consolation*.[6] Others have suggested that Boethius in the *Consolation* avoids theological issues and confines himself to philosophical ones because of the way in which theological controversy had involved him in political trouble.[7] The problem is one to which we will simply never know the answer.[8]

14. The influence of the *Consolation of Philosophy*.

14.1 Even to begin to give an indication of the influence of the *Consolation* on subsequent thought and literature in the space available is impossible. Aspects of its content caused problems for Christian orthodoxy;[9] but it *could* be interpreted as a Christian work,[10] and it became a central focus for medieval thought and literary study. Between the ninth and fifteenth centuries the *Consolation* was translated into fourteen different languages[11] and was the subject of nearly three dozen commentaries.[12] The solution to the problem of reconciling divine fore-

---

1. Chadwick 15.

2. Merlan 203. An extreme version of this view is expressed by Arnaldo Momigliano, who argues that Boethius' Christianity "collapsed so thoroughly that perhaps he did not even notice its disappearance" ('Cassiodorus and the Italian culture of his time', *Proc. Brit. Acad.* 41 [1955] 207-245, at 213.)

3. Crabbe 262-3 argues that Boethius lacks the zeal of the convert (or rather, re-convert) found in Augustine, and that his enthusiasms were directed rather towards philosophy.

4. See on V.6.48.

5. So Reiss 95-9.

6. So Obertello [1974] 748. On the circumstances of Boethius' imprisonment and the chronology of his arrest and execution see above, Introduction §10.6-7.

7. So Bark 425, suggesting that Boethius may still have hoped for release, and Liebeschütz 552-3.

8. So Shanzer [1984] 358.

9. See above, §§13.1-2.

10. As for example by Alcuin; Chadwick 251.

11. Reiss, 155.

12. Ibid.; cf. also Courcelle [1967] 22-99, 135-158, 177-199, 241-322, 337 n.1; Gruber 13-16.

knowledge and human freedom advanced by Boethius in V.6 was further developed by Aquinas and others.[1]

14.2. In the Renaissance interest in Boethius lessened, with the rejection of the medieval culture of which his work seemed to be part.[2] It has been left for modern times, and perhaps for our own day in particular, to see it in the context of a new understanding both of the philosophy of late antiquity and of the complexities of literary form and literary allusion which the work so well exemplifies.[3]

15. On the texts

The Latin texts in this volume make no claim to constitute new editions. I have worked from printed editions, and I have not consulted original manuscripts. My aim, in the case of Cicero in particular, has been to present readers with a Latin text and minimal apparatus which gives a more accurate impression of what Cicero probably wrote, and of the evidence on which our text rests where there are significant doubts, than has hitherto been available in combination with an English translation; I thus offer this text as an improvement on that in Rackham's Loeb, based (Rackham p.191) on Nobbe's edition of 1827. Rackham introduces needless conjectures, does not always clearly indicate the sense by his punctuation, and sometimes follows earlier printed editions without comment against all the main manuscripts.[4]

In constructing the text and apparatus of Cicero's treatise I have consulted the Teubner editions of Ax and Giomini, the edition by Bayer and the Budé of Yon. Variant readings have been noted only where the correct reading is open to some doubt or the sense of the argument could be affected; I have not noted, for example, the omissions by a first hand, corrected by a second, that are fundamental for Clark's reconstruction of the manuscript tradition (cf. Clark 341ff). I have noted the reported readings of the earlier MSS, ABFMPV and (where

---

1. Aquinas, *Summa Theologiae* 1 q.14 art.13; cf. Sorabji [1980,2] 125-6, and Commentary on V.6.17 below.

2. Courcelle [1967] 332.

3. On the influence of the *Consolation* see also Patch [1935,2] (especially 41-3 on the themes of free will and providence); Chadwick 251-3; chs. 11, 13, 14 of Gibson (q.v.); and Reiss, 154-161.

4. For example, in §2 Rackham has *eis studiis* and *eis deliberationibus* without comment, where the early MSS all have *his* and later ones *hiis, iis* being due to Davies, according to Bayer, and not even being mentioned by Ax, Yon or Giomini. In §17 Rackham's *ea posse* seems to be a simple mistake for *posse ea; futura sint,* which he prints without comment, is Moser's conjecture for *futura* of the MSS; and his *facta sint* is an error for *facta sunt.* In §19 the omission of *Epicurus* after *Morietur* seems to be simple carelessness. At the start of §32 Rackham prints *haec* with the footnote "*hoc* Turnebus", implying that the MSS have *haec;* but in fact *hoc* is the reading of all the early MSS and all but three of the later ones cited by Bayer. *haec* is the reading of Davies' edition (1721) but is not even mentioned by Yon, Ax or Giomini.

relevant) H, as does Giomini, though in two cases (P and H) I have used Bayer's sigla rather than Giomini's as closer to the names of the MSS. Readings of later MSS are reported, where they seemed relevant given the purposes of this apparatus, simply as "rec." or "recc."; those who seek more information on these readings, and on variations between my text and Rackham's (not all of which have been noted) should consult the apparatus of Giomini and especially the very full apparatus of Bayer, which takes account of 33 MSS and early printed editions and is longer than the text. Bayer provides a complete *stemma* on p.111 of his edition. I have not attempted to indicate the contributions of different hands in the MSS, something which would in any case not be possible without personal inspection since the printed editions often come to different conclusions; like Yon, I have simply indicated whether a reading is original or a correction. Inevitably there are places, both in Cicero and Boethius, where the printed editions disagree over the actual reading of a MS; here, given the purpose of the present text, I can only point out that my apparatus cannot be stronger than the foundations on which it is based.

In the case of Boethius my text and apparatus are based on a comparison of those of Weinberger, Bieler and Büchner, Bieler's apparatus being the fullest. The punctuation is my own. There are only ten places in the chapters here included where there is a divergence, except in matters of punctuation or orthography, between any of these texts, including my own; in two of these (V m.3.18 and V m.4.1) I have gone against all three editors, in the former case reverting to an earlier conjecture, in the latter incorporating a suggestion of my colleague Alan Griffiths. My apparatus is highly selective; Bieler observes (p.xii: my translation) that "whoever reads the variants ... with attention will easily be convinced that he should consider not so much the MSS as the readings themselves", and I have noted simply those variations that could substantially affect the sense of the argument, making no attempt to provide the reader with all the evidence on which a study of the affiliations of the MSS would have to be based.[1] Given the purposes of this apparatus, I have been sparing in citations of the secondary MSS (those indicated, following Bieler, with an abbreviation rather than a single letter) where a variant is already present in the primary MSS; those who require more information should consult Bieler's edition.

---

1. An attempt to construct a *stemma* was made by Klingner [1940] 27-9, but rejected by Bieler; Gruber 47 argues that none can be constructed.

Sigla

CICERO, ON FATE

A	Leidensis Vossianus 84 (9th-10th cent.)
B	Leidensis Vossianus 86 (10th cent.)
F	Florentinus Marcianus lat. 257 (10th cent.)
H	Excerpta Hadoardi, Vaticanus Reg. lat. (9th-10th cent.) (Giomini's R)
M	Monacensis lat. 528 (11th cent.)
P	Parisinus lat. 17812 (12th cent.) (Giomini's N)
V	Vindobonensis 189 (9th-10th cent.)

Ven = first Venetian printed edition, 1471

codd. = agreement of ABFMV

cett. = agreement of all of codices ABFMV not otherwise cited

rec., recc. = reading of one or more of MSS of the 13th century or later

V^a = V before correction
V^c = V after correction

BOETHIUS CONSOLATION OF PHILOSOPHY

A	Antuerpiensis M.16.8 (early 10th cent.)[1]
D	Bonnensis 175 (9th-10th cent.)
E	Emmeranus Clm 14324 (10th-11th cent.)
L	Laurentianus XIV.15 (early 9th cent.)
K	Bernensis 179 (9th-10th cent.)
M	Turonensis 803 (end of 9th cent.)
N	Neopolitanus IV.G.68 (later 9th cent.)
O	Aurelianensis 270 (c. 820 A.D.)
P	Parisinus Bibl. Nat. lat. 7181 (mid-9th cent.)
T	Tegernseensis Clm 18765 (early 9th cent.)
V	Vaticanus lat. 3363 (9th cent.)

Bam.	Bambergensis M.IV.2 (11th cent.)
Goth.	Gothanus 103 + 104 (11th-12th cent.)
Harl.	Harleianus 3095 (9th-10th cent.)
Hib.	Laurentianus LXXVIII.19 (12th cent.)
Laud.	Laudunensis 439 (9th cent.)
Met.	Metensis 377 (11th cent.)
Rehd.	Rehdigeranus S I 4,3 (early 12th cent.)
Vind.	Vindobonensis 271 (9th-10th cent.)

Planudes Planudis versio Graeca (ed. E.A. Bétant, Geneva 1871)

cett. = agreement of all of codices ADELKMNOPTV not otherwise cited

Rand = Loeb ed. (see Stewart, H.F. and Rand, E.K. in the Bibliography)

---

1. See Bieler xiii n.22.

M. TULLI CICERONIS
DE FATO

[I][1] ... quia pertinet ad mores, quod ἦθος illi vocant, nos eam partem philosophiae de moribus appellare solemus, sed decet augentem linguam Latinam nominare moralem. explicandaque vis est ratioque enuntiationum, quae Graeci ἀξιώματα vocant; quae de re

5 futura cum aliquid dicunt deque eo quod possit fieri aut non possit, quam vim habeant obscura quaestio est, quam περὶ δυνατῶν philosophi appellant; totaque est λογική, quam rationem disserendi voco. quod autem in aliis libris feci, qui sunt de natura deorum, itemque in iis, quos de divinatione edidi, ut in utramque partem

10 perpetua explicaretur oratio, quo facilius id a quoque probaretur quod cuique maxime probabile videretur, id in hac disputatione de fato casus quidam ne facerem impedivit. [2] nam cum essem in Puteolano, Hirtiusque noster consul designatus isdem in locis, vir nobis amicissimus et his studiis in quibus nos a pueritia viximus

15 deditus, multum una eramus, maxime nos quidem exquirentes ea consilia quae ad pacem et ad concordiam civium pertinerent. cum enim omnes post interitum Caesaris novarum perturbationum causae quaeri viderentur, iisque esse occurrendum putaremus, omnis fere nostra in his deliberationibus consumebatur oratio,

20 idque et saepe alias, et quodam liberiore quam solebat et magis vacuo ab interventoribus die. cum ille ad me venisset, primo ea quae erant cotidiana et quasi legitima nobis, de pace et de otio.

[II][3] Quibus actis, Quid ergo? inquit ille, quoniam oratorias exercitationes non tu quidem ut spero reliquisti, sed certe philos-

25 ophiam illis anteposuisti, possumne aliquid audire?

Tu vero, inquam, vel audire vel dicere; nec enim, id quod recte existimas, oratoria illa studia deserui, quibus etiam te incendi, quamquam flagrantissimum acceperam, nec ea quae nunc tracto

---

3 moralem $F^c(?)V^c$: morabilem ABF^aMV^aB: cf. Quintiliani Inst. 6.2.8

21 die. cum *sic interpunxit Giomini:* die, quo cum *Wopkens:* die. nam cum *Plasberg*

ON FATE

[I][1] ... because it relates to character, which they (the Greeks) call *êthos*, while we usually call this part of philosophy "concerned with character" *(mores)*, but it is appropriate to enhance the Latin language and call (this) "moral" (philosophy). It is also necessary to explain the force and the logic of propositions, which the Greeks call *axiômata*. What force they have when they say something about a matter in the future and about what can come about or not is an obscure question, which the philosophers call "concerning possibles" *(peri dunatôn)*; and the whole question is a matter of "logic" *(logikê)*, which I call "reason in speaking".

A chance occurrence prevented me from doing, in this discussion about fate, what I have done in my other books which are concerned with the nature of the gods, and likewise in those which I published on divination; that is, that a continuous speech should be set out on each side, so that each person should more easily recommend what seemed most acceptable to each. [2] I was at my villa at Pozzuoli, and my friend Hirtius, who was consul-designate, was in the same area, a man who is a very great friend of mine and devoted to these studies, in which I have spent my life since boyhood. We were together a great deal, principally for our part looking for plans for peace and harmony among the citizens. After the death of Julius Caesar people seemed to be looking for every reason for new turmoil, and we thought we should counter these; so almost all our talk was spent in these deliberations. In particular on a day when we had more leisure than usual and were more free from interruptions. When he came to me, first (we talked about) those things that were our daily concern and as it were obligatory for us, about peace and tranquillity.

[II][3] When we had done this, he said, "Well, since you indeed have not - I hope - abandoned rhetorical exercises, though you have certainly given philosophy priority over them, can I hear something from you?"

"You can indeed," I said, "either listen or speak yourself. For, as you rightly judge, I have not abandoned that enthusiasm for rhetoric, which I fired in you too, even though it was already blazing in you when you came to me. Nor do the things I am now dealing with diminish that

minuunt sed augent potius illam facultatem. nam cum hoc genere
philosophiae quod nos sequimur magnam habet orator societatem,
subtilitatem enim ab Academia mutuatur et ei vicissim reddit
ubertatem orationis et ornamenta dicendi. quam ob rem, inquam,
5   quoniam utriusque studii nostra possessio est, hodie utro frui
malis optio sit tua.

Tum Hirtius, Gratissimum, inquit, et tuorum omnium simile; nihil
enim umquam abnuit meo studio voluntas tua. [4] sed quoniam
rhetorica mihi vostra sunt nota teque in iis et audivimus saepe et
10   audiemus, atque hanc Academicorum contra propositum disputandi
consuetudinem indicant te suscepisse Tusculanae disputationes,
ponere aliquid ad quod audiam, si tibi non est molestum, volo.

An mihi, inquam, potest quidquam esse molestum quod tibi gratum
futurum sit? sed ita audies ut Romanum hominem, ut timide in-
15   gredientem ad hoc genus disputandi, ut longo intervallo haec
studia repetentem.

Ita, inquit, audiam te disputantem ut ea lego quae scripsisti;
proinde ordire.

Considamus hic.

* * *

20   [fr.5 (4 Ax)] *Et ne vilior sit testis poeta, accipite adsertore Cicer-*
one in quo honore fuerit hic piscis apud P. Scipionem Africanum
illum et Numantinum. haec sunt in dialogo de fato verba Ciceronis:
nam cum esset apud se ad Lavernium Scipio unaque Pontius,
allatus est forte Scipioni acipenser, qui admodum raro capitur sed
25   est piscis, ut ferunt, in primis nobilis. cum autem Scipio unum et
alterum ex eis qui eum salutatum venerant invitavisset plures-

---

9 vostra *Yon*: nostra *codd.*: vestra *Ald., recc.*: ura *?P, recc.*

14 futurum est] futurumst *Madvig*

19 considamus hic A^CB^CM: consida musici B^a: considamusici V^a:
considamus ici A^a: considamus ii $V^C(vel$ ic?)P: consideramus hic F
Davies: consideramus Hirti *Ramus*: considamus igitur *Ax. verba
Ciceroni tribuunt Ax, Rackham, Bayer; Hirtio tribuunt Yon, Giomini.
post haec verba lacunam indicant $ABFM^C$ atque edd. omnes*

fr.5 (4 Ax) per errorem libro De fato attributum esse a Macrobium
susp. *Christ*

faculty; rather, they increase it. For there is a great affinity between the orator and the type of philosophy which I follow; he borrows subtlety in argument from the Academy, and gives back to it in return richness of expression and rhetorical ornament. For this reason," I said, "since both subjects are in my possession, let it be for you to choose today which you prefer to employ."

Hirtius then said, "That is most welcome, and characteristic of all that you do; for you have always been willing to grant me whatever I was eager for. [4] But since I am familiar with your rhetoric and have often both heard and will hear you practising it, and since your discussions at Tusculum show that you have adopted this Academic practice of arguing against something proposed, I would like, if you don't mind, to propose something on which I can hear you.

"Can I mind anything," I said, "which is going to be welcome to you? But you will be listening to me as to a Roman, to one who is timidly entering upon this kind of discussion, to one who is taking up these studies again after a long interval."

"I shall listen to your discussion," he said, "in the same way as I read what you have written. So begin."

"Let us sit down here ..."

* * *

[fr.5 (4 Ax)] *And in case a poet should not be a sufficiently worthy witness, learn from the evidence of Cicero in what honour this fish was held by the famous Publius Scipio, victor over Africa and Numantia. These are Cicero's words in his dialogue on fate: "...* For when Scipio was at home at Lavernium and Pontius was with him, as it happened there was brought to Scipio a sturgeon, a fish which is caught pretty rarely but is, they say, particularly esteemed. But when Scipio invited first one and then another of the people who had come to call on

que etiam invitaturus videretur, in aurem Pontius, "Scipio," inquit, "vide quid agas: acipenser iste paucorum hominum est."
[Macrobius, Saturnalia 3.16.3ff.]

* * *

[fr.1] *M. Cicero in libro quem de fato conscripsit, cum quaestio-*
nem istam diceret obscurissimam esse et implicatissimam, Chrysip-
5 *pum quoque philosophum non expedisse se in ea ⟨ait⟩ his verbis:*
Chrysippus, aestuans laboransque quonam ⟨hoc modo⟩ explicet et
fato omnia fieri et esse aliquid in nobis, intricatur [hoc modo].
[Gellius, Noct. Att. 7.2.15.]

* * *

[fr.2] "volvitque vices": *Definitio fati secundum Tullium, qui ait:*
Fatum est conexio rerum per aeternitatem se invicem tenens, quae
10 suo ordine et lege variatur, ita tamen ut ipsa varietas habeat
aeternitatem.
[Servius ad Vergilii Aeneida 3.376]

* * *

[fr.3] *Illi quoque versus Homerici (Od.18.136-7) huic sententiae*
suffragantur, quam Cicero in Latinum vertit:
tales sunt hominum mentes quali pater ipse
15 Iuppiter auctiferas lustravit lumine terras.
nec in hac quaestione auctoritatem haberet poetica sententia; sed
quoniam Stoicos dicit vim fati adserentes istos ex Homero versus
solere usurpare, non de illius poetae sed de istorum philosopho-
rum opinione tractatur, cum per istos versus quos disputationi
20 *adhibent quam de fato habent quid sentiant esse fatum apertis-*
sime declaratur, quoniam Iovem appellant, quem summum deum
putant, a quo connexionem dicunt pendere fatorum.
[Augustinus, De civitate dei 5.8]

---

fr.1 = Chrysippus, SVF 2.977   5 ait *add. Lion:* refert *Gronov*
6 hoc modo *post* quonam *transtulit Hertz:* quonam ⟨pacto⟩ *Christ*

fr.2. 10 lege sic *F:* lege *cett.:* lege ⟨sua⟩ *Ax*

fr.3. 12 huic sententiae] ducunt volentem fata, nolentem trahunt
(Seneca, Ep. Mor. 107.9)

him, and looked as if he was going to invite more, Pontius whispered in his ear, "Scipio, take care what you are doing; that sturgeon of yours is a dish for the few. ..."

[Macrobius, Saturnalia 3.16.3ff.]

* * *

[fr.1] *Marcus Cicero in the book which he composed on fate, saying that that question was most obscure and complicated, says that Chrysippus the philosopher too did not disentangle himself in it, in the following words:* "... Chrysippus, agitated and struggling as to how he might explain this, both that all things come about by fate and that something depends on us, gets entangled ..."

[Gellius, Attic Nights 7.2.15]

* * *

[fr.2] *"And (Jupiter) turns the changes (of fate)": the definition of fate according to Tullius (Cicero), who says:* "... Fate is a reciprocal connection of things through all perpetuity, which varies in accordance with an order and law of its own, but in such a way that the very variation has a perpetual character. ..."

Servius on Virgil, Aeneid 3.376]

* * *

[fr.3] *Those verses of Homer too* (Odyssey 18.136-7) *support this opinion, the ones which Cicero turned into Latin:* "... The minds of men are as the light with which father Jupiter himself illuminates the fruitful earth ..." *The opinion of a poet would not have authority in this question; but since he says that the Stoics, asserting the power of fate, were in the habit of using those verses of Homer, it is not the opinion of that poet but the opinion of those philosophers that is under discussion. For through those verses which they applied in their discussion of fate it is most clearly declared what they think fate to be; for they call it Jupiter, whom they think to be the supreme god, and it is from him that they say the continuity of fate derives.*

[Augustine, City of God 5.8]

* * *

[fr.4] *Cicero dicit* Hippocratem, nobilissimum medicum, scriptum
reliquisse quosdam fratres, cum simul aegrotare coepissent et
eorum morbus eodem tempore ingravesceret, eodem levaretur,
geminos suspicatum; quos Posidonius Stoicus multum astrologiae
5   deditus eadem constitutione astrorum natos eademque conceptos
solebat adserere. *ita, quod medicus pertinere credebat ad similli-
mam temperiem valetudinis, hoc philosophus astrologus ad vim
constitutionemque siderum, quae fuerat quo tempore concepti
natique sunt.*

                            [Augustinus, De civitate dei 5.2]

[de fr.6 quod fertur vid. comm.]

10   [III][5] ... quorum in aliis, ut in Antipatro poeta, ut in brumali die
natis, ut in simul aegrotantibus fratribus, ut in urina, ut in
unguibus, ut in reliquis eiusmodi, naturae contagio valet, quam
ego non tollo, vis est nulla fatalis; in aliis autem fortuita quaedam
esse possunt, ut in illo naufrago, ut in Icadio, ut in Daphita;
15   quaedam etiam Posidonius – pace magistri dixerim – comminisci
videtur; sunt quidem absurda. quid enim? si Daphitae fatum fuit
ex equo cadere atque ita perire, ex hocne equo, qui cum equus
non esset nomen habebat alienum? aut Philippus hasce in capulo
quadrigulas vitare monebatur? quasi vero capulo sit occisus. quid
20   autem magnum est naufragum illum sine nomine in rivo esse
lapsum? – quamquam huic quidem hic scribit praedictum in aqua
esse pereundum. ne hercule Icadii quidem praedonis video fatum
ullum; nihil enim scribit ei praedictum. [6] quid mirum igitur ex
spelunca saxum in crura eius incidisse? puto enim, etiam si
25   Icadius tum in spelunca non esset, saxum tamen illud casurum
fuisse. nam aut nihil omnino est fortuitum aut hoc ipsum potuit
evenire fortuna. quaero igitur, atque hoc late patebit: si fati
omnino nullum nomen, nulla natura, nulla vis esset, et forte

---

fr.4. om. Ax

12 contagio *codd.:* cognatio *Luck AJPh 99 [1978] 175–8*

13 vis] an *(superscr.)* vis *V*   18 hasce *codd.:* hasne *Christ*

20 est *F.A. Wolf:* aut *codd.:* et *Manutius:* om. *recc.,* del. *Lambinus*

[fr.4] *Cicero says that* Hippocrates, the most distinguished doctor, left a record that, when two brothers began to be ill simultaneously and their illness grew more serious and was alleviated at the same time, he suspected that they were twins. Posidonius the Stoic, who was greatly devoted to astrology, used to assert that they were born and conceived under the same arrangement of the stars. *So what the doctor thought was a matter of their very similar medical constitution, this the philosophical astrologer thought was a matter of the power and condition of the stars which had existed at the time when they were conceived and born.*

[Augustine, City of God *5.2]*

[For the so-called fr.6 see the Commentary].

[III][5] ... In some of these cases, as in that of the poet Antipater, of those born on the shortest day, of the brothers who fell ill at the same time, of urine, nails and the other things of that sort, natural connection has an effect - I am not doing away with it - but there is no influence of fate. In others, however, some things can be the results of chance, as in the case of that shipwrecked (sailor), or of Icadius or of Daphitas. Some cases, if the master will excuse my saying it, Posidonius actually seems to have made up; they are beside the point. Why, if Daphitas was fated to fall from a horse and perish in that way, should it be from this Horse (a rock), which, not being a horse, had the name of something other than itself? Or was it these little four-horse chariots on the sword-hilt that Philip was warned to avoid? As if he was killed by a sword-hilt! What great significance is there in that shipwrecked (sailor) without a name having fallen into a stream? - although (Posidonius) writes that to this man it had been foretold that he must perish in water. Nor do I even see any fate in the case of the pirate Icadius; for he does not write that anything was foretold to him. **[6]** So what is surprising in a rock having fallen on his legs from the roof of a cave? I suppose that even if Icadius had not been in the cave then, that rock would still have fallen. For either nothing at all is a result of chance, or else this itself could have come about as a result of chance. So I ask - and this will have wide implications: if no-one had ever heard of fate, if it did not exist, and if it had no influence, and most or all

temere casu aut pleraque fierent aut omnia, num aliter ac nunc eveniunt evenirent? quid ergo attinet inculcare fatum, cum sine fato ratio omnium rerum ad naturam fortunamve referatur?

[IV][7] sed Posidonium sicut aequum est cum bona gratia
5 dimittamus, ad Chrysippi laqueos revertamur. cui quidem primum de ipsa rerum contagione respondeamus, reliqua postea persequemur. inter locorum naturas quantum intersit videmus: alios esse salubris, alios pestilentis, in aliis pituitosos et quasi redundantis, in aliis exsiccatos atque aridos; multaque sunt alia quae inter
10 locum et locum plurimum differant. Athenis tenue caelum, ex quo etiam acutiores putantur Attici; crassum Thebis, itaque pingues Thebani et valentes. tamen neque illud tenue caelum efficiet ut aut Zenonem quis aut Arcesilam aut Theophrastum audiat, neque crassum ut Nemea potius quam Isthmo victoriam petat. [8] diiunge
15 longius; quid enim loci natura afferre potest ut in porticu Pompeii potius quam in campo ambulemus, tecum quam cum alio, Idibus potius quam Kalendis? ut igitur ad quasdam res natura loci pertinet aliquid, ad quasdam autem nihil, sic astrorum adfectio valeat, si vis, ad quasdam res, ad omnis certe non valebit.

20 at enim, quoniam in naturis hominum dissimilitudines sunt, ut alios dulcia alios subamara delectent, alii libidinosi alii iracundi aut crudeles aut superbi sint, alii <a> talibus vitiis abhorreant – quoniam igitur, inquit, tantum natura a natura distat, quid mirum est has dissimilitudines ex differentibus causis esse factas?

25 [V][9] haec disserens qua de re agatur et in quo causa consistat non videt. non enim si alii ad alia propensiores sunt propter causas naturalis et antecedentis, idcirco etiam nostrarum voluntatum atque appetitionum sunt causae naturales et antecedentes; nam nihil esset in nostra potestate si ita se res haberet. nunc

---

6 contagione *codd.:* cognatione *Bremi, quod in quibusdam libris exstitisse affirmat etiam Turnebus: ita quoque Luck AJPh 99 [1978] 175-8*

8 *ante* pituitosos *exhib.* esse *recc., Davies*

14 Nemeae *coni. Rackham*   in Isthmo *coni. Rackham*

22 <a> *add. Lambinus*

things came about by chance, at random, and fortuitously, would they happen in a different way from that in which they do now? What then is the relevance of forcing fate upon us, when in the absence of fate everything can be explained by nature or chance?

[IV][7] But let us dismiss Posidonius on friendly terms, as is fair, and return to the snares of Chrysippus. First let us reply to him about the connection among things itself; then we will pursue the other points. We can see how great a difference there is in the natures of different regions; some are healthy, others plague-ridden, in some people are phlegmatic and as it were overflowing with moisture, in others they are dried up and parched; and there are many other things which differ greatly between one place and another. At Athens the air is thin, and for this reason the people of Attica too are thought to be more sharp-witted, while at Thebes it is dense, and for this reason the Thebans are stupid but strong. However, that thin air will not make anyone listen to Zeno or Arcesilaus or Theophrastus; nor will that thick air make anyone seek victory at Nemea rather than at the Isthmus. [8] Continue the distinction further; what influence can the nature of the place have over our walking in Pompey's portico rather than in the Campus Martius, with you rather than with somebody else, on the Ides rather than on the Kalends? So, just as the nature of the place has some bearing on some things, but none on others, just so the position of the stars may have power over some things, if you like, but it will certainly not have power over all of them.

'But,' someone may say, 'there are differences in the natures of men: some are pleased by things that are sweet, others by those that are rather bitter; some are licentious, some inclined to anger, or cruel, or arrogant, while others recoil from such vices. So since one nature differs so much from another, what is there surprising in these differences being brought about by causes that differ from one another?'

[V][9] In saying this he fails to see what matter we are dealing with, and what the issue amounts to. For it is not the case that, if different people are more inclined to different things because of natural antecedent causes, there are also for that reason natural and antecedent causes of our wishes and desires. For if that were how the matter stood, nothing would be in our power. As it is, however, we assert that

vero fatemur, acuti hebetesne, valentes inbellicine simus, non esse
id in nobis; qui autem ex eo cogi putat, ne ut sedeamus quidem
aut ambulemus voluntatis esse, is non videt quae quamque rem
res consequatur. ut enim et ingeniosi et tardi ita nascantur
5   antecedentibus causis itemque valentes et imbecilli, non sequitur
tamen ut etiam sedere eos et ambulare et rem agere aliquam
principalibus causis definitum et constitutum sit. [10] Stilponem,
Megaricum philosophum, acutum sane hominem et probatum temporibus illis accepimus. hunc scribunt ipsius familiares et ebriosum
10   et mulierosum fuisse, neque haec scribunt vituperantes sed potius
ad laudem; vitiosam enim naturam ab eo sic edomitam et compres-
sam esse doctrina ut nemo umquam vinolentum illum, nemo in eo
libidinis vestigium viderit. quid? Socraten nonne legimus quemadmodum notarit Zopyrus physignomon, qui se profitebatur hominum
15   mores naturasque ex corpore oculis vultu fronte pernoscere?
stupidum esse Socratem dixit et bardum, quod iugula concava non
haberet, obstructas eas partes et obturatas esse dicebat; addidit
etiam mulierosum, in quo Alcibiades cachinnum dicitur sustulisse.
[11] sed haec ex naturalibus causis vitia nasci possunt, exstirpari
20   autem et funditus tolli, ut is ipse qui ad ea propensus fuerit a
tantis vitiis avocetur, non est positum in naturalibus causis, sed
in voluntate studio disciplina. quae tolluntur omnia, si vis et
natura fati ex divinationis ratione firmabitur.

[VI] etenim si est divinatio, qualibusnam a perceptis artis
25   proficiscitur ('percepta' appello quae dicuntur Graece θεωρήματα)?
non enim credo nullo percepto aut ceteros artifices versari in suo
munere aut eos qui divinatione utantur futura praedicere. [12]
sint igitur astrologorum percepta huiusmodi: 'Si quis' – verbi
causa – 'oriente Canicula natus est, is in mari non morietur'.
30   vigila, Chrysippe, ne tuam causam, in qua tibi cum Diodoro
valente dialectico magna luctatio est, deseras. si enim est verum
quod ita conectitur, 'Si quis oriente Canicula natus est, in mari
non morietur', illud quoque verum est, 'Si Fabius oriente Canicula
natus est, Fabius in mari non morietur.' pugnant igitur haec

---

22 tollentur *C.F.W. Müller et (suis ipsius auspiciis) Rackham*

28 sint] sunt *recc., Moser*

32 *ante* in mari *add.* is *supra lineam* $B^{c}P^{a}$: *probant Yon, Bayer, Giomini*

it does not depend on us whether we are sharp or dull-witted, strong or weak; but the person who thinks that from this it can be proved that whether we sit or walk is not a matter of our will either, does not see what follows from each thing. Granted that the talented and the slow are born like that from antecedent causes, and similarly the strong and the weak; still it does not follow that their sitting and walking and doing anything is also defined and decided by primary causes. [10] We hear that Stilpo, the Megarian philosopher, was certainly sharp, and approved of in those times. Yet his associates write that he was inclined both to drink and to womanising, and they write this not in censure but rather in order to praise him; for his vicious nature was tamed and restrained by him through learning in such a way that no-one ever saw him drunk or saw any trace of lust in him. After all, do we not read how Socrates was stigmatized by Zopyrus the physiognomist, who claimed that he could recognise the characters and natures of men from their bodies, eyes, faces and foreheads? He said that Socrates was stupid and dull, because he did not have hollows in his neck above the collar-bone; he said that those parts were blocked and closed up, and also added that he was inclined to womanising, at which it is said that Alcibiades burst out laughing. [11] But these faults may have their origin from natural causes; their eradication and complete removal, so that the very person who was inclined to such faults is called back from them, depends not on natural causes but on will, application, and discipline. All this is done away with, if the explanation of divination is going to confirm the natural influence of fate.

[VI] Indeed, if divination exists, from what skilled observations does it take its start? (I call "observations" what in Greek are called *theôremata.*) For I do not believe either that the practitioners of other skills engage in their occupation without employing any observation, or that those who employ divination foretell the future thus. [12] Let us suppose,) then, that the observations of the astrologers are like this: "If anyone has been born with the Dogstar rising," for example, "that man will not die at sea." Take care, Chrysippus, that you do not desert your own cause, over which there is a great struggle between you and the powerful dialectician Diodorus. For if the conditional "If anyone has been born with the Dogstar rising, he will not die at sea" is true, then so too is "If Fabius has been born with the Dogstar rising, Fabius will not die at sea." So these things are incompatible, namely that Fabius

inter se, Fabium oriente Canicula natum esse et Fabium in mari
moriturum; et quoniam certum in Fabio ponitur natum esse eum
Canicula oriente, haec quoque pugnant, et esse Fabium et in mari
esse moriturum. ergo haec quoque coniunctio est ex repugnanti-
5   bus, 'Et est Fabius et Fabius in mari morietur,' quod ut propositum est ne fieri quidem potest. ergo illud 'Morietur in mari Fabius' ex eo genere est quod fieri non potest. omne igitur, quod
falsum dicitur in futuro, id fieri non potest.

[VII][13] at hoc, Chrysippe, minime vis, maximeque tibi de hoc
10   ipso cum Diodoro certamen est. ille enim id solum fieri posse
dicit, quod aut sit verum aut futurum sit verum, et quicquid
futurum sit, id dicit fieri necesse esse, et quicquid non sit futurum, id negat fieri posse. tu et quae non sint futura posse fieri
dicis, ut frangi hanc gemmam etiam si id numquam futurum sit,
15   neque necesse fuisse Cypselum regnare Corinthi, quamquam id
millensimo ante anno Apollinis oraculo editum esset. at si ista
conprobabis divina praedicta, et quae falsa in futuris dicentur in
iis habebis, ut ea fieri non possint, ut si dicatur Africanum
Carthagine non potiturum; et si vere dicatur de futuro idque ita
20   futurum sit, dicas esse necessarium; quae est tota Diodori vobis
inimica sententia. [14] etenim si illud vere conectitur, 'Si oriente
Canicula natus es, in mari non moriere,' primumque quod est in
conexo, 'Natus es oriente Canicula,' necessarium est - omnia enim
vera in praeteritis necessaria sunt, ut Chrysippo placet dissenti-
25   enti a magistro Cleanthe, quia sunt inmutabilia nec in falsum e
vero praeterita possunt convertere - si igitur quod primum in
conexo est necessarium est, fit etiam quod consequitur necessarium. quamquam hoc Chrysippo non videtur valere in omnibus; sed
tamen si naturalis est causa, cur in mari Fabius non moriatur, in
30   mari Fabius mori non potest.

----

17 conprobabis] *e* conprobamus *fecit A ut vid.*

18 iis *B:* his *AFMPV*   habebis *recc.:* habemus *codd.*

19 Carthagine non *(i.e.* carthagine n̄) *Plasberg:* carthaginem
A^aB^aV: carthagine A^CB^C: Carthagine <non esse> *Alanus:* ut si ...
potiturum *secl. Christ, Bayer*

20 necessarium] non necessarium V^CP: necessarium <est> *Rackham,
sed cf. comm.*

23 es *recc.:* est *codd.*

25-6 falsum e vero F^CM: falsume vero A^a: falsu(m)me vero A^C:
falsum me vero BF^a: falsum ne vero V^a: falsum nec in verum V^CP

has been born with the Dogstar rising and that Fabius will die at sea; and since it is supposed as certain in the case of Fabius that he *has* been born with the Dogstar rising, these things also are incompatible, namely that Fabius exists and that he will die at sea. So the following conjunction, too, is a combination of things that are incompatible: "Fabius exists, and Fabius will die at sea". Put forward in this way, this cannot actually happen. So "Fabius will die at sea" belongs to the class of what cannot happen. Therefore everything which is said to be false in the future cannot happen.

[VII][13] But this, Chrysippus, is what you least want, and there is a great dispute about this very point between you and Diodorus. For he says that only what either is true or will be true can happen, and he says that whatever is going to happen must necessarily happen, and that whatever will not happen cannot happen. *You* say that things that will not happen, too, *can* happen, for example that this precious stone should be broken can happen, even if this is never going to happen, and that it was not necessary for Cypselus to rule in Corinth although this had been declared by the oracle of Apollo a thousand years before. But if you accept those divine predictions, you will have false statements about future events in such cases, with the result that it will be impossible for those things to happen, for example if it were said that Scipio will not capture Carthage. And if a true statement were made about the future and that thing were going to happen in that way, you would have to say that it is necessary. But all this is the view of Diodorus, which is opposed to you. [14] For if this is a true conditional, "If you were born with the Dogstar rising, you will not die at sea," and the first clause in the conditional, "You were born with the Dogstar rising", is necessary – for all true statements about past things are necessary, in the view of Chrysippus who disagrees with his teacher Cleanthes, because they are unchangeable and cannot be turned from true to false – well then, if the first clause in the conditional is necessary, what follows becomes necessary as well. True, Chrysippus does not think this applies in every case; but nevertheless, if there is a cause in nature for Fabius not dying at sea, Fabius *cannot* die at sea.

[VIII][15] hoc loco Chrysippus aestuans falli sperat Chaldaeos ceterosque divinos, neque eos usuros esse con\<exis sed con>iunctionibus, ut \<non> ita sua percepta pronuntient, 'Si quis natus est oriente Canicula, is in mari non morietur,' sed potius ita dicant,

5 'Non et natus est quis oriente Canicula et is in mari morietur.' o licentiam iocularem! ne ipse incidat in Diodorum, docet Chaldaeos quo pacto eos exponere percepta oporteat. quaero enim, si Chaldaei ita loquentur ut negationes infinitarum coniunctionum potius quam infinita conexa ponant, cur idem medici, cur geometrae, cur

10 reliqui facere non possint? medicus in primis quod erit ei perspectum in arte non ita proponet, 'Si cui venae sic moventur, is habet febrim', sed potius illo modo, 'Non et \<cui> venae sic moventur et is febrim non habet.' itemque geometres non ita dicet, 'In sphaera maximi orbes medii inter se dividuntur,' sed

15 potius illo modo, 'Non et sunt in sphaera maximi orbes et ii non medii inter se dividuntur.' [16] quid est quod non possit isto modo ex conexo transferri ad coniunctionum negationem? et quidem aliis modis easdem res efferre possumus. modo dixi, 'In sphaera maximi orbes medii inter se dividuntur'; possum dicere 'Si

20 in sphaera maximi orbes erunt', possum dicere 'Quia in sphaera maximi orbes erunt.' multa genera sunt enuntiandi, nec ullum distortius quam hoc quo Chrysippus sperat Chaldaeos contentos Stoicorum causa fore. [IX][17] illorum tamen nemo ita loquitur; maius est enim has contortiones orationis quam signorum ortus

25 obitusque perdiscere.

sed ad illam Diodori contentionem quam περὶ δυνατῶν appellant revertamur, in qua quid valeat id quod fieri possit anquiritur. placet igitur Diodoro id solum fieri posse quod aut verum sit   aut verum futurum sit. qui locus attingit hanc quaestionem, nihil fieri

2 con\<exis sed con>iunctionibus *Szymánski:* con\<exis potius quam con>iunctionibus *Plasberg:* coniunctionibus *codd.:* conexionibus *Madvig*

3 non *add. Szymánski*   percepta] praecepta *AFM*

4 dicant *recc.:* dicent *codd.*

8 loquentur *codd.:* loquantur *Ven.*

12 non et \<cui> venae *Giomini:* non ei venae *codd.* (et *supr.* ei scr. M^c): non cui venae *Hottinger:* non et ei venae *Baiter*

cui *post* sic *add. Müller*   15 ii *BVP:* hi *F:* hii A^cM

20 quia B^cF^c: qua AB^aF^a *Plasberg* (possum – erunt *om.V*)

[VIII][15] At this point Chrysippus, becoming agitated, hopes that the astrologers and the other diviners can be foiled, and that they will not make use of conditionals but rather of conjunctions, so that they will not declare their observations as follows, "If someone was born with the Dogstar rising, that man will not die at sea", but rather will speak as follows, "It is not the case both that someone was born with the Dogstar rising and that that man will die at sea." What amusing presumption! So that he shall not himself fall into Diodorus' position, he instructs the astrologers how they ought to express their observations. For I ask, if the astrologers are going to speak in such a way as to assert negations of indefinite conjunctions, rather than indefinite conditionals, why should the doctors, the geometricians and all the rest not be able to do this? The doctor, first of all, will not put forward what has been observed by him in his skill as follows, "If someone's pulse is like this, that person has a fever", but rather, in the manner described, "it is not the case both that someone's pulse is like this and that that person does not have a fever." Similarly the geometrician will not say "Greatest circles on a sphere bisect one another", but rather, in the manner described, "it is not the case both that there are greatest circles on a sphere and that they do not bisect one another". [16] What is there that could not in this way be transformed from a conditional to the negation of a conjunction? And indeed we can express the same things in other ways. Just now I said "Greatest circles on a sphere bisect one another"; I could say "If there are greatest circles on a sphere", I could say "Since there are greatest circles on a sphere." There are many types of expression, but none is more tortuous than this one which Chrysippus hopes the astrologers will accept for the Stoics' sake. [IX][17] However, none of them does talk like that; for it is a bigger undertaking to learn these contorted expressions than to learn the risings and settings of the constellations.

But let us return to that argument of Diodorus which they call "concerning possibles", in which the meaning of "what can happen" is examined. Well, Diodorus' position is that only that which either is or will be true can happen. This topic touches on the following problem, that

quod non necesse fuerit, et quicquid fieri possit, id aut esse iam
aut futurum esse, nec magis commutari ex veris in falsa posse ea
quae futura quam ea quae facta sunt; sed in factis immutabilita-
tem apparere, in futuris quibusdam, quia non appareat, ne inesse
5 quidem videri: ut in eo qui mortifero morbo urgeatur verum sit
'Hic morietur hoc morbo,' at hoc idem si vere dicatur in eo, in
quo vis morbi tanta non appareat, nihilo minus futurum sit. ita fit
ut commutatio ex vero in falsum ne in futuro quidem ulla fieri
possit. nam 'Morietur Scipio' talem vim habet ut, quamquam de
10 futuro dicitur, tamen ut id non possit convertere in falsum; de
homine enim dicitur, cui necesse est mori. [18] sic si diceretur,
'Morietur noctu in cubiculo suo vi oppressus Scipio,' vere diceretur; id enim fore diceretur quod esset futurum, futurum autem
fuisse ex eo, quia factum est, intellegi debet. nec magis erat
15 verum 'Morietur Scipio' quam 'Morietur illo modo,' nec magis
necesse mori Scipioni quam illo modo mori, nec magis inmutabile ex
vero in falsum 'Necatus est Scipio' quam 'Necabitur Scipio'; nec,
cum haec ita sint, est causa cur Epicurus fatum extimescat et ab
atomis petat praesidium easque de via deducat, et uno tempore
20 suscipiat res duas inenodabiles, unam ut sine causa fiat aliquid,
ex quo exsistet ut de nihilo quippiam fiat, quod nec ipsi nec
cuiquam physico placet, alteram ut, cum duo individua per inani-
tatem ferantur, alterum e regione moveatur, alterum declinet.

[19] licet enim Epicuro, concedenti omne enuntiatum aut verum aut
25 falsum esse, non vereri ne omnia fato fieri sit necesse; non enim
aeternis causis naturae necessitate manantibus verum est id quod
ita enuntiatur, 'Descendit in Academiam Carneades,' nec tamen sine

---

3 futura] futura sint *Moser*

4 appareat *Bremi:* appareret *ABPV:* apparent *FHM:* apparet *rec.
Davies*

7 futurum sit] futurumst *coni. Halm*   10 ut *om. recc., del. Davies*

12 <non minus> vere diceretur *Stüve, approb. Hamelin*

15 magis *Ramus:* minus *codd.*

16 quam illo modo] illo modo quam *Davies (qui* minus *retinet):* nec
minus, quam necesse mori Scipioni, illo modo mori *Turnebus*

Scipioni *codd.:* Scipionem *recc. Davies*

26 <ex> aeternis *Davies*

naturae] a naturae *V^C P:* naturae <e> *Baiter*

emanantibus *coni. Christ*

27 descendit *codd.:* descendet *coni. Lörcher*

nothing happens that was not necessary, and that whatever can happen either is already or is going to be, and that things that will be can no more be turned from true to false than those that have happened. But in the case of things that have happened the unchangeability is evident, whereas in certain future cases, because it is not evident, it does not even seem to be present. Thus in the case of someone who is beset by a terminal illness "This man will die of this illness" is true, but if this same thing is said truly in the case of someone in whom the power of the illness is not yet evident to so great an extent, it will happen none the less. Thus it happens that there can be no change from true to false even in what is future. For "Scipio will die" has such a force that, although it is a statement about what is future, nevertheless it cannot turn into falsehood; for it is a statement about a human being, who must necessarily die. [18] Thus, if someone were to say "Scipio will die at night in his bedroom from a violent attack," this would be said truly; for it would be said that what was going to be was going to be, and that it was going to be should be understood from the fact that it did indeed happen. "Scipio will die" was no more true than "Scipio will die in that way", nor was it more necessary for Scipio to die than for him to die in that way; nor is it more impossible for "Scipio has been killed" to turn from true to false than for "Scipio will be killed" to do so. But neither, just because these things are so, is there any reason for Epicurus to tremble before fate, seek help from the atoms and turn them aside from their path, and for him to commit himself at one and the same time to two things that cannot be proved: first that something should happen without a cause, from which it will follow that something comes from nothing, which neither he himself nor any natural philosopher accepts; and second that, when two indivisible bodies travel through the void, one moves in a straight line and the other swerves aside.

[19] For it is possible for Epicurus to grant that every proposition is either true or false, without fearing that it will be necessary for all things to come about by fate. For it is not through causes that have always existed, deriving from natural necessity, that such a proposition as "Carneades is going down into the Academy" is true; nor yet is it

causis, sed interest inter causas fortuito antegressas et inter
causas cohibentes in se efficientiam naturalem. ita et semper
verum fuit 'Morietur Epicurus cum duo et septuaginta annos
vixerit, archonte Pytharato,' neque tamen erant causae fatales cur
5   ita accideret, sed quod ita cecidit certe casurum, sicut cecidit,
fuit. [20] nec ii qui dicunt immutabilia esse quae futura sint, nec
posse verum futurum convertere in falsum, fati necessitatem
confirmant, sed verborum vim interpretantur; at qui introducunt
causarum seriem sempiternam, ii mentem hominis voluntate libera
10   spoliatam necessitate fati devinciunt.

[X] sed haec hactenus; alia videamus. concludit enim Chrysippus
hoc modo; 'Si est motus sine causa, non omnis enuntiatio (quod
ἀξίωμα dialectici appellant) aut vera aut falsa erit. causas enim
efficientis quod non habebit, id nec verum nec falsum erit. omnis
15   autem enuntiatio aut vera aut falsa est; motus ergo sine causa
nullus est. [21] quod si ita est, omnia quae fiunt causis fiunt
antegressis; id si ita est, omnia fato fiunt. efficitur igitur fato
fieri quaecumque fiant.' hic primum si mihi libeat adsentiri Epicuro et negare omnem enuntiationem aut veram esse aut falsam, eam
20   plagam potius accipiam, quam fato omnia fieri comprobem; illa enim
sententia aliquid habet disputationis, haec vero non est tolerabi-
lis.

itaque contendit omnis nervos Chrysippus ut persuadeat omne
ἀξίωμα aut verum esse aut falsum. ut enim Epicurus veretur ne,
25   si hoc concesserit, concedendum sit fato fieri quaecumque fiant
(si enim alterum utrum ex aeternitate verum sit, esse id etiam
certum, et si certum, etiam necessarium: ita et necessitatem et
fatum confirmari putat), sic Chrysippus metuit ne, si non obtinu-
erit omne quod enuntietur aut verum esse aut falsum, non teneat
30   omnia fato fieri et ex causis aeternis rerum futurarum. [22] sed
Epicurus declinatione atomi vitari necessitatem fati putat; itaque
tertius quidam motus oritur extra pondus et plagam, cum declinat

---

5 ita cecidit *Bremi*: ita cecidisset *ABFM*: ita accidisset *VP*

casurum *A^C BFM*: causarum *A^a V^a*: a serie causarum *V^C P*

6 fuit *A^a VP*: fuerit *A^C BFM*

8 at qui *recc.*: atque *codd.*

without causes, but there is a difference between causes that precede by chance and those that contain within themselves a natural effectiveness. Thus "Epicurus will die when he has lived 72 years, in the archonship of Pytharatus" was always true, and yet there were no fated causes why it should so happen; but because it *did* so happen it was certainly going to happen just as it did happen. [20] Nor do those who say that the things that are going to be are unchangeable, and that a future truth cannot be turned into a falsehood, establish the necessity of fate; rather, they are explaining the meanings of words. It is those who introduce an eternal series of causes who rob the mind of free will and bind it in the necessity of fate.

[X] But enough of these matters; let us consider others. Chrysippus argues to his conclusion as follows: 'If there is movement without a cause, it is not the case that every proposition (what the dialecticians call an *axiôma*) will be either true or false. For what does not have any causes that bring it about will be neither true nor false. But every proposition *is* true or false; so there is no movement without a cause. [21] But if this is so, all the things that come about do so through antecedent causes; and if this is so, all things come about through fate. So it is brought about that whatever things come about do so through fate.' Now here, first of all, if it were my desire to agree with Epicurus and deny that every proposition is either true or false, I would rather accept that blow than agree that all things come about through fate; for the former opinion gives some scope for discussion, but the latter is intolerable.

So, Chrysippus strains every sinew in order to convince us that every proposition is either true or false. Epicurus is afraid that, if he grants this, he will have to grant that whatever comes about does so through fate; for if either the assertion or the denial is true from eternity, it will also be certain, and if certain, also necessary; thus he thinks that both necessity and fate will be confirmed. Just so Chrysippus fears that, if he does not maintain that every proposition that is made is either true or false, he will not uphold his claim that all things come about through fate and through eternal causes of the things that are going to be. [22] Epicurus, however, thinks that the necessity of fate is avoided by the swerve of the atom; and so a certain third movement arises, apart from weight and collision, when the atom swerves by a

atomus intervallo minimo (id appellat ἐλάχιστον). quam declinationem sine causa fieri, si minus verbis, re cogitur confiteri. non
enim atomus ab atomo pulsa declinat; nam qui potest pelli alia ab
alia si gravitate feruntur ad perpendiculum corpora individua
5   rectis lineis, ut Epicuro placet? sequitur enim ut, si alia ab alia
numquam depellatur, ne contingat quidem alia aliam; ex quo efficitur, etiam si sit atomus eaque declinet, declinare sine causa.

[23] hanc Epicurus rationem induxit ob eam rem quod veritus est
ne, si semper atomus gravitate ferretur naturali ac necessaria,
10   nihil liberum nobis esset, cum ita moveretur animus ut atomorum
motu cogeretur. id Democritus auctor atomorum accipere maluit,
necessitate omnia fieri, quam a corporibus individuis naturalis
motus avellere. [XI] acutius Carneades, qui docebat posse Epicu-
reos suam causam sine hac commenticia   declinatione defendere.
15   nam cum doceret esse posse quendam animi motum voluntarium, id
fuit defendi melius quam introducere declinationem, cuius praesertim causam reperire non possunt; quo defenso facile Chrysippo
possent resistere. cum enim concessissent motum nullum esse sine
causa, non concederent omnia quae fierent fieri causis anteceden-
20   tibus; voluntatis enim nostrae non esse causas externas et antecedentis.

[24] communi igitur consuetudine sermonis abutimur cum ita
dicimus, velle aliquid quempiam aut nolle sine causa; ita enim
dicimus 'sine causa' ut dicamus sine externa et antecedente causa,
25   non sine aliqua. ut cum vas inane dicimus, non ita loquimur ut
physici, quibus inane esse nihil placet, sed ita ut verbi causa
sine aqua, sine vino, sine oleo vas esse dicamus; sic, cum sine
causa animum dicimus moveri, sine antecedente et externa causa
moveri, non omnino sine causa dicimus. de ipsa atomo dici potest,
30   cum per inane moveatur gravitate et pondere, sine causa moveri,
quia nulla causa accedat extrinsecus. [25] rursus autem, ne omnes

---

5 enim *codd.:* autem *Davies, Rackham, sed perperam*
5-6 ut si ... ne] ut ... si ne *Madvig, similiter Christ*
7 etiam si *Davies:* ut iam si *codd.:* ut iam [si] *rec. Ven. Manutius*
15 doceret *codd.:* docere B^a: docerent *Meyer*
17 possunt *ABFM:* possent V^cP: possem V^a

72

very small distance (this he calls a "minimum"). That this swerve comes about without a cause he is compelled to admit, if not by his own words, by the facts themselves. For it is not the case that an atom swerves when struck by another; for how can one be struck by another if individual bodies are carried downwards by their weight in straight lines, as Epicurus supposes? For, if one is never struck from its course by another, it follows that none even touches another; and from this it results that, even if there is an atom and it swerves, it does so without a cause.

[23] Epicurus introduced this theory because he was afraid that,if the atom was always carried along by its weight in a natural and necessary way, we would have no freedom, since our mind would be moved in the way in which it was constrained by the movement of the atoms. Democritus, the inventor of the atoms, preferred to accept this, that all things come about through fate, rather than to remove the natural movements of individual bodies from them. [XI] More acutely, Carneades taught that the Epicureans could have maintained their position without this fictitious swerve. For, seeing that (Epicurus) taught that there could be some voluntary movement of the mind, it would have been better to defend that than to introduce the swerve, especially as they cannot find a cause for it. And by defending this they could easily have resisted Chrysippus. For in having admitted that there was no movement without a cause, they would not be admitting that all things that came about did so through *antecedent* causes. For (they could have said), there are no external and antecedent causes of our will.

[24] We are therefore misusing the common manner of speaking when we say that somebody wants or does not want something "without a cause"; for we say "without a cause" meaning without an *external* and *antecedent* cause, not without *any* cause. Just as when we speak of an empty vessel, we are not speaking as natural scientists, who hold that emptiness is absolutely *nothing*, but so as to say, for example, that the vase contains no water, no wine, no oil. Just so, when we say that the mind is moved without a cause, we are saying that it is moved without an antecedent and external cause, not without any cause. Of the atom itself it can be said, when it is moved through the void by heaviness and weight, that it is moved without a cause, because no cause comes to it from outside. [25] On the other hand, so that all the natural philoso-

physici inrideant nos, si dicamus quicquam fieri sine causa, dis-
tinguendum est et ita dicendum, ipsius individui hanc esse naturam ut pondere et gravitate moveatur, eamque ipsam esse causam
cur ita feratur. similiter ad animorum motus voluntarios non est
5   requirenda externa causa; motus enim voluntarius eam naturam in
se ipse continet ut sit in nostra potestate nobisque pareat, nec id
sine causa; eius enim rei causa ipsa natura est.

[26] quod cum ita sit, quid est cur non omnis pronuntiatio aut
vera aut falsa sit nisi concesserimus fato fieri quaecumque fiant?
10   'quia futura vera,' inquit, 'non possunt esse ea quae causas cur
futura sint non habent; habeant igitur causas necesse est ea quae
vera sunt; ita, cum evenerint, fato evenerint.' [XII] confectum
negotium, siquidem concedendum tibi est aut fato omnia fieri aut
quicquam fieri posse sine causa. [27] an aliter haec enuntiatio
15   vera esse non potest, 'Capiet Numantiam Scipio,' nisi ex aeternitate causa causam serens hoc erit effectura? an hoc falsum po-
tuisset esse si esset sescentis saeculis ante dictum? et si tum non
esset vera haec enuntiatio, 'Capiet Numantiam Scipio', ne illa
quidem eversa esset vera haec enuntiatio, 'Capiet Numantiam
20   Scipio.' potest igitur quicquam factum esse quod non verum fuerit
futurum esse? nam ut praeterita ea vera dicimus quorum super-
iore tempore vera fuerit instantia, sic futura quorum consequenti
tempore vera erit instantia, ea vera dicemus. [28] nec si omne
enuntiatum aut verum aut falsum est, sequitur ilico esse causas

31-1 omnes physici inrideant nos *Müller:* omnes phisici inrideamur
ABF^aV: omnes a phisicis inrideamur F^CHM: omnibus a physicis
inrideamur *censor Jenensis ed. Bremi, Christ:* omnes physici
inrideant *Baiter:* omnes ⟨nos⟩ physici inrideant *Bremi*

11-12 quae vera ⟨futura⟩ sunt *Christ*

15 non *om. recc., secl. Rackham, sed perperam*

16 erit] erat V^CP

18-20 ne illa - Scipio *in mg. add. recentiss. man. V*

19 quidem eversa esset vera haec enuntiatio *Montanari Caldini:*
quidem eversa vera est haec enuntiatio V^C(ē; *cf. Montanari Caldini
85 n.11), edd. plerique:* quidem eversa *(ut. vid.: cf. Montanari
Caldini 84)* esse vera est haec enuntiatio A^a *ut vid.:* quidem vera
esset vera haec enuntiatio B^a: quidem vera esset vera est haec
enuntiatio A^C(?; *cf. Introd. §14)*B^CFM: quidem vera esset [vera est
haec enuntiatio] *Skassis, Baiter, Yon*

capiet *codd., probat Caldini:* cepit *Ramus, edd. plerique*

phers may not ridicule us, if we say that something comes about without a cause, we must make a distinction and say that it is the nature of the individual atom itself to be moved by weight and heaviness, and this itself is the cause for its being carried along in this way. Similarly in the case of the voluntary movements of mind an external cause is not to be looked for; for voluntary movement has this nature in itself, that it is in our power and is obedient to us. And this is not without a cause, for the nature of that thing itself is the cause of that thing.

[26] Since this is so, what reason is there why every proposition should not be either true or false if we do not grant that whatever comes about does so by fate? 'Because,' he says, 'those things cannot be true in the future that do not have causes for their future being; so those things that are true necessarily have causes; and thus when they have come about, they will have done so through fate.' [XII] That is the end of the matter, *if* we have to grant to you that either all things come about through fate or something can come about without a cause. [27] Or can this proposition, 'Scipio will capture Numantia,' really not be true unless one cause sowing another from eternity was going to bring this about? Could this have been false(, given that it happened,) if it was said countless centuries before(, even though it was not brought about by an eternal series of antecedent causes)? And, if this proposition, 'Scipio will capture Numantia,' was not true at that time, then even when that city was overthrown this proposition, 'Scipio will capture Numantia,' would not have been true. Can anything have come about which was not truly going to be (even if not predetermined)? For, just as we say those past things are true which truly occurred at an earlier time, just so we will say that those future things are true that will truly occur in future time. [28] Nor, if every proposition is either true or false, does it for that reason follow that there are

75

immutabiles easque aeternas quae prohibeant quicquam secus
cadere atque casurum sit; fortuitae sunt causae quae efficiant ut
vere dicantur quae ita dicentur, 'Veniet in senatum Cato,' non
inclusae in rerum natura atque mundo; et tamen tam est immuta-
5 bile venturum, cum est verum, quam venisse, nec ob eam causam
fatum aut necessitas extimescenda est. etenim erit confiteri necesse: si haec enuntiatio, 'Veniet in Tusculanum Hortensius" vera
non est, sequitur ut falsa sit. quorum isti neutrum volunt: quod
fieri non potest.

10 nec nos impediet illa ignava ratio quae dicitur; appellatur enim
quidam a philosophis ἀργὸς λόγος, cui si pareamus nihil omnino
agamus in vita. sic enim interrogant: 'Si fatum tibi est ex hoc
morbo convalescere, sive tu medicum adhibueris sive non adhibueris, convalesces; [29] item si fatum tibi est ex hoc morbo non
15 convalescere, sive tu medicum adhibueris sive non adhibueris, non
convalesces; et alterutrum fatum est; medicum ergo adhibere nihil
attinet.' [XIII] recte genus hoc interrogationis ignavum atque
iners nominatum est, quod eadem ratione omnis e vita tolletur
actio. licet etiam inmutare, ut fati nomen ne adiungas et eandem
20 tamen teneas sententiam, hoc modo: 'Si ex aeternitate verum hoc
fuit, "Ex isto morbo convalesces," sive adhibueris medicum sive
non adhibueris, convalesces; itemque, si ex aeternitate falsum hoc
fuit, "Ex isto morbo convalesces," sive adhibueris medicum sive
non adhibueris, non convalesces'; deinde cetera.

25 [30] haec ratio a Chrysippo reprehenditur. 'Quaedam enim sunt,'
inquit, 'in rebus simplicia, quaedam copulata; simplex est, "Morietur illo die Socrates"; huic, sive quid fecerit sive non fecerit,
finitus est moriendi dies. at si ita fatum sit, "Nascetur Oedipus
Laio," non poterit dici "sive fuerit Laius cum muliere sive non
30 fuerit"; copulata enim res est et confatalis.' sic enim appellat quia
ita fatum sit, et concubiturum cum uxore Laium et ex ea Oedipum

---

7 haec enuntiatio *codd. (sed* -tio *in rasura A):* hoc enuntiatum
Ramus

7-8 vera ... falsa *recc., Davies:* verum ... falsum AV^CB (fal V^p)

12 agamus] agemus V^CP

23 non *ante* convalesces *exhib. sed del. AB,* Ñ *in rasura ubi erat*
**n *exhib.* V

30 quia] quasi V^C *in mg.*

unchangeable and eternal causes which prevent anything from coming about in a different way from that in which it will in fact come about. The causes which make true those statements which will be made like "Cato will come into the senate" are fortuitous, not inherent in the nature of things and the universe; nevertheless, it is as unchangeable that he will come, when it is true that he will come, as that he *has* come; and fate or necessity should not for that reason be feared. And indeed, if the following proposition, 'Hortensius will come to his villa at Tusculum' is not true, it will be necessary to admit that it follows that it is false. *They* want neither of these to apply; but that is impossible.

And we will not be hindered, either, by the so-called Lazy Argument; for there is a certain argument which is caused the 'Lazy Argument' by the philosophers; if we obeyed this we would do nothing at all in life. For they argue as follows: 'If it is fated for you to recover from this disease, then you will recover, whether you call in a doctor or not; [29] similarly, if it is fated for you not to recover from this disease, then you will not recover, whether you call in a doctor or not. But one or the other is fated; so there is no point in calling in a doctor.' [XIII] This kind of argument is rightly named lazy and idle, since by the same argument all activity will be removed from life. For one can change the argument so as not to bring in the name of 'fate' and still maintain the same position, as follows: 'If this has been true from eternity, that "You will recover from this disease," then you will recover, whether you call in a doctor or not; and similarly, if this has been false from eternity, "You will recover from this disease," then you will not recover, whether you call in a doctor or not"; and the rest follows.

[30] This argument is criticised by Chrysippus. 'For,' he says, 'there are some cases in things that are simple, others complex. A case of what is simple is "Socrates will die on that day"; whether he does anything or not, there is a fixed day for his death. But if it is fated that "Oedipus will be born to Laius", one will not be able to say "whether Laius has slept with a woman or not"; the matter is complex and "co-fated" ' - for that is what he calls it, because it is fated, *both* that Laius will sleep with his wife *and* that he will beget Oedipus

procreaturum. ut si esset dictum, 'Luctabitur Olympiis Milon,' et referret aliquis, 'Ergo sive habuerit adversarium sive non habuerit, luctabitur,' erraret; est enim copulatum 'luctabitur,' quia sine adversario nulla luctatio est. omnes igitur istius generis captiones
5 eodem modo refelluntur. 'Sive tu adhibueris medicum sive non adhibueris, convalesces' captiosum; tam enim est fatale medicum adhibere quam convalescere. haec, ut dixi, confatalia ille appellat.

[XIV][31] Carneades genus hoc totum non probabat et nimis inconsiderate concludi hanc rationem putabat. itaque premebat alio
10 modo, nec ullam adhibebat calumniam; cuius erat haec conclusio: 'Si omnia antecedentibus causis fiunt, omnia naturali conligatione conserte contexteque fiunt; quod si ita est, omnia necessitas efficit; id si verum est, nihil est in nostra potestate. est autem aliquid in nostra potestate. at, si omnia fato fiunt, omnia causis
15 antecedentibus fiunt. non igitur fato fiunt quaecumque fiunt.'

[32] hoc artius adstringi ratio non potest. nam si quis velit idem referre, atque ita dicere, 'Si omne futurum ex aeternitate verum est, ut ita certe eveniat quemadmodum sit futurum, omnia necesse est conligatione naturali conserte contexteque fieri,' nihil dicat.
20 multum enim differt utrum causa naturalis ex aeternitate futura vera efficiat, an etiam sine aeternitate naturali futura quae sint ea vera esse possint intelligi. itaque dicebat Carneades ne Apollinem quidem futura posse dicere nisi ea quorum causas natura ita contineret ut ea fieri necesse esset. [33] quid enim spectans deus
25 ipse diceret Marcellum eum qui ter consul fuit in mari esse periturum? erat quidem hoc verum ex aeternitate, sed causas id efficientis non habebat. ita ne praeterita quidem ea, quorum nulla signa tamquam vestigia exstarent, Apollini nota esse censebat; quo minus futura. causis enim efficientibus quamque rem cognitis
30 posse denique sciri quid futurum esset. ergo nec de Oedipode potuisse Apollinem praedicere, nullis in rerum natura causis praepositis cur ab eo patrem interfici necesse esset, nec quicquam eiusmodi.

---

16 hoc *codd.*: haec *recc.*   ratio *codd.*: ratione *recc.*

21 sine ⟨causa ex⟩ aeternitate naturali *Moser: fort.* sine ⟨causa⟩ naturali ⟨ex⟩ aeternitate *Christ*

28 quo] quanto *Davies*

by her. Just as if someone had said "Milo will wrestle in the Olympic games", and someone else answered "So, whether he has an opponent or not, he will wrestle," he would be wrong, for "he will wrestle" is complex. For without an opponent there is no wrestling. So all captious arguments of that sort can be refuted in the same way. "Whether you call in the doctor or not, you will get well" is captious; it is as fated to call in the doctor as it is to get well. These cases, as I said, Chrysippus calls "co-fated".

[XIV][31] Carneades disapproved of this whole type of argument, and considered that this reasoning was brought to its conclusion with too little consideration. And so he urged his case in another way, without involving any misrepresentation; and this argument was as follows. 'If all things come about through antecedent causes, all things come about in such a way that they are joined and woven together by a natural connection. But if that is so, all things are brought about by necessity; and if that is true, nothing is in our power. However, there is something in our power. But if all things come about through fate, all things come about through antecedent causes. So it is not the case that whatever comes about does so through fate.'

[32] An argument cannot be made more binding than this. For if someone were to want to make the same point in reply, and to speak as follows, 'If everything that will be in the future is true from eternity, so that it will certainly come about in the way in which it is going to be, it is necessary for all things to come about in such a way that they are joined and woven together by a natural connection,' he would be talking nonsense. For it makes a great difference whether a natural cause makes future things true from eternity, or whether even those things which are going to be in the future *without* a natural eternity (of preceding causes) can be understood to be true. And so Carneades used to say that not even Apollo could say what was going to be in the future, except for those things whose causes were contained in nature in such a way that it was necessary for them to come to be. [33] For what could the god himself look to in saying that the Marcellus, who was consul three times, was going to die at sea? This had indeed been true from all eternity, but it did not yet have causes bringing it about. In this way he judged that not even those past things of which there existed no signs – traces, as it were – were known to Apollo; how much less future ones! For it was, in short, by knowing the causes that brought each thing about that it was possible to know what was going to be in the future. Therefore Apollo could not have made a prediction about Oedipus, since there were no causes laid down beforehand in the nature of things making it necessary for his father to be killed by him; nor could he make any other prediction of that sort.

[XV] quocirca si Stoicis qui omnia fato fieri dicunt consentaneum est huiusmodi oracula ceteraque quae a divinatione ducuntur conprobare, iis autem qui quae futura sunt ea vera esse ex aeternitate dicunt non idem dicendum est, vide ne non eadem sit
5 illorum causa et Stoicorum; hi enim urguentur angustius, illorum ratio soluta ac libera est.

[34] quod si concedatur nihil posse evenire nisi causa antecedente, quid proficiatur si ea causa non ex aeternis causis apta dicatur? causa autem ea est quae id efficit cuius est causa,
10 ut vulnus mortis, cruditas morbi, ignis ardoris. itaque non sic causa intellegi debet ut quod cuique antecedat id ei causa sit, sed quod cuique efficienter antecedat, nec quod in Campum descenderim id fuisse causae cur pila luderem, nec Hecubam causam interitus fuise Troianis quod Alexandrum genuerit, nec Tyndareum
15 Agamemnoni quod Clytemestram. hoc enim modo viator quoque bene vestitus causa grassatori fuisse dicetur cur ab eo spoliaretur. [35] ex hoc genere illud est Ennii,
　　utinam ne in nemore Pelio securibus
　　caesae accedissent abiegnae ad terram trabes!
20 licuit vel altius, "Utinam ne in Pelio nata ulla umquam esset arbor!" etiam supra "Utinam ne esset mons ullus Pelius!" similiterque superiora repetentem regredi infinite licet.
　　Neve inde navis inchoandi exordium
　　coepisset.

2 a divinatione BF^CM^C: ad divinatione AF^aM^a: ad divinationem A^aVP

ducuntur *recc., Madvig:* dicuntur *AVB:* ad ·divinationem pertinent *Davies :* ad divinationem pertinere dicuntur *recc., Bremi*

3 iis *rec., Davies, ?F (cf. Introd. §14):* his *codd.:* ⟨de⟩ eis *coni. Rackham*

5 angustius V^CP: angustus V^a: angustiis *ABFM*

9 dicetur A^CBFM: diceretur A^aVP

19 accedissent *VP, Ciceronis De inventione codd. plerique;* accedisset *Varro, Priscianus 7.40;* accidissent B^a, *Cic. Topic. (codd. AaV), Cic. De Nat. Deorum (sed* cecidissent *eius corrector B^2):* cecaedissent F^a: cecidissent $A^CB^CF^CM$, *Cic. Top. codd. plerique, et similiter Quintilianus, Julius Victor, Donatus, Priscianus De metris Terentii: codd. Rhet. ad Herenn. alii alia.*

23 inchoandi] incohandae *rec., Rhet. ad Herenn.(codd.CP^{2}d), Davies:* incohanda *Priscianus, Rhet. ad Herenn.(cod.B)*

24 coepisset *VFM:* caepisset B^C: cepisset B^aP

[XV] So it is appropriate for the Stoics, who say that all things come about by fate, to accept oracles of this sort and the other things which are derived from divination; but the same cannot be said by those who say that the things that are going to be in the future have been true from eternity (*sc*. whether there have been antecedent *causes* of them or not). See therefore that their case is not the same as that of the Stoics; for these (the Stoics) are harder pressed, while *their* account is free from such restrictions.

[34] But even if it were granted that nothing can happen except by an antecedent cause, what would be achieved if that cause were not said to be attached to an eternal sequence of causes? A cause, however, is what brings about that of which it is said to be the cause, as a wound is the cause of death, undigested food of illness, fire of heat. So "cause" should not be understood in such a way that what *precedes* each thing is the cause for that thing, but what precedes each thing *and brings it about;* we should not suppose that the fact that I went down to the Campus was the cause of my playing ball, nor that Hecuba was the cause of destruction for the Trojans because she gave birth to Alexander, nor that Tyndareus was the cause of destruction for Agamemnon because he was the father of Clytemnestra. For on this basis the well-dressed traveller will be said to have been the cause for the highwayman's robbing him. [35] Of this sort is that passage in Ennius,

Would that never in the groves of Pelion

had the axe-hewn fir-timbers fallen to earth!

He could have gone back further, "Would that no tree had ever sprouted on Pelion!", or even further, "Would that there had never been a mountain Pelion!"; and if one goes back to what was earlier in this way one can go back to infinity.

And would that the construction of a ship

had not begun there.

quorsum haec praeterita? quia sequitur illud,

  nam numquam era errans mea domo ecferret pedem,

    Medea, animo aegro, amore saevo saucia,

non ut eae res causam adferrent amoris.

5 [XVI][36] interesse autem aiunt utrum eiusmodi quid sit, sine quo
effici aliquid non possit, an eiusmodi cum quo effici aliquid necesse sit. nulla igitur earum est causa, quoniam nulla eam rem sua
vi efficit [in] cuius causa dicitur; nec id sine quo quippiam non
fit causa est, sed id quod cum accessit id cuius est causa efficit
10 necessario. nondum enim ulcerato serpentis morsu Philocteta quae
causa in rerum natura continebatur, fore ut is in insula Lemno
linqueretur? post autem causa fuit propior et cum exitu iunctior.
[37] ratio igitur eventus aperit causam. sed ex aeternitate vera
fuit haec enuntiatio, "Relinquetur in insula Philoctetes", nec hoc
15 ex vero in falsum poterat convertere.

necesse est enim in rebus contrariis duabus - contraria autem
hoc loco ea dico quorum alterum ait quid, alterum negat - ex iis
igitur necesse est invito Epicuro alterum verum esse, alterum
falsum, ut "Sauciabitur Philocteta" omnibus ante saeculis verum
20 fuit, "Non sauciabitur" falsum; nisi forte volumus Epicureorum
opinionem sequi, qui tales enuntiationes nec veras nec falsas esse
dicunt, aut, cum id pudet, illud tamen dicunt, quod est impuden-
tius, veras esse ex contrariis diiunctiones, sed quae in his enun-

---

2 ecferret $A^C B^C FMV^C$: haec ferret $A^a B^a V^a$

4 non <erat> ut *Rackham: ante* non ut *pauca deesse suspicatur
Lambinus*

6 effici aliquid *(alt.)*] aliaquid (del.) effici aliquid *V:* aliquid effici
recc.

7 earum <rerum> *coni. Plasberg, noluit Ax*

8 in *om. Ven., eds.*

12 propior $M^C V^C P$: proprior $ABFMV^a P$

13 aperit] aperuit *Rackham*

15 convertere $A^a V$: converti $A^C B^C FM$: converte B^a

18 invito Epicuro *secl. Bremi*

19 Philocteta *delendum censuit Madvig*

23 diiunctiones] disiunctiones *M*

What is the point of these things in the past? That this follows,

> For never would my mistress have set foot
> outside her home and wandered, Medea, sick at heart,
> wounded by a fierce love,

but not this, that those things supplied the *cause* of her love.

[XVI][36] But they say it makes a great difference whether something is of such a sort that something cannot be brought about without it, or whether it is of such a sort that something must be brought about along with it. So none of *those* things is a cause, because none of them brings about by its own power that of which it is said to be a cause; nor is that, without which something does not come about, a cause, but rather that which, when it comes to apply, necessarily brings about that of which it is the cause. For when Philoctetes had not yet been given a festering sore by the bite of the serpent, what cause was there included in the nature of things for his being abandoned on the island of Lemnos? Afterwards, however, the cause was closer at hand and more closely linked with the outcome. [37] So the way in which the event comes about reveals the cause; nevertheless, this statement, "Philoctetes will be abandoned on the island," was true from all eternity, and this could not change from true to false.

For it is necessary in the case of two opposed things – and by "opposed" here I mean those one of which asserts something and the other denies it – it is necessary, against Epicurus' wishes, that one of these be true, the other false, as "Philoctetes will be wounded" was true for all ages beforehand, "he will not be wounded" false – unless perhaps we wish to follow the Epicureans, who say that such statements are neither true nor false, or, when they are embarrassed to say *that*, say what is even more shameless, that disjunctions from opposites (e.g.: "*Either* Philoctetes will be wounded or he will not be") are true, but of

83

tiata essent, eorum neutrum esse verum. [38] O admirabilem licen-tiam et miserabilem inscientiam disserendi! si enim aliquid in eloquendo nec verum nec falsum est, certe id verum non est; quod autem verum non est, qui potest non falsum esse? aut quod falsum non est, qui potest non verum esse? tenebitur id quod a Chrysippo defenditur, omnem enuntiationem aut veram aut falsam esse; ratio ipsa coget et ex aeternitate quaedam esse vera et ea non esse nexa causis aeternis et a fati necessitate esse libera.

[XVII][39] ac mihi quidem videtur, cum duae sententiae fuissent veterum philosophorum, una eorum qui censerent omnia ita fato fieri ut id fatum vim necessitatis afferret, in qua sententia Democritus, Heraclitus, Empedocles, Aristoteles fuit, altera eorum quibus viderentur sine ullo fato esse animorum motus voluntarii, Chrysippus tamquam arbiter honorarius medium ferire voluisse, sed applicat se ad eos potius qui necessitate motus animorum liberatos volunt; dum autem verbis utitur suis, delabitur in eas difficultates ut necessitatem fati confirmet invitus.

[40] atque hoc, si placet, quale sit videamus in adsensionibus, quas prima oratione tractavi. eas enim veteres illi, quibus omnia fato fieri videbantur, vi effici et necessitate dicebant. qui autem ab eis dissentiebant, fato adsensiones liberabant negabantque fato adsensionibus adhibito necessitatem ab his posse removeri, iique ita disserebant: "Si omnia fato fiunt, omnia fiunt causa antece-dente; et si adpetitus, illa etiam quae adpetitum sequuntur; ergo etiam adsensiones. at si causa adpetitus non est sita in nobis, ne ipse quidem adpetitus est in nostra potestate; quod si ita est, ne illa quidem quae adpetitu efficiuntur sunt sita in nobis. non sunt igitur neque adsensiones neque actiones in nostra potestate. ex quo efficitur ut nec laudationes iustae sunt nec vituperationes nec honores nec supplicia." quod cum vitiosum sit, probabiliter concludi putant non omnia fato fieri quaecumque fiant.

---

1 essent] sint *Rackham*

5 *post* tenebitur *add.* igitur *Lambinus*, ergo *Fabricius, Davies:* <si> tenebitur *von Arnim, SVF 2.952*

12 Aristoteles] Anaxagoras *Karsten*

15 animorum *Davies:* animos *AVB:* animi *Casaubon*

24 adpetitum] adpetitus *Hamelin*

the statements included in them *neither* is true. [38] What amazing presumption and pitiful ignorance of logical discourse! For if something that is stated is neither true nor false, it certainly is not true; but how can what is not true not be false? Or how can what is not false not be true? So what Chrysippus defended will be maintained, that every statement is either true or false; for reason itself compels us to accept *both* that certain things are true from eternity *and* that those things are not bound up with causes from eternity and are free from the necessity of fate.

[XVII][39] I indeed see it like this. There were two opinions among the old philosophers; one that held by those who judged that all things came about by fate, in such a way that that fate imposed the force of necessity. This was the opinion of Democritus, Heraclitus, Empedocles and Aristotle. The other was the opinion of those who thought that there were voluntary movements of minds not involving fate at all. Chrysippus, like a respected arbitrator, seems to have wanted to strike a balance, but in fact inclines rather to those who want the movements of the mind to be free from necessity. However, by the expressions he uses he slips into difficulties such that he unwillingly supports the necessity of fate.

[40] Let us, if you like, see how this is in the case of "assentings", which I dealt with in the first part of my speech. Those men of old, to whom it seemed that everything came about by fate, said that assentings were brought about by force and necessity. Those however who disagreed with them freed assentings from fate, and said that if fate applied to assentings it would be impossible for necessity to be removed from them. They argued as follows: "if all things come about by fate, all things come about by an antecedent cause; and if impulses do, so too do those things which follow on impulse; and therefore so too do assentings. But if the cause of impulse is not located in us, impulse itself too is not in our power; and if this is so, neither do those things which are brought about by impulse depend on us. So neither assentings nor actions are in our power; and from this it follows that neither praise nor blame nor honours nor punishments are just." But since this is wrong, they think that the conclusion can persuasively be drawn that it is not the case that all things that come about do so by fate.

[XVIII][41] Chrysippus autem, cum et necessitatem improbaret et nihil vellet sine praepositis causis evenire, causarum genera distinguit, ut et necessitatem effugiat et retineat fatum. "Causarum enim," inquit, "aliae sunt perfectae et principales, aliae adiuvantes et proximae. quam ob rem cum dicimus omnia fato fieri causis antecedentibus, non hoc intellegi volumus, causis perfectis et principalibus, sed causis adiuvantibus [antecedentibus] et proximis." itaque illi rationi quam paullo ante conclusi sic occurrit; si omnia fato fiant, sequi illud quidem, ut omnia causis fiant antepositis, verum non principalibus causis et perfectis sed adiuvantibus et proximis. quae si ipsae non sunt in nostra potestate, non sequitur ut ne adpetitus quidem sit in nostra potestate. at hoc sequeretur, si omnia perfectis et principalibus causis fieri diceremus, ut cum eae causae non essent in nostra potestate, ne ille quidem esset in nostra potestate.

[42] quam ob rem qui ita fatum introducunt ut necessitatem adiungant, in eos valebit illa conclusio; qui autem causas antecedentis non dicent perfectas neque principalis, in eos nihil valebit. quod enim dicantur adsensiones fieri causis antepositis, id quale sit facile a se explicari putat; nam quamquam adsensio non possit fieri nisi commota viso, tamen cum id visum proximam causam habeat, non principalem, hanc habet rationem, ut Chrysippus vult, quam dudum diximus: non ut illa quidem fieri possit nulla vi extrinsecus excitata (necesse est enim adsensionem viso commoveri), sed revertitur ad cylindrum et ad turbinem suum, quae moveri incipere nisi pulsa non possunt, id autem cum accidit, suapte natura quod superest et cylindrum volvi et versari turbinem putat. [XIX][43] "Ut igitur," inquit, "qui protrusit cylindrum dedit ei principium motionis, volubilitatem autem non dedit, sic visum obiectum imprimet illud quidem et quasi signabit in animo suam speciem, sed adsensio nostra erit in potestate, eaque, quemadmodum in cylindro dictum est, extrinsecus pulsa

7 antecedentibus *del. Davies*

11 sunt *recc., editores plerique:* sint *codd.*

14 eae] hae V^c

14-15 ne ... potestate *om. ABFM, add. man. rec. in marg.* V, *deinde, supra* ne ille quidem, *eadem manu vel* ne appetitus *suprascr.*

[XVIII][41] But Chrysippus, since he both disapproved of necessity and wanted nothing to come about without causes laid down beforehand, distinguished types of causes so that he could both escape necessity and retain fate. "For," he said, "some causes are perfect and primary, others auxiliary and proximate; and for this reason, when we say that everything comes about by fate through antecedent causes, we do not want this to be understood as "through perfect and primary causes", but as "through auxiliary and proximate causes". And so he meets the argument, which I set out a short while ago, as follows.   If all things come about by fate (he says), it does indeed follow that all things come about by causes that precede them, but these are not perfect and primary causes, rather auxiliary and proximate ones. And [even] if these themselves are not in our power, it does not follow that impulse too is not in our power. This <u>would</u> follow, if we said that all things come about through perfect and primary causes, so that, since those causes are not in our power, impulse too would not be in our power.

[42] For this reason, those who introduce fate in such a way that they add necessity to it will have to accept that conclusion, but against those who are not going to speak of antecedent causes that are perfect or primary it will have no force. For as for the statement that assentings come about through causes laid down beforehand, (Chrysippus) thinks that he can easily explain this. For although assenting could not occur unless aroused by a sense-impression, nevertheless, since it has this sense-impression as proximate and not as primary cause it may be explained, as Chrysippus would have it, in the way that we described some time ago; not indeed that the assenting could occur without being aroused by any external force – for it is necessary that assenting should be caused by a sense-impression – but he goes back to his cylinder and spinning-top; these cannot begin to move unless pushed, but, when this has happened, he thinks that for the rest it is by their own nature that the cylinder rolls and the top moves in a curve.
[XIX][43] "As therefore," he says, "he who pushes a cylinder gives it the beginning of its motion, but does not give it the power of rolling; so a sense-impression when it strikes will, it is true, impress and as it were stamp its appearance on the mind, but assenting will be in our power, and, in the same way as was said in the case of the cylinder, it is pushed from outside but for the rest moves by its own force and

quod reliquum est suapte vi et natura movebitur. quod si aliqua
res efficeretur sine causa antecedente, falsum esset omnia fato
fieri; sin omnibus quaecumque fiunt verisimile est causam an-
tecedere, quid adferri poterit cur non omnia fato fieri fatendum
5   sit? modo intellegatur quae sit causarum distinctio ac dissimilitu-
do."

[44] haec cum ita sint a Chrysippo explicata, si illi qui negant
adsensiones fato fieri fateantur tamen eas non sine viso antecedente fieri, alia ratio est; sed si concedunt anteire visa, nec
10   tamen fato fieri adsensiones quod proxima illa et continens causa
non moveat adsensionem, vide ne idem dicant. neque enim Chrysippus, concedens adsensionis proximam et continentem causam
esse in viso positam neque eam causam esse ad adsentiendum
necessariam, concedet ut, si omnia fato fiant, omnia fiant causis
15   antecedentibus et necesariis; itemque illi qui ab hoc disssentiunt,
confitentes non fieri adsensiones sine praecursione visorum,
dicent, si omnia fato fierent eiusmodi ut nihil fieret nisi praegres-
sione causae, confitendum esse fato fieri omnia. ex quo facile
intellectu est, quoniam utrique patefacta atque explicata sententia
20   sua ad eundem exitum veniant, verbis eos non re dissidere. [45]
omninoque cum haec sit distinctio, ut quibusdam in rebus vere
dici possit, cum hae causae antegressae sint non esse in nostra
potestate quin illa eveniant quorum causae fuerint, quibusdam
autem in rebus causis antegressis in nostra tamen esse potestate
25   ut illud aliter eveniat, hanc distinctionem utrique adprobant; sed
alteri censent quibus in rebus cum causae antecesserint non sit

---

4 quid V^C: quod V^aA^a: del. A^C: om. BFM

poterit A^aV: potest A^CBFM

8 fateantur tamen] <non> fateantur [tamen] *Bremi*: infitiantur
tamen *Heine*

non sine] [non] sine *Valla*: non nisi *Bremi (cf. Gercke p.703)*

9 ratio] oratio *Kleywegt*

13 neque *om. ed. Veneta 1496, del. Lambinus: defendit Gercke p.704*
esse *om.* B   14 concedet AF^aVP: concedit B^CF^C

15 itemque] neque *Lambinus*

21 cum *secl. Lambinus*   22 hae *del. Hamelin*

26 non sit A^CB^CFM: non sint $A^aV^aB^a$: ita ut non sit V^CP *Lambinus*

nature. If something were to occur without an antecedent cause, it would not be true that everything occurred by fate; if however er it seems likely that everything which happens is preceded by a cause, what reason can be adduced for not admitting that everything occurs by fate? - provided only that it is understood what is the distinction and difference among causes."

[44] Since this is how Chrysippus explains these things, if those who deny that assentings come about by fate nevertheless admit that they do not come about without a preceding sense-impression, it is another argument. But if they grant that sense-impressions precede, but [say] that assentings do not come about by fate because that proximate and contiguous cause does not [itself] bring about the assenting, see whether they are not saying the same thing. For Chrysippus too concedes that the proximate and contiguous cause of the assenting is located in the sense-impression, but not that this is a necessitating cause of assenting; and so he will not concede that, if all things come about by fate, all things come about as a result of necessitating antecedent causes. And again those who disagree with him do assert that assentings do not come about without sense-impressions preceding them; [and so they] will say that, if all things come about by fate of such a sort that nothing comes about except by a cause having preceded, then it must be admitted that all things come about by fate. From this it is easy to understand that, since both sides, when their opinion is explained and set forth, come to the same result, they disagree about words and not about the facts. [45] In general there is this distinction: in some matters it can truly be said that, since these causes have preceded, it is not in our power to prevent those things happening of which they were the causes; but in some matters, [although] causes have preceded, it is nevertheless in our power that that thing should turn out differently. Both sides approve this distinction; but the one group think that those things come about by fate in which, since the

in nostra potestate ut aliter illa eveniant, eas fato fieri; quae
autem in nostra potestate sint, ab iis fatum abesse * * *

[XX][46] hoc modo hanc causam disceptari oportet, non ab atomis
errantibus et de via declinantibus petere praesidium. "Declinat,"
5   inquit, "atomus." Primum cur? aliam enim quandam vim motus
habebunt a Democrito inpulsionis quam plagam ille appellat, a te,
Epicure, gravitatis et ponderis. quae ergo nova causa in natura
est quae declinet atomum? aut num sortiuntur inter se quae
declinet, quae non? aut cur minimo declinent intervallo, maiore
10   non, aut cur declinent uno minimo, non declinent duobus aut
tribus? optare quidem est, non disputare.

[47] nam neque extrinsecus inpulsam atomum loco moveri et declinare dicis, neque in illo inani, per quod feratur atomus, quicquam
fuisse causae cur ea non e regione ferretur, nec in ipsa atomo
15   mutationis aliquid factum est quam ob rem naturalem motum sui
ponderis non teneret. ita cum attulisset nullam causam quae istam
declinationem efficeret, tamen aliquid sibi dicere videtur cum id
dicat quod omnium mentes aspernentur ac respuant.

[48] nec vero quisquam magis confirmare mihi videtur non modo
20   fatum verum etiam necessitatem et vim omnium rerum sustulis-
seque motus animi voluntarios, quam hic qui aliter obsistere fato
fatetur se non potuisse nisi ad has commenticias declinationes
confugisset. nam ut essent atomi, quas quidem esse mihi probari
nullo modo potest, tamen declinationes istae numquam explicaren-
25   tur; nam si atomis ut gravitate ferantur tributum est necessitate
naturae, quod omne pondus nulla re impediente moveatur et
feratur necesse est, illud quoque necesse est, declinare, quibusdam atomis, vel si volunt omnibus, naturaliter ...

---

2 *post* abesse *lacunam indicant AB:* ⟨alteri, sive hae sive illae
causae antecesserint, a rebus fatum abesse⟩ *suppl. Lambinus:*
fatum omne relegari *cod. Harl., ex quo* ⟨alteri volunt a rebus
fatum omne relegari⟩ *suppl. Allen*

8 qua declinet atomus *coni. Davies*

15 est] esse *Davies*   19 confirmasse *Rackham*

23 probari *Ven.:* probare *ABFM (commenticias – tamen declina-*
tio[nes *erasa in V)*

28 omnibus ⟨tributum esse⟩ naturaliter *suppl. Lambinus*

causes have preceded, it is not in our power that they should turn out otherwise, while fate is not involved in things which are in our power * * *

[XX][46] This is how this case ought to be argued; one ought not to seek help from atoms that swerve and deviate from their path. "The atom swerves," he says. First, why? For the atoms will have one force to move them from Democritus, the force of an impulse which he calls a blow, and from you, Epicurus, the force of weight and heaviness. So what new cause is there in nature to make the atom swerve? Or do they draw lots among themselves which will swerve and which not? Or why do they swerve by a minimum interval and not by a larger one, or why do they swerve by one minimum and not by two or three? This is wishful thinking, not argument.

[47] For you do not say that the atom is moved from its position and swerves through an impulse from outside, nor that in that void through which the atom travels there was any cause for its not travelling in a straight line; nor has there been any change in the atom itself as a result of which it might not preserve the motion natural to its weight. So, although (Epicurus) has not brought forward any cause which might cause that swerve of his, nevertheless he thinks he has a point to make when he says the sort of thing which the minds of all reject and repudiate.

[48] Nor, indeed, does anyone seem to me more to confirm not only fate, but also necessity applying forcibly to all things, and to do away with voluntary movements of the mind, than this man, who admits that he cannot resist fate in any other way than by recourse to these fictitious swerves. For if it were granted that there are atoms (and there is no way it can be proved to me that they exist); still, those swerves would never be explained. For if it is granted to atoms by the necessity of nature that they are carried along by weight, because it is necessary that every weight should be moved and carried along if nothing impedes it; and that alleged swerving too <is> naturally necessary for some atoms, or, if they like, for all ...

APPENDIX

A. Origen, Contra Celsum 2.20 (= *SVF* 2.957: cf. *De fato* 28-30)

καὶ πρὸς Ἕλληνας δὲ χρησόμεθα τῷ εἰρημένῳ τοῦτον τὸν τρόπον πρὸς
τὸν Λάϊον ... λέγεται τοίνυν πρὸς αὐτὸν ὑπὸ τοῦ προεγνωκότος δὴ τὰ
ἐσόμενα·

Μὴ σπεῖρε παίδων ἄλοκα δαιμόνων βίᾳ·

5   εἰ γὰρ τεκνώσεις παῖδ᾽, ἀποκτενεῖ σ᾽ ὁ φύς
καὶ πᾶς σὸς οἶκος βήσεται δι᾽ αἵματος.

καὶ ἐν τούτῳ τοίνυν δηλοῦται, ὅτι δυνατὸν μὲν ἦν τῷ Λαΐῳ μὴ
σπείρειν τέκνων ἄλοκα· οὐκ ἂν γὰρ τὸ μὴ δυνατὸν προσέταξεν αὐτῷ ὁ
χρησμός· δυνατὸν δὲ ἦν καὶ τὸ σπείρειν καὶ οὐδέτερον αὐτῶν
10   κατηνάγκαστο. ἠκολούθησε δὲ τῷ μὴ φυλαξαμένῳ σπεῖραι παίδων ἄλοκα
παθεῖν ἐκ τοῦ ἐσπαρκέναι τὰ τῆς κατὰ Οἰδίποδα καὶ Ἰοκάστην καὶ
τοὺς υἱοὺς τραγῳδίας.

ἀλλὰ καὶ ὁ ἀργὸς καλούμενος λόγος, σόφισμα ὤν, τοιοῦτός ἐστι,
λεγόμενος ἐπὶ ὑποθέσεως πρὸς τὸν νοσοῦντα, καὶ ὡς σόφισμα
15   ἀποτρέπων αὐτὸν χρῆσθαι τῷ ἰατρῷ πρὸς ὑγίειαν, καὶ ἔχει γε οὕτως ὁ
λόγος· εἰ εἵμαρταί σοι ἀναστῆναι ἐκ τῆς νόσου, ἐάν τε εἰσαγάγῃς
τὸν ἰατρὸν ἐάν τε μὴ εἰσαγάγῃς, ἀναστήσῃ· ἀλλὰ καὶ εἰ εἵμαρταί σοι
μὴ ἀναστῆναι ἐκ τῆς νόσου, ἐάν τε εἰσαγάγῃς τὸν ἰατρὸν ἐάν τε μὴ
εἰσαγάγῃς, οὐκ ἀναστήσῃ· ἤτοι δὲ εἵμαρταί σοι ἀναστῆναι ἐκ τῆς
20   νόσου ἢ εἵμαρταί σοι μὴ ἀναστῆναι· μάτην ἄρα εἰσάγεις τὸν ἰατρόν.

ἀλλὰ χαριέντως τούτῳ τῷ λόγῳ τοιοῦτόν τι παραβάλλεται· εἰ εἵμαρταί
σοι τεκνοποιῆσαι, ἐάν τε συνέλθῃς γυναικὶ ἐάν τε μὴ συνέλθῃς,
τεκνοποιήσεις· ἀλλὰ καὶ εἰ εἵμαρταί σοι μὴ τεκνοποιῆσαι, ἐάν τε
συνέλθῃς γυναικὶ ἐάν τε μὴ συνέλθῃς, οὐ τεκνοποιήσεις· ἤτοι δὲ
25   εἵμαρταί σοι τεκνοποιῆσαι ἢ μὴ τεκνοποιῆσαι· μάτην ἄρα συνέρχῃ
γυναικί. ὡς γὰρ ἐπὶ τούτου, ἐπεὶ ἀμήχανον καὶ ἀδύνατον
τεκνοποιῆσαι τὸν μὴ συνελθόντα γυναικί, οὐ μάτην παραλαμβάνεται τὸ
συνελθεῖν γυναικί, οὕτως εἰ τὸ ἀναστῆναι ἐκ τῆς νόσου ὁδῷ τῇ ἀπὸ
ἰατρικῆς γίνεται, ἀναγκαίως παραλαμβάνεται ὁ ἰατρὸς καὶ ψεῦδος τὸ
30   "μάτην εἰσάγεις τὸν ἰατρόν."

ὅλα δὲ ταῦτα παρειλήφαμεν δι᾽ ἃ παρέθετο ὁ σοφώτατος Κέλσος εἰπών·

4-6 *Euripides, Phoenissae 18-20*

24 ἐάν τε BCDEH: ἢ cett., von Arnim, sed cf. *Barnes (1985,1) 238 n.19*

APPENDIX

A. Origen, *Against Celsus* 2.20 (= *SVF* 2.957: cf. *On Fate* 28-30)

And against the Greeks (i.e. pagans) we will employ what was said in the following way to Laius ... well, it was said to him by the one who foreknew, indeed, what was to be:

> Do not sow the furrow that bears children in despite of the gods:
> For if you beget a child, he who is born will slay you,
> And all your house will fall amid bloodshed.

And in this it is shown that it was possible for Laius *not* to sow the furrow that bears children, for the oracle would not have commanded him to do what was impossible. It was also possible for him to sow it, and neither of these had been made necessary. But it followed, if he did not take care not to sow the furrow that bears children, that he would suffer from having sown it what happens in the tragedy concerning Oedipus and Jocasta and their sons.

And the so-called Lazy Argument, which is sophistical, is like this, arguing on the basis of hypotheses with a man who is ill, and sophistically discouraging him from using the doctor to get healthy; and the argument is as follows. If it is fated for you to recover from the disease, then whether you call in the doctor or whether you do not, you will recover. But if it is fated for you not to recover from the disease, too, then whether you call in the doctor or whether you do not, you will not recover. But, either it is fated for you to recover from the disease or it is fated for you not to recover. So there is no point in your calling in the doctor.

However, something like the following is pleasingly set alongside this argument. If it is fated for you to beget children, then whether you sleep with a woman or whether you do not, you will beget children. But if it is fated for you not to beget children, too, then whether you sleep with a woman or whether you do not, you will not beget children. But, either it is fated for you to beget children or it is fated for you not to beget children. So there is no point in your sleeping with a woman. – For in this case, since it is impossible and inconceivable for someone who does not sleep with a woman to beget children, sleeping with a woman is not undertaken pointlessly; just so, if recovery from the disease comes about by the medical route, the doctor is brought in necessarily, and "there is no point in your calling in the doctor" is false.

We have brought in all this because of what the most wise Celsus al-

θεὸς ὢν προεῖπε καὶ πάντως ἐχρῆν γενέσθαι τὸ προειρήμενον. εἰ γὰρ
τὸ πάντως ἀκούει ἀντὶ τοῦ κατηναγκασμένως, οὐ δώσομεν αὐτῷ·
δυνατὸν γὰρ ἦν καὶ μὴ γενέσθαι· εἰ δὲ τὸ πάντως λέγει ἀντὶ τοῦ
ἔσται, ὅπερ οὐ κωλύεται εἶναι ἀληθές, κἂν δυνατὸν ᾖ τὸ μὴ
5   γενέσθαι, οὐδὲν λυπεῖ τὸν λόγον.

B. Cicero, *Topics* 58–61 (cf. *De fato* 34–7)

[58] Proximus est locus rerum efficientium, quae causae appellan-
tur; deinde rerum effectarum ab efficientibus causis. harum
exempla, ut reliquorum locorum, paulo ante posui equidem ex iure
civili; sed haec patent latius.

10   causarum enim genera duo sunt; unum, quod vi sua id quod sub
eam vim subiectum est certe efficit, ut ignis accendit; alterum,
quod naturam efficiendi non habet sed sine quo effici non possit,
ut si quis aes statuae causam velit dicere, quod sine eo non posit
effici. [59] huius generis causarum, sine quo non efficitur, alia
15   sunt quieta, nihil agentia, stolida quodam modo, ut locus, tempus,
materia, ferramenta, et cetera generis eiusdem; alia autem prae-
cursionem quandam adhibent ad efficiendum et quaedam afferunt
per se adiuvantia, etsi non necessaria, ut: amori congressio
causam attulerat, amor flagitio. ex hoc genere causarum ex aeter-
20   nitate pendentium fatum a Stoicis nectitur.

atque ut earum causarum sine quibus effici non potest genera
divisi, sic etiam efficientium dividi possunt. sunt enim aliae causae
quae plane efficiant nulla re adiuvante, aliae quae adiuvari velint,
ut sapientia efficit sapientis sola per se; beatos efficiat necne sola
25   per se quaestio est. [60] qua re cum in disputationem inciderit
causa efficiens aliquid necessario, sine dubitatione licebit quod
efficitur ab ea causa concludere. cum autem erit talis causa, ut in
ea non sit efficiendi necessitas, necessaria conclusio non sequitur.
atque illud quidem genus causarum quod habet vim efficiendi
30   necessariam errorem afferre non fere solet; hoc autem sine quo
non efficitur saepe conturbat. non enim, si sine parentibus filii
esse non possunt, propterea in parentibus causa fuit gignendi
necessaria.

---

4 ᾖ] ἦν *BCDEH*

leged, saying "Being God he has foretold it, and what is foretold must certainly *(pantôs)* come about". If he intends "certainly" in the sense of "necessarily", we will not grant him this; for it was possible for it also not to happen. But if he intends "certainly" in the sense of "it will happen", which is not prevented from being true even if it was also possible for it not to happen, this does not trouble our argument.

B. Cicero, *Topics* 58-9.

The next topic is concerned with things that bring something about, and are called causes; and then with the things brought about by the causes that bring them about. I did indeed give examples of these, as of the other topics, a short while ago, derived from the civil law; but their application is wider.

There are two kinds of causes: one, that which by its own power brings about with certainty what is subject to it, as fire burns; the other that which does not have a nature that brings something about, but without which something cannot be brought about, as if someone wanted to call bronze the cause of a statue, because the statue cannot be brought about without it. [59] Of this kind of causes without which something is not brought about, some are inactive, do nothing, and are in a way inert, like place, time, material, iron implements and the other things of the same kind; others however provide a certain beginning for bringing about the effect, and contribute certain things that in themselves assist, even if they do not necessitate, as "meeting had provided the cause of love, love of disgrace". It is from this kind of causes, linked together from eternity, that fate is bound together by the Stoics.

And just as I have distinguished the kinds of those causes without which a thing cannot be brought about, so also the kinds of those that bring things about can be distinguished. For there are some causes which bring about a result simply, with nothing assisting them, and others that require assistance, as wisdom on its own makes wise men wise by itself, but as to whether it makes men happy on its own by itself there is a question. [60] Therefore, when there enters into an argument a cause that brings something about necessarily, it will be possible to infer without hesitation what is brought about by that cause; but when the cause is such that there is in it no necessity of bringing about the result, the necessary inference does not follow. And indeed that kind of causes which has a necessary power of bringing about the result does not usually introduce error; but this kind, without which a result is not brought about, often causes confusion. For it is not the case, if sons cannot exist without parents, that for that reason there is in the parents a necessary cause of begetting.

[61] hoc igitur sine quo non fit, ab eo in quo certe fit diligenter est separandum. illud enim est tamquam

    Utinam ne in nemore Pelio –;

nisi enim

5   accedissent abiegnae ad terram trabes,

Argo illa facta non esset; nec tamen fuit in his trabibus efficiendi vis necessaria. at cum

    in Aiacis navim crispisulcans igneum

fulmen iniectum est, inflammatur navis necessario.

C. Aulus Gellius, *Noctes Atticae* 7.2.1–14 (= SVF 2.1000: cf. *De Fato* 41–43)

10 [1] Fatum, quod εἱμαρμένην Graeci vocant, ad hanc ferme sententiam Chrysippus, Stoicae princeps philosophiae, definit: "Fatum est" inquit "sempiterna quaedam et indeclinabilis series rerum et catena, volvens semetipsa sese et implicans per aeternos consequentiae ordines, ex quibus apta nexaque est." [2] ipsa autem
15 verba Chrysippi, quantum valui memoria, ascripsi, ut, si cui meum istud interpretamentum videtur esse obscurius, ad ipsius verba animadvertat. [3] in libro Περὶ προνοίας quarto εἱμαρμένην esse dicit φυσικήν τινα σύνταξιν των ὅλων ἐξ ἀϊδίου τῶν ἑτέρων τοῖς ἑτέροις ἐπακολουθούντων καὶ μεταπολουμένων ἀπαραβάτου οὔσης τῆς
20 τοιαύτης ἐπιπλοκῆς.

[4] aliarum autem opinionum disciplinarumque auctores huic definitioni ita obstrepunt: [5] "Si Chrysippus" inquiunt "fato putat omnia moveri et regi nec declinari transcendique posse agmina fati et volumina, peccata quoque hominum et delicta non suscen-
25 senda neque inducenda sunt ipsis voluntatibusque eorum, sed necessitati cuidam et instantiae, quae oritur ex fato, omnium quae sit rerum domina et arbitra, per quam necesse sit fieri quicquid futurum est; et propterea nocentium poenas legibus inique constitutas, si homines ad maleficia non sponte veniunt, sed fato tra-
30 huntur."

[6] contra ea Chrysippus tenuiter multa et argute disseruit; sed omnium fere, quae super ea re scripsit, huiuscemodi sententia

---

5 accedissent *Fleckeisen:* accidissent *AaV:* cecidissent *MSS plerique: cf. ad De fato §35*

19 μεταπολουμένων *Kumanudes:* ΜΕΛΠΟΑΥΜΕΝΩΝ *codd.:* μὴ ἀπολυομένων *Usener*

96

[61] So this without which a thing does not come about must be carefully separated from that in the case of which a thing certainly comes
about. For the former is like

    Would that never in the groves of Pelion –;
for unless

    the fir-timbers had fallen to the earth
the famous Argo would not have been built; and yet there was not in
these timbers a necessary power of bringing it about. But when

    the fiery thunderbolt with its curving path
is hurled onto Ajax' ship, the ship is set on fire necessarily.

C. Aulus Gellius, *Attic Nights* 7.2.1–14 (SVF 2.1000: cf. *On Fate* 41–43)

[1] Fate, which the Greeks call *heimarmenê,* Chrysippus the chief Stoic
philosopher defines in approximately the following way: "Fate," he says,
"is a certain everlasting and unalterable sequence and ,haining of
things, involving and entwining itself with itself through the eternal
laws of sequence from which it is fitted and bound together." [2] I
have added Chrysippus' actual words, as far as I have been able to
from memory, so that if that translation of mine seems too obscure to
anyone, he may attend to the man's own words. [3] In the fourth book
On Providence Chrysippus says that fate is "a certain natural connected ordering of all things, one group of things following on and involved with another from eternity, such a weaving-together allowing no
avoidance."

[4] However, the supporters of other views and teachings criticised this
definition as follows. [5] "If Chrysippus," they said, "thinks that all
things are moved and ruled by fate, and that the marches and turnings
of fate cannot be turned aside or surmounted, then the failings and
crimes of men too should not be a cause for anger and should not be
attributed to them and to their wills, but rather to a certain necessity
and pressure, which arises from fate and is the mistress of and decides
all the things that there are; through this it is necessary for whatever
is going to be to come about. And for this reason the penalties for
those who do wrong are laid down by the laws unjustly, if men do not
come to commit misdeeds of their own accord, but are dragged by fate."

[6] Against this Chrysippus brought many acute and subtle arguments;
but the sense of almost everything which he wrote on that topic is of

est: [7] "Quamquam ita sit" inquit "ut ratione quadam necessaria et principali coacta atque conexa sint fato omnia, ingenia tamen ipsa mentium nostrarum proinde sunt fato obnoxia ut proprietas eorum est ipsa et qualitas. [8] nam si sunt per naturam primitus salubriter utiliterque ficta, omnem illam vim quae de fato extrinsecus ingruit inoffensius tractabiliusque transmittunt. sin vero sunt aspera et inscita et rudia nullisque artium bonarum adminiculis fulta, etiamsi parvo sive nullo fatalis incommodi conflictu urgeantur, sua tamen scaevitate et voluntario impetu in assidua delicta et in errores se ruunt. [9] idque ipsum ut ea ratione fiat, naturalis illa et necessaria rerum consequentia efficit quae fatum vocatur. [10] est enim genere ipso quasi fatale et consequens, ut mala ingenia peccatis et erroribus non vacent."

[11] huius deinde fere rei exemplo non hercle nimis alieno neque inlepido utitur. "Sicut" inquit "lapidem cylindrum si per spatia terrae prona atque derupta iacias, causa quidem ei et initium praecipitantiae fueris, mox tamen ille praeceps volvitur, non quia tu id iam facis, sed quoniam ita sese modus eius et formae volubilitas habet: sic ordo et ratio et necessitas fati genera ipsa et principia causarum movet, impetus vero consiliorum mentiumque nostrarum actionesque ipsas voluntas cuiusque propria et animorum ingenia moderantur." [12] infert deinde verba haec, his quae dixi congruentia:

Διὸ καὶ ὑπὸ τῶν Πυθαγορείων εἴρηται·
Γνώσει δ᾽ ἀνθρώπους αὐθαίρετα πήματ᾽ ἔχοντας,
ὡς τῶν βλαβῶν ἑκάστοις παρ᾽ αὐτοὺς γινομένων καὶ καθ᾽ ὁρμὴν αὐτῶν
ἁμαρτανόντων τε καὶ βλαπτομένων καὶ κατὰ τὴν αὐτῶν διάνοιαν καὶ
⟨διά⟩θεσιν.

[13] propterea negat oportere ferri audirique homines aut nequam aut ignavos et nocentes et audentes, qui, cum in culpa et in maleficio revicti sunt, perfugiunt ad fati necessitatem tamquam in aliquod fani asylum, et quae pessime fecerunt, ea non suae temeritate sed fato esse attribuenda dicunt.

---

14 fere rei *Hertz:* fieri *VP:* rei *recc.*

26 αὐτοὺς *V:* αὐτοῖς *recc.*

28 ⟨διά⟩θεσιν *suppl. Sedley*

the following sort. [7] Although it is the case," he said, "that all things are constrained and bound together by fate through a certain necessary and primary principle, yet the way in which the natures of our minds themselves are subject to fate depends on their own individual quality. [8] For if they have been fashioned through nature originally in a healthy and expedient way, they pass on all that force, which assails them from outside through fate, in a more placid and pliant manner. If however they are harsh and ignorant and uncultured, and not sustained by any supports from good practices, then even if they are pressed on by little or no necessity from an adverse fate, through their own perversity and voluntary impulse they hurl themselves into constant crimes and errors. [9] And that this very thing should come about in this way is a result of that natural and necessary sequence which is called fate. [10] For it is as it were a fated consequence of their type itself, that bad natures should not lack crimes and errors.

[11] Then he employs an illustration of approximately this point which is certainly not lacking in relevance or wit. "It is," he says, "just as if you throw a cylindrical stone across a region of ground which is sloping and steep; you were the cause and beginning of headlong fall for it, but soon it rolls headlong, not because *you* are now bringing that about, but because that is how its fashion and the capacity for rolling in its shape are. Just so the order and rule and necessity of fate sets types and beginnings of causes in motion, but the impulses of our minds and deliberations, and our actions themselves, are governed by each person's own will and by the natures of our minds." [12] Then he introduces the following words, which are in agreement with what I have said:

'And this is why it has also been said by the Pythagoreans,
    "You shall know that men suffer woes that they choose themselves",
since harm comes to them on their own account in each case, when they themselves go wrong and come to harm in accordance with their impulse and in accordance with their own thought and disposition.'

[13] For these reasons he says that one should not endure or listen to people who are wicked or idle, and both harmful and bold, who when they are convicted of guilt and wrong-doing, have recourse to the necessity of fate as if to some sanctuary in a temple, and say that the worst things they have done should be attributed not to their own rashness but to fate.

[14] primus autem hoc sapientissimus ille et antiquissimus poeta-
rum dixit hisce versibus:

Ὦ πόποι, οἷον δή νυ θεοὺς βροτοὶ αἰτιόωνται.
ἐξ ἡμέων γάρ φασι κάκ' ἔμμεναι· οἱ δὲ καὶ αὐτοὶ
5   σφῆσιν ἀτασθαλίῃσιν ὑπὲρ μόρον ἄλγε' ἔχουσιν.

D. Plutarch, *De Stoicorum Repugnantibus* 47 1056B (= SVF 2.997:
cf. *De fato* 41)

Ὁ δὲ λέγων ὅτι Χρύσιππος οὐκ αὐτοτελῆ τούτων αἰτίαν (sc. τοῦ
κατορθοῦν καὶ φρονεῖν) ἀλλὰ προκαταρκτικὴν μόνον ἐποιεῖτο τὴν
εἱμαρμένην, ἐκεῖ πάλιν αὐτὸν ἀποδείξει μαχόμενον πρὸς αὐτόν, ὅπου
τὸν μὲν Ὅμηρον ὑπερφυῶς ἐπαινεῖ περὶ τοῦ Διὸς λέγοντα
10   Τῷ ἔχεθ' ὅττι κεν ὕμμι κακὸν πέμπῃσιν ἑκάστῳ
ἢ ἀγαθόν· καὶ τὸν Εὐριπίδην
       Ὦ Ζεῦ, τί δῆτα τοὺς ταλαιπώρους βροτοὺς
       φρονεῖν λέγοιμ' ἄν; σοῦ γὰρ ἐξηρτήμεθα,
       δρῶμέν τε τοιάδ', ἃ σύ <γε> τυγχάνεις φρονῶν.
15   αὐτὸς δὲ πολλὰ τούτοις ὁμολογούμενα γράφει, τέλος δέ φησι μηδὲν
ἴσχεσθαι μηδὲ κινεῖσθαι μηδὲ τοὐλάχιστον ἄλλως ἢ κατὰ τὸν τοῦ Διὸς
λόγον· ὃν τῇ εἱμαρμένῃ τὸν αὐτὸν εἶναι. ἔτι τοίνυν τὸ μέν προκα-
ταρκτικὸν αἴτιον ἀσθενέστερον εἶναι τοῦ αὐτοτέλους, καὶ οὐκ
ἐξικνεῖται κρατούμενον ὑπ' ἄλλων ἐξανισταμένων· τὴν δ' εἱμαρμένην
15   αἰτίαν ἀνίκητον καὶ ἀκώλυτον καὶ ἄτρεπτον ἀποφαίνων, αὐτὸς Ἄτρο-
πον καλεῖ καὶ Ἀδράστειαν καὶ Ἀνάγκην καὶ Πεπρωμένην, ὡς πέρας
ἅπασιν ἐπιτιθεῖσαν.

3-5 *Homer, Odyssey* 1.32-4

10 *Homer, Iliad* 15.109

12-14 *Euripides, Suppliants* 734-6

[14] And the wisest and most ancient of poets (i.e. Homer) said this first in these lines:

"Alas, how mortals now blame the gods.
They say evils are from us; but they themselves
through their own folly have sufferings beyond what is fated."

D. Plutarch, *On Stoic Self-Contradictions* **47 1056B (= SVF 2.997: cf.** *On Fate* **41)**

He who says that Chrysippus made fate not a sufficient cause of these (*sc.* of acting rightly and being wise), but only an initiating one, will show him being inconsistent with himself again where he gives exceeding praise to Homer for saying about Zeus

So accept whatever evil he sends to each of you

or whatever good, and Euripides who says

Zeus, how should I say wretched mortals

Have wisdom? For it is on you that we depend,

And what we do depends on how you may be minded,

and himself writes many things that agree with these, and in sum says that nothing is maintained or changed even in the smallest respect other than in accordance with the reasoning of Zeus, which is the same as fate. Moreover, the initiating cause is (he says) weaker than the sufficient one, and does not arrive at its goal when it is overcome by others that rise up against it; but fate he declares to be a cause that is unconquerable and cannot be hindered or turned aside, himself calling it Atropos and Adrasteia and Necessity and Peprômenê, since it imposes a limit *(peras)* on everything.

PHILOSOPHIAE CONSOLATIONIS

[IV.5] [1] Hic ego: Video, inquam, quae sit vel felicitas vel miseria in ipsis proborum atque improborum meritis constituta. [2] sed in hac ipsa fortuna populari non nihil boni malive inesse perpendo; neque enim sapientum quisquam exsul, inops ignominiosusque esse
5 malit potius quam pollens opibus, honore reverendus, potentia validus in sua permanens urbe florere. [3] sic enim clarius testatiusque sapientiae tractatur officium cum in contingentes populos regentium quodam modo beatitudo transfunditur, cum praesertim carcer, nex ceteraque legalium tormenta poenarum perniciosis
10 potius civibus, propter quos etiam constitutae sunt, debeantur. [4] cur haec igitur versa vice mutentur scelerumque supplicia bonos premant, praemia virtutum mali rapiant, vehementer ammiror, quaeque tam iniustae confusionis ratio videatur ex te scire desidero. [5] minus etenim mirarer, si misceri omnia fortuitis casibus
15 crederem. nunc stuporem meum deus rector exaggerat. [6] qui cum saepe bonis iucunda malis aspera, contraque bonis dura tribuat malis optata concedat, nisi causa deprehenditur quid est quod a fortuitis casibus differre videatur?

[7] Nec mirum, inquit, si quid ordinis ignorata ratione temerarium
20 confusumque credatur; sed tu quamvis causam tantae dispositionis ignores, tamen quoniam bonus mundum rector temperat, recte fieri cuncta ne dubites.

[IV metr. 5] Si quis Arcturi sidera nescit
propinqua summo cardine labi,
cur regat tardus plaustra Bootes
mergatque seras aequore flammas

[IV.5] 6 enim ⟨ut⟩ *P:* enim ⟨vel⟩ *coni. Bieler*

8 eodem quo regentium modo *Merkelbach 71*

9 carcer nex *Rehd., Valenciennes 298 (Tronçarelli 139): post* carcer *lacunam exhibent D(ex superscr.)KOᵃ(et erasum ut vid.):* carceres *Laud., cod. Bernensis 421:* carcer lex nexus *Hib.:* carcer lex *cett.:* carcer nexus *Vulpius:* carcer *Weinberger*

[IV metr. 5] 3 regat *superscr. Paris 7183:* legat *cett.*

CONSOLATION OF PHILOSOPHY

[IV.5] [1] At this point I said, "I see what the happiness or wretchedness is that is a matter of the actual deeds of good or bad men. [2] But in fortune itself as popularly understood I judge that there is a certain amount of good or evil; for none of the wise would prefer to be an exile, needy and in disgrace, rather than to remain and flourish in his own city, powerful in wealth, revered in honour, and strong in power. [3] For the duties of wisdom are performed more notably and evidently, when the happiness of the rulers is in a way transferred to the people in contact with them, and especially when prison, death, and the other tortures of punishment imposed by law are reserved rather for the harmful citizens on account of whom they were indeed set up. [4] So I wonder greatly why these things are turned about and punishments for crimes oppress the good while the wicked seize the rewards of virtue, and I long to know from you what reason there may appear for so unjust a confusion. [5] I would indeed wonder less if I thought that all things were thrown into confusion by the chances of fortune; but as it is, the fact that God is the ruler increases my amazement. [6] Seeing that he often assigns pleasant things to the good and harsh to the wicked, but conversely also assigns hardships to the good and grants the wicked what they desire, then, unless a reason is found, what is there in this that would seem different from the chances of fortune?"

[7] "It is not surprising," she said, "that something should be thought random and confused when the principle of its ordering is not known; but for your part, although you do not know the reason in so great a design, nevertheless, do not doubt that all things come about rightly, since a good ruler governs the world.

[IV metr. 5] If someone does not know that the stars of Arcturus glide close to the highest pole, and why the Ox-driver is slow to steer his cart and sinks his light late into the sea, although he reveals his

5   cum nimis celeres explicet ortus,
       legem stupebit aetheris alti.
       palleant plenae cornua lunae
       infecta metis noctis opacae,
       quaeque fulgenti texerat ore,
10   confusa Phoebe detegat astra:
       commovet gentes publicus error
       lassantque crebris pulsibus aera.
       nemo miratur flamina Cori
       litus frementi tundere fluctu
15   nec nivis duram frigore molem
       fervente Phoebi solvier aestu;
       hic enim causas cernere promptum est,
       illic latentes pectora turbant.
       cuncta quae rara provehit aetas
20   stupetque subitis mobile vulgus,
       cedat inscitiae nubilus error,
       cessent profecto mira videri.

[IV.6][1] Ita est, inquam; sed cum tui muneris sit latentium rerum causas evolvere velatasque caligine explicare rationes, quaeso, uti, quae hinc decernas, quoniam hoc me miraculum maxime perturbat, edisseras.

5   [2] tum illa paulisper arridens: Ad rem me, inquit, omnium quaesitu maximam vocas, cui vix exhausti quicquam satis sit. [3] talis namque materia est, ut una dubitatione succisa innumerabiles aliae velut hydrae capita succrescant; nec ullus fuerit modus, nisi quis eas vivacissimo mentis igne coherceat. [4] in hac enim de provi-
10   dentiae simplicitate, de fati serie, de repentinis casibus, de cognitione ac praedestinatione divina, de arbitrii libertate quaeri solet, quae quanti oneris sint ipse perpendis. [5] sed quoniam haec quoque te nosse quaedam medicinae tuae portio est, quamquam angusto limite temporis saepti tamen aliquid deliberare conabimur.
15   [6] quodsi te musici carminis oblectamenta delectant, hanc oportet paulisper differas voluptatem, dum nexas sibi ordine contexo rationes.

[V.6] 14 deliberare] delibare *Pulman*

17 rationes] orationes *ALN^{a}T^{a}V*

rising too swiftly, this person will be amazed by the law of high heaven. Should the full moon's horns lose their colour, stained with the cones of shadowy night, and Phoebe, thrown into confusion, reveal the stars which she had hidden with her shining face; then a general misunderstanding stirs the peoples, and they weary bronze with frequent striking. No-one wonders that the blasts of the north-west wind beat the shore with roaring wave, or that the mass of snow, hard with the cold, is melted by the boiling heat of Phoebus; for here the reasons may be readily seen, but there they are hidden and disturb our hearts. All the things which time brings forth infrequently and the common people are amazed at when they happen suddenly, would indeed, if the mist of erring ignorance were overcome, cease to seem marvellous."

[IV.6][1] "Yes," I said; "but since it is your task to lay open the causes of hidden things and to unfold reasons that are hidden in obscurity, I ask you to explain to me what conclusions you draw concerning this, since the strangeness of this disturbs me most of all."

[2] Then, smiling briefly, she said: "You summon me to a matter which is the greatest of all to enquire into, for which even completeness would scarcely be enough. [3] For the subject is such that, when one doubt has been removed, countless others grow up like the heads of the Hydra; nor is there any limit to them, except to check them with the most lively fire of the mind. [4] In this connection there is customarily enquiry about the singleness of providence, the sequence of fate, sudden chances, divine knowledge and predestination, and freedom of choice; and how weighty these are you yourself judge. [5] But since for you to know these things too is a part of your treatment, we will try to consider them to some extent even though hemmed in by narrow limits of time. [6] If the delights of musical song charm you, you must put off this pleasure for a time, while I weave arguments bound together in sequence."

Ut libet, inquam.

[7] Tunc velut ab alio orsa principio ita disseruit: Omnium genera-
20 tio rerum cunctusque mutabilium naturarum progressus et, quicquid aliquo movetur modo, causas, ordinem, formas ex divinae
mentis stabilitate sortitur. [8] haec in suae simplicitatis arce
composita multiplicem rebus gerendis modum statuit. qui modus
cum in ipsa divinae intellegentiae puritate conspicitur, providentia
25 nominatur; cum vero ad ea quae movet atque disponit refertur,
fatum a veteribus appellatum est. [9] quae diversa esse facile
liquebit, si quis utriusque vim mente conspexerit; nam providentia
est ipsa illa divina ratio in summo omnium principe constituta,
quae cuncta disponit, fatum vero inhaerens rebus mobilibus
30 dispositio, per quam providentia suis quaeque nectit ordinibus.
[10] providentia namque cuncta pariter quamvis diversa, quamvis
infinita complectitur; fatum vero singula digerit in motum locis,
formis ac temporibus distributa, ut haec temporalis ordinis expli-
catio in divinae mentis adunata prospectum providentia sit, eadem
35 vero adunatio digesta atque explicata temporibus fatum vocetur.

[11] quae licet diversa sint, alterum tamen pendet ex altero; ordo
namque fatalis ex providentiae simplicitate procedit. [12] sicut
enim artifex faciendae rei formam mente praecipiens movet operis
effectum et quod simpliciter praesentarieque prospexerat per
40 temporales ordines ducit, ita deus providentia quidem singulariter
stabiliterque facienda disponit, fato vero haec ipsa quae disposuit
multipliciter ac temporaliter amministrat. [13] sive igitur famulan-
tibus quibusdam providentiae divinis spiritibus fatum exercetur
seu anima seu tota inserviente natura seu caelestibus siderum
45 motibus seu angelica virtute seu daemonum varia sollertia seu
aliquibus horum seu omnibus fatalis series texitur, illud certe
manifestum est immobilem simplicemque gerendarum formam rerum
esse providentiam, fatum vero eorum quae divina simplicitas
gerenda disposuit mobilem nexum atque ordinem temporalem.

---

23 rebus gerendis *E, F mg., Harl.ᵃ Hib. Met.ᶜ Vind.:* gerendi
Harl.ᶜ: rebus generandis *Machan MS Cantab. Bibl. Univ. Ii.3.21
secutus:* rebus regendis *cod. Wallersteinianus I.2.Lat.4˚, n.3:*
regerendis *Vᵃ Laud.ᵃ:* regendi *AᶜMᶜ:* regendis *cett.*

38 praecipiens] percipiens *EKLN(sscr.pr(a)e-)OᶜPTᶜVᶜ:* concipiens
M

"As you wish," I said.

[7] Then, as if making a fresh start, she spoke as follows: "All coming-to-be of things, all development of natural things subject to change, and whatever is in movement in any way at all derives its causes, order and forms from the permanence of the divine mind. [8] This, settled in the citadel of its own singleness, has laid down a complex rule for the things that come about. When this rule is considered in the context of the very purity of the divine intelligence, it is named providence; but when it is referred to those things which it sets in motion and arranges, it has been called fate by the ancients. [9] That these are different will be easily apparent, if one considers in his mind the power of each; for providence is that very divine reason established in the highest ruler of all, which arranges all things, but fate is the arrangement present in things subject to movement, through which providence binds each thing in its own proper order. [10] For providence embraces all things, however diverse and however infinite; but fate arranges individual things, in their movement distributed as to places, forms and times, so that this whole temporal unfolding, when united in the view of the divine mind, is providence, but the same uniting of things, when arranged and unfolded in time, is called fate.

[11] Although these are different, one depends on the other; for the sequence of fate proceeds from the singleness of providence. [12] For just as the craftsman grasps the form of the thing to be made in his mind first and sets the realisation of the work in motion, carrying out in temporal sequence what he had foreseen in singleness and in present time, just so God by his providence arranges in a single and fixed way the things that are to be brought about, but by fate he manages, in their plurality and in time, these very same things which he arranged. [13] So, whether fate is carried on by certain divine spirits which are servants of providence, or whether the sequence of fate is woven together through the service of the world-soul or the whole of nature, or by movements of the heavenly bodies or by the power of angels or by the varied offices of *daemones,* by some of these things or by all of them, what at any rate is certain is that the unmoved and single pattern of things that come about is providence, while fate is the moving connection and sequence in time of the things whose coming-about has been arranged by the divine simplicity.

50   [14] quo fit ut omnia quae fato subsunt providentiae quoque
subiecta sint, cui ipsum etiam subiacet fatum; quaedam vero, quae
sub providentia locata sunt, fati seriem superent. ea vero sunt
quae primae propinqua divinitati stabiliter fixa fatalis ordinem
mobilitatis excedunt. [15] nam ut orbium circa eundem cardinem
55   sese vertentium qui est intimus ad simplicitatem medietatis accedit
ceterorumque extra locatorum veluti cardo quidam circa quem
versentur exsistit; extimus vero maiore ambitu rotatus quanto a
puncti media individuitate discedit, tanto amplioribus spatiis expli-
catur; si quid vero illi se medio conectat et societ, in simplici-
60   tatem cogitur diffundique ac diffluere cessat: simili ratione quod
longius a prima mente discedit maioribus fati nexibus implicatur et
tanto aliquid fato liberum est quanto illum rerum cardinem vici-
nius petit. [16] quodsi supernae mentis haeserit firmitati, motu
carens fati quoque supergreditur necessitatem. [17] igitur uti est
65   ad intellectum ratiocinatio, ad id quod est id quod gignitur, ad
aeternitatem tempus, ad punctum medium circulus, ita est fati
series mobilis ad providentiae stabilem simplicitatem.

[18] ea series caelum ac sidera movet, elementa in se invicem
temperat et alterna commutatione transformat; eadem nascentia
70   occidentiaque omnia per similes fetuum seminumque renovat
progressus. [19] haec actus etiam fortunasque hominum indissolu-
bili causarum conexione constringit, quae cum ab immobilis providentiae proficiscatur exordiis, ipsas quoque immutabiles esse
necesse est. [20] ita enim res optime reguntur, si manens in
75   divina mente simplicitas indeclinabilem causarum ordinem promat,
hic vero ordo res mutabiles et alioquin temere fluituras propria
incommutabilitate coherceat. [21] quo fit ut, tametsi vobis hunc
ordinem minime considerare valentibus confusa omnia perturba-
taque videantur, nihilo minus tamen suus modus ad bonum diri-
80   gens cuncta disponat. [22] nihil est enim quod mali causa ne ab
ipsis quidem improbis fiat; quos, ut uberrime demonstratum est,
bonum quaerentes pravus error avertit, nedum ordo de summi
boni cardine proficiens a suo quoquam deflectat exordio.

---

59 illi se] illis e LO^aT^aV^a: illis est P: illis K

64 supergreditur] supergredietur Bases: ὑπεραναβήσεται Planudes

73 ipsas ... immutabiles] ipsam ... immutabilem N^CT^CV^C

83 proficiens] proficiscens L^CO sscr.A

[14] Thus it comes about that all things which are subject to fate are also subject to providence, to which fate itself is subordinate; but certain things which are situated subject to providence rise above the ordering of fate. These are those which, close to the first divinity, are firmly fixed and are outside the sequence of movement subject to fate. [15] When circles turn around the same pivot, that which is innermost comes close to the singleness of the centre and is as it were a pivot for the others round which they can turn; but the outermost turns in a larger circle and covers a greater distance to the extent that it is further removed from the simplicity of the central point. If anything binds and unite itself to the centre, it is gathered together in single-ness and ceases to be broken up and dissipated. In a similar way what departs further from the supreme Mind is bound in greater bonds of fate, and a thing is free from fate to the extent that it draws closer to that Pivot of things. [16] If it clings to the stability of the mind above, it is free from movement and surpasses also the necessity of fate. [17] So, as reasoning is to understanding, what comes to be to what is, time to eternity, a circle to its central point, so is the moving se-quence of fate to the fixed singleness of providence.

[18] That sequence moves the heaven and the stars, creates the mutual blending of the elements and transforms them one into another in turn; it too renews, through the development of corresponding seeds and offspring, all things that are born and perish. [19] It also constrains the actions and fortunes of human beings by an indissoluble connecting of causes; since this has its starting-points in the immobility of provi-dence, the causes too must be unalterable. [20] For this is how things are best governed, if the singleness that abides in the divine mind produces the undeviating sequence of causes, and this sequence in its own proper unalterability controls the things that are subject to change and would otherwise pass away at random. [21] Thus it comes about that, although all things seem confused and in disarray to you who have very little ability to see this ordering, nevertheless all things are arranged by their own rule which directs them towards what is best. [22] For there is nothing which is brought about for the sake of what is bad, not even by the wicked; as has been most amply shown, they are seeking what is good but are turned aside by vicious error. It is certainly *not* the case that the sequence that starts from the su-preme good as its centre turns aside in any direction from the way in which it started.

[23] quae vero, inquies, potest ulla iniquior esse confusio, quam
85   ut bonis tum adversa tum prospera, malis etiam tum optata tum
odiosa contingant? [24] num igitur ea mentis integritate homines
degunt ut, quos probos improbosve censuerunt, eos quoque uti
existimant esse necesse sit? [25] atqui in hoc hominum iudicia
depugnant et, quos alii praemio, alii supplicio dignos arbitrantur.

90   [26] sed concedamus ut aliquis possit bonos malosque discernere;
num igitur poterit intueri illam intimam temperiem, velut in corporibus dici solet, animorum? [27] non enim dissimile est miraculum
nescienti cur sanis corporibus his quidem dulcia, illis vero amara
conveniant, cur aegri etiam quidam lenibus, quidam vero acribus
95   adiuvantur. [28] at hoc medicus, qui sanitatis ipsius atque ae-
gritudinis modum temperamentumque dinoscit, minime miratur. [29]
quid vero aliud animorum salus videtur esse quam probitas, quid
aegritudo quam vitia? quis autem alius vel servator bonorum vel
malorum depulsor quam rector ac medicator mentium deus? [30]
100 qui cum ex alta providentiae specula respexit, quid unicuique
conveniat agnoscit et quod convenire novit accommodat. [31] hic
iam fit illud fatalis ordinis insigne miraculum, cum ab sciente
geritur quod stupeant ignorantes.

[32] nam ut pauca quae ratio valet humana de divina profunditate
105 perstringam, de hoc quem tu iustissimum et aequi servantissimum
putas omnia scienti providentiae diversum videtur. [33] et victri-
cem quidem causam dis, victam vero Catoni placuisse familiaris
noster Lucanus ammonuit. [34] hic igitur quicquid citra spem
videas geri, rebus quidem rectus ordo est, opinioni vero tuae
110 perversa confusio.

[35] sed sit aliquis ita bene moratus ut de eo divinum iudicium
pariter humanumque consentiat; sed est animi viribus infirmus;
cui si quid eveniat adversi, desinet colere forsitan innocentiam,
per quam non potuit retinere fortunam. [36] parcit itaque sapiens
115 dispensatio ei quem deteriorem facere possit adversitas, ne cui
non convenit laborare patiatur. [37] est alius cunctis virtutibus
absolutus sanctusque ac deo proximus; hunc contingi quibuslibet
adversis nefas providentia iudicat adeo ut ne corporeis quidem

---

87 censuerunt] censuerint $A^CCMN^CT^CV^C$

95 adiuvantur] adiuventur CN^CT^C

[23] But, you will say, what confusion can be more unjust, than that good men sometimes enjoy adverse fortune, sometimes favourable, and bad men too sometimes what is wished for and sometimes what is hateful? [24] Well, surely human beings do not enjoy such sureness of judgement that it is necessary for those whom they judge to be righteous or unrighteous actually to be as they think them to be? [25] Indeed in this respect the judgements of men conflict, and those who are thought to deserve reward by some are thought to deserve punishment by others.

[26] But let us grant that someone could distinguish between the good and the bad; surely he will not be able to see into that inmost temperament - as we are accustomed to put it in the case of bodies - of their minds? [27] To someone who does not know it is like a marvel, why sweet things are suitable for some healthy bodies and bitter things for others, or again why some sick people are helped by gentle remedies and others by fierce ones. [28] But the doctor, who distinguishes the measure and temperament both of health and of sickness, certainly does not marvel at this. [29] But what else does the health of minds appear to be than righteousness, the sickness than vices? And who is the preserver of good men or the suppressor of bad ones, other than God, the ruler and physician of minds? [30] When he observes from the lofty observation-post of providence, he recognises what is suitable for each individual and supplies what he knows to be suitable. [31] And it is here that there occurs that marvellous and striking ordering of fate, when he who knows brings about that at which the ignorant are amazed.

[32] For, to touch on a few points concerning the profundity of the divine for which human reason has the strength: to providence, which has knowledge, everything appears different concerning the person whom *you* think most just and most observant of what is right. [33] We are reminded by our Lucan that the victorious cause pleased the gods, the defeated one Cato. [34] So whatever you may see happening here falling short of your hope is a right ordering as far as the things themselves are concerned; it is in your opinion that there is distortion and confusion.

[35] Suppose that there should be someone who behaves so well that divine and human judgement are completely in agreement about him, but who lacks strength in his mind; if anything adverse should happen to him, perhaps he will cease to cultivate innocence, which has not enabled him to preserve his good fortune. [36] So a wise dispensation spares the man who could be made worse by suffering, so as not to allow that person to struggle for whom it is not suitable. [37] Another man is completely endowed with all the virtues, holy and close to God; providence judges it so wrong for him to be touched by any misfortune that it does not even allow him to be vexed by bodily diseases. [38]

morbis agitari sinat. [38] nam ut quidam me quoque excellentior:

120   ἀνδρὸς δὴ ἱεροῦ δέμας αἰθέρες οἰκοδόμησαν.

[39] fit autem saepe, uti bonis summa rerum regenda deferatur, ut exuberans retundatur improbitas. [40] aliis mixta quaedam pro animorum qualitate distribuit; quosdam remordet, ne longa felici-tate luxurient; alios duris agitat, ut virtutes animi patientiae usu 125 atque exercitatione confirment. [41] alii plus aequo metuunt quod ferre possunt, alii plus aequo despiciunt quod ferre non possunt; hos in experimentum sui tristibus ducit. [42] nonnulli venerandum saeculis nomen gloriosae pretio mortis emerunt, quidam suppliciis inexpugnabiles exemplum ceteris praetulerunt invictam malis esse 130 virtutem; quae quam recte atque disposite et ex eorum bono quibus accedere videntur fiant, nulla dubitatio est.

[43] nam illud quoque quod improbis nunc tristia nunc optata proveniunt ex eisdem ducitur causis. [44] ac de tristibus quidem nemo miratur, quod eos male meritos omnes existimant; quorum 135 quidem supplicia tum ceteros ab sceleribus deterrent, tum ipsos quibus invehuntur emendant. laeta vero magnum bonis argumen-tum loquuntur, quid de huius modi felicitate debeant iudicare quam famulari saepe improbis cernant. [45] in qua re illud etiam dispensari credo, quod est forsitan alicuius tam praeceps atque 140 importuna natura ut eum in scelera potius exacerbare possit rei familiaris inopia; huius morbo providentia collatae pecuniae reme-

---

120 δέμας αἰθέρες *vulg.:* δυνάμεις δέμας Shanzer: *codices alii aliter corrupti.* ἀνδρὸς ἱηροῦ σῶμα δυνάμεις οἰκονομοῦσι Planudes *(Shanzer 280)*

123 remordet] *sscr.* rerum V: *corruptum censuit Bases, Planudis* ἀηδοῦς συγχωρεῖ πειραθῆναι *conferens:* <rerum mutatione> remordet *ex gr. coni. Weinberger:* obelis inclusit Bieler <iniucundo sinit interdum> remorderi *dubitanter coniciens*

124 duris] *sscr.* permittit V Hib. Vind.

agitat Büchner: agitari *codd.:* agitari <sinit> Goth. quidam Obbarii *saec. XV:* <sinit> agitari Rand *(fort.),* Weinberger

128 saeculis *Bases:* saeculi *codd.*

131 accedere] accidere AᵃCLᶜNᶜTᶜ

accedere <mala> videntur *coni.* Tränkle [1968] 286

134 male ACLᶜN(*sscr.* -o)OᶜP(?)T: malo *cett.*

112

For as someone even better than me said,

The heavens have built the body of a holy man.

[39] Moreover it often happens that the greatest things are entrusted to the control of good men, so that flourishing wickedness can be beaten down. [40] To others it gives mixed fortune according to the nature of their souls; some it vexes, so that long-lasting happiness should not make them self-indulgent; others it harries with harsh circumstances, so that they may strengthen the virtues of their minds by experience of endurance and struggle. [41] Some fear more than they should what they can in fact endure, others despise more than they should what they cannot in fact endure; these she leads by misfortune to make trial of themselves. [42] Not a few have purchased, at the price of a glorious death, a name to be revered by the ages; some, who could not be overcome by tortures, have provided an example for others to show that virtue is not overcome by evils. There is no doubt how rightly these things come about, in how organised a way, and for the good of those to whom they are seen to happen.

[43] For that the wicked at one time enjoy misfortune, at another time what they have wished for – this too derives from the same causes. [44] Concerning their misfortunes no-one is surprised, because all judge that they have deserved ill; indeed their punishments at one time deter others from crimes, at another correct the very people on whom they fall. But their good fortune too provides the good with ample evidence of what they ought to judge concerning happiness of this sort, which they see often attends upon the wicked. [45] In this regard I think that this arrangement is also made, that because someone's nature is perhaps so rash and savage that lack of property could actually urge him on to crimes; providence cures this man's disease by

113

dio medetur. **[46]** hic foedatam probris conscientiam spectans et se cum fortuna sua comparans forsitan pertimescit ne, cuius ei iucundus usus est, sit tristis amissio; mutabit igitur mores ac dum 145 fortunam metuit amittere nequitiam derelinquit. **[47]** alios in cladem meritam praecipitavit indigne acta felicitas; quibusdam permissum puniendi ius, ut exercitii bonis et malis esset causa supplicii. **[48]** nam ut probis atque improbis nullum foedus est, ita ipsi inter se improbi nequeunt convenire. **[49]** quidni, cum a 150 semet ipsis discerpentibus conscientiam vitiis quisque dissentiat faciantque saepe quae, cum gesserint, non fuisse gerenda decernant?

[50] ex quo saepe summa illa providentia protulit insigne miraculum, ut malos mali bonos facerent. **[51]** nam dum iniqua sibi a 155 pessimis quidam perpeti videntur, noxiorum odio flagrantes ad virtutis frugem rediere, dum se eis dissimiles student esse, quos oderant. **[52]** sola est enim divina vis cui mala quoque bona sint, cum eis competenter utendo alicuius boni elicit effectum. **[53]** ordo enim quidam cuncta complectitur ut quod adsignata ordinis ratione 160 decesserit hoc licet in alium tamen ordinem relabatur, ne quid in regno providentiae liceat temeritati.

[54] ἀργαλέον δέ με ταῦτα θεὸν ὣς πάντ' ἀγορεύειν,

[55] neque enim fas est homini cunctas divinae operae machinas vel ingenio comprehendere vel explicare sermone. **[56]** hoc tantum 165 perspexisse sufficiat, quod naturarum omnium proditor deus idem ad bonum dirigens cuncta disponat, dumque ea quae protulit in sui similitudinem retinere festinat, malum omne de rei publicae suae terminis per fatalis seriem necessitatis eliminet. **[57]** quo fit ut quae in terris abundare creduntur, si disponentem providenti-170 am spectes, nihil usquam mali esse perpendas. **[58]** sed video te

---

142 spectans *LNO^CT^C:* αἰσθανόμενος *Planudes:* expectans *cett.*

146 *ante* acta *lacunam exhib.* T (auct *erasum esse putavit Peiper):* aucta *F:* ducta *N^CT^C in mg.:* ac *P:* ἐπενεχθεῖσα *Planudes*

148-9 foedus est, ita ipsi] foedus ita ut ipsi *P:* foedus est, ita et ipsi *coni. Bieler*

165 proditor] conditor *Tränkle [1968] 286*

170 mali] mala *Tränkle [1977] 155*

the remedy of bestowing money on him. [46] Another, considering his conscience which is defiled by disgraceful deeds and comparing his own condition with his good fortune, perhaps grows fearful that he will find it grievous to lose what he enjoys with pleasure; so he will change his ways and, fearing to lose his good fortune, abandon his wickedness. [47] Others are hurled into the ruin they deserve by good fortune they have handled unworthily; some are allowed the right to punish, in order to exercise the good and punish the bad. [48] For just as there is no agreement between the upright and the wicked, just so the wicked themselves cannot reach agreement among themselves. [49] How could they, seeing that they are each at variance with themselves as their faults tear their conscience apart, and that they often do things which when they have done them they judge ought not to have been done?

[50] As a result of this, that supreme providence often produces the outstanding marvel that bad men make other bad men good. [51] For certain people seem to themselves to be suffering things they do not deserve at the hands of very bad men; burning with hatred of those responsible, they have returned to the excellence of virtue, in their desire to be unlike those they hated. [52] To the divine power alone evil things too are good, since by using them skilfully it brings forth some good result. [53] For a certain ordering embraces all things, so that what departs from its place in that order falls back into an order, admittedly a different one, so that in the kingdom of providence nothing should be permitted to random chance.

[54] 'But it is difficult for me to utter all these things like a god'; [55] nor is it right for a human being either to grasp in his mind all the contrivances of the divine working or to explain them in speech. [56] Let it be sufficient just to have seen this, that the same God who produces all things also arranges all things, guiding them to what is good, and that as he hastens to preserve all those things which he has produced in his own likeness, he banishes all evil from the boundaries of his commonwealth through the ordering of fated necessity. [57] So it

iam dudum et pondere quaestionis oneratum et rationis prolixitate fatigatum aliquam carminis exspectare dulcedinem; accipe igitur haustum, quo refectus firmior in ulteriora contendas.

[IV metr. 6] Si vis celsi iura Tonantis
              pura sollers cernere mente,
              aspice summi culmina caeli;
              illic iusto foedere rerum
5   veterem servant sidera pacem.
              non sol rutilo concitus igne
              gelidum Phoebes impedit axem
              nec quae summo vertice mundi
              flectit rapidos Ursa meatus,
10   numquam occiduo lota profundo,
              cetera cernens sidera mergi
              cupit Oceano tinguere flammas;
              semper vicibus temporis aequis
              Vesper seras nuntiat umbras
15   revehitque diem Lucifer almum.
              sic aeternos reficit cursus
              alternus amor, sic astrigeris
              bellum discors exsulat oris.
              haec concordia temperat aequis
20   elementa modis, ut pugnantia
              vicibus cedant humida siccis
              iungantque fidem frigora flammis,
              pendulus ignis surgat in altum
              terraeque graves pondere sidant.
25   his de causis vere tepenti
              spirat florifer annus odores,
              aestas cererem fervida siccat,
              remeat pomis gravis autumnus,
              hiemem defluus inrigat imber.
30   haec temperies alit ac profert,
              quicquid vitam spirat in orbe;
              eadem rapiens condit et aufert
              obitu mergens orta supremo.

171 rationis] orationis *Orth*: rationum *coni. Bieler*

[IV metr.6] 25 his de *MNT^C*: hisdem *cett.*: iisdem *Vulpius*: isdem
Peiper

comes about that if you were to watch providence arranging the evils that are believed to abound on the earth, you would judge that there is no evil anywhere. [58] But I see that for a long time now you have been burdened by the weightiness of the question and wearied by the length of the reasoning, and have been waiting for the sweetness of song; so accept a draught by which you may be refreshed and go on strengthened to what lies beyond.

[IV metr. 6]

If you wish to look carefully with pure mind on the laws of the Thunderer on high, look at the summit of the highest heaven; there by the just law that governs things the stars preserve their ancient peace. The sun, travelling swiftly with its ruddy fire, does not hinder the cold rotation of the moon, nor does the Bear which turns swiftly round the topmost point of the universe, never bathed in the western deep but seeing the other stars sink, desire to moisten its flames in the Ocean; and always, with equal alternations of time, the Evening Star heralds the shadows of night and the Morning Star brings back kindly day. Thus an alternating desire renews the eternal courses, thus discordant strife is banished from the country of the stars. This harmony tempers the elements in equal measures, so that in their rivalry moisture yields by turns to dryness and there is a treaty between cold and hot. Fire, suspended, rises up on high, and earth, heavy with its weight, sinks down. For these reasons in warm spring the season of flowers breathes forth fragrance, hot summer dries out the corn, autumn follows heavy with fruit, and winter is wet with pouring showers. These things the tempering nourishes and produces, whatever breathes with life in the world; it also swiftly hides away and removes the things that have arisen, plunging them into their last perishing. Meanwhile the

                    sedet interea conditor altus
        35   rerumque regens flectit habenas
                    rex et dominus, fons et origo,
                    lex et sapiens arbiter aequi,
                    et, quae motu concitat ire,
                    sistit retrahens ac vaga firmat;
        40   nam nisi rectos revocans itus
                    flexos iterum cogat in orbes,
                    quae nunc stabilis continet ordo
                    dissaepta suo fonte fatiscant.
                    hic est cunctis communis amor
        45   repetuntque boni fine teneri,
                    quia non aliter durare queant
                    nisi converso rursus amore
                    refluant causae quae dedit esse.

[IV.7][1] Iamne igitur vides, quid haec omnia, quae diximus, consequatur?

Quidnam? inquam.

[2] Omnem, inquit, bonam prorsus esse fortunam.

5   Et qui id, inquam, fieri potest?

[3] Attende, inquit. Cum omnis fortuna vel iucunda vel aspera tum remunerandi exercendive bonos, tum puniendi corrigendive impro-bos causa deferatur, omnis bona, quam vel iustam constat esse vel utilem.

10   [4] Nimis quidem, inquam, vera ratio et, si quam paulo ante do-cuisti providentiam fatumve considerem, firmis viribus nixa sen-tentia. [5] sed eam, si placet, inter eas quas inopinabiles paulo ante posuisti numeremus.

Qui? inquit.

15   [6] Quia id hominum sermo communis usurpat, et quidem crebro, quorundam malam esse fortunam.

[7] Visne igitur, inquit, paulisper vulgi sermonibus accedamus, ne nimium velut ab humanitatis usu recessisse videamur?

[IV.7] 11 fatumque *P*

Founder is seated on high and guides things steering them by their reins, the King and Lord, Source and Origin, Law and wise Judge of what is fair; the things that he urges on to move he stops, brings them back and makes firm what wavers: for if he did not call them back from their straight courses and compel them into curved circles again, the things which are now held together in a stable order would be separated from their source and fall to pieces. This is the common love of them all, and they seek to be held by the good as their end, since they could not survive otherwise than by turning back with love returned to the cause which gave them their being.

[IV.7][1] Then do you now see what follows on all these things which we have said?"

"What?" I said.

[2] "That all fortune is surely good," she said.

"How can this be?" I said.

[3] "Listen," she said. "Since all fortune, whether pleasant or harsh, is conferred for the sake of rewarding or exercising the good and punishing or correcting the wicked, it is all good, it being agreed that it is either just or useful."

[4] "That is a very true argument," I said, "and, if I were to bear in mind the providence and fate which you taught me of a short while ago, a judgement that rests on firm foundations. [5] But if you will, let us count it among those which you laid down a short while ago as unthinkable."

"Why?" she said.

[6] "Because people's common way of speaking asserts that some people's fortune *is* bad, and indeed does so frequently."

[7] "Then would you like us," she said, "for a while to approach the way of speaking of ordinary people, so that we should not seem to have departed too far from human usage, as it were?"

Ut placet, inquam.

20 [8] Nonne igitur bonum censes esse, quod prodest?

Ita est, inquam.

[9] Quae vero aut exercet aut corrigit, prodest?

Fateor, inquam.

Bona igitur?

25 Quidni?

[10] Sed haec eorum est, qui vel in virtute positi contra aspera bellum gerunt vel a vitiis declinantes virtutis iter arripiunt.

Negare, inquam, nequeo.

[11] Quid vero iucunda, quae in praemium tribuitur bonis, num
30 vulgus malam esse decernit?

Nequaquam, verum uti est, ita quoque esse optimam censet.

[12] Quid reliqua, quae cum sit aspera, iusto supplicio malos cohercet, num bonam populus putat?

[13] Immo omnium, inquam, quae excogitari possunt, iudicat esse
35 miserrimam.

[14] Vide igitur, ne opinionem populi sequentes quiddam valde inopinabile confecerimus.

Quid? inquam.

[15] Ex his enim, ait, quae concessa sunt evenit eorum quidem,
40 qui [vel] sunt vel in possessione vel in provectu vel in adeptione virtutis, omnem quaecumque sit bonam, in improbitate vero manentibus omnem pessimam esse fortunam.

[16] Hoc, inquam, verum est, tametsi nemo audeat confiteri.

[17] Quare, inquit, ita vir sapiens moleste ferre non debet, quoti-
45 ens in fortunae certamen adducitur, ut virum fortem non decet indignari, quotiens increpuit bellicus tumultus. [18] utrique enim huic quidem gloriae propagandae, illi vero conformandae sapientiae difficultas ipsa materia est. [19] ex quo etiam virtus vocatur,

---

40 vel *primum om. EL*ᵃ*NT*ᶜ*, del. O Büchner; alterum om. CKV*ᶜ

"As you like," I said.

[8] "Well, do you not judge that to be good which is beneficial?"

"Yes," I said.

[9] "But fortune that either exercises or corrects, is beneficial?"

"I agree," I said.

"Then it is good?"

"Of course."

[10] "But this is the fortune of those who are either in a virtuous condition and wage war against adversity, or else are turning away from wickedness and setting foot on the road to virtue."

"I cannot deny it," I said.

[11] "What about pleasant fortune, which is assigned to the good as their reward? Surely the ordinary people do not judge this to be bad?"

"In no way; rather they judge it to be the best, as indeed it is."

[12] "What of the remaining type which, although it is harsh, restrains the wicked by justly punishing them? Surely the people do not think that good?"

[13] "On the contrary," I said, "they judge it the most wretched of all that can be conceived."

[14] "Consider, then, that by following popular opinion we may not have ended with something *really* unthinkable."

"What?" I said.

[15] "From what has been agreed," she said, "it turns out that all fortune, whatever it is, of those who possess virtue or are on the way to it or are grasping it is good, all fortune of those who remain in wickedness, very bad."

[16] "This is true," I said, "even if no-one would dare to admit it."

[17] "For this reason, she said, a wise man ought not to bear it ill, whenever he is brought into a trial of fortune, just as it is not fitting for a brave man to complain when the strife of war grows noisy. [18] For the difficulty is itself an opportunity to both, to the latter for spreading his glory, to the former for fashioning his wisdom. [19] This is why virtue is so called, on the grounds that virtue, resting on its

121

quod virtus suis viribus nitens non superetur adversis; neque
50 enim vos in provectu positi virtutis diffluere deliciis et emarce-
scere voluptate venistis. [20] proelium cum omni fortuna animis
acre conseritis, ne vos aut tristis opprimat aut iucunda corrum-
pat. [21] firmis medium viribus occupate; quicquid aut infra
subsistit aut ultra progreditur, habet contemptum felicitatis, non
55 habet praemium laboris. [22] in vestra enim situm manu, qualem
vobis fortunam formare malitis; omnis enim quae videtur aspera,
nisi aut exercet aut corrigit, punit.

[IV metr. 7] Bella bis quinis operatus annis
                 ultor Atrides Phrygiae ruinis
                 fratris amissos thalamos piavit.
                 ille dum Graiae dare vela classi
5   optat et ventos redimit cruore,
                 exuit patrem miserumque tristis
                 foederat natae iugulum sacerdos.
                 flevit amissos Ithacus sodales,
                 quos ferus vasto recubans in antro
10   mersit immani Polyphemus alvo;
                 sed tamen caeco furibundus ore
                 gaudium maestis lacrimis rependit.
                 Herculem duri celebrant labores:
                 ille Centauros domuit superbos,
15   abstulit saevo spolium leoni,
                 fixit et certis volucres sagittis,
                 poma cernenti rapuit draconi
                 aureo laevam gravior metallo,
                 Cerberum traxit triplici catena.
20   victor immitem posuisse fertur
                 pabulum saevis dominum quadrigis.
                 Hydra combusto periit veneno,
                 fronte turpatus Achelous amnis

---

51 animis] ac nimis *KL^C:* nimis *MN^CT^C:* μάχην ἐκτόπως δριμεῖαν
Planudes: a nimis *Peiper:* animis ac re *Damsté*

[IV metr. 7] 7 foederat *A^CC^aDV^C:* f(o)ederat *F^CEC^C:* foderat *T^CN:*
σφαγίασσε *Planudes:* foedera *cett.* (turparat *superscr. V*)

own strength, is not overcome by adversity; for neither have you, situated on the road to virtue, come this far in order to be abandoned to delights and weakened by pleasure. [20] You are joined in fierce battle in your spirit with every sort of fortune, so that neither shall adverse fortune overwhelm you nor pleasant fortune corrupt you. [21] Hold the middle ground with sure strength; whatever stops too soon or goes beyond involves contempt of happiness, but not reward for effort. [22] It rests with you what sort of fortune you prefer to fashion for yourselves; for all fortune that seems adverse, if it does not exercise or correct, is punishment.

[IV metr. 7]

Having waged war for ten years Agamemnon the avenger by the ruin of Troy enacted retribution for his brother's lost wife. While he wished to give the Greek fleet an opportunity to sail and purchased fair winds by bloodshed, he put off the role of father and as a grim priest defiled the wretched throat of his daughter. The man from Ithaca wept for his lost comrades whom the monster Polyphemus, lying in his huge cave, plunged into his savage belly; but maddened, with blinded countenance, he paid for his pleasure with sad tears. Hercules is made famous by his stern labours. He tamed the proud Centaurs; he took his trophy from the savage lion; he pierced the birds with unerring arrows; he stole the apples as the dragon watched, his left hand weighted with the golden metal; he dragged up Cerberus on a triple chain. It is said that as victor he gave to the savage teams of horses their own master as food. The Hydra perished, its poison burned up; the river Achelous, his

ora demersit pudibunda ripis.
25 stravit Antaeum Libycis harenis,
Cacus Euandri satiavit iras,
quosque pressurus foret altus orbis,
saetiger spumis umeros notavit.
ultimus caelum labor inreflexo
30 sustulit collo pretiumque rursus
ultimi caelum meruit laboris.
ite nunc, fortes, ubi celsa magni
ducit exempli via. cur inertes
terga nudatis? superata tellus
35 sidera donat.

Liber V

[V.1] [1] Dixerat orationisque cursum ad alia quaedam tractanda atque expedienda vertebat. [2] tum ego: Recta quidem, inquam, exhortatio tuaque prorsus auctoritate dignissima, sed quod tu dudum de providentia quaestionem pluribus aliis implicitam esse
5 dixisti re experior. [3] quaero enim an esse aliquid omnino et quidnam esse casum arbitrere.

[4] tum illa: Festino, inquit, debitum promissionis absolvere viamque tibi qua patriam reveharis aperire. [5] haec autem etsi perutilia cognitu tamen a propositi nostri tramite paulisper aversa
10 sunt, verendumque est ne deviis fatigatus ad emetiendum rectum iter sufficere non possis.

[6] Ne id, inquam, prorsus vereare; nam quietis mihi loco fuerit ea quibus maxime delector agnoscere. [7] simul, cum omne disputationis tuae latus indubitata fide constiterit, nihil de sequentibus
15 ambigatur.

[8] tum illa: Morem, inquit, geram tibi, simulque sic orsa est: Si quidem, inquit, aliquis eventum temerario motu nullaque causarum conexione productum casum esse definiat, nihil omnino casum esse confirmo et praeter subiectae rei significationem inanem prorsus
20 vocem esse decerno. quis enim cohercente in ordinem cuncta deo

---

31 caelum $A(sscr.)CL^CMT^CV$: caelo *cett.*: caelos *Peiper*

forehead disfigured, plunged his face between his banks for shame. Hercules laid Antaeus out on the Libyan sands. Evander's anger at Cacus was satisfied, and the bristling boar marked with its foam the shoulders on which the lofty sphere of the sky would press. As his last labour Hercules supported heaven on unbending neck, and conversely earned heaven as the reward for his last labour. Go now, brave ones, where the lofty road of great example leads. Why do you hesitate with bare backs? The reward for conquering earth, is heaven."

Book V

[V.1] [1] The Lady Philosophy had spoken, and was now directing what she was saying towards dealing with and disentangling certain other matters. [2] Then I said, "Your exhortation is indeed correct and certainly most worthy of your authoritative position; but I am experiencing in practice what you said some time ago, that the question about providence is intertwined with several others. [3] For I am asking whether you think that chance exists at all and what you think it is."

[4] Then she said, "I am hurrying to discharge the debt incurred by my promise and to open for you a way by which you may return to your fatherland. [5] However, though it is thoroughly advantageous to know about these matters, nevertheless they are somewhat aside from the path that leads to our intended goal, and there must be a fear that you will be tired by the detours and not have sufficient strength to complete the direct route."

[6] "Don't be afraid of that at all," I said, "for to become acquainted with the things in which I take most delight will have been like rest for me; [7] and at the same time, when every aspect of your argument has been established by undoubted proof, there can be no doubt about what follows."

[8] Then she said "I will do what you want," and at once began as follows: "If indeed," she said, "someone defined chance as an outcome produced by random motion and by no connection of causes, then I do assert that chance does not exist at all, and without indicating any subject the word is, I judge, absolutely empty. For when God directs

locus esse ullus temeritati reliquus potest? **[9]** nam nihil ex nihilo exsistere vera sententia est, cui nemo umquam veterum refragatus est, quamquam id illi non de operante principio sed de materiali subiecto hoc omnium de natura rationum quasi quoddam iecerint
25 fundamentum. **[10]** at si nullis ex causis aliquid oriatur, id de nihilo ortum esse videbitur; quodsi hoc fieri nequit, ne casum quidem huius modi esse possibile est qualem paulo ante definivimus.

[11] Quid igitur, inquam, nihilne est quod vel casus vel fortuitum
30 iure appellari queat? an est aliquid, tametsi vulgus lateat, cui vocabula ista conveniant?

[12] Aristoteles meus id, inquit, in Physicis et brevi et veri propinqua ratione definivit.

Quonam, inquam, modo?

35 **[13]** Quotiens, ait, aliquid cuiuspiam rei gratia geritur aliudque quibusdam de causis quam quod intendebatur obtingit casus vocatur, ut si quis colendi agri causa fodiens humum defossi auri pondus inveniat. **[14]** hoc igitur fortuitu quidem creditur accidisse, verum non de nihilo est; nam proprias causas habet,
40 quarum inprovisus inopinatusque concursus casum videtur operatus. **[15]** nam nisi cultor agri humum foderet, nisi eo loci pecuniam suam depositor obruisset, aurum non esset inventum. **[16]** hae sunt igitur fortuiti causae compendii, quod ex obviis sibi et confluentibus causis, non ex gerentis intentione provenit. **[17]**
45 neque enim vel qui aurum obruit vel qui agrum exercuit ut ea pecunia repperiretur intendit, sed, uti dixi, quo ille obruit hunc fodisse convenit atque concurrit. **[18]** licet igitur definire casum esse inopinatum ex confluentibus causis in his quae ob aliquid geruntur eventum. **[19]** concurrere vero atque confluere causas

---

23 id *del. Tränkle [1977]* 155

38 fortuitu $EM^CO^CPT^aV^C$: fortuito *cett.*

42 hae] haec $A^aD^aL^aOT^a$

43 fortuiti] fortuitu PV^a; fortuita V^C

causae] causa $A^CDL^aM^aOPT^aV^a$

all things into an ordered pattern, what place at all can there be left for randomness? [9] For that nothing comes from nothing is a true judgement which none of the ancients opposed, although they laid this as the foundation, as it were, for all their reasoning about nature not in relation to the principle that acts, but in relation to the underlying matter. [10] Nevertheless, if something were to arise from no causes, it will seem that that thing arose from nothing; and if this cannot happen, nor is it possible for chance of the sort that we defined a little while ago to exist."

[11] "What then?" I said, "Is there nothing which can rightly be called either chance or fortuitous? Or is there something, even if it is generally unknown, to which those words are suited?"

[12] "My Aristotle," she said, "defined this in his *Physics* in an account that is both short and close to the truth."

"How?" I said.

[13] "Whenever something is being done for the sake of anything," she said, "and for certain reasons something other than what was intended happens, this is called chance. For example, if someone were to dig the ground in order to cultivate a field, and discovered a quantity of buried gold. [14] This then is believed to happen fortuitously, but it does not come from nothing; for it has its own proper causes, the unforeseen and unexpected coincidence of which appears to have produced the chance result. [15] For if the cultivator were not digging the ground, or if the person who hid his money had not buried it at that precise point, the gold would not have been found. [16] So these are causes of the fortuitous gain, which results from causes which met each other and came together, not from the intention of the agent. [17] For neither the man who buried the gold nor the man who tilled the field had the intention that that money should be found, but, as I said, it happened coincidentally that the one dug where the other had buried it. [18] So chance may be defined as an unexpected outcome, as the result of causes that come together, in these things that are being done for the sake of something. [19] But the coincidence and coming

50 facit ordo ille inevitabili conexione procedens qui de providentiae
  fonte descendens cuncta suis locis temporibusque disponit.

[V metr. 1] Rupis Achaemeniae scopulis, ubi versa sequentum
   pectoribus figit spicula pugna fugax,
  Tigris et Euphrates uno se fonte resolvunt
   et mox abiunctis dissociantur aquis.
5 si coeant cursumque iterum revocentur in unum,
   confluat alterni quod trahit unda vadi,
  conveniant puppes et vulsi flumine trunci
   mixtaque fortuitos implicet unda modos;
  quos tamen ipsa vagos terrae declivia casus
10 gurgitis et lapsi defluus ordo regit.
  sic quae permissis fluitare videtur habenis
  fors patitur frenos ipsaque lege meat.

[V.2] [1] Animadverto, inquam, idque, uti tu dicis, ita esse consen-
tio. [2] sed in hac haerentium sibi serie causarum estne ulla
nostri arbitrii libertas an ipsos quoque humanorum motus animorum fatalis catena constringit?

5 [3] Est, inquit; neque enim fuerit ulla rationalis natura, quin
eidem libertas adsit arbitrii. [4] nam quod ratione uti naturaliter
potest, id habet iudicium, quo quidque discernat; per se igitur
fugienda optandave dinoscit. [5] quod vero quis optandum esse
iudicat, petit; refugit vero, quod aestimat esse fugiendum. [6]
10 quare, quibus in ipsis inest ratio, inest etiam volendi nolendique
libertas, sed hanc non in omnibus aequam esse constituo. [7] nam
supernis divinisque substantiis et perspicax iudicium et incorrup-
ta voluntas et efficax optatorum praesto est potestas. [8] humanas
vero animas liberiores quidem esse necesse est, cum se in mentis
15 divinae speculatione conservant, minus vero, cum dilabuntur ad
corpora, minusque etiam, cum terrenis artubus colligantur. [9]
extrema vero est servitus, cum vitiis deditae rationis propriae
possessione ceciderunt. [10] nam ubi oculos a summae luce verita-

---

[V metr.1] 7 conveniant *M*^{cp}: conveniunt *K*: convenient *cett.*

[V.2] 7 quo] quod *A*^{a}N

10 in ipsis *del. Tränkle [1977] 156: om. ET*^{a}: *del. sed restituit A*^{C}: *post* inest *transpos. Hib.*

together of causes is brought about by that order, advancing by unavoidable connections, which descends from providence as its source and arranges all things in their proper times and places.

[V metr.1] From the cliffs of the Persian crags, in the land where the fleeing warriors turn and pierce the breasts of their pursuers with their darts, the Tigris and Euphrates flow from a single source and are soon separated, their waters parted. If they were to come together and were again united in a single course, the things that the waters of each river carry would come together; the boats and the trees torn up by the current would meet, and the mingled waters would combine their chance measures. Nevertheless, these chance wanderings are governed by the very slopes of the land and the ordered course of the stream as it flows down. Just so fortune, which seems to waver with reins slackened, suffers the bridle and itself proceeds according to law."

[V.2] [1] "I realise this," I said, "and I agree that it is as you say. [2] But in this sequence of causes that are fastened together, is there any freedom for our choice, or are the very movements of human minds also constrained by the chain of fate?"

[3] "There is [freedom]," she said; "for there could not be any rational nature that did not have freedom of choice. [4] For what is naturally able to make use of reason has judgement by which it distinguishes each thing; so by itself it knows what things are to be avoided and what wished for. [5] But what anyone judges is to be wished for, that he seeks; but he shrinks from what he judges is to be avoided. [6] So those [beings] that have reason in themselves have also a freedom of willing and not willing; but I judge that this is not equal in all of them. [7] For the divine beings above have judgment with insight and an uncorrupted will and a power ready to hand that brings about what they wish for. [8] Human souls however must indeed be more free when they keep themselves in contemplation of the divine mind, but less so when they descend to bodies, and less still when they are bound in earthly limbs. [9] But the ultimate enslavement is when they surrender to vices and fall from possession of the reason that is theirs. [10] For when they turn their eyes away from the light of the highest truth and

tis ad inferiora et tenebrosa deiecerint, mox inscitiae nube cali-
gant, perniciosis turbantur affectibus, quibus accedendo consenti-
endoque, quam invexere sibi, adiuvant servitutem et sunt quodam
modo propria libertate captivae. [11] quae tamen ille ab aeterno
cuncta prospiciens providentiae cernit intuitus et suis quaeque
meritis praedestinata disponit.

[V metr. 2] Πάντ' ἐφορᾶν καὶ πάντ' ἐπακούειν
        puro clarum lumine Phoebum
        melliflui canit oris Homerus;
        qui tamen intima viscera terrae
        non valet aut pelagi radiorum
   5   infirma perrumpere luce.
        haud sic magni conditor orbis;
        huic ex alto cuncta tuenti
        nulla terrae mole resistunt,
        non nox atris nubibus obstat.
  10   quae sint, quae fuerint veniantque,
        uno mentis cernit in ictu;
        quem, quia respicit omnia solus,
        verum possis dicere solem.

[V.3] [1] Tum ego: En, inquam, difficiliore rursus ambiguitate
confundor.

[2] Quaenam, inquit, ista est? iam enim, quibus perturbere, coniec-
to.

[3] Nimium, inquam, adversari ac repugnare videtur praenoscere
universa deum et esse ullum libertatis arbitrium. [4] nam si
cuncta prospicit deus neque falli ullo modo potest, evenire necesse est, quod providentia futurum esse praeviderit. [5] quare si
ab aeterno non facta hominum modo, sed etiam consilia volunta-
tesque praenoscit, nulla erit arbitrii libertas; neque enim vel
factum aliud ullum vel quaelibet exsistere poterit voluntas, nisi
quam nescia falli providentia divina praesenserit. [6] nam si aliorsum quam provisae sunt detorqueri valent, non iam erit futuri
firma praescientia, sed opinio potius incerta, quod de deo credere
nefas iudico.

[V.2] 19 inscitiae] inscientiae *EV*
[V.3] 3 perturbere *A^aDLNOV^a:* perturbaere *E:* perturbare *cett.*
13 provisae] provisa *P*

cast them downwards towards inferior and shadowy things, they are soon darkened by the cloud of ignorance and thrown into confusion by destructive passions; by assenting and agreeing to these they assist the enslavement which they have brought upon themselves and are in a certain way prisoners through their own freedom. [11] But that gaze of providence, looking on all things from eternity, sees these things and arranges what is predestined according to what each individual deserves.

[V metr.2] Phoebus, bright in his clear light, sees and hears all things; so sings Homer of the honeyed voice. But he is not able to break through the inmost parts of earth or sea with the feeble light of his rays. Not so he who established the great sphere of the universe; as he observes all things from on high the earth does not resist him at all with its bulk, night does not stand in his way with its black clouds. What is, what has been and what is to come, all these he sees in a single glance of his mind; and since he looks on all things in his solitude, you could call him the true Sun."

[V.3] [1] Then I said, "Well, I am thrown into confusion again by an uncertainty that is harder to deal with."

[2] "What is that?" she said. "For I can already guess what disturbs you."

[3] "It seems to me," I said, "that there is a complete opposition and inconsistency between God's foreknowing everything and there being any free choice. [4] For if God foresees all things and cannot in any way be mistaken, it is necessary that that should happen which he with his providence has foreseen will happen. [5] Therefore if from eternity he foresees not only the deeds of men, but also their deliberations and wishes, there will be no freedom of choice; for no deed or wish will be able to exist other than that which divine providence, which cannot be deceived, has foreseen. [6] For if wishes could be turned in a different direction from that in which they were foreseen, there will no longer be sure foreknowledge of the future, but rather an uncertain opinion, and I judge it wrong to believe this about God.

[7] neque enim illam probo rationem, qua se quidam credunt hunc quaestionis nodum posse dissolvere. **[8]** aiunt enim non ideo quid esse eventurum, quoniam id providentia futurum esse prospexerit, sed e contrario potius, quoniam quid futurum est, id divinam providentiam latere non posse eoque modo necessarium hoc in contrariam relabi partem. **[9]** neque enim necesse esse contingere quae providentur, sed necesse esse quae futura sunt provideri – quasi vero quae cuius rei causa sit, praescientiane futurorum necessitatis an futurorum necessitas providentiae, laboretur ac non illud demonstrare nitamur, quoquo modo sese habeat ordo causarum, necessarium esse eventum praescitarum rerum, etiam si praescientia futuris rebus eveniendi necessitatem non videatur inferre.

[10] etenim si quispiam sedeat, opinionem quae eum sedere coniectat veram esse necesse est; atque e converso rursus, si de quopiam vera sit opinio quoniam sedet, eum sedere necesse est. **[11]** in utroque igitur necessitas inest, in hoc quidem sedendi, at vero in altero veritatis. **[12]** sed non idcirco quisque sedet quoniam vera est opinio, sed haec potius vera est quoniam quempiam sedere praecessit. **[13]** ita cum causa veritatis ex altera parte procedat, inest tamen communis in utraque necessitas. **[14]** similia de providentia futurisque rebus ratiocinari patet; nam etiam si idcirco quoniam futura sunt providentur, non vero ideo quoniam providentur eveniunt, nihilo minus tamen a deo vel ventura provideri vel provisa necesse est evenire [provisa], quod ad perimendam arbitrii libertatem solum satis est.

[15] iam vero quam praeposterum est, ut aeternae praescientiae temporalium rerum eventus causa esse dicatur! **[16]** quid est autem aliud arbitrari ideo deum futura quoniam sunt eventura providere, quam putare quae olim acciderunt causam summae illius esse providentiae? **[17]** ad haec, sicuti cum quid esse scio id ipsum esse necesse est, ita cum quid futurum novi id ipsum futurum esse necesse est; sic fit igitur, ut eventus praescitae rei nequeat evitari.

---

40 provisa (alt.) *om. AN, eras.* E^{C}OT^{C}V^C

45 acciderint *Merkelbach 71*

[7] For I do not approve that argument, either, by which certain people believe the knot of this problem can be undone. **[8]** For they say that something is not going to come about for the reason that providence has foreseen that it will, but rather on the contrary it is because something is going to be that it cannot escape the notice of divine providence; and in this way, they say, this necessity passes over to the other side. **[9]** For they say it is not necessary for those things to happen that are foreseen; rather, it is necessary for those things to be foreseen that are going to be. – As if the difficulty was over which thing was the cause of which, foreknowledge the cause of the necessity of future things or the necessity of future things the cause of providence, and we were not striving to show that, whatever the order of causation, the coming about of things that are foreknown is necessary, even if it does not seem that it is the *foreknowledge* that imposes on future things the necessity of coming about.

[10] For indeed, if anyone should be sitting, the opinion which conjectures that he is sitting must be true, and conversely if, concerning anyone, the opinion that he is sitting is true, it is necessary that he be sitting. **[11]** So there is necessity present in both, in the one the necessity of sitting, in the other the necessity of truth. **[12]** But it is not the case that the *reason* for each person's sitting is that the opinion is true; rather, the opinion is true, because the person's sitting came first. **[13]** So, although the *cause* of truth proceeds from one side, nevertheless there is common necessity in both. **[14]** It is clear that similar reasoning applies to providence and things that are going to be; for even if they are foreseen for this reason, that they are going to come about, and do not come about *because* they are foreseen, nevertheless this does not make it any less necessary either that things that are coming should be foreseen by God or that things that have been foreseen should come about, and this on its own is sufficient to do away with freedom of choice.

[15] But how back-to-front this is, that the outcome of temporal things should be said to be the cause of eternal foreknowledge! **[16]** For what else is thinking that the reason for God's foreknowing the things that are going to be is the fact that they are going to come about, than to think that things which have happened in the past were the cause of his supreme providence? **[17]** Moreover, when I know that something is the case, it is necessary that it is the case; just so, when I know that something is going to be, it is necessary that that same thing is going to be. Thus it happens that the coming about of a thing that has been foreknown cannot be avoided.

50   [18] postremo si quid aliquis aliorsum atque sese res habet ex-
      istimet, id non modo scientia non est, sed est opinio fallax ab
      scientiae veritate longe diversa. [19] quare si quid ita futurum
      est, ut eius certus ac necessarius non sit eventus, id eventurum
      esse praesciri qui poterit? [20] sicut enim scientia ipsa impermixta
55   est falsitati, ita id quod ab ea concipitur esse aliter atque conci-
      pitur nequit. [21] ea namque causa est cur mendacio scientia ca-
      reat, quod se ita rem quamque habere necesse est uti eam sese
      habere scientia comprehendit. [22] quid igitur? quonam modo deus
      haec incerta futura praenoscit? [23] nam si inevitabiliter eventura
60   censet quae etiam non evenire possibile est, fallitur, quod non
      sentire modo nefas est, sed etiam voce proferre. [24] at si ita, uti
      sunt, ita ea futura esse decernit, ut aeque vel fieri ea vel non
      fieri posse cognoscat, quae est haec praescientia, quae nihil
      certum, nihil stabile comprehendit? [25] aut quid hoc refert vati-
65   cinio illo ridiculo Tiresiae, "Quicquid dicam, aut erit aut non"?
      [26] quid etiam divina providentia humana opinione praestiterit, si
      uti homines incerta iudicat quorum est incertus eventus? [27]
      quodsi apud illum rerum omnium certissimum fontem nihil incerti
      esse potest, certus eorum est eventus, quae futura firmiter ille
70   praescierit. [28] quare nulla est humanis consiliis actionibusque
      libertas, quas divina mens sine falsitatis errore cuncta prospici-
      ens ad unum alligat et constringit eventum.

      [29] quo semel recepto quantus occasus humanarum rerum conse-
      quatur, liquet. [30] frustra enim bonis malisque praemia poenaeve
75   proponuntur, quae nullus meruit liber ac voluntarius motus
      animorum. [31] idque omnium videbitur iniquissimum, quod nunc
      aequissimum iudicatur, vel puniri improbos vel remunerari probos,
      quos ad alterutrum non propria mittit voluntas, sed futuri cogit
      certa necessitas. [32] nec vitia igitur nec virtutes quicquam
80   fuerint, sed omnium meritorum potius mixta atque indiscreta
      confusio; quoque nihil sceleratius excogitari potest, cum ex provi-
      dentia rerum omnis ordo ducatur nihilque consiliis liceat humanis,
      fit ut vitia quoque nostra ad bonorum omnium referantur aucto-
      rem. [33] igitur nec sperandi aliquid nec deprecandi ulla ratio
85   est; quid enim vel speret quisque vel etiam deprecetur, quando

      ───────────────────────────────

      64 refert] fert *P:* distat *Hib.:* differt *Bentley*

      75 <nisi> liber *Wiede*

      85 est] potest *P:* esset *Schepss:* potest <esse> *coni. Bieler*

[18] Finally, if anyone judges otherwise than the matter is, that is not only not knowledge, but false opinion, far removed from the truthfulness of knowledge. [19] Therefore, if anything is going to be in such a way that its coming about is not certain and necessary, how will it be possible for it to be foreknown that this will come about? [20] For just as knowledge itself is unmixed with falsehood, just so that which is grasped by it cannot be otherwise than it is grasped as being. [21] This indeed is the reason why there is no deception in knowledge, that each thing must be as knowledge understands it to be. [22] What then? In what way does God have foreknowledge that these uncertain things are going to be? [23] For if he judges that those things will come about inevitably which can also *not* come about, he is mistaken - a view that it is wrong (for us) not only to hold but even to utter. [24] But if he judges that these things are going to be in the way that they actually are going to be, so that he realises that they can equally well come about or not come about, what is this "foreknowledge", which grasps nothing firm or certain? [25] Or how is this different from that ridiculous prophecy of Tiresias, "Whatever I say either will happen or won't"? [26] And how would divine providence be superior to human opinion, if, like human beings, it judged those things as uncertain of which the outcome is uncertain? [27] But if there can be no uncertainty with that most certain source of all things, the outcome is certain of those things which he has foreknown as surely going to be. [28] And for this reason there is no freedom for human decisions or actions; the divine mind, looking forth on all things without the error of falsehood, binds and constrains them to a single outcome.

[29] When this has once been accepted, it is clear how human affairs will collapse in consequence. [30] In vain will rewards or punishments for good and bad men be set forth, since no free and voluntary movement of minds has deserved them. [31] And what is now judged most just will seem the most unjust of all things, that the wicked should be punished or the upright rewarded, when they were not sent to each sort of action by their own will, but compelled by the sure necessity of the future. [32] Nor therefore would vices or virtues exist at all, but rather there will be a mixed and indeterminate confusion of all deserving, and - than which nothing more wicked can be conceived - when all the order of things is derived from providence and nothing is allowed to human decisions, it comes about that our faults, too, are imputed to the author of all good things. [33] So there is no reason to hope for anything or pray for anything; for what should each person either hope for or even pray for, when all the things that are to be prayed

optanda omnia series indeflexa conectit? **[34]** auferetur igitur unicum illud inter homines deumque commercium sperandi scilicet et deprecandi, si quidem iustae humilitatis pretio inaestimabilem vicem divinae gratiae promeremur; qui solus modus est, quo cum
90 deo colloqui homines posse videantur illique inaccessae luci prius quoque quam impetrent ipsa supplicandi ratione coniungi. **[35]** quae si recepta futurorum necessitate nihil virium habere credantur, quid erit quo summo illi rerum principi conecti atque adhaerere possimus? **[36]** quare necesse erit humanum genus, uti paulo
95 ante cantabas, dissaeptum atque disiunctum suo fonte fatiscere.

[V metr.3] Quaenam discors foedera rerum
            causa resolvit? quis tanta deus
            veris statuit bella duobus,
            ut, quae carptim singula constent,
5   eadem nolint mixta iugari?
            an nulla est discordia veris
            semperque sibi certa cohaerent,
            sed mens caecis obruta membris
            nequit oppressi luminis igne
10   rerum tenues noscere nexus?
            sed cur tanto flagrat amore
            veri tectas reperire notas?
            scitne, quod appetit anxia nosse?
            sed quis nota scire laborat?
15   at si nescit, quid caeca petit?
            quis enim quicquam nescius optet
            aut quis valeat nescita sequi?
            quove inveniat? quisve repertam
            queat ignarus noscere formam?
20   an, cum mentem cerneret altam,
            pariter summam et singula norat?
            nunc membrorum condita nube
            non in totum est oblita sui
            summamque tenet singula perdens.
25   igitur quisquis vera requirit,

88 pretio] praeconio *P*

[V metr.3] 12 reperire *N Hib.:* repperire *cett.*

18 quisve *Pulman, Peiper:* quisque *L^C:* quis *cett.*

reppertam *Weinberger*

for are bound together in an undeviating sequence? **[34]** Therefore that single sort of commerce between gods and human beings will be done away with, I mean that of hoping and praying for things, if indeed just humility purchases for us the inestimable reward of divine grace; this is the only way in which it seems that human beings can converse with God and be joined with that inaccessible light before they obtain it, by the act of praying itself. **[35]** If these things should be believed to have no power, when the necessity of future things is accepted, in what way could we be united to and cleave to that highest Prince of all things? And for this reason the human race, as you sang a short while ago, must fall to pieces, being cut off and separated from its Source.

[V metr.3] What is this discordant cause which undoes the laws of things? What god instituted such wars between two truths, so that the very things, which are agreed individually when taken separately, refuse to be mingled and united together? Or is there no disagreement among things that are true, and they are always sure and consistent with one another, but our mind, overwhelmed by the blindness of our body, cannot by the glow of her diminished light recognise the subtle connections of things? But why then does our mind burn with such desire to discover the hidden signs of the truth? Does it know the things which it anxiously desires to know? But who struggles to know things that are known already? If however it does not know, what is it seeking in its blindness? For who would wish for anything when he did not know it, or who would have the strength to pursue what he did not know? And where would he find it? Or who would be able in his igno-rance to know its form when he found it? Or is it that, when our soul beheld the Mind on high, it knew the whole and its parts alike? Now, hidden in the body's mist, it does not entirely forget itself, and keeps hold of the whole while losing the parts. Therefore whoever seeks for

neutro est habitu; nam neque novit
nec penitus tamen omnia nescit,
sed, quam retinens meminit, summam
consulit alte visa retractans,
30   ut servatis queat oblitas
addere partes.

[V.4] [1] Tum illa: Vetus, inquit, haec est de providentia querela
Marcoque Tullio, cum divinationem destruit, vehementer agitata
tibique ipsi res diu prorsus multumque quaesita, sed haudqua-
quam ab ullo vestrum hactenus satis diligenter ac firmiter expedi-
5   ta. [2] cuius caliginis causa est quod humanae ratiocinationis
motus ad divinae praescientiae simplicitatem non potest ammoveri;
quae si ullo modo cogitari queat, nihil prorsus relinquetur ambi-
gui. [3] quod ita demum patefacere atque expedire temptabo, si
prius ea quibus moveris expendero.

10   [4] quaero enim cur illam solventium rationem minus efficacem
putes, quae quia praescientiam non esse futuris rebus causam
necessitatis existimat, nihil impediri praescientia arbitrii libertatem
putat. [5] num enim tu aliunde argumentum futurorum necessitatis
trahis, nisi quod ea quae praesciuntur non evenire non possunt?
15   [6] si igitur praenotio nullam futuris rebus adicit necessitatem,
quod tu etiam paulo ante fatebare, quid est quod voluntarii exitus
rerum ad certum cogantur eventum? [7] etenim positionis gratia,
ut quid consequatur advertas, statuamus nullam esse praescientiam. [8] num igitur, quantum ad hoc attinet, quae ex arbitrio
20   veniunt ad necessitatem cogantur?

Minime.

[9] Statuamus iterum esse, sed nihil rebus necessitatis iniungere;
manebit, ut opinor, eadem voluntatis integra atque absoluta
libertas. [10] sed praescientia, inquies, tametsi futuris eveniendi
25   necessitas non est, signum tamen est necessario ea esse ventura.

[V.4] 2 destruit *coni. Theiler:* de * * * *Vat. lat. 5956 ante correc-*
tionem (vid. Troncarelli 148): distruit L^aT^aV: describit L^C: distribuit *cett.:* disseruit *coni. Büchner: obelos posuit Bieler*

20 veniunt] eveniunt *T Bam.*

cogantur A^CEPT^a: coguntur *codd.*

the truth is in neither condition; for he neither knows nor yet completely fails to know everything, but he thinks of the whole which he remembers and retains, recalling the things seen on high, so that he can add the forgotten parts to those that are retained."

[V.4] [1] Then she said: "This is an old complaint about providence, one that was forcefully urged by Marcus Tullius, when he did away with divination, and a matter that has certainly for a long time now been investigated extensively by you yourself; but it has not up to now been explained by any of you with sufficient care and assurance. [2] The cause of this obscurity is that the movement of human reasoning cannot attain to the simplicity of divine foreknowledge; if this could in any way be thought of, there will certainly be no doubt left. [3] So I will eventually try to reveal and explain this, after first weighing up those things by which you are perturbed.

[4] "I ask why you think that method of solving the problem less effective, which judges that foreknowledge is not the cause of the necessity of future things, and therefore supposes that freedom of choice is in no way hindered by foreknowledge. [5] Surely you do not yourself base your argument for the necessity of future things on anything other than the fact that those things which are foreknown cannot fail to come about? [6] If then foreknowledge adds no necessity to future things, which you too admitted a short while ago, what reason is there for the voluntary outcomes of things to be compelled to a fixed result? [7] Indeed, for the sake of argument, so that you can observe what follows, let us suppose that there is no foreknowledge. [8] Surely, as far as this is concerned, the results of choice would not be compelled to be necessary?"

"Certainly not."

[9] "Let us again suppose that there is foreknowledge, but that it adds no necessity to things; there will, as I suppose, remain the same whole and complete freedom of the will. [10] But, you will say, although foreknowledge does not make it necessary for future things to come about, nevertheless it is a sign that they will necessarily come about.

[11] hoc igitur modo, etiam si praecognitio non fuisset, necessarios futurorum exitus esse constaret; omne etenim signum tantum quid sit ostendit, non vero efficit quod designat. [12] quare demonstrandum prius est nihil non ex necessitate contingere, ut praenotionem signum esse huius necessitatis appareat; alioquin si haec nulla est, ne illa quidem eius rei signum poterit esse, quae non est. [13] iam vero probationem firma ratione subnixam constat non ex signis neque petitis extrinsecus argumentis, sed ex convenientibus necesariisque causis esse ducendam.

[14] sed qui fieri potest ut ea non proveniant quae futura esse providentur? quasi vero nos ea, quae providentia futura esse praenoscit, non esse eventura credamus, ac non illud potius arbitremur, licet eveniant, nihil tamen ut evenirent sui natura necessitatis habuisse. [15] quod hinc facile perpendas licebit; plura etenim dum fiunt subiecta oculis intuemur, ut ea quae in quadrigis moderandis atque flectendis facere spectantur aurigae, atque ad hunc modum cetera. [16] num igitur quicquam illorum ita fieri necessitas ulla compellit?

Minime; frustra enim esset artis effectus, si omnia coacta moverentur.

[17] Quae igitur cum fiunt carent exsistendi necessitate, eadem prius quam fiant sine necessitate futura sunt. [18] quare sunt quaedam eventura quorum exitus ab omni necessitate sit absolutus. [19] nam illud quidem nullum arbitror esse dicturum, quod quae nunc fiunt prius quam fierent eventura non fuerint; haec igitur etiam praecognita liberos habent eventus. [20] nam sicut scientia praesentium rerum nihil his quae fiunt, ita praescientia futurorum nihil his quae ventura sunt necessitatis importat.

[21] sed hoc, inquis, ipsum dubitatur, an earum rerum quae necessarios exitus non habent ulla possit esse praenotio. [22] dissonare etenim videntur, putasque si praevideantur consequi necessitatem, si necessitas desit minime praesciri, nihilque scientia comprehendi posse nisi certum. [23] quodsi quae incerti sunt exitus, ea quasi certa providentur, opinionis id esse caliginem, non scientiae veritatem; aliter enim ac sese res habeat arbitrari ab integritate scientiae credis esse diversum.

---

59 certa] incerta $C^a P T^a$: ⟨s⟩in⟨t⟩ certa *Engelbrecht*

[11] So in this way, even if there had not been foreknowledge, it would be agreed that the outcomes of future things are necessary; for every sign only shows what is the case, it does not bring about what it indicates. [12] So it must first be shown that nothing comes about except from necessity, so that it may be clear that foreknowledge is a sign of this necessity; otherwise, if this necessity does not exist, neither indeed will it be possible for foreknowledge to be a sign of that which does not exist. [13] However, it is agreed that a proof which rests on sure reasoning should be drawn not from signs or from arguments brought in from outside, but rather from appropriate and necessary reasons.

[14] But [you will protest], how can it happen that those things do not come about which are foreseen as going to be? - As if we believed that those things, which providence foreknows will come about, are not going to come about, and did not rather think that, even if they do come about, nevertheless they do not in their own nature possess any necessity of coming about. [15] You can easily consider this on the following basis. There are many things which we see before our eyes while they are happening, like the things which charioteers are seen to do in controlling and steering their chariots, and other things like this. [16] Surely none of these is compelled to happen in this way by any necessity?"

"Certainly not; for what skill produces would be in vain, if all these movements were brought about by compulsion."

[17] "So the things which are free from any necessity of occurring *while* they are happening, are also, before they happen, *going to be* without necessity. [18] And for this reason there are certain things that are going to come about, the outcome of which is free from all necessity. [19] For I do not think that anyone will say that the things which are now happening were, before they happened, not going to come about; so these things have free outcomes, even if they were known beforehand. [20] For just as the knowledge of present things does not introduce any necessity in these things which are happening, just so the foreknowledge of future things does not introduce any necessity in these things which are to come.

[21] But it is this very thing, you say, that is in doubt, whether there *can* be any foreknowledge of those things which do not have necessary outcomes. [22] For these things do not seem in harmony with one another, and you think that, if things are foreseen, their necessity follows, while if necessity is absent they are certainly not foreknown, and nothing can be grasped by knowledge unless it is certain. [23] If however those things whose outcome is uncertain are foreseen as if certain, that, you suppose, is the obscurity of mere opinion, not the truthfulness of knowledge; for you believe that it is at variance with the completeness of knowledge to suppose otherwise than the matter actually is.

[24] cuius erroris causa est quod omnia quae quisque novit ex ipsorum tantum vi atque natura cognosci aestimat quae sciuntur.
[25] quod totum contra est; omne enim, quod cognoscitur, non
65 secundum sui vim, sed secundum cognoscentium potius comprehenditur facultatem. [26] nam ut hoc brevi liqueat exemplo, eandem corporis rotunditatem aliter visus, aliter tactus agnoscit; ille eminus manens totum simul iactis radiis intuetur, hic vero cohaerens orbi atque coniunctus circa ipsum motus ambitum
70 rotunditatem partibus comprehendit. [27] ipsum quoque hominem aliter sensus, aliter imaginatio, aliter ratio, aliter intellegentia contuetur. [28] sensus enim figuram in subiecta materia constitutam, imaginatio vero solam sine materia iudicat figuram. [29] ratio vero hanc quoque transcendit speciemque ipsam quae singularibus
75 inest universali consideratione perpendit. [30] intellegentiae vero celsior oculus exsistit; supergressa namque universitatis ambitum ipsam illam simplicem formam pura mentis acie contuetur.

[31] in quo illud maxime considerandum est: nam superior comprehendendi vis amplectitur inferiorem, inferior vero ad superiorem
80 nullo modo consurgit. [32] neque enim sensus aliquid extra materiam valet vel universales species imaginatio contuetur vel ratio capit simplicem formam, sed intellegentia quasi desuper spectans concepta forma quae subsunt etiam cuncta diiudicat, sed eo modo quo formam ipsam, quae nulli alii nota esse poterat, comprehendit.
85 [33] nam et rationis universum et imaginationis figuram et materiale sensibile cognoscit nec ratione utens nec imaginatione nec sensibus, sed illo uno ictu mentis formaliter, ut ita dicam, cuncta prospiciens. [34] ratio quoque cum quid universale respicit nec imaginatione nec sensibus utens imaginabilia vel sensibilia comprehendit. [35] haec est enim quae conceptionis suae universale
90 ita definit: homo est animal bipes rationale. [36] quae cum universalis notio sit, tum imaginabilem sensibilemque esse rem nullus ignorat, quod illa non imaginatione vel sensu sed in rationali conceptione considerat. [37] imaginatio quoque, tametsi ex sensibus visendi formandique figuras sumpsit exordium, sensu tamen
95 absente sensibilia quaeque collustrat non sensibili sed imaginaria ratione iudicandi.

75 intellegentiae] intellegentia NPT^C

91 definit] definivit LT: διορισάμενος Planudes

92 tum] tamen coni. Bieler

[24] The reason for this error is that each person judges that all the things which he knows are known only in accordance with the nature and power of the things which are known. [25] In fact it is completely the reverse; for everything which is known is grasped not according to its own power but rather according to the capacity of those who know it. [26] For, to make this clear by a short example, the same roundness of a body is recognised by sight in one way, by touch in another; the former, remaining at a distance, observes the whole together by casting its rays, but the latter, clinging to the curvature and joined with it, moves round the circumference itself and apprehends the roundness part by part. [27] Man too himself is observed in one way by sensation, in another by imagination, in another by reasoning, in another by understanding. [28] For sensation judges the shape in the underlying matter, imagination the shape alone without the matter. [29] Reasoning rises above this too and considers in universal terms the form itself which is present in the individuals. [30] The eye of understanding rises still higher; for passing above the circumference of the universe it observes the simple form itself with the pure sight of the mind.

[31] What should above all be considered in this is that the higher power of apprehension includes the lower, but the lower in no way rises to the level of the higher. [32] For sensation has no power except in matter, nor does imagination observe the universal forms, nor does reasoning grasp the simple form; but understanding, as if looking down from above, when it has grasped the form also discerns all the things which are beneath it, but does so in the way in which it apprehends the form itself, which could not be known to any of the other powers. [33] For it knows reasoning's universal and imagination's shape and the material object of sensation not by using reasoning or imagination or the senses, but looking forth on all things in the manner of forms, if I may put it that way, by that single cast of the mind. [34] Reasoning too, when it looks at any universal, grasps the objects of imagination and the senses without using either imagination or the senses. [35] For it is reasoning that defines as follows the universal that it conceives: 'Man is a rational biped animal.' [36] Although this is a universal notion, everyone knows that the thing is an object of imagination and sensation; but reasoning considers it not by imagination or sensation, but by a rational conceiving. [37] Imagination too, although it takes its starting-point of considering and forming shapes from the senses, even when sensation is absent surveys each of the objects of sensation with a manner of judging that involves not sensation but imagination.

[38] videsne igitur ut in cognoscendo cuncta sua potius facultate quam eorum quae cognoscuntur utantur? [39] neque id iniuria: 100 nam cum omne iudicium iudicantis actus exsistat, necesse est ut suam quisque operam non ex aliena sed ex propria potestate perficiat.

[V metr. 4] Quosdam Porticus attulit
    obscuros nimium senes,
    qui sensus et imagines
    e corporibus extimis
5   credant mentibus imprimi,
    ut quondam celeri stilo
    mos est aequore paginae
    quae nullas habeat notas
    pressas figere litteras.
10 sed mens si propriis vigens
    nihil motibus explicat,
    sed tantum patiens iacet
    notis subdita corporum
    cassasque in speculi vicem
15 rerum reddit imagines,
    unde haec sic animis viget
    cernens omnia notio?
    quae vis singula perspicit
    aut quae cognita dividit?
20 quae divisa recolligit
    alternumque legens iter
    nunc summis caput inserit,
    nunc decedit in infima,
    tum sese referens sibi
25 veris falsa redarguit?
    haec est efficiens magis
    longe causa potentior,
    quam quae materiae modo
    impressas patitur notas.
30 praecedit tamen excitans

---

100 actus] actu *Met.*[C]

[V metr.4] 1 quosdam *A.H. Griffiths:* quondam *codd.*

6 quondam *suspicatus est Bieler:* quodam *Graziano di S. Teresa (vid. Troncarelli 139)*

23 decedit] decidit $A^aEKM^CPT^a$: descendit *Hib.:* desidit *Th. Wolf*

[38] Do you see therefore how in apprehending all use their own capacity rather than that of the things which are apprehended? **[39]** And rightly so; for since every judgement is an act of the one who judges, it is necessary that each should carry out its task not on the basis of the power of something else, but on the basis of its own.

[V Metr. 4]

The Porch contributed certain excessively obscure old men, who believed that sensations and images are imprinted on minds from external bodies, as the custom is sometimes with a swift stylus to make impressed letters on the smooth surface of a page which has no marks. But if the mind explains nothing through the power of its own movements, but is simply subjected passively to the marks imprinted by bodies, and reproduces empty images of things in the manner of a mirror, how is this thought that sees all things so strong in minds? What power perceives individual things or distinguishes the things that are known? What power gathers together again the things that are distinguished, and, travelling now this way, now that, now raises its head to the highest point, now goes down to the lowest parts, and then bringing itself back to comparison with itself rejects what is false by means of what is true? These things are produced rather by a cause which is far more powerful than one which like matter experiences marks impressed upon it. What comes first, indeed, is an experience

ac vires animi movens
vivo in corpore passio,
cum vel lux oculos ferit
vel vox auribus instrepit.
35   tum mentis vigor excitus,
quas intus species tenet
ad motus similes vocans
notis applicat exteris
introrsumque reconditis
40   formis miscet imagines.

[V.5][1] Quodsi in corporibus sentiendis, quamvis afficiant instru-
menta sensuum forinsecus obiectae qualitates animique agentis
vigorem passio corporis antecedat, quae in se actum mentis
provocet excitetque interim quiescentes intrinsecus formas, si in
5   sentiendis, inquam, corporibus animus non passione insignitur,
sed ex sua vi subiectam corpori iudicat passionem, quanto magis
ea quae cunctis corporum affectionibus absoluta sunt in discer-
nendo non obiecta extrinsecus sequuntur, sed actum suae mentis
expediunt? [2] hac itaque ratione multiplices cognitiones diversis
10   ac differentibus cessere substantiis. [3] sensus enim solus cunctis
aliis cognitionibus destitutus immobilibus animantibus cessit,
quales sunt conchae maris quaeque alia saxis haerentia nutriun-
tur; imaginatio vero mobilibus beluis, quibus iam inesse fugiendi
appetendive aliquis videtur affectus. [4] ratio vero humani tantum
15   generis est sicut intellegentia sola divini; quo fit, ut ea notitia
ceteris praestet, quae suapte natura non modo proprium, sed
ceterarum quoque notitiarum subiecta cognoscit.

[5] quid igitur, si ratiocinationi sensus imaginatioque refragentur
nihil esse illud universale dicentes quod sese intueri ratio putet?
20   [6] quod enim sensibile vel imaginabile est, id universum esse non
posse; aut igitur rationis verum esse iudicium nec quicquam esse
sensibile aut, quoniam sibi notum sit plura sensibus et imaginationi
esse subiecta, inanem conceptionem esse rationis, quae quod sensibile sit ac singulare quasi quiddam universale consideret. [7] ad
25   haec si ratio contra respondeat se quidem et quod sensibile et quod
imaginabile sit in universitatis ratione conspicere, illa vero ad

---

6 corpori] corporis *Tränkle [1977] 156*

15 sola] solius *Hib.* (sola *v.l.*)

in a living body which awakes and sets in motion the powers of the mind, when light strikes the eyes or a voice sounds in the ears. Then the strength of the mind is aroused, and summoning the forms it holds within it to similar movements it applies them to the marks from outside, and mingles the images with the forms stored within itself.

[V.5] [1] In the case of the perception of bodies, their properties, situated outside us, are presented to our sense-organs, and the effect upon the body precedes the activity of the mind, calling the mind to activity within itself and arousing the forms within that have previously been quiet. But if in the case of perceptible bodies the mind is not marked by some effect upon it, but by its own power passes judgement on the effect added to the body, how much more do those things which are free from all bodily feelings not follow in their act of discernment what is situated outside them, but rather carry out the activity of their own mind? [2] So it is in this way that the many different ways of apprehending are given to the various and differing beings. [3] Sensation alone, deprived of all other ways of apprehending, is given to creatures that are unable to move, like mussels and other things that feed while clinging to the rocks; imagination to creatures that can move, in which already there seems to be present some response of avoidance or pursuit. [4] Reasoning however belongs to the human race alone, as understanding alone does to the divine; and so it comes about that that way of apprehending excels over the others, which by its own nature knows not only its proper object but also those to which the other ways of apprehending apply.

[5] What then, if sensation and imagination should challenge reasoning saying that the universal which reasoning thinks it contemplates does not exist at all? [6] For they might say that what can be sensed or imagined cannot be universal; so either the judgement of reasoning is correct and nothing that can be sensed exists, or, since they know that many things *are* objects of sensation and imagination, reasoning's conceiving is empty, since it considers what can be sensed and is singular as some sort of universal. [7] Reasoning might reply to this that it perceives, in the manner of a universal, also what can be sensed and what can be imagined, while they cannot aspire to knowledge of the

universitatis cognitionem aspirare non posse, quoniam eorum notio
corporales figuras non posset excedere, de rerum vero cognitione
firmiori potius perfectiorique iudicio esse credendum: in huius modi
30   igitur lite nos, quibus tam ratiocinandi quam imaginandi etiam senti-
endique vis inest, nonne rationis potius causam probaremus?

[8] simile est, quod humana ratio divinam intellegentiam futura, nisi
ut ipsa cognoscit, non putat intueri. [9] nam ita disseris: si qua
certos ac necessarios habere non videantur eventus, ea certo even-
35   tura praesciri nequeunt. [10] harum igitur rerum nulla est praescientia; quam si etiam in his esse credamus, nihil erit, quod non ex
necessitate proveniat. [11] si igitur uti rationis participes sumus ita
divinae iudicium mentis habere possemus, sicut imaginationem sen-
sumque rationi cedere oportere iudicavimus, sic divinae sese menti
40   humanam summittere rationem iustissimum censeremus. [12] quare
in illius summae intelligentiae cacumen, si possumus, erigamur;
illic enim ratio videbit quod in se non potest intueri, id autem est
quonam modo etiam quae certos exitus non habent certa tamen
videat ac definita praenotio, neque id sit opinio sed summae
45   potius scientiae nullis terminis inclusa simplicitas.

[V metr. 5]   Quam variis terras animalia permeant figuris!
namque alia extento sunt corpore pulveremque verrunt
continuumque trahunt vi pectoris incitata sulcum;
sunt quibus alarum levitas vaga verberetque ventos
5   et liquido longi spatia aetheris enatet volatu;
haec pressisse solo vestigia gressibusque gaudent
vel virides campos transmittere vel subire silvas.
quae variis videas licet omnia discrepare formis,
prona tamen facies hebetes valet ingravare sensus;
10   unica gens hominum celsum levat altius cacumen,
atque levis recto stat corpore despicitque terras.
haec, nisi terrenus male desipis, ammonet figura;
qui recto caelum vultu petis exserisque frontem,
in sublime feras animum quoque, ne gravata pessum
15   inferior sidat mens corpore celsius levato.

[V.6][1] Quoniam igitur, uti paulo ante monstratum est, omne quod
scitur non ex sua, sed ex comprehendentium natura cognoscitur,

---

38 possemus] possimus $A^c KO^a T^a V^a$, sscr. N ut vid.

universal since their apprehension cannot go beyond bodily shapes; and that where the knowledge of things is concerned it is the more sure and perfect judgement that should rather be believed. In such a dispute would not we, who possess the power both of reasoning and of imagining and also of sensation, not decide in favour of reasoning's case?

[8] Similarly with the fact that human reasoning thinks that divine understanding can only observe future things in the way that it itself knows them. [9] For what you are saying is as follows: if certain things should not appear to have sure and necessary outcomes, it cannot be known certainly beforehand that those things will come about. [10] So you say there is no foreknowledge of these things; and if we should believe that there *is* foreknowledge even in these cases, there will be nothing which will not come about of necessity. - [11] Well, if we were able, just as we now have a share in reasoning, so to have judgement of the divine mind, then, just as we judged that imagination and sensation must yield to reasoning, so we would judge it most right that human reasoning should yield to the divine mind. [12] So let us rise up to that highest summit of understanding, if we can; for there reasoning will see what it cannot in itself observe, and that is how even those things which do not have sure outcomes are seen by a sure and definite foreknowledge, and how this is not opinion, but rather the simplicity of the highest knowledge, not confined within any limits.

[V metr. 5] In what varied shapes do living creatures move on the face of the earth! For some have elongated bodies and sweep the dust and moved on by the force of their breasts dig out a continuous furrow; for some the wandering lightness of wings beats the winds and swims across the wide expanse of air in fluid flight. Some rejoice to press their footstep on the earth and with their steps either to cross green plains or enter under the woods. Though you see they are all different, with varied shapes, nevertheless their downcast gaze has the power to weigh down their sluggish senses; only the race of man lifts its head up higher, stands lightly upright and looks down on the earth. This image contains a lesson. If earth has not greatly dulled your senses, you who look upright at the sky and raise your forehead, raise your thoughts on high too, lest your mind weighed down should sink down to ruin below your body raised up high.

[V.6][1] Since therefore, as was shown a short while ago, everything which is known is known not as a result of its own nature but as a

intueamur nunc, quantum fas est, quis sit divinae substantiae
status, ut quaenam etiam scientia eius sit, possimus agnoscere. [2]
5   deum igitur aeternum esse cunctorum ratione degentium commune
iudicium est. [3] quid sit igitur aeternitas, consideremus; haec
enim nobis naturam pariter divinam scientiamque patefaciet. [4]
aeternitas igitur est interminabilis vitae tota simul et perfecta
possessio, quod ex collatione temporalium clarius liquet. [5] nam
10   quicquid vivit in tempore, id praesens a praeteritis in futura
procedit, nihilque est in tempore constitutum quod totum vitae
suae spatium pariter possit amplecti, sed crastinum quidem
nondum apprehendit, hesternum vero iam perdidit; in hodierna
quoque vita non amplius vivitis quam in illo mobili transitorioque
15   momento. [6] quod igitur temporis patitur condicionem, licet illud,
sicuti de mundo censuit Aristoteles, nec coeperit umquam esse nec
desinat vitaque eius cum temporis infinitate tendatur, nondum
tamen tale est ut aeternum esse iure credatur. [7] non enim totum
simul infinitae licet vitae spatium comprehendit atque complectitur,
20   sed futura nondum, transacta iam non habet. [8] quod igitur
interminabilis vitae plenitudinem totam pariter comprehendit ac
possidet, cui neque futuri quicquam absit nec praeteriti fluxerit,
id aeternum esse iure perhibetur idque necesse est et sui compos
praesens sibi semper assistere et infinitatem mobilis temporis
25   habere praesentem.

[9] unde non recte quidam, qui, cum audiunt visum Platoni
mundum hunc nec habuisse initium temporis nec habiturum esse
defectum, hoc modo conditori conditum mundum fieri coaeternum
putant. [10] aliud est enim per interminabilem duci vitam, quod
30   mundo Plato tribuit, aliud interminabilis vitae totam pariter com-
plexum esse praesentiam, quod divinae mentis proprium esse manifestum est. [11] neque deus conditis rebus antiquior videri debet
temporis quantitate, sed simplicis potius proprietate naturae. [12]
hunc enim vitae immobilis praesentarium statum infinitus ille
35   temporalium rerum motus imitatur, cumque eum effingere atque
aequare non possit, ex immobilitate deficit in motum, ex simplicitate praesentiae decrescit in infinitam futuri ac praeteriti quanti-
tatem et, cum totam pariter vitae suae plenitudinem nequeat
possidere, hoc ipso quod aliquo modo numquam esse desinit, illud
40   quod implere atque exprimere non potest aliquatenus videtur

---

7 patefaciet *cod. Fribourg 378:* patefecit, *super* c *scr.* r, *T (cf.*
Klingner [1940] 31-2): patefecerit *N:* patefaecit A^c: patefacit *vulg.*

result of that of those who know it, let us now consider, in so far as it is right to do so, what is the condition of the divine being, so that we may be able to recognise what his knowledge is. [2] Well, it is the common judgement of all who live their lives by reason that God is eternal. [3] So let us consider what eternity is; for this will at the same time reveal to us the divine nature and its knowledge. [4] Eternity, then, is the unbounded simultaneous and complete possession of life; this is made clearer by comparison with temporal things. [5] For whatever lives in time proceeds in the present from past things to future ones; and there is nothing established within time which can embrace the whole duration of its life at the same time – rather, it does not yet apprehend what will be tomorrow, and it has already lost what was yesterday, and in your life today too you live only in that single fleeting moment. [6] So even if something that is subject to the conditions of time should never have begun to exist nor cease, as Aristotle supposed about the world, and even if its life should be stretched out in an infinity of time, nevertheless it is not yet such as rightly to be believed eternal. [7] For it does not simultaneously grasp and embrace the whole duration of its life, unending though that life may be; it does not yet possess future things, and it does not now possess those that have been completed. [8] So it is what grasps and possesses simultaneously the whole fullness of unbounded life, nothing of what is future being absent from it and nothing of what is past having slipped away, that is rightly called eternal, and it is necessary that this should both, being in control of itself, always be present to itself, and also possess as present the unending duration of flowing time.

[9] It is for this reason that certain people are wrong who, when they hear that in Plato's opinion this world neither had a beginning of time nor will have an ending, think that in this way the world that is fashioned comes to be co-eternal with the one who fashions it. [10] For it is one thing to travel through an unending life, which is what Plato assigns to the world, another to have embraced simultaneously the whole of unending life as present, which is clearly what is proper to the divine mind. [11] Nor is it through length of time that God should seem prior to things that have been fashioned, but rather through the simplicity of the nature that he possesses. [12] This present condition of unchanging life is imitated by that unending changing of temporal things. Since it cannot reproduce and equal this, it descends from changelessness to change; from the simplicity of the present it is reduced to the unending extension of future and past; and, since it cannot possess the whole fullness of its life simultaneously, by this very fact, that it never ceases to exist in some way, it seems up to a point to imitate that which it cannot fully express, binding itself to

151

aemulari, alligans se ad qualemcumque praesentiam huius exigui
volucrisque momenti, quae quoniam manentis illius praesentiae
quandam gestat imaginem quibuscumque contigerit id praestat ut
esse videantur. [13] quoniam vero manere non potuit, infinitum
45   temporis iter arripuit, eoque modo factum est ut continuaret
eundo vitam cuius plenitudinem complecti non valuit permanendo.
[14] itaque si digna rebus nomina velimus imponere, Platonem
sequentes deum quidem aeternum, mundum vero dicamus esse
perpetuum.

50   [15] quoniam igitur omne iudicium secundum sui naturam quae sibi
subiecta sunt comprehendit, est autem deo semper aeternus ac
praesentarius status, scientia quoque eius omnem temporis supergressa motionem in suae manet simplicitate praesentiae infinitaque
praeteriti ac futuri spatia complectens omnia, quasi iam gerantur,
55   in sua simplici cognitione considerat. [16] itaque si praevidentiam
pensare velis, qua cuncta dinoscit, non esse praescientiam quasi
futuri sed scientiam numquam deficientis instantiae, rectius aesti-
mabis. [17] unde non praevidentia, sed providentia potius dicitur,
quod porro a rebus infimis constituta quasi ab excelso rerum
60   cacumine cuncta prospiciat. [18] quid igitur postulas ut necessaria
fiant quae divino lumine lustrentur, cum ne homines quidem
necessaria faciant esse quae videant? [19] num enim quae praesentia cernis aliquam eis necessitatem tuus addit intuitus? Minime.
[20] Atqui si est divini humanique praesentis digna collatio, uti
65   vos vestro hoc temporario praesenti quaedam videtis, ita ille
omnia suo cernit aeterno. [21] quare haec divina praenotio naturam rerum proprietatemque non mutat taliaque apud se praesentia
spectat, qualia in tempore olim futura provenient. [22] nec rerum
iudicia confundit unoque suae mentis intuitu tam necessarie quam
70   non necessarie ventura dinoscit, sicuti vos cum pariter ambulare
in terra hominem et oriri in caelo solem videtis, quamquam simul
utrumque conspectum tamen discernitis et hoc voluntarium, illud
esse necessarium iudicatis. [23] ita igitur cuncta dispiciens divinus intuitus qualitatem rerum minime perturbat apud se quidem
75   praesentium, ad condicionem vero temporis futurarum. [24] quo fit

---

55 praevidentiam *CV^a*: praescientiam *L^CLaud.Rehd.^C*: πρόγνωσιν
Planudes: praesentiam *cett.*

63 minime *Philosophiae ipsi sibi tribuit respondenti Bieler; Boethio
tribuunt Weinberger Büchner editores plerique*

73 dispiciens] despiciens *A^aLMNOT^CV^C*

whatever present it can, that of this tiny and fleeting moment, which, since it displays a certain image of that permanent present, provides a semblance of being to the things to which it applies. [13] Since however it cannot be at rest, it takes up the unending journey through time, and in this way it comes about that it makes continuous by travelling that life whose fullness it does not have the power to grasp while at rest. [14] So, if we wanted to give things the names they deserve, we would follow Plato and say that God indeed is eternal, but the world is everlasting.

[15] Since therefore it is in accordance with its own nature that all judgement comprehends the things that are subject to it, and God's condition is always eternal and present, his knowledge too, surpassing all temporal change, abides in the simplicity of its own present, embracing the infinite extent of past and future, and in its simple act of knowing considers all things as if they were happening now. [16] And so, if you are prepared to consider the "foresight", by which God discerns all things, not as the foreknowledge, as it were, of what is going to be in the future, but rather as knowledge of a never-failing present, you will judge more correctly. [17] And for this reason it is more correctly called not *praevidentia* (foresight) but *providentia* (looking forth), because, established far above the lowliest things, it looks forth on all things as if from a high peak among things. [18] Why therefore do you insist that things which are surveyed by the divine sight should be necessary, when not even men make the things that they see necessary? [19] Surely, when you see present things, your gazing does not impart any necessity to them? Certainly not. [20] But, if it is right to compare the divine present with the human, then, just as you see some things in this temporal present of yours, just so does God see all things in his eternal present. [21] And for this reason this divine foreknowledge does not change the nature and character of things, and sees things present to itself in the same way as they are going to come to be in time at some future time. [22] And he does not make confused judgements about things; rather, with a single gaze of his mind he distinguishes both things that are going to come to be necessarily and those that are not, just as, when you see together a man walking on the earth and the sun rising in the sky, although you see both at the same time, you make a distinction and say that the one is voluntary, the other necessary. [23] So the divine gaze, discerning all things in this way, certainly does not disturb the quality possessed by things which are indeed present to him, but as far as the condition of time is concerned are going to be in the future. [24] And thus it

ut hoc non sit opinio, sed veritate potius nixa cognitio, cum
exstaturum quid esse cognoscit, quod idem exsistendi necessitate
carere non nesciat.

[25] hic si dicas, quod eventurum deus videt, id non evenire non
80   posse, quod autem non potest non evenire, id ex necessitate
contingere, meque ad hoc nomen necessitatis adstringas, fatebor
rem quidem solidissimae veritatis, sed cui vix aliquis nisi divini
speculator accesserit. [26] respondebo namque idem futurum, cum
ad divinam notionem refertur, necessarium, cum vero in sua
85   natura perpenditur liberum prorsus atque absolutum videri. [27]
duae sunt etenim necessitates, simplex una, veluti quod necesse
est omnes homines esse mortales, altera condicionis, ut, si aliquem
ambulare scias, eum ambulare necesse est. [28] quod enim quisque
novit id esse aliter ac notum est nequit, sed haec condicio minime
90   secum illam simplicem trahit. [29] hanc enim necessitatem non
propria facit natura, sed condicionis adiectio; nulla enim necessitas cogit incedere voluntate gradientem, quamvis eum tum cum
graditur incedere necessarium sit. [30] eodem igitur modo, si quid
providentia praesens videt, id esse necesse est, tametsi nullam
95   naturae habeat necessitatem. [31] atqui deus ea futura, quae ex
arbitrii libertate proveniunt, praesentia contuetur; haec igitur ad
intuitum relata divinum necessaria fiunt per condicionem divinae
notionis, per se vero considerata ab absoluta naturae suae libertate non desinunt. [32] fient igitur procul dubio cuncta, quae
100 futura deus esse praenoscit, sed eorum quaedam de libero profi-
ciscuntur arbitrio, quae quamvis eveniant, exsistendo tamen
naturam propriam non amittunt, qua prius quam fierent etiam non
evenire potuissent.

[33] quid igitur refert non esse necessaria, cum propter divinae
105 scientiae condicionem modis omnibus necessitatis instar eveniet?
[34] hoc scilicet quod ea quae paulo ante proposui, sol oriens et
gradiens homo, quae dum fiunt non fieri non possunt, eorum
tamen unum prius quoque quam fieret necesse erat exsistere,
alterum vero minime. [35] ita etiam quae praesentia deus habet
110 dubio procul exsistent, sed eorum hoc quidem de rerum necessi-

---

97 fiunt] fiant K^{a}T^a

105 eveniet] eveniat L^{C}M: evenient *Goth.*: eveniant *Bam.*

110 exsistent] existunt A^{C}CL^{a}N^{C}T

154

comes about that this is not opinion, but rather knowledge resting upon truth, when it knows that something is going to exist, but does not fail to know that there is no necessity of this same thing's existing.

[25] Here you may say that what God sees is going to happen cannot not happen, and that what cannot not happen happens of necessity. If you tie me to this term of "necessity", I will admit that it is a matter of the firmest truth, but one to which scarcely anyone other than a student of the divine has attained. [26] For I will reply that the same thing that is going to be in the future is seen to be necessary, in relation to divine knowledge, but absolutely free and unrestricted when it is considered in its own nature. [27] For there are two types of necessity; one is simple, as with its being necessary that all men are mortal, the other depends on a condition, as, if you know that someone is walking, it is necessary that he be walking. [28] For what each person knows cannot be other than it is known to be; but this condition certainly does not bring that other simple necessity with it. [29] For this necessity is not produced by the proper nature of the thing concerned, but by the addition of the condition; no necessity compels the person who walks voluntarily to move forward, although it *is* necessary that he move forward at the time when he walks. [30] So in the same way, if providence which is present sees anything, it is necessary that that thing be, even though it has no natural necessity. [31] But God sees those things, which proceed from free choice, as being present; so these things come to be necessary in relation to the divine gaze, through the condition that they are known by God, but considered in themselves they do not cease from the complete freedom of their own nature. [32] And so all the things which God knows beforehand will happen do without doubt come about, but some of them proceed from free choice; and these, although they *do* come about, do not by existing lose their own proper nature, through which, before they came about, they were also able not to come about.

[33] What difference does it make, then, that these things are not necessary, seeing that, through the condition that God knows them, in all ways the exact equivalent of necessity will come about? [34] This, clearly: the things that I mentioned a short while ago, the sun's rising and the man's walking, cannot not occur while they do occur, but even before one of them existed it was necessary that it exist, but in the case of the other certainly not. [35] So too those things which are present for God will without doubt exist, but some of them result

155

tate descendit, illud vero de potestate facientium. [36] haud igitur
iniuria diximus haec si ad divinam notitiam referantur necessaria,
si per se considerentur necessitatis esse nexibus absoluta; sicuti
omne quod sensibus patet, si ad rationem referas universale est,
115 si ad se ipsa respicias singulare.

[37] sed si in mea, inquies, potestate situm est mutare propositum,
evacuabo providentiam, cum quae illa praenoscit forte mutavero.
[38] respondebo propositum te quidem tuum posse deflectere, sed
quoniam et id te posse et an facias quove convertas praesens
120 providentiae veritas intuetur, divinam te praescientiam non posse
vitare, sicuti praesentis oculi effugere non possis intuitum,
quamvis te in varias actiones libera voluntate converteris.

[39] Quid igitur, inquies, ex meane dispositione scientia divina
mutabitur, ut cum ego nunc hoc nunc illud velim, illa quoque
125 noscendi vices alternare videatur? [40] minime. omne namque
futurum divinus praecurrit intuitus et ad praesentiam propriae
cognitionis retorquet ac revocat; nec alternat, ut aestimas, nunc
hoc, nunc aliud praenoscendi vice, sed uno ictu mutationes tuas
manens praevenit atque complectitur. [41] quam comprehendendi
130 omnia visendique praesentiam non ex futurarum proventu rerum,
sed ex propria deus simplicitate sortitus est. [42] ex quo illud
quoque resolvitur, quod paulo ante posuisti, indignum esse si
scientiae dei causam futura nostra praestare dicantur. [43] haec
enim scientiae vis praesentaria notione cuncta complectens rebus
135 modum omnibus ipsa constituit, nihil vero posterioribus debet.

[44] quae cum ita sint, manet intemerata mortalibus arbitrii libertas nec iniquae leges solutis omni necessitate voluntatibus praemia
poenasque proponunt. [45] manet enim spectator desuper cunctorum praescius deus visionisque eius praesens semper aeternitas
140 cum nostrorum actuum futura qualitate concurrit bonis praemia,
malis supplicia dispensans. [46] nec frustra sunt in deo positae
spes precesque, quae cum rectae sunt, inefficaces esse non
possunt. [47] aversamini igitur vitia, colite virtutes, ad rectas
spes animum sublevate, humiles preces in excelsa porrigite. [48]
145 magna vobis est, si dissimulare non vultis, necessitas indicta
probitatis, cum ante oculos agitis iudicis cuncta cernentis.

---

115 ipsa] ipsum CV^c
128 aliud] illud $AMNOT^a$
143 aversamini] adversamini T^a Hib.

from the necessity in things, others from the power of those who perform them. [36] So we were not wrong in saying that these things are necessary in relation to divine knowledge, but, if they are considered in themselves, free from the bonds of necessity, just as everything which is apparent to the senses is universal if you relate it to reasoning, but particular if you consider the things in themselves.

[37] But, you will say, if it rests in my power to change my intention, I will make providence empty, when I will perhaps have changed things that it foreknows. [38] I shall reply that you can indeed divert your intention; but, since providence, being present, truly sees both that you can do this and whether you do so or where you direct it. So you cannot avoid divine foreknowledge, just as you cannot escape the gaze of a present eye, although you direct yourself to different actions by free will.

[39] What, then, you will say, will divine knowledge be changed by my arranging, so that, when I wish now this and now that, it too seems to change its knowledge? [40] Certainly not. For the divine gaze overtakes everything that is going to be in the future and bends and summons it back to the present of its own proper knowing; and it does not change, as you think, by foreknowing in turn now this and now something else, but in one glance, remaining unchanged itself, it anticipates and embraces your changes. [41] This present grasping and seeing of all things God derives not from the outcome of the future events, but from his own proper simplicity. [42] This also resolves the point you made a little earlier, that it is unworthy if our future actions are said to be the cause of God's knowledge. [43] This power of knowledge, embracing all things in its present knowledge, has itself established a limit for all things, and owes nothing to things that come after it.

[44] Since these things are so, human freedom of choice remains unassailed, and it is not unjustly that the laws impose rewards and punishments for wills that are free from all necessity. [45] God remains unchanged above as an observer, foreknowing all things, and the always-present eternity of his vision concurs with the future quality of our actions, distributing rewards to the good and punishments to the bad. [46] Nor are hopes placed in God and prayers made to him in vain; if they are righteous they cannot be without effect. [47] So turn aside from vices, cultivate virtues, lift up your mind to righteous hopes, extend humble prayers on high. [48] A great necessity to be good is laid upon you, if you do not want to pretend otherwise, when you act before the eyes of a judge who sees all things.

COMMENTARY

Cicero, *On Fate*

On the probable amount of material lost before the start of the extant text see Introduction, §§4.1.3-4.

1 because it relates to character] The text as we have it opens with references to ethical philosophy and to logic. The Stoics, and Hellenistic philosophers in general, divided philosophy into three main parts, logic, physics and ethics; (cf. Diogenes Laertius 7.41 (= LS 26B) and Cicero *On the Orator* 1.68, *Academics* 1.19, *Lucullus* 116 (Eisenberger 158). If there was a reference to physics as well here, presumably it came in the missing section before our text starts. Philippson 1032 suggested that, as in the case of logic we have not only an explanation of the term but also a statement of the philosophical issue ("What force they have ...)", so in the case of ethics too the question of whether we possess free will or not was indicated before our text opens.

Our terms "ethical" and "moral" derive respectively from the Greek and Latin words, *êthos* and *mores*, for a person's character and mode of living; Aristotle's *Nicomachean Ethics* is not so much a study of what is *morally right* as of *what sort of person* one should be and how one should behave. Cicero here first paraphrases the sense of the Greek term *êthikos* in Latin and then coins the new Latin word *moralis*. See the Introduction, §1.3.

propositions, which the Greeks call *axiômata*] Literally the Greek term means "claims" about something; it was used by the Stoics to indicate assertions, whether positive or negative, as opposed to questions or commands (Diogenes Laertius 7.66 = SVF 2.186). The correspondence to the "propositions" of modern logic is not exact; see further LS vol.1 p.205, Mignucci [1985] 219-224, and below on §14. Cicero's Latin equivalent *enuntiatio* literally means "utterance" or "statement", and replaced an earlier use of *effatum;* on this see Johansen and Londey.

which the philosophers call "concerning possibles"] This title, for which Cicero does not attempt a Latin equivalent, also occurs in *Letters to his Friends (ad Fam.)* 9.4; see Introduction §1.1, note. The topic is given the same technical name by Alexander *In an. pr.* 183.34 = LS 38B; cf. Simplicius *In cat.* 195.31.

a matter of logic] Ramus and Kayser read the genitive, "(a part of) logical (philosophy)". "Which I call reason in speaking" must refer to the *whole* of logical philosophy, but the slight shift does not seem too awkward. In creating a Latin equivalent for "logic(al)" Cicero does not coin a new word, as he did with *moralis*, but takes the existing word *ratio* and specifies a particular sense of it; Stoic *logikê* included not only dialectic but rhetoric (Diogenes Laertius 7.41 = SVF 2.48 = LS 31), and the idea of thought as silent speech with oneself is widespread in Greek philosophy (e.g. Plato *Sophist* 263e; Sextus Empiricus *Adv. math.* 8.275 = SVF 2.223 = LS 53T). At *On Ends* 1.22 Cicero describes *logikê* as the part of philosophy concerned with inquiry and discussion *(quaerendi ac disserendi).* Cf. Introduction §1.3.

A chance occurrence prevented me] Cicero does not say in so many words what this occurrence was. He does however indicate in section 2 that he was preoccupied, in his conversations with Hirtius, with political rather than philosophical matters. See Introduction §§2.3-4.

my other books] Cicero is never averse to referring, in the course of one of his works, to others (see also below, §4); and indeed gives the exact titles, for those who might want to look the books up or order copies *(De natura deorum* and *De divinatione* here; *Tusculanae disputationes* in §4.)

so that each person should more easily recommend what seemed most acceptable] "Recommend" *(probare)* and "acceptable" *(probabile)* derive from the same root, which is the one regularly used by Cicero to render Carneades' key term *pithanon;* on this and its relation to English "probable" see LS vol.1 p.459, and on the general approach see Introduction §1.2.

2 my villa at Pozzuoli] just west of Naples, and between Naples and Baiae, in the area that was more favoured than any other as a summer resort and for leisure *(otium,* the word translated in a political context "tranquillity" at the end of this paragraph). Cf. for example Propertius 1.11.

Hirtius, who was consul-designate] Aulus Hirtius was an officer of Julius Caesar, who added the eighth book to Caesar's *Gallic War* and was probably the author of the *Alexandrian War* ascribed to Caesar. In 43, as consul, with his colleague Pansa he joined with Octavian in attacking Antony, who was besieging the conspirator Decimus Brutus at Modena, but although Antony was driven off Hirtius was killed in the battle.

in particular on a day] More literally "and we did this both on other occasions (understanding *fecimus;* so Bremi, cited by Hamelin 18) and on a certain day ...". "Both on other occasions and on a certain day" is an imitation of Greek constructions of the *allôs te kai* type, "both otherwise and ..." being a way of saying "especially".

3 I have not abandoned that enthusiasm for rhetoric] At *Tusc. Disp.* 2.9 Cicero describes himself as practising rhetorical declamation in the morning and philosophical discussion in the afternoon.

when you came to me] At *Letters to his Friends* 9.16.7 Cicero refers to Hirtius and Dolabella as his pupils in rhetoric but teachers in dining.

there is a great affinity between the orator and the type of philosophy which I follow] The relation between philosophy and oratory had been a matter of debate since Plato and Isocrates in the fourth century B.C. Cicero's belief that philosophy assists the orator, and that the separation between philosophy and oratory had been unfortunate, is set out especially in *On the Orator* 3.55ff.; see also *Tusculan Disputations* 2.9 and Douglas [1964] 154. In these passages too he stresses that the Academic philosophy is the most suitable for the orator, because it is advantageous for the orator to practise discussing both sides of a question.

4 your rhetoric] Hamelin suggested "the rhetoric of (your school)", i.e. following Academic principles; but that makes the sentence less forceful by anticipating the reference to Academic practice in its second part.

your discussions at Tusculum] That is, the *Tusculan Disputations,* written in the summer of 45 B.C. See above on §1. For the way in which the *Tusculans* follow Academic practice cf. *Tusc. Disp.* 1.8.

to propose something on which I can hear you] Clearly the discussion in the lacuna after §4 started with Hirtius proposing fate as the topic for discussion. But how far he went into detail, rather than simply stating the theme and leaving it for Cicero to develop, is open to question. See Introduction, §4.1.7.

which is going to be welcome to you] The subjunctive *sit* is generic.

as to a Roman, etc.] that is, to one who cannot be expected to be as subtle as the Greeks in these matters. "after a long interval" refers to Cicero's resumption of philosophical activity in 45 B.C.

in the same way as I read what you have written] We, the readers, are indeed about to read something Cicero has written rather than to hear a live discussion. The relation between philosophical argument and its exposition in written form had been an issue since Plato *(Phaedrus* 275-8), and will be particularly significant in the case of Boethius (see Introduction §11).

Let us sit down, then] The manuscripts lead in a more or less confused fashion straight from the end of section 4 into section 5 below; A and B note a lacuna. See Introduction, §§4.1.5-8.

Fragment 5: When Scipio was at home at Lavernium] Scipio Africanus the younger, the principal speaker in Cicero's *Republic.* Titus Pontius is also mentioned at *On Ends* 1.9 and *On Old Age* 33. The point of the anecdote, which Yon following the editor Christ rejected as irrelevant to our dialogue, is probably not that the fish *happened* to be brought to Scipio *by chance,* being rarely caught, but rather that the fish that was a dish for few men provides an analogy with what Cicero regards as a difficult branch of philosophy with restricted appeal (cf. Eisenberger 160 n.17). The fish in question (*Acipenser sturio:* D'Arcy Thompson, *A Glossary of Greek Fishes,* London 1947, 7-8) was not prized by the Romans for its roe in particular, and so we do not have as close an anticipation of Shakespeare's "caviar to the general" as might at first appear. Since Cicero is still developing the theme of the difficulty and obscurity of the subject, it seems likely that fragment 5 came near the start of Cicero's reply to Hirtius. (Philippson 1032 placed it rather in the lacuna before §1; but when our text opens it is the importance of the subject that is being emphasised rather than its difficulty.)

Fragment 1: Chrysippus ... gets entangled.] This text immediately follows Gellius' discussion of Chrysippus in *Attic Nights* 7.2.1-14 (below, Appendix (C)) and concludes Gellius' whole essay. Its most obvious affinity with what we have of Cicero's *On Fate* is with what is said about Chrysippus' position in §39. It could thus have come in the lacuna after §45, and is placed there by Eisenberger (167 and n.40) and Schröder 150-1, following Schmekel [1938] 271 and Philippson 1035f. However, it would be odd if Chrysippus' attempt to reconcile fate and freedom was not even hinted at until §39. Moreover, as Alan Griffiths points out to me, the remark in §7 about "returning to the snares of Chrysippus" could well be a reference back to the present passage.

Fragment 2: Fate is a reciprocal connection] This is Cicero's rendering of a Stoic definition, as can be shown by comparison with the Stoic definitions in SVF 2.912-927, some of which are reproduced in LS 55J-M, and especially with that in Gellius *Attic Nights* 7.2 =SVF 2.1000 (see Appendix (C)). That it comes from our treatise is a matter of conjecture, but seems likely enough. Eisenberger 155 places this fragment in the lacuna before §1, arguing that Cicero would need to define his topic at the outset, as in *On Divination* 1.1, and that the attribution by Servius of the definition to Cicero himself, rather than to the Stoics, may reflect this. He also compares the attribution of a Stoic definition of fate to "the Greeks" in general, in *On Divination* 1.125, with the surviving reference to "they (the Greeks)" in §1 of our treatise. But I suspect the topic was introduced in simpler terms before §1 and that the present text belongs somewhere after §4. So Philippson, 1033.

Fragment 3: The minds of men are as the light] The position the Stoics are said to defend with this text is the one that Cicero is arguing against in §§7-11; since fragment 4 below is picked up in §5, and it is clear from §7 that Cicero stated the view of Chrysippus before that of Posidonius and then replied to them in reverse order in §§5-6 and 7-11 respectively, fragment 3 belongs in the present lacuna and before fragment 4. Cicero's translation does not really bring out the point of Homer's lines, which is that men's minds and attitudes vary with the *differing* fortunes (the kinds of "day") that Zeus brings to each one.

Fragment 4: Hippocrates, the most distinguished doctor] This text is not explicitly attributed to the treatise *On Fate,* and is included by Yon, Bayer and Giomini but not by Ax or Rackham. Cicero refers back to the example in §5, so if this fragment is part of the missing text it must come from the lacuna between §§4 and 5. Augustine goes on to argue that the medical explanation is the more plausible, as many more people than the one pair of twins would have been born in the same astrological conditions; he returns to the example in *City of God* 5.5. (Our text, and the following discussion by Augustine, form Posidonius F111 EK.) As EK vol.2 437 point out, if the reference to Hippocrates was to *Epidemics* 1.20, it was somewhat inaccurate; the two brothers there are not referred to as twins, but as older and younger, and the first crisis of their illnesses was on successive days, though the subsequent relapse and final crisis were on the same day.

The context in Augustine is part of a lengthy discussion of astrology, and especially of the problems raised for it by the different destinies of twins (*City of God* 5.1-7) which is followed by a discussion of fate as conceived by the Stoics (5.8), in which our fr.3 is cited, and then by a discussion of divine foreknowledge (5.9-10) in the course of which Cicero's *On Fate* is repeatedly alluded to, though not by name (cf. Introduction §6.2). This raises the question how far Augustine may have derived other material in the discussion of astrology in 5.1-7, as well as fragment 4, from the lost part of *On Fate;* it is clear that astrology had been discussed there (see below on §8). Augustine in 5.3 refers to Cicero's contemporary and associate, the Neo-Pythagorean Nigidius Figulus, who had supported Pompey against Caesar in the Civil War and died in exile in 45 B.C.; Hagendahl 529-30 suggests that this reference too comes from *On Fate.*

An argument against astrology from the different destinies of those born under the same sign was used by Carneades and appears in Sextus Empiricus *Adv. math.* 5.89 and in Favorinus cited by Gellius 14.1.26 (cf. Amand 51-3); and the Homeric text in our fragment 3 is cited not only by Augustine but also by Sextus, *Adv. math.* 5.4. These facts have led some to suppose not only that Augustine is dependent on Cicero but also that Cicero, Sextus and Gellius have a common source, Carneades himself being the obvious candidate (Schmekel [1892] 162-5 and 172-7; Yon xxxviii f.; Hagendahl 528-9 and 529 n.2).

However, these arguments are not conclusive. Sextus does not specifically mention *twins,* who form only one instance of those conceived under the same horoscope, and devotes much more space to the fact that many people born at *different* times may suffer the *same* fate (*Adv. math.* 5.90ff.; cf. Gellius 14.1.27, Amand 53-5). And Augustine may be developing his own argument rather than following a single source closely throughout. He certainly introduces non-classical examples, such as Jacob and Esau from *Genesis* at the start of 5.4; and his use of Cicero's *On Divination* and *On Fate* in 5.9 is a free one, developing his own view of the significance of the arguments and the issues involved (see Introduction §6). His citation of our fragment 3 is, as Eisenberger 164 n.31 points out, not in the context of astrology; and sitting and walking, cited as examples of what cannot be regarded as fated both in Augustine 5.3 and in

Cicero *On Fate* §9 (Yon xxxviii n.5), are commonplaces (Aristotle *On Generation and Corruption* 2.11 337b7; [Plutarch] *On Fate* 571cd; Alexander of Aphrodisias *On Fate* 9 175.22ff.; Nemesius *On the Nature of Man* 34 p.104.4 Morani; cf. also the Stoics reported by Nemesius in SVF 2.991, Ammonius *On* On Interpretation 142.5, and below on Boethius *Consolation* V.6.22ff.). Moreover, what Augustine actually cites Cicero for in Fragment 4 is the use of the example of twins to support belief in divination in general and astrology in particular. If the arguments *against* astrology in Augustine come from the lost part of Cicero's *On Fate*, we would have to suppose that Cicero both cited the example *and* criticised it at length in the lacuna before §5, and then returned to it and criticised it along with other non-astrological examples in §5 below.

Yon, Bayer and Giomini print a sixth fragment; the grammarian Nonius (p.35) cites "Cicero in *On Fate* and in *On Ends (De finibus bonorum et malorum)* book 4" for *praestringere* in the sentence "you *dazzle* the eyes of our minds with the brightness of your virtue." But this actually occurs in *De finibus* 4.37, and Lindsay was surely right to suppose that *De Fato et* was an incorrect doublet arising from the abbreviation *De fi(nibus) bo(norum) et.*

5 In some of these cases] When the MSS text resumes, Cicero is arguing against the Stoic Posidonius (c.135-51 B.C.), who had apparently given various examples of the supposed influence of fate. (§§5-6 are Posidonius F104 EK.) One of the examples had already been stated more fully in the lacuna (see above on fr.4), and another seems to have been (see below on "that shipwrecked sailor without a name"); it is probable that they all were.

In the first group of cases Cicero is prepared to allow some connection in terms of natural causes, but denies that this has to be interpreted in terms of *fate*. Antipater of Sidon the poet suffered fever yearly on his birthday, and eventually died on his birthday (Valerius Maximus 1.8.ext.16; cf. Pliny *Nat. Hist.* 7.172). To be born on the shortest day had special astrological significance (EK vol.2 p.419). For the twins falling ill on the same day see fragment 4 above. For urine in medical diagnosis cf. Hippocrates, *Epidemics* 1.23, Pliny *Natural History* 28.68-9, and Celsus *On Medicine* 2.7 p.40.21-41.7 Daremberg; for growth of fingernails as a symptom of phthisis Aristotle, *History of Animals* 3.2 518b23 (Hamelin, 20). Turnebus ap. Bayer 124 cites Celsus *On Medicine* 2.6 (p.36.6-7 Daremberg) for pallor in fingernails as a sign of impending death; hooked fingernails are a sign of suppuration, ibid. 2.7 p.44.9.

natural connection] The Stoic doctrine of *sumpatheia*, emphasised by Posidonius but not unique to him (cf. Introduction §3.1.6, and Duhot 117ff.). The MSS, here and in §7, have *contagio*, "contact"; Luck proposed *cognatio*, "common origin". *cognatio* and *contagio* are both apparently used by Cicero in *On Divination* 2.33-4 = EK F106 (though Plasberg saw signs that *contagio* was an emendation of *cognatio* in one MS). *contagio* appears at *On Divination* 2.92; *cognatio* at 1.64, 2.142, *On the Nature of the Gods* 3.28.

In others, however] In the second group of cases, Posidonius seems to have pointed to instances where a prophecy was fulfilled in an unexpected way. This is a common motif in ancient literature: cf. Fontenrose 58-62 (who entitles his discussion "The Jerusalem Chamber" after the example of the type in Shakespeare, *Henry IV part 2,* IV.5.231-9. I am grateful to my colleague Alan Griffiths for drawing my attention to this discussion). A famous ancient example is Cambyses' death at Ecbatana - but an obscure Ecbatana in Syria, not Ecbatana in Media (Herodotus 3.64.3-5). Cicero attacks the idea that such happenings should be taken as fulfilling the prophecies at all.

if the master will excuse my saying it] The reference to Posidonius as "Master" probably reflects his having taught Cicero in Rhodes in 78 B.C. (*On the Nature of the Gods* 1.6); EK vol. 2 pp.23-4.

beside the point] That this is the sense of *absurdus* is pointed out by Hamelin 21; so Yon *(hors de propos)*.

if Daphitas was fated to fall from a horse] Daphitas teased the oracle at Delphi by asking if he would find his horse when he did not in fact possess one; the oracle replied that he would die by being thrown from a horse, and King Attalus of Pergamum, whom he had angered earlier, had him thrown from a rock called the Horse (Valerius Maximus 1.8.ext.8; Hesychius of Miletus, *On Famous Men* 16, p.14.2ff. Flach; Suda s.v. Daphidas, vol.2 p.11.2ff. Adler; Q239 in Fontenrose, p.346. Valerius gives the name as Daphnites [corr. Kempf; Daphanites MSS]; Hesychius and the Suda as Daphidas.)

or was it these little four-horse chariots] Philip of Macedon, the father of Alexander the Great, was warned to beware of four-horse chariots, and was either killed at a place in Boeotia called Harma, the Chariot, or killed with a sword with a chariot engraved on the hilt (Aelian *Miscellaneous History* 3.45, saying that the second version, as here, was the more common one; Valerius Maximus 1.8.ext.9 conflates the two stories, saying that Philip avoided the place but was killed by the sword. Fontenrose Q214, p.338). In a rather feeble piece of sarcasm Cicero points out that Philip was not killed by the *hilt*.

that shipwrecked sailor without a name] Presumably the sailor suffered shipwreck but survived, and then consulted the oracle and was warned that he would die in water; he gave up seafaring as a result of the warning, but could not escape his fate. The use of *illum,* and the obscurity of the story as narrated here, suggest that it had been told more fully in the missing part of the work before §5, Cicero is again being sarcastic (EK vol. 2 p.419) – if Posidonius is going to use stories like this, he should at least know the name of the person involved.

in the case of the pirate Icadius] For whom cf. Festus, *On the meaning of Words* p.94.7 and 322.26 Lindsay. The point could be that it was surprising for a pirate to die through a rock-fall rather than by drowning (so Turnebus and Yon) – though one would have thought that hiding in caves with consequent dangers from rock-falls was an occupational hazard for a pirate. In all these cases Cicero's reply is that the events could have come about through chance or natural causes, and thus provide no evidence for the influence of fate.

7 But let us dismiss Posidonius on friendly terms ... and return to the snares of Chrysippus] *cum bona gratia* is a technical term in Roman law for the settlement of a dispute (Hamelin, 21). Chrysippus' arguments were presumably stated before those of Posidonius, in the lacuna before §5. They turn on the influence of climate and other natural causes upon human character; Cicero replies that it is one thing to say that these factors influence our behaviour, another to say that they determine it in every detail. For the "snares" of Stoic arguments – i.e. fine-meshed complexities from which it is difficult to escape even though one is convinced the Stoic position is wrong – *Tusculan Disputations* 5.76 and *On the Orator* 1.43; also fr.1 above, and more generally the complaints about Stoic arguments of Alexander of Aphrodisias, *On Fate* 36 208.12, 38 212.1.

The influence of locality and climate upon health and character had often been stressed, notably in the Hippocratic treatise *Airs Waters Places*. Cf. also Cicero *On the Nature of the Gods* 2.17, 2.42, and *On Divination* 1.79 with Pease's note. The healthy climate of Athens is noted at Plato, *Timaeus* 24c.

the connection among things] see above on §5.

The Thebans are stupid but strong] There is a double word-play here; not only does *crassus* mean "dense" both literally and in intelligence, but *pinguis*, here rendered "stupid", also means "rich", "thick", "fertile" (of soil) and "sturdy or strong" of people; the strength and the "thickness" of the Thebans go together. Given the reference to the Nemean and Isthmian games in the next sentence, one may see here a reflection of the hostility between mind and muscle, especially with regard to athletics, that goes back at least to Xenophanes, fr.2 Diehl. For the proverbial slow-wittedness of the Boeotians (as in Offenbach's *Orpheus in the Underworld*) cf. Horace, *Epistles* 2.1.244, and Strabo 2.3.7 p.103 (= Posidonius F49 lines 322ff. EK; cf. EK vol.2 p.267).

Zeno or Arcesilaus or Theophrastus] Zeno of Citium (335-263), the founder of the Stoic school; Arcesilaus (316/5-242/1), the seventh head of Plato's Academy and the first to embrace Scepticism; Theophrastus (c.370-288/5), the associate and successor of Aristotle. The philosophers cited represent three of the four main philosophical schools, with the exception of the Epicureans.

at Nemea rather than at the Isthmus] The Latin literally means *from* Nemea, a victory being *brought back* from the place of the contest; but that is not natural English idiom. Games are presumably as appropriate to strong and slow-witted Thebans as philosophy is to Athenians.

8 the nature of the place] Pompey's portico and the Campus Martius are hardly far enough apart for the difference in their nature to have any effect (Hamelin, 8). This might be intended precisely as a *reductio ad absurdum*. If not, the reference might be to the nature of Rome in general; Yon translates "the climate".

in Pompey's portico ... on the Ides] Julius Caesar was assassinated in Pompey's adjacent theatre on the Ides of March; Bayer 127 suggests that there may be an allusion here to Caesar's fate, but if so it may be very much in passing (cf. Introduction §4.1.7). It is not clear from the text whether we are dealing with three separate sets of alternatives or with one complex one; if the latter, and if there was some significance in Cicero's walking with Hirtius in Pompey's portico on the Ides of March, we cannot now tell what it was.

the position of the stars] This comes in rather abruptly here; it must have been mentioned in the earlier statement of Chrysippus' position. *adfectio* was a technical term in astrology for the position of the stars in relation to one another; it does not itself refer to the "influence" of the stars on men, though that is indeed implied in the context. See Cicero *On Divination* 2.98-9, especially 2.98, *quo modo caelo adfecto compositisque sideribus quodque animal oriatur;* also Eisenberger, 163 n.25, and the *Oxford Latin Dictionary* s.v., 6.

may have power over some things] Unlike omens from the livers of sacrificial animals for example (see Introduction §3.1.6), the connection between the stars and terrestrial events is not just a matter of "sympathy" but of actual causal influence – a point which will be important in the interpretation of §§15-16. Cf., with Sedley [1993] to whom I owe this point, Cicero *On Divination* 2.89, Manilius 4.105, and fr.4 above.

9 what the issue amounts to] The Latin could also be rendered "in what a cause consists"; Sedley [1993] suggests a deliberate pun.

defined and decided by primary causes] It is not ruled out that natural causes may have *some* bearing on our decisions and actions. On the meaning of "primary" see further below, on §41, and the Excursus at the end of this commentary. The present passage might suggest, as Sedley [1993] points out, that Chrysippus held that environmental factors *were* among the *primary* causes not only of our characters but also (through them) of our decisions and actions. However, Cicero (or his source) could be providing his own formulation, borrowing Stoic language, of the position he rejects. Cf. Duhot 193-4.

10 Stilpo the Megarian philosopher] c.380-300 B.C. Our text is no.158 in K. Döring, *Die Megariker*, Amsterdam 1972, who discusses it in relation to the other evidence for Stilpo's life and character (Döring p.143).

Socrates was stigmatized by Zopyrus the physiognomist] The same anecdote appears at *Tusculan Disputations* 4.80, Alexander of Aphrodisias *On Fate* 6, and elsewhere. It may have originated in a fourth-century Socratic dialogue by Phaedo of Elis, the associate of Socrates after whom Plato's *Phaedo* is named, and have originally been intended to encourage people to take up philosophy by showing how it would enable them to overcome faults of character; its use in anti-determinist polemic would then be secondary, perhaps due to Carneades. See P.R. Foerster, *Scriptores Physiognomici Graeci*, Leipzig, Teubner, 1893, I viixiii, and L. Rosetti, 'Ricerche sui "Dialoghi Socratici" di Fedone e di Euclide', *Hermes* 108 (1980) 183-99.

Alcibiades burst out laughing] Alcibiades attempted to seduce Socrates (Plato, *Symposium* 217-219); he failed because Socrates, as represented by Plato in that dialogue and elsewhere, regarded the physical expression of love as characterising inferior forms of passion (cf. *Phaedrus* 256).

11 if the explanation of divination is going to confirm the natural existence of fate] The reference to divination seems to come in oddly here, though it is essential for the transition to Cicero's next topic. But the "natural connection" mentioned at the start of this discussion was used by the Stoics to explain divination (see Introduction §3.1.6), and the topic may have been mentioned in the lacuna before §5 (Bayer, 130; Eisenberger 163-4).

Indeed, if divination exists, from what skilled observations] The predictions of diviners are based, according to the Stoics, on correlations between events, so that the observation of one justifies the prediction of another; see Introduction §3.1.6. This must have been expounded in the missing part of the text before §5 (Eisenberger 163-4). Cicero's intention is to force Chrysippus to accept that, once the sign has occurred, the outcome is necessary and the alternative impossible; which conflicts with Chrysippus' position on possibility (below, §13).

skilled observations] literally "observations of the art". Here and in §15 *praecepta* "precepts" appears as a variant, but *percepta* "observations" is better attested, and is the translation of the Greek *theorêmata*. For the explanation of art or skill in terms of *theoremata* cf. Sextus *Outlines of Pyrrhonism* 3.269, and for art as based on observations *(katalêpseis/perceptiones)* SVF 1.73, 2.93-4, Cicero *On the Nature of the Gods* 2.148 and *Lucullus* 22. Cf. LS vol.1 263-6.

12 with the Dogstar rising] i.e. at the heliacal rising of Sirius, the first point at which, as it rises earlier and earlier on successive days, it can be seen above the horizon before hidden by daylight at dawn. In the latitude of Athens in 43 B.C. this would be on the 29th of July; E.J. Bickerman, *Chronology of the Ancient World*, London ²1980, 54.

the powerful dialectician Diodorus] Diodorus Cronus; see Introduction §3.2.4. He has in the past been described as a member of the Megarian school of philosophy, but Sedley [1977] 75-6 has argued that he should rather be classified with the Dialectical school. Hamelin 99 points out that the example of dying at sea turns up in discussions of Diodorus' position also at Plutarch *On Stoic Self-Contradictions* 46 1055e and Boethius *On On Interpretation*[2] 235.12; it is likely that it early became part of the topic.

For if the conditional] The Stoics divided statements into definite, intermediate and indefinite (Diogenes Laertius 7.70 = SVF 2.204 = LS 34K; cf. Sextus Empiricus *Adv. math.* 8.96-8, 100 = SVF 2.205 = LS 34H,I, with LS vol.1 p.205 n.1). Indefinite propositions are those with an indefinite subject, like "anyone" here; definite are those with a demonstrative pronoun as subject, such as "this man"; intermediate are those where the subject is referred to by a proper name, such as Fabius. An indefinite proposition is true only if a corresponding definite one is (Sextus *Adv. math.* 8.98; Hamelin 98). "Fabius" is the Latin equivalent of John Smith or John Doe where just a sample name is required (cf., with Turnebus, Cicero *Topics* 14).

So these things are incompatible] Sextus Empiricus, *Outlines of Pyrrhonism* 2.110-113 (= LS 35B) lists four different views on what is required for a conditional sentence to be true. The third, which is probably that of Chrysippus, is that a conditional is true if the contradictory of its consequent is incompatible with its antecedent. So, here, Fabius' being born with the Dogstar rising and Fabius' dying at sea are incompatible - which means that, if one is true, the other *cannot* be.

since it is supposed as certain in the case of Fabius] Once Fabius has been born, the astrological context of his birth is fixed. The very fact that he exists, having come to be in the way he has, is thus incompatible with his dying at sea. But one might ask why Cicero introduces the fact of Fabius' existing *now;* his having been born when he was would seem sufficient for the argument. LS vol.2 p. 235 criticise this argument as "garbled" and as introducing "essentialist" ideas which do not occur elsewhere in ancient thought, supposing that it is an essential part of Fabius' existing that he be born at a particular time.

Put forward in this way, this cannot (actually) happen] or "this cannot happen in the way supposed". The point may be that, while both propositions are possible in themselves, the supposition that one is actually true excludes the possibility of the other (see Introduction §3.2.4, and Yon 34-5).

Therefore everything which is said to be false in the future] That is, as the argument requires, everything which a diviner correctly predicts will not happen - which might have been a clearer way of putting it.

13 But this, Chrysippus, is what you least want] Although Chrysippus held that everything that happened was predetermined by fate, he nevertheless maintained that not everything that was going to happen in the future was necessary, and that some things were possible even though they were not in fact going to happen. See Introduction §3.2.6.

For he says that only what either is true or will be true can happen] Diodorus supported this view by the Master Argument; see Introduction §3.2.4.

for example that this precious stone should be broken] That is, Chrysippus says that it is *possible* for this stone to be broken even if it never will be: *posse dicis* must be understood again with *frangi.* A precious stone hardly seems a natural example for what is breakable even if only in principle; but *gemma* can be applied to cups and other objects made of semi-precious stone.

and that it was not necessary for Cypselus to rule in Corinth] Cypselus became tyrant of Corinth in the seventh century B.C.; as Alan Griffiths points out to me, the fact that he did not inherit his position but gained it unexpectedly (as far as human judgement, as opposed to oracles, could tell) gives the example added point. See Herodotus, 5.92ε. LS vol.1 pp.229 and 234 point out that a number of ancient logical paradoxes have titles which relate both to the nature of the argument and to the example used - for instance, the *Horned* Argument was a *dilemma* about whether one has lost horns or still has them, on the same basis as the question "Have you stopped beating your wife?" - and suggest that the *Master* or "Ruling" Argument originally had someone's *ruling* as its central example. See also Sedley [1977] 115 n.132. The tense of "it *was* not necessary for Cypselus to rule in Corinth" is important; now that Cypselus *has* ruled, Chrysippus accepts that it is necessary that he ruled (cf. Introduction § 3.2.5), but that is not the same as asserting that it *was* necessary (before the event) that he *rule* (Bayer, 133).

a thousand years before] Not according to Herodotus; Turnebus suggests that Cicero speaks loosely.

you will have statements of falsity about the future in (such cases)] What Cicero means is that, if an oracle predicts that something will not happen, it will be possible to say truly beforehand that it will not happen, i.e. it will be possible to say truly that it is false that it will happen. But the consideration of *negative* predictions has made his expression unclear. See above on §13 ad fin. Cicero is in effect allowing that for Chrysippus, though not for Diodorus or himself, the existence of false (or true) statements about such future events depends on the acceptance of divination; he does not himself think this (see below, §§17ff.), but Chrysippus does (§§20ff.). (The Latin here might be taken to mean "you will have false statements about the future in those predictions", but that suggests that the oracles themselves make the false predictions, and while ancient oracles might equivocate they did not lie. Yon and Rackham take *iis* rather as referring forward to *ea* - "you will reckon false statements as to future events as being *in the class* of things impossible".)

with the result that it will be impossible for those things to happen] Why? Not just because it is claimed that the truth of a prediction in itself renders the event necessary; that is a claim that Cicero will in a sense accept from Diodorus, while insisting that it has nothing to do with *causal* determinism (below, §§17ff.) Rather, as the preceding argument shows, what renders Chrysippus liable to this conclusion in a *damaging* sense is his commitment to divination, and to the causal determinism which underlies the correlations of portents and what they signify. See further below.

for example if it were said that Scipio will not capture Carthage] He did, of course, in 146 B.C.; the "not" apparently dropped out of the MSS, being written as an abbreviation which was misunderstood, and the editor Christ therefore deleted the clause. Yon follows him, regarding it as a gloss.

you would have to say that it is necessary] Cicero assumes that "not possibly not" amounts to "necessary" (and thus "impossible" to "necessarily not", and "not necessarily not" to "possibly"). (Mignucci [1978] has argued that Chrysippus did not accept these implications; but it is not clear that this is right. Cf. Sorabji [1980,1] 265, and [1980,2] 73; White 110-12).

14 For if this is a true conditional] What follows is essentially a statement of Diodorus' Master Argument; but, as the preceding context shows, its use by Cicero rests upon Chrysippus' commitment to divination. Cf. Introduction §§3.2.4-5 and White 86-90.

in the view of Chrysippus who disagrees with his teacher Cleanthes] see Introduction §3.2.5.

Chrysippus does not think this applies in every case] Chrysippus made *two* moves against the imputation of necessity to everything that happens and impossibility to everything that does not. (A) He rejected the second proposition of the Master Argument and claimed that what is impossible can follow from what is possible (Epictetus, *Diss.* 2.19.3 and 5 = LS 38A; above, Introduction §3.2.6); that is, the antecedent of a true conditional may be possible and the consequent nevertheless impossible. (B) He argued that in certain cases a conditional was not the appropriate formulation at all (§§15ff. below). Here Cicero is clearly alluding to (A); for to deny, as Chrysippus is said to here, that

(i) what follows from what is necessary must itself be necessary

is logically equivalent to claiming that

(ii) what is impossible can follow from what is possible

(if q follows from p, not-p follows from not-q; if p is necessary and q is not, not-q is possible but not-p is impossible).

Chrysippus based his argument for (A) on the example "if Dion is dead, this (man) is dead", arguing that while "Dion is dead" may be true, "this (man) is dead" *cannot* be, because a corpse cannot be referred to as "this man" (SVF 2.202a = LS 38F). It might be supposed that this simply shows that the conditional is false, but Chrysippus claimed that the proposition "this man is dead" simply ceases to exist when the man dies, because "this man" no longer refers to anything, and that the conditional "if Dion is dead, this man is dead" is thus not *falsified* by Dion's death, for the consequent is then not false but nonexistent. Cf. White 107-115.

but nevertheless, if there is a cause in nature for Fabius not dying at sea] This could at first glance be taken to imply that Chrysippus' rejection of the second proposition in the Master Argument, outlined in the preceding note, applied only to cases where there was no natural cause. But this is probably misleading; it is rather the *second* move (B), discussed in §§15-16, which turns on the presence or absence of a natural cause, and there it is a matter not of (A) denying that what follows from what is necessary is itself necessary, but rather of (B) denying that the relation is one of *following* at all.

15 Chrysippus hopes that the astrologers ... can be foiled] The Latin could mean either "he hopes that their predictions are sometimes mistaken" or "he hopes that he can escape the consequences for his own position of the truth of their predictions". Both make good sense; the double meaning may be intentional.

that they will not make use of conditionals but rather of conjunctions] Chrysippus, according to Cicero, thinks that the unpalatable consequences for his own position can be avoided if astrological observations are stated not in the form of conditionals, "if p then q", but in the form of negated conjunctions, "not both p and not q". The criterion for the truth of a conditional that was probably Chrysippus' (see above, on §12) amounts to saying that "if p, then q" is true if not-q and p are *incompatible; that is, "not possibly both* p and not-q", as opposed to the simple negated conjunction "*not both* p and not-q". And that suggests that the difference turns on the question of modality; conditionals should in Chrysippus' view be reserved for correlations that *cannot* happen as opposed to those that just *don't* happen. The question is, what is the sense of "cannot" here? Donini [1973] 34ff. suggests that conditionals are used for all

169

causal relations, the negated conjunction being reserved for empirically observed correlations. Sambursky [1959] 78f. argued rather that conditionals were reserved for cases where there is a logical or conceptual connection; however, ancient thinkers did not distinguish between logical and other necessities or impossibilities as sharply as is common in modern philosophy (cf. R. Sorabji, 'On Aristotle and Oxford Philosophy', *American Philosophical Quarterly* 6 (1969) 127-135, and Sorabji [1980,2] 75; White 103-4, 260, and on some difficulties for the modern view e.g. M. Smithurst, 'Hume on Existence and Possibility', *Proc. Aristotelian Soc.* n.s. 81 [1980-81] 17-37). And this makes more plausible the intermediate position of Sedley, that conditionals were used by Chrysippus for connections derived *from the nature of the things involved,* whether the necessity is logical or causal in our terms, and negated conjunctions in cases where a correlation is asserted on the basis of observation rather than of an analysis of the nature of the things involved, and is thus convincing *(pithanon)* rather than certain, whether it is in fact a case of direct causal connection or not. (Sedley [1982] 253-5: cf. id. 'The negated conjunction in Stoicism', *Elenchos* 5 (1984) 311-316.)

Cicero mentions three cases, from astrology, medicine and geometry, suggesting that Chrysippus should advocate the negated conjunction in all of them. Unfortunately it is not clear that Cicero is here concerned to report Chrysippus' *actual* views on when one formulation or the other is appropriate; he did after all argue throughout §§12-14 as if Chrysippus *allowed* the conditional in the astrological case. The geometrical example of circles on a sphere certainly seems to involve a logical type of necessity in the narrower modern sense. In the case of a person's pulse and his having fever, the causal relation, if there is a direct one at all, is in the reverse direction, not from pulse to fever but from fever to pulse. The astrological example might seem to be one where there is simply an observed correlation; but see above on §8.

Even if a sign does not cause what it foretells but is simply related to it as another part of the universal causal nexus, that does not alter the fact that in Chrysippus' view the outcome is causally predetermined, even if not predetermined *by the sign;* indeed this is why Chrysippus used divination as an argument for determinism in the first place (Introduction, §3.1.6). So nothing is achieved against determinism by Chrysippus' argument; but it may be his critics, rather than Chrysippus himself, who have that as their chief preoccupation.

The issues dealt with in this note have been extensively discussed; in addition to the works already cited cf. M. Frede, 'Stoic versus Aristotelian Syllogistic', *Archiv für Geschichte der Philosophie* 56 (1974) 1-32, at 25 = his *Essays in Ancient Philosophy,* Minneapolis 1987, 99-124, at 118, and id. [1980] 246-8; I. Mueller, 'An Introduction to Stoic Logic', in J.M. Rist, ed., *The Stoics,* Berkeley 1978, 1-26, at 18ff., 24f.; J. Moreau, 'Immutabilité du vrai, necessité logique et lien causal', in *Les Stoïciens et leur logique, Actes du colloque de Chantilly,* Paris 1978, 347-360, at 355f.; F. Caujolle-Zaslawsky, 'Le style stoïcien et la "paremphasis"', ibid. 425-448, at 432-4; Mignucci [1978]; Sorabji [1980,2] 74-8; Barnes [1982] 28-9, and id. [1985,2]; White 106; LS vol.1 236 and 265. *coniunctionibus* of the MSS might seem a plausible rendering of *sunêmmenon,* the Stoic term for a conditional, "if p then q" (so Turnebus); but in §12 Cicero has used *conectitur* for a conditional and *coniunctio* for a conjunction in our sense of the term, "both p and q". In §14 he uses *conexum* for a conditional, and later in §15 *conexa* for "conditionals" and *coniunctiones* for "conjunctions". Hence the emendations of Madvig, Plasberg and Szymánski. Against Madvig, Yon p.34 points out that *conexio,* as opposed to *conexum,* is not found elsewhere in Cicero; Szymánski's emendation makes the corruption easier to understand, *conexis sed coniunctionibus* having first been miscopied through the scribe's eye having jumped from one word to the other, and the following *non* then omitted in an attempt to restore consistency to the text. The alternative to emendation is to suppose that Cicero has been careless. (Gercke, *Chrysippea* fr.85, defends the transmitted text by suggesting that *coniunctio* is a generic term covering both conditionals and conjunctions, *conexum* the specific term for conditionals; this has been accepted by Ax, Giomini and Mignucci.)

fall into Diodorus' position] For this use of *incidere* cf. Cicero *On Ends* 4.78 (I owe this point to David Sedley). On Diodorus see Introduction §3.2.4.

indefinite conjunctions ... indefinite conditionals] See above on §12.

If anyone's pulse is like this] Literally, "if anyone's veins move in this way". The systematic study of the pulse as an aid to medical diagnosis was begun by Praxagoras and Herophilus, in the later fourth and earlier third centuries B.C. respectively. The failure to distinguish between veins and arteries is characteristic in antiquity, as Turnebus pointed out.

Greatest circles on a sphere bisect one another] Take any two of the largest circles that can be drawn on a sphere (for example, on the earth, the equator or the meridian circle, but not the tropics of Cancer or Capricorn or any other circle of latitude apart from the equator; what are still called "great circles"). They will intersect each other at two diametrically opposed points, and thus each will divide the circumference of the other in half.

it is not the case both that there are greatest circles on a sphere] "It is not the case that certain circles on a sphere are greatest and that these do not bisect one another" would be closer to the preceding astrological and medical examples, and so too with "If there are greatest circles on a sphere" and "Because there are greatest circles on a sphere" in §16 below; but it is harder to extract this from the Latin.

16 it is a bigger undertaking to learn these contorted expressions] The Stoics are often criticised for their cramped and "thorny" style of expression; cf. e.g. Cicero *Lucullus* 112.

17 let us return to that argument of Diodorus] Cicero has already in the preceding sections been arguing that Chrysippus as a determinist is compelled to accept Diodorus' equation of the necessary and the actual. In §§17-20 he himself accepts this in a sense, allowing that the truth of a prediction *necessarily* involves the occurrence of the event predicted, while emphasising that this sort of necessity (for which see below on Boethius, *Consolation* book 5 prose 6 §25) has no deterministic implications *in itself* for one who is not – as Chrysippus was – *already* and *independently* committed to causal determinism.

things that will be can no more be turned from true to false] This is not a claim that we cannot affect the future; rather, Cicero is making the point, in a context which has now left causal determinism aside, that *che sarà, sarà: if* something is going to happen, then it is certainly going to happen. But whether it is going to happen or not may depend on human choices or on chance; so the fact that it is going to happen does not mean that it is *predetermined* now that it will.

if this same thing is said truly ... it will happen none the less.] The claim is *not* that it will happen because it is said truly; rather, the prediction is true because the event will occur. The truth of the prediction and the occurrence of the event each imply the other, but the direction of causation is from the occurrence of the event to the truth of the prediction, and not vice versa. Aristotle himself had pointed out, though not in the context of future contingents, that the truth of a statement depends on the occurrence of the event, not vice versa; *Metaphysics* Θ 10 1051b6ff., *Categories* 12 14b14. What is less clear is whether we are to suppose that the man's death is already predetermined, though not obviously so, or whether both possibilities, death and recovery, are still open. "The power of the illness is not yet evident" might suggest that it is already in fact inevitable that the man will die of the disease; but §19 below indicates that there are occurrences which are not predetermined at all.

a human being, who must necessarily die] The one certainty in human life, used similarly as an example of a necessary, rather than contingent future event by Aristotle, *Metaphysics* E3 1027b9. Donini [1989] 134–5 n.33 argues that the example is an obvious one and that it is not evidence for knowledge of *Metaphysics* E3 by Carneades, which would be incompatible with his being the source of §39 below, where Aristotle is classified as a determinist. Sorabji [1980,2] 110 suggests that the passage may show knowledge of the Aristotle passage on the part of *Diodorus*. Cf. also Cicero *Topics* 62.

18 Scipio will die at night in his bedroom from a violent attack] Scipio Africanus the Younger was found dead in bed in 129 B.C., and it was thought that he had been poisoned. It may be that he died of natural causes but his death was exploited for political purposes (see I. Worthington, 'The death of Scipio Aemilianus', *Hermes* 117 [1989] 125–6). Cicero appears to accept the assassination theory also in book 6 of his *Republic* and at *On Friendship* 41; elsewhere Cicero refers to the suspicion of assassination without himself taking a position one way or the other (*On the Orator* 2.170, *Letters to his Friends* 9.21.3 and *Letters to his brother Quintus* 2.3.3).

nor was it more necessary for Scipio to die than for him to die in that way] Scipio's dying in one way or another was inevitable; *how* he died was not predetermined. Cicero is insisting with Diodorus that "what happens, necessarily happens", in a sense of "necessarily" that carries no causally deterministic implications (see above); and from *that* point of view there is no distinction to be drawn between Scipio's dying and his dying in a particular way. (So Yon, 10 n.1.) *magis* "more" is Ramus' emendation for *minus* "less" of the MSS, which seems to give little sense.

neither … is there any reason for Epicurus to tremble before fate] Cicero alludes to *one* of the two aspects he, following Carneades, objects to in Epicurus' position, the introduction of the atomic swerve as a way of denying determinism (see Introduction, §3.1.4), and makes two points against this before moving on to the second, and more immediately relevant point, Epicurus' denial of the truth of future contingents (§§19–20; Introduction §3.2.2). He then returns to the atomic swerve at §22. The implication that misunderstandings over the truth of future contingents were the factor that prompted Epicurus to introduce the swerve is a misleading piece of rhetoric; Epicurus saw the inexorable succession of atomic movements, each caused by its predecessor, as in itself a threat to freedom (see §23 below), and showing that the truth of statements about the future does not in itself imply determinism will not answer *that* anxiety.

that something should happen without a cause] This is how Cicero, at least, presents the atomic swerve throughout. See further below on §§22-3.

that something comes from nothing] Cicero is right in that Greek philosophers, and the Atomists in particular, had generally rejected this possibility; see below on Boethius V.1.9. But the atomic swerve - on the interpretation adopted here - is an exception to the general rule and *is* a case of something "coming from nothing" in the sense of happening without a cause.

two indivisible (bodies)] i.e. atoms. Cicero uses the Greek term in §22 below; at *On Ends* 1.17 he uses and explains the Greek term.

in a straight line] *e regione* often has this sense; cf. below §47, *On Ends* 1.19, and Lucretius 6.823.

19 It is possible for Epicurus to grant that every statement is either true or false] Epicurus, like the Stoics and unlike Carneades, accepted that a future-tense statement could only be true or false if the event were already predetermined, and therefore asserted, to Cicero's indignation, that some future-tense statements were neither true nor false. See Introduction, §3.2.2, and below on §38.

there is a difference between causes that precede by chance and those that contain within themselves a natural effectiveness] This is one of the two key points in the Carneadean answer to the Stoic dilemma of determinism or uncaused motion, the other being the claim that free human action has its cause in the nature of voluntary action itself (below, §25, and Introduction, §3.1.8). But the question arises whether a "cause that precedes by chance" is really a cause or explanation at all. To take the Aristotelian example *(Metaph.* Δ 30 1025a5ff.), my digging in a particular place in order to plant a tree may be the chance cause of my finding buried treasure, but it is certainly not a sufficient cause or explanation, and a coincidence may as such have *no* explanation (there may be good reasons explaining why each of five airliners crashed on a given day, but that does not necessarily mean that there is any reason beyond sheer coincidence, why they all, for different reasons, crashed on the *same* day. Sorabji [1980,2] 10-13; criticised by Fine). Nor is it clear that examples of chance like this are in any way incompatible with determinism as such; it could be entirely predetermined that one man would bury the treasure in a given place, and the other dig there in order to plant, without there being any further reason for the coincidence. See also below on Boethius, *Consolation* V.1.

Carneades is going down into the Academy] As Donini [1989] 135 points out, this is hardly natural as an example of *chance*, since Carneades was head of the Academy. His happening to go there at a particular time, or at the same time as someone else did, might provide more natural examples of chance events. See below on §28; also Talanga, 127-8. The tense of *descendit* could be taken as either present or perfect; either way it may serve (unless changed to the future with Lörcher) to emphasise that the truth of future-tense propositions has no more deterministic implications than that of present- or past-tense ones.

(Epicurus) will die when he has lived 72 years] He was born in Samos in 341 B.C. and died in Athens in 270 B.C. Cf. Diogenes Laertius 10.15.

20 rather, they are explaining the meaning of words] To say that a prediction is or was true is simply to say that it predicts or predicted what is or was going to happen, whether predetermined or not; and that is all. To some Carneades' ability to distinguish between linguistic and non-linguistic issues may seem a high-water-mark in ancient philosophy; to others it has seemed a mark of insensitivity to underlying metaphysical questions. See Introduction, §3.2.3 n.

those who introduce an eternal series of causes] The Stoic definition of fate; cf. fr.2 above and commentary there.

But enough of these matters; let us consider others] Cicero now moves on to the question of uncaused motion, and in particular to Epicurus' assertion of its existence in the form of the atomic swerve (see Introduction §§3.1.4-5). The discussion is still however being conducted in the context of the truth of future-tense statements, to which the question of causation has already been linked in §§18-20. There the emphasis was on the question of future truth as such; here it is on that of causation and in particular of human action.

Chrysippus argues to his conclusion as follows] The argument runs as follows:
(1) if there is uncaused movement, all propositions are not true or false. For
(2) if something is not caused, propositions about it will not be true or false before the event.
(3) But all propositions *are* true or false. So [from (2) and (3), by *modus tollens*],
(4) there is no uncaused movement. So
(5) all things that come about do so through antecedent causes, and so
(6) all things that come about do so through fate.

It is important that Chrysippus is *not* presented as arguing that the truth of a prediction *itself causally necessitates* the event; for the argument from (3) to (4) depends on (2), and to say that being caused is a *necessary condition* for future truth is not the same as to say that future truth itself causes the event. No reason is given for the assertion of (3), but the claim that all propositions are either true or false is one regularly made by the Stoics (Diogenes Laertius 7.65 = SVF 2.193 = LS 34A; cf. Gellius *Attic Nights* 16.8.8 = SVF 2.194, Cicero *Lucullus* 95 = SVF 2.196 = LS 37H(5), and SVF 2.195, 197-8; see further Johansen and Londey 325-7 and 331). The move from (4) to (5) and (6) depends on the assumption that whatever is caused must have antecedent causes of the type postulated by the Stoic doctrine of fate (cf. Introduction §3.1.3); it is this assumption that will be challenged in the following discussion. Duhot plausibly claims (196-7) that what we have here is not so much a verbatim report of Chrysippus as an Academic formulation of his position for the sake of criticism.

Every proposition (what the dialecticians call an *axiôma*)] See above on §1.

21 I would rather accept that blow] The Latin word rendered "blow", *plaga*, is the same used in §22 for the collisions of atoms. Whether this is deliberate word-play is uncertain; Yon argues that it is not (p.36).

The former opinion gives some scope for discussion, but the latter is intolerable] Cicero here contrasts the Stoic assertion of causal determinism not with Epicurus' denial of causal determinism but with the denial that all future-tense statements are either true or false. He is going to break the link between the issues of causal determinism and future truth, by arguing that one can still assert the truth or falsity of future-tense statements while denying causal determinism; but, for the present, feigned readiness to accept the aspect of the Epicurean position he has chiefly been arguing against, the denial of universal future truth, has the rhetorical effect of making his opposition to Stoic causal determinism all the more forceful. A similar tactic had already been used by Epicurus himself in *Letter to Menoeceus* 134: "it would be better to follow the story about the gods than to be a slave to the fate of the natural philosophers; for the former sketches out (some) hope of intercession with the gods by honouring them, but the latter involves inexorable necessity." And Augustine, *City of God* 5.9, in turn says that it would be better to accept astrological determinism than Cicero's denial of divine foreknowledge (Henry 40; cf. Introduction, §6.2).

Chrysippus strains every sinew in order to convince us that every proposition is either true or false] In fact Chrysippus has just been reported as taking this, (3), as the apparently self-evident basis *from which* he argued for universal causal determinism; Johansen and Londey, loc. cit. Cicero's presentation has been influenced by the rhetorical contrast with Epicurus' *denial* that all propo-

174

sitions are true or false, which *is* controversial.

22 a certain third movement arises, apart from weight and collision] For Epicurus, atoms are carried downwards in parallel lines by their own weight, but on this downward movement there are as it were superimposed the movements that result from the collisions and reboundings of atoms as a result of the swerve or swerves that produce collisions in the first place (cf. Lucretius, 2.216-250 = LS 11H).

by a very small distance (this he calls a "minimum")] Lucretius, 2.244-50 = LS 11H(4) spells out the argument, in complete accordance with Epicurean epistemological principles, that a very small deviation of a falling body from a vertical path is not contradicted by the senses, and should therefore be accepted in the case of the atoms if reason requires it (cf. Epicurus, *Letter to Herodotus* 51 = LS 15A(12), Sextus Empiricus *adv. math.* 7.211ff. = LS 18A on what is "uncontested" [LS vol.1 pp.94-6], and J.P. Dumont, 'Confirmation et disconfirmation' in J. Barnes et al. (eds.) *Science and Speculation*, Cambridge and Paris, 1982, 273-303). "Minimum" here probably relates to a doctrine that there were indivisible minima of space as well as of matter. In this case we should not think of the swerve as a continued oblique motion; the atom as it were steps sideways and then continues on its previous trajectory unless and until it strikes another atom. Cf. LS 11G and vol.1 51-2; Asmis 277-9, Sedley [1983] 41-2, Englert 16-25.

That this swerve comes about without a cause he is compelled to admit] On the atomic level at least atomic swerves must be uncaused, for the only possible cause for them, the impact of other atoms, *itself* in Epicurus' view depends on the swerves that cause collision; see above. What is less clear is that Cicero needs to argue the point as if it were one that Epicurus would be reluctant to accept. Epicurus' insight, for which he deserves more credit than Cicero is prepared to give him, is that the swerve *must* be uncaused, at least on the level of individual atoms, if it is to preserve freedom of the will. Cicero argues as a lawyer; to imply that his opponent finds unpalatable views that he actually accepts serves the double purpose of suggesting both that the views *are* unpalatable and that the opponent is in difficulties over them. – This interpretation differs from that of Sedley, who accepts that the swerves of individual atoms are uncaused on the atomic level but argues that they are caused by our volitions, and therefore argues that this and other passages where the swerve is said to be *totally* uncaused are misrepresentations by critics which Epicurus would not himself endorse. Cicero *On Ends* 1.19 is the only place where absence of cause is explicitly said to be asserted by Epicurus himself. (Cf. Sedley [1983] 42, [1989] 318, and LS vol.1 110-11.) Cf. Introduction §3.1.5, and, against Sedley, Mitsis 160 n.73, 166 n.85, Asmis 289-291.

driven from its course by the striking of another] This renders *depellatur*, from the same root as *pulsa* and *pelli* which were translated by "struck" above. In the absence of a swerve, atoms will not even touch one another unless previously diverted from their parallel courses by blows from other atoms; that is *the reason why* one atom cannot "be struck by another if individual bodies are carried downwards ... in straight lines". The MSS *enim* is thus correct, and emendation to *autem* is unnecessary. Cf. also Yon pp.36-8.

even if there is an atom and it swerves] As a sceptic, Cicero is not committing himself to the actual truth or falsity of the atomic theory. Cf. §48 below, *On Ends* 1.21, and *On the Nature of the Gods* 1.65.

23 Epicurus introduced this theory ... Democritus preferred] cf. Introduction §3.1.4. It might be fairer historically to say that it is not clear how far Democritus himself saw his theory of atomic motion as raising problems for human freedom of action; his ethical doctrines seem to assume that we are in control of our actions (but then so, in a sense, do those of the Stoics), and it is not clear that the problem of determinism was even formulated in Laplacean terms in Democritus' time (cf. Balme [1941]). But *Epicurus* saw Democritus' position as threatening freedom; and Epicurus and Cicero have it in common that they are concerned with the implications of philosophical doctrines as they themselves perceive them, not with accurate historical reconstruction of the thoughts of those who initially proposed them.

Carneades taught that the Epicureans could have maintained their position without this fictitious swerve] See Introduction §§ 3.1.8-9. Sedley takes this to mean that the Epicureans could have maintained a recognisably *Epicurean* position on free will without the swerve. To me however it seems that Cicero's Carneades is regarding the Epicureans, for the purpose of the present argument, as people whose main concern is to maintain free will against Chrysippus, and is offering them a way of doing *that* which fails to preserve an aspect of the Epicurean answer, the swerve, which he (mistakenly, in my view) regards as unnecessary and undesirable. LS vol.2 p.110 argue, surely rightly, that the plural "the Epicureans" is not intended to introduce a distinction between Epicurus and his followers, but simply to avoid anachronism. - I am grateful to David Sedley for discussion of the issues in this paragraph.

seeing that (Epicurus) taught that there could be some voluntary movement of the mind] Sedley [1983] 50-1, [1989] 301 argues that this shows that the Epicureans recognised voluntary movement of the mind in its own right, without immediate reference to the atomic level, and that Carneades' suggestion that it could be detached from the atomic swerve is a reasonable one in Epicurean terms. But our passage may only be evidence for Carneades' recognising that a voluntary movement of the mind was what the swerve was intended to introduce. LS vol.2 p.110 claim that, as Carneades is only himself presenting an account of how free will is possible for dialectical purposes against Chrysippus, he must argue on the basis of Epicurean premises, and that the claim that acts of will can be free from external and antecedent causes even without the introduction of the atomic swerve must therefore be intelligible in Epicurean terms. But Carneades is criticising both the Stoic *and* (here) the Epicurean positions, and it does not follow from the fact that he is arguing dialectically that *all* the premises of his argument must be acceptable to the Epicureans. Carneades certainly makes a point of using illustrations that would be acceptable to Epicureans in §§24-5 below (Sedley [1983] 50), but that is hardly conclusive. I hope to discuss these issues in more detail elsewhere.

there are no external and antecedent causes of our will] Carneades suggests that, rather than accepting the Stoic dilemma of determinism or uncaused motion as valid, Epicurus - and anyone else concerned to uphold our freedom - could have attacked the dilemma itself; for to deny that our will has external and antecedent causes is not to say that it has no cause at all. (See above on §20.) As will become clear in §25, for him the cause of voluntary movements of our mind being in our power is, simply, the nature of voluntary movement itself.

"there are no external and antecedent causes of our will" should only be understood as saying that our will is not *completely* governed or determined by such causes. There is no reason why even Epicurus, in advancing the theory of the swerve, should have been committed to the bizarre view that our decisions are in *no way* related to antecedent factors in our own character and to the situation in which the need for a decision arises. Cf. Long [1974] 61.

24 We are therefore misusing the common manner of speaking] "Movement without a cause" means "without an external and antecedent cause", not "without any cause", just as saying that a vessel is empty means that there is no wine or oil in it, not that there is a complete vacuum empty of air as well. And - ingeniously using an example from Epicurus' own theory - the downwards fall of the atom (*not* the swerve) is uncaused only in the sense that it has no external cause; it is the natural movement of the atom, caused by its own weight, in the absence of collisions with other atoms impinging on it from outside. (One might however question whether anyone *would* naturally say that the downwards fall was "without a cause" just because it was caused by the weight of the atom rather than by an external cause.)

who hold that emptiness is absolutely nothing] i.e., they will only use "empty" to refer to absolute void. This translation, proposed by Sedley [1983] 50 n.70, gives the remark more point than "who hold that no vacuum exists" (Rackham; similarly Yon).

25 in the case of the voluntary movements of mind an external cause is not to be looked for] Carneades' emphasis on the contrast between external causes and the nature of the thing itself could give the impression that, although our voluntary decisions are not predetermined by external and antecedent causes alone, they are entirely predetermined if one takes the two together. But this is the position of Chrysippus himself rather than of his critics (see Introduction §3.1.7). And that this is not what Carneades means to suggest is shown by his referring to the absence of determination by *antecedent* causes, as well as by external ones; the causes within us that primarily determine our actions for Chrysippus may not be external, but they are still *antecedent*, for the whole Stoic picture of fate as a series or network of causes depends on causes succeeding one another in time, and it is this that Carneades wants to challenge.

Carneades' argument is very similar to one put forward, in a similar context, by Alexander of Aphrodisias, *On Fate* ch.15. Alexander, however, places the cause of free human action not in the nature of voluntary *action* (§25 below) but in that of human beings as free *agents*. He does not explicitly mention either Carneades or the Epicurean atomic swerve, anywhere in his treatise; and he does not make the same point as Carneades in §24 about the two ways of understanding "without a cause", or use the same comparisons of the empty vessel or the downwards fall of the atom. Whether one should assert categorically with Pierre Thillet (*Alexandre d'Aphrodise, Traité du Destin;* Paris, Budé, 1984, cix) that Alexander used *no* neo-Academic sources is perhaps questionable. Cf. further Sharples [1983,1] 146-8, and [1987,2] at 211-215.

26 Since this is so, what (reason) is there why every proposition should not be either true or false] Cicero returns to the question of future truth, and now links this with the claim that events can be caused without being predetermined. His analysis of the truth of future-tense statements in fact makes it as compatible with the random contingency of the uncaused Epicurean atomic swerve as with Carneades' own view of causation; but it is hardly in his interest to emphasise this. Rather, he stresses that events that are truly predicted, though not causally predetermined, may still have causes; the Stoic account of what it means for something to be caused is not the only possible one.

'Because,' he says] Who is "he"? Both Epicurus and Chrysippus held that determinism was a necessary condition for the truth or falsity of all propositions (Introduction §3.2.2). But Yon in his translation rightly supplies the name of Chrysippus here, pointing out (p.13 n.1) that Carneades at the end of §23 substituted himself for Epicurus *as Chrysippus' adversary*, and (p.14 n.1) that the present argument repeats Chrysippus' argument at the end of §20 (p.14 n.1). So too Turnebus and Bayer (146).

those things cannot be true in the future that do not have causes for their being in the future] The natural way to take this, and the one that Carneades attributes to his opponents, is that statements about future events can only be true now if there are *already* causes which will, directly or indirectly, bring these events about; in other words, if the outcome is already predetermined. Carneades accepts that future contingent events depending on human decisions are not uncaused – but in the sense that they *will have* causes, not that they *already have them*. Having an antecedent cause at every preceding time is not, Carneades argues, the only way for an event to be caused.

27 Or can this proposition ... (really) not be true] So the manuscripts. Rackham deletes the "not", but wrongly, for Carneades has already started his counter-argument. "Or" (*an*) introduces the second half of an alternative question; when as here the first alternative is not expressed, the effect is ironical (cf. R. Kühner and C. Stegmann, *Ausführliche Grammatik der lateinischen Sprache,* Hannover 1914, 519).

'Scipio will capture Numantia'] As he did in 133 B.C. An eight-month siege may be an example of something whose outcome is uncertain, but it is not perhaps the most obvious example of something depending in a simple and straightforward way on a free human decision (the Numantians had little option but to surrender in the end). Here as elsewhere Carneades does not seem to distinguish clearly between human agency and other exceptions to determinism; see Introduction §3.1.8.

unless one cause sowing another from eternity] as in the Stoic doctrine of fate (cf. fr.2 above and §§32, 34 below). There is a wordplay on *serens* "sowing" and the Stoic *series* of causes (cf. Cicero *On Divination* 1.125 = SVF 2.921 = LS 55L, and [Plutarch] *On Fate* 570B), in imitation perhaps of the Greek derivation of *heimarmenê* "fate" from *eirein* "string together" (Diogenes Laertius 7.149 = SVF 2.915).

Could this have been false ... if it was said countless centuries before] Cf. Aristotle, *On Interpretation* 9 18b34. The use of *sescenti* (literally "six hundred") to indicate some very large number is commonplace.

If this proposition, 'Scipio will capture Numantia', was not true at that time, then even when that (city) was overthrown this proposition, 'Scipio will capture Numantia,' would not have been true] The Latin text is corrupt. Skassis, followed by Yon and Bayer, argued that the text of A and B resulted from dittography in Q, that the text of Q had originally been *et si tum non esset vera haec enuntiatio "Capiet Numantiam Scipio" ne illa quidem vera esset "Cepit Numantiam Scipio* – "If this proposition, 'Scipio will capture Numantia', was not true at that time, then even that proposition, 'Scipio captured Numantia,' would not be true" (i.e. after the city was captured)", that a repetition of *vera haec enuntiatio "Capiet Numantiam Scipio"* ousted the original *"Cepit Numantiam Scipio"*, and that the version in the margin of V was simply an attempt to patch things up, replacing one superfluous *vera* by "overthrown", *eversa.* Carneades would then be arguing by *reductio ad absurdum;* if a prediction of a future contingent event was not true *before* the event, then why should a past-tense proposition about it after the event be true either? (This sense could be made even clearer if "when that (city) was overthrown" were retained in the text while reading "captured" *(cepit)*, and this is what Ax and Giomini do; but this involves abandoning the explanation in terms of the alleged dittography).

However, Montanari Caldini (see Bibliography) points out that Skassis' reconstruction fails to take account of the fact that *eversa* is not only found in the margin of V, but seems originally to have been present in A as well. If the

178

alleged dittography is in doubt, then it cannot be used to support the claim that an original *cepit* has been ousted by *capiet*. That could indeed have happened through a slip of the eye relating to just that one word; but, as Montanari Caldini shows, the future *capiet* makes good sense. If the prediction was not true before the event, then, Carneades argues, not even the occurrence of the event can make it true. One cannot say after the event that it was true beforehand that it would happen, if one cannot say *before* the event that it is true that it will happen. This will not convince anyone who is committed to the view that predictions of future events were neither true nor false before the event; but neither will the argument of the text as emended by Skassis convince anyone who is not already disposed to accept Carneades' view that past and future truth should be on the same footing. In the absence of any decisive argument to the contrary it seems best to accept the future *capiet* from the MSS in the second quoted sentence as well as the first.

28 Nor ... does it ... follow that there are unchangeable and eternal causes] Events that are not predetermined do have causes, but not causes of the type that make up Stoic fate. "unchangeable and eternal causes" is short for "an eternal and unchangeable sequence of causes".

The causes which make true ... propositions ... like 'Cato will come into the senate' are fortuitous] Again a Roman example; that Cato the Younger is intended is suggested by the mention of Hortensius below. Cato the Elder is too early in date to be suggested by the references in the context to Scipio the Younger. For fortuitous or chance causes cf. §19 above; the example here too hardly seems an apt instance of a chance event, given that Cato was a member of the senate, unless what is fortuitous is the cause of Cato coming into the senate at a particular time. On the other hand Cato's regularly coming into the senate might be fortuitous from the point of view of "the nature of things and the universe"; it is not part of the general order of the universe that Cato should be a senator - though the Stoics, for whom *everything* is part of the universal plan, would disagree. Cf. Introduction §3.1.8, and Donini [1989] 135-6.

It is as unchangeable that he will come ... as that he *has* come] Past and future are alike; see above on §27, and for "unchangeable" - which does *not* mean that we cannot affect the course of events - see on §17.

***They* want neither of these (to apply)]** "They" must be Epicurus and his followers, though Epicurus has not been explicitly mentioned in connection with future truth since §21.

We will not be hindered ... by the so-called Lazy Argument] The Lazy Argument is an attempt by opponents of determinism to suggest that it leads to unacceptable fatalistic consequences (cf. Introduction, §3.1.7). Cicero records Chrysippus' defence, but (as Eisenberger 161 points out) does not emphasise, in the way Diogenianus (SVF 2.998 = LS 62F) does, Chrysippus' positive emphasis on the need for us to take action, treating the reply rather as defensive. However, this may reflect different original discussions by Chrysippus; see below on §30. In §31 Cicero will go on to report Carneades' more radical attack on Chrysippean determinism; so the sense in which the Lazy Argument "will not hinder us" is that, rejecting determinism altogether, we will not need to defend ourselves against it in the way that Chrysippus has to. Cf. Yon, xxv n.1; Bayer 147.

The statement of the Lazy Argument here and of Chrysippus' rebuttal of it are closely parallelled by Origen, *contra Celsum* 2.20 (SVF 2.957: Appendix (A) below). Barnes [1985,1] argues that since Origen is highly unlikely to have used Cicero's Latin there must be a common Greek source, and that this source is Chrysippus himself. See Introduction §4.2.4.

29 One can change the argument ... and still maintain the same position, as follows] By substituting, for the claim that what is *fated* to happen will happen regardless of other relevant considerations, the claim that what is *truly* going to happen is going to happen regardless of other relevant considerations. It has however already been argued that the truth of future-tense statements has no fatalistic implications; and indeed, the fact that similar absurdities can be generated from the Lazy Argument and from the claim that what is truly going to happen must happen is itself an indication that to infer the necessity of future events from the truth of predictions is to get matters the wrong way round. One should start with the event and its preconditions, not with the truth of the prediction.

30 "Socrates will die on that day."] This is odd; that Socrates will die *eventually* is certain, since he is mortal, but one might have thought that *when* he dies will depend on other occurrences just as much as do the cases that follow. There is a long-standing popular belief that the time of death, especially for soldiers in battle, is fixed in advance, presumably just because it is something beyond the individual's control; in modern times the belief that "there is a bullet with your name on it", but for antiquity cf. Homer, *Iliad* 6.488, Callinus 1.8-15 and A.W.H. Adkins, *Merit and Responsibility* (Oxford 1960) 17-22 and 119. Sedley [1993] suggests that Chrysippus had in mind a belief by Socrates that his death was fore-ordained, resulting from the prophetic dream at *Crito* 44ab (referred to at Cicero *On Divination* 1.52).

If it is fated that "Oedipus will be born to Laius"] On the face of it this, like the following example of Milo only wrestling if he has an opponent, is just a case of something that cannot happen in the absence of certain necessary preconditions. But the choice of mythical example may be significant. Not surprisingly, the story of Laius and Oedipus is often mentioned in ancient discussions of fate; there is, however, evidence for Chrysippus' interest in more than one stage of the story.

The oracle itself is cited from Euripides' *Phoenician Women* not only by Origen, immediately before his account of the Lazy Argument (see Appendix (A)), but also by Middle Platonist writers who use it to exemplify their doctrine that fate is conditional, our free choices being followed by inexorable consequences (Alcinous, *Didascalicus* 26 179.13ff. Hermann; Maximus of Tyre 13.5, p.164 Hobein; Calcidius, *On Plato's* Timaeus 153 188.9f. Waszink; cf. the Cynic Oenomaus in SVF 2.978). For Chrysippus too it was Laius' decision whether to take the risk of sleeping with a woman or not; he chose, and the fated consequences followed. The difference between the Stoic and the Platonist positions is that in the former Laius' choice itself is predetermined. Alexander *(On Fate* 31) says that opponents of determinism cite the determinists' use of it (again in the version from Euripides) and object when the determinists', far from saying that Apollo did not know that Laius would disobey the oracle, stress the fact that Apollo's giving of the oracle was itself crucial in bringing the subsequent events about – thus, in Alexander's view, impiously making Apollo the cause of evil. (If Laius had not been warned by the oracle, he would not have tried to destroy the infant Oedipus by exposing him; Oedipus would not then have grown up in Corinth and slain Laius through failure to recognise him.) What Alexander characteristically disregards is that from a *Stoic* point of view the oracle was not the decisive cause of the subsequent events, only a necessary condition. It was Laius' choice to sleep with Jocasta (even though it was predetermined that he would), and thus he was more the cause of what followed than Apollo was.

Once Laius had disobeyed and had a son, indeed, he could not escape his fate. We know from Diogenianus (SVF 2.939 ad fin.) that Chrysippus noted that Laius and Priam were unable to evade fate by attempting to kill their sons. Indeed

Laius' attempt to evade his fate was instrumental in bringing it about, for it ensured that Oedipus would not recognise him. Moreover Oedipus would not have killed Laius in the way he did if he too had not tried to avert what was fated by fleeing from those he thought were his parents and so meeting his real father. We do not know whether Chrysippus noted these points too; but for as much of the story as he did discuss, he will have stressed *both* the inescapability of fate *and* the way in which what happened resulted from human decisions. As for Alexander's complaint that the story does not show the gods in a favourable light Chrysippus may have had in mind the story (for which cf. H. Lloyd-Jones, *The Justice of Zeus,* Berkeley 1971, 120-3) that the original oracle was itself a punishment of Laius, who had offended Apollo by seducing the son of Pelops - whose name, by a coincidence worthy of the Oedipus story itself, was Chrysippus. Apollo, in making the oracle conditional, is in a sense giving Laius a chance to escape deserved punishment, even if he knows that the chance will not in fact be taken.

Milo will wrestle in the Olympic games] Milo of Croton, in the later sixth century B.C., won six victories in wrestling at the Olympic games and six at the Pythian. White 123 points out that the relation between wrestling and having an opponent, like that between Laius' sleeping with a woman and his having a son, could be viewed as in some sense one of conceptual necessity, while that between calling in a doctor and recovering from illness is not, in modern terms at least (see above on §15). This fact makes the logical absurdity of the Lazy Argument more apparent, but reduces the emphasis on the need for practical action - in Cicero Milo will not compete unless there is an opponent, while in Diogenianus (above, on §28) Hegesarchus the boxer will not *win* unless he *keeps up his guard* (Donini [1974-5] 216). Chrysippus must have made the point in more than one passage with different examples and emphases.

31. Carneades disapproved of this whole type of argument] Carneades' objection is that the Stoic doctrine of co-fated events, in trying to reject fatalism while retaining determinism, does not go far enough. For Carneades, unlike the Stoics, nothing can be in our power if all things are brought about by antecedent causes; since some things are in our power, things cannot all be brought about by antecedent causes as the Stoic doctrine of fate implies. The claim that some things are in our power could be an assertion of Carneades' own belief; but it may rather be an *ad homines* argument based on the Stoics' own admission that some things are in our power, even though their requirements for this to be so are not the same as Carneades'. See Introduction §3.1.9.

without involving any misrepresentation *(calumnia)*] The implication is that the Lazy Argument is indeed invalid against Chrysippus, but that for Carneades Chrysippus' position is untenable anyway. Carneades *would* have misrepresented Chrysippus if he had maintained that Chrysippus had no answer to the Lazy Argument at all. Cf. Turnebus, and Yon xxv n.2.

and this argument was as follows] Literally "its argument", i.e. the argument of "another way"; or "his argument", but this gives a more disjointed structure. *conclusio* is strictly the conclusion of an argument, but Cicero here spells out the stages leading to the conclusion as well.

32. An argument cannot be made more binding than this] The case against the determinists ultimately rests on the experience of things being in our power - which they too accept - plus our intuitions of what this requires.

If someone were to want to make the same point in reply] What follows is a repetition of the claim in §§20-21 that the truth of predictions depends on the events predicted being causally determined; and that argument has already been countered by Carneades in §§19 and 28. But at the end of §32 and in §33 this leads on to a new point about divine foreknowledge. Hamelin 33 suggests "to argue in reverse on the same point", but the following argument from future truth to determinism does not cover *exactly* the same ground as the argument from something's being in our power to the rejection of determinism in §31.

a natural cause, existing from eternity] Probably a compressed expression for "a series of natural causes extending from eternity" (see above, on §28).

without a natural eternity (of preceding causes)] So, rightly, Yon 17 n.1, noting that the brevity of Cicero's expression is at the expense of clarity; "without an eternity of naturally preceding causes" would have been clearer still.

And so Carneades used to say that not even Apollo ...] A distinction is here drawn between the question of future *truth* and that of *foreknowledge*. It may be *true* before the event that what is going to happen contingently is going to happen, but just because it is not, or not yet, causally determined, no-one, not even a god, can yet know that it would happen. The Stoics would agree that undetermined events cannot be foreknown, but deny that any such undetermined events exist. Cf. Cicero *On Divination* 2.15-18, and Introduction, §7.1.

33. Marcellus, who was consul three times] Marcus Claudius Marcellus, grandson of the general of the second Punic war and himself consul in 166, 155 and 152 B.C., died in a shipwreck in 148 B.C. while on an embassy to Masinissa, king of Numidia. Cicero refers to him in very similar words not only at *On Divination* 2.14 but also in the speech *Against Piso* of 55 B.C.(§44), where he is cited simply as a stock example of someone who suffered shipwreck. It is worth emphasising how far Cicero's eloquence not only in speeches but also in his philosophical works depends on his ability to draw on an abundant repertoire of examples; this may serve as a corrective to the picture of him slavishly following a particular Greek source in each philosophical work. See Introduction, §1.1.

not even those past things of which there existed no signs] In the case of knowledge as in that of truth, Carneades' position involves a symmetry between past and future. Even a god cannot have foreknowledge of what is truly going to happen unless there are grounds for this knowledge, in the form of already existing causes; and in the same way even a god cannot know what has truly happened in the past unless it has left behind some evidence in the form of effects. These however may presumably include traces in the gods' own memories, even where no other traces exist; and the Stoics argued that the gods' knowledge of the future derives from their having seen it already, since time repeats itself in an endless cycle (SVF 2.625 = LS 52C,4). The relevance of determinism for divine foreknowledge is then that it ensures that what happens in every cycle is the same, for only then will the gods' experience of the past be an absolutely certain guide to the future. – I am grateful to David Sedley for discussion of these points.

Apollo could not have made a prediction about Oedipus] Even though it might seem that by the time of the second oracle, the categorical statement to Oedipus that he was fated to kill his father and marry his mother, the machinery of fate was already set up and simply waiting to be set in motion, it was still, it may be supposed, Oedipus' *choice* to kill the unknown man he met on the road from Delphi to Thebes. In what is actually attributed to Carneades himself (at the end of §32) there is no categorical assertion that there *are* in fact things which are not predetermined and so cannot be foreknown; in §33 this claim does seem to be made, but the formulation could be Cicero's rather than Carneades'. See above on §32, and Introduction §3.1.9.

these (the Stoics) are harder pressed] "These" *(hi)* could be taken to refer either to the Stoics (so Turnebus), who have been mentioned more recently, or to their opponents (so Rackham), who have been the subject of discussion and are closer to the readers' minds. However, §34 begins with a further attack on the Stoic position, which suggests that it is the Stoics who are "harder pressed" here; and Cicero describes an Academic position as less restricted than a dogmatist one also at *Lucullus* §8. Moreover, taking "these are harder pressed" as referring to the Stoics gives the two occurrences of *illorum* the same reference and preserves the contrast between *illorum* and *hi*. Why the Stoics are "harder pressed" is not immediately clear, for, as Duhot 200 points out, one can hardly suppose that the Stoics would be reluctant to accept the universal applicability of divination. *angustius* is the reading adopted by most editors, though Schröder 138 n.6 argues for *angustiis*.

34 (even) if it is granted that nothing can happen except by an antecedent cause] Cicero will argue that not everything that precedes an event is its cause, even if it is a necessary condition. This enables him to make the concession here; for even if A is the antecedent cause of B, and B of C, it does not follow, if one restricts the notion of cause as it is restricted in §§34-36, that either A or anything else earlier than B was itself the cause of C. This does not in itself provide an escape from determinism; for it is perfectly possible that, sufficiently far in advance of an event, there should be a number of circumstances none of which individually qualifies as a *cause* of the event in the sense now specified, but that nevertheless their *conjunction* is sufficient to bring the event about necessarily. Indeed there is some evidence for the Stoics themselves making a similar point to that in §§34-6 (for a fuller discussion cf. Sharples [1995]). Cicero in *Topics* 58-9 (below, Appendix (B)) argues that Stoic fate is made up of causes in the sense of necessary conditions; Hamelin interpreted the Academics as taking the distinction between necessary and sufficient conditions from the Stoics and, by introducing the notion of *chance* causes, forcing it further than the Stoics would wish (Yon xxvii n.1). See also Duhot 200.

"cause" should not be understood in such a way that what precedes each thing is the cause for that thing] One may compare the rather different discussion of this point in Alexander of Aphrodisias, *On Fate* 24-5; cf. Sharples [1983,1] 155-7.

I went down to the Campus] The Campus Martius in Rome, used for sport and military exercises. Going to the Campus was not the cause of playing ball; rather, the *intention* of playing ball was the cause of going to the Campus. Cicero was in his early sixties at the time of writing the *De fato;* but Petronius' Trimalchio still plays ball (*Satyricon* 27).

nor that Hecuba was the cause of destruction for the Trojans because she gave birth to Alexander] Alexander is Paris, son of Priam and Hecuba, who seduced Helen and thus caused the Trojan War. In Euripides' *Trojan Women* (919-922) Helen herself blames Hecuba for the war on similar grounds, and Priam for not killing the child. On the face of it the charge is grotesquely far-fetched. However, Priam and Hecuba had disobeyed an oracle warning them not to have children (as Laius too did, above §30). Euripides' play was the third of a trilogy, and Hecuba's dream and the consultation of the oracle were narrated in the prologue of the first play, *Alexandros* (cf. T.B.L. Webster, *The Tragedies of Euripides,* 165-7; R.A. Coles, *A new Oxyrhynchus papyrus: the Hypothesis of Euripides' Alexandros, Bulletin of the Institute of Classical Studies* suppl. 32 [1974], at 23-4).

the well-dressed traveller] It was the victim's fault for being obviously wealthy; if he had looked poor the highwayman wouldn't have bothered to rob him. As

Juvenal put it (10.22, cited by Boethius at *Consolation of Philosophy* II.5.34), "the empty-handed traveller will sing in the presence of the highwayman" *(cantabit vacuus coram latrone viator).*

35 Of this sort is that passage in Ennius] The opening of the *Medea* by the Roman playwright Ennius (239-169 B.C.), closely modelled on the opening of Euripides' *Medea;* the tutor of Medea's children laments that, if Jason had not built the *Argo* of wood from mount Pelion and sailed to Colchis, Medea's elopement with him to Greece and subsequent desertion by him in Corinth would never have occurred. Cicero uses the same example to illustrate the difference between necessary and sufficient conditions in his *Topics,* 61 (below, Appendix (B)); however, necessary conditions are there allowed to be causes of a type. The example is cited in the *Greek* tradition – not therefore dependent on Cicero – to make a similar point to that here in Clement of Alexandria, *Stromateis* 8.9 596A = SVF 2.347. But it was also, in Ennius' translation, a standard example in Latin of far-fetched considerations which it is counter-productive to include in an argument: *Rhetorica ad Herennium* 2.34, Cicero's (early) *On (Rhetorical) Invention* 1.91, Quintilian, *Education of the Orator* 5.10.84, Julius Victor 12 (*Rhet. Lat.* p.415,33 Halm. At *In Defence of Caelius* 18 Cicero mentions its use in a speech by Crassus. At *On the Nature of the Gods* 3.75 it is applied to the gods' alleged responsibility for human wrongdoing; and at *On Ends* 1.4-5 it is cited as an example of Latin literature based on Greek. (It also occurs in illustration of *trabes* as a *singular,* with a singular verb, in Varro, *On the Latin Language* 7,33 and Priscian 7.40 *(Gramm. Lat.* vol.2 p.320,16 Keil; in illustration of *utinam* at Donatus on Terence, *Phormio* 157, vol.2 p.391.18ff. Wassner; and in Priscian *On the Metres of Terence* 14, *Gramm. Lat.* vol.3 p.424.1 Keil). Cf. Yon, loc. cit. *accedissent* (with a short second syllable) is a variant archaic spelling for *accidissent.*

(He) could have gone back even further] "He" referring to Ennius as author; or "she", referring to the nurse. In the Latin there is no need to specify.

one can go back to infinity] The present tense is used because this is a generalising statement about all such cases, even though it is immediately followed by continued quotation from Ennius and a return to the particular case of Medea.

And would that the construction of a ship had not begun there] the building of the *Argo* was the beginning of all ship-building.

not this, that those things supplied the cause of her love] The *ut* clause is a result clause, and depends, like what precedes it, on *sequitur;* it does not follow, from the fact that the building of the Argo was a *necessary condition* for Medea's elopement ("never would my mistress ..."), that it was therefore the *cause* of it.

36 But they say that it makes a difference] The reference may be to the Stoics themselves; if so, the point is that they make a distinction between necessary and sufficient conditions (see above on §34) which Carneades will use against them in a way they did not intend. See further Sharples [1995].

of such a sort that something must be brought about along with it] whenever X occurs Y is necessarily brought about along with X; in other words, X is a sufficient condition for Y, or a *necessitating* cause of Y.

So none of *those* things is a cause] *earum* refers not to *both* the types of condition just mentioned, the necessary and the sufficient, but to the first type only, the necessary but not sufficient conditions exemplified by the remote factors of §34. *nulla* and *earum* may be attracted into the feminine by *causa*, even though it is being denied that these things *are* causes; or else the feminine picks up *eae res* at the end of section 34 (so Hamelin 34 and Ax, arguing against Plasberg; see the *apparatus*).

when Philoctetes had not yet been given a festering sore] Philoctetes was bitten by a serpent on his way to the Trojan War; the wound festered, and the smell caused the other Greeks to abandon him on the island of Lemnos. Sophocles' *Philoctetes* tells how Odysseus tried to get Achilles' son Neoptolemus to trick Philoctetes into giving up Heracles' bow, which was in his possession and by which alone Troy could be captured.

the cause was closer at hand] Is Cicero committed to saying that once the bite had festered it was *inevitable* that Philoctetes would be abandoned on the island? The preceding discussion would seem to suggest it; but it was still up to the other Greeks whether they should abandon him or not. At any rate, if one were to ask for "the cause" of his being abandoned there, the festering of the wound is the natural answer to give, rather than anything earlier in the story; what counts as a cause will be relative to the context in which the question was asked. (Cf. Sorabji [1980,2] 29-30).

37 the way in which the event (comes about) reveals the cause] To be understood by contrast with what follows. It was always true that Philoctetes was going to be abandoned on the island, even though it was not predetermined (reverting to the point of §§19, 28 and 32); but even though it was always *true*, no-one could say that the snake-bite was the *cause* of his being abandoned – even once the snake-bite or the festering had occurred – until he actually was abandoned. Only then did it become clear, with hindsight, why he had been. Rackham emends "reveals" to "revealed"; but the present can stand as illustrating a general principle of which the Philoctetes story is one example. A similar point is made by Cicero, *Topics* 67 (Yon p.39).

and this could not change from true to false] See above, on §17.

unless perhaps we wish to follow the Epicureans] Cicero distinguishes two positions. The first is the denial of the truth or falsity of future contingents familiar from §§19 and 21 and there attributed to Epicurus himself. But he then goes on to refer to a different claim, that "Either p will occur or not-p will occur" is true, even though neither "p will occur" or "not-p will occur" is true in the case of future contingents. This preserves the law of excluded middle – "either p or not-p" – while denying the logical link between the truth of a disjunction and the truth of one or other of its members; hence Cicero's indignation, bolstered by his general hostility to Epicurus. At *Lucullus* 97 = LS 20I Cicero says that Epicurus denies the truth of the disjunction; at *On the Nature of the Gods* 1.70 we are told that Epicurus denied the *necessity* both of the whole disjunction and of its parts.

38 So what Chrysippus defended will be maintained] Both Chrysippus and Carneades maintained that every statement was true or false; but Chrysippus, unlike Carneades, also claimed that all events were predetermined, and *that* Cicero promptly goes on to deny. (See above on §§20-21.) Lambinus added *igitur* and Davies *ergo*, both meaning "therefore", at the start of this sentence, but Ax rightly argues that this is unnecessary, comparing the asyndeton at *ratio ipsa* just below.

causes from eternity] literally "eternal causes"; see above, on §§28 and 32.

39 I indeed see it like this] §§39-45 of Cicero's speech contain a compromise solution to the problem of reconciling fate and human agency. On the question of Cicero's own attitude to this compromise see below on §45 and Introduction §§4.2.1-2.

Democritus, Heraclitus, Empedocles and Aristotle] Although Fate or the fates (*Moirai*) appear often enough in literature, *universal* determinism does not become a philosophical issue before the fourth century, and references to the views of the Presocratics on fate in secondary sources reflect later attempts to classify their implicit views on the topic, rather than historically accurate reports of their own explicit views. On the present passage cf. G. Verbeke, 'Aristotélisme et Stoïcisme dans le *De fato* d'Alexandre d'Aphrodise', *Archiv für Geschichte der Philosophie* 50 (1968) 73-100, at p.75 n.10; Mansfeld [1988] 194; Donini [1989] 124-125.

Democritus (second half of the fifth century B.C.; on his date cf. W.K.C. Guthrie, *A History of Greek Philosophy*, vol.2 p.386 n.2) was a follower of Leucippus, who had asserted that nothing comes about at random but everything by necessity (Leucippus fr.67B2 DK). There is no sign that Democritus himself saw his atomistic system as threatening human responsibility or freedom, and what Aristotle (*Physics* 2.4 196a24ff.; see on Boethius *Consolation* V.1.9) finds objectionable in his views is the denial of purpose in nature, rather than that of freedom. However Epicurus saw Democritus' atomism, unlike his own, as deterministic; see Introduction §3.1.4 and above §22 (where, as here, the issue is put in terms of the *necessity* of fate; cf. Donini [1989] 130). Democritus is also presented as saying that everything comes about by necessity by "Aëtius" (in the doxographical work reconstructed by Diels) 1.25.3 (DG p.321 = 28A32 DK) and Diogenes Laertius 9.45 (Hamelin 35). **Heraclitus** (c.540-480 B.C.) did not speak explicitly of fate, to judge from our sources, but he did say that all things happen according to strife and necessity (*chreôn*; fr. 22B80 DK) and described all things as governed by the single divine *Logos;* and the Stoics, who certainly were determinists, adopted him as a precursor and borrowed imagery from him. Cf. also Diogenes Laertius 9.8 and "Aëtius" 1.27.2 (Stobaeus; DG p.303. Hamelin 36). **Empedocles** (c.495-435 B.C.) described the world as ruled over by Love and Strife in turn with an oath determining their succession (fr. 31B30 DK), and attributed the fall of the divine spirit into the cycle of reincarnation in mortal bodies to "a decree of Necessity" (fr. 31B115 DK).

The really surprising figure in the list is **Aristotle**. It seems likely - though not all modern scholars would agree - that he would reject universal determinism but had not worked out a detailed position. See Introduction, §3.1.3 and §3.2.2. Thus Cicero, or his source, might have in mind deterministic implications that could be drawn from Aristotle's writings because he had not explicitly guarded against them. But there is in any case a question about the basis of Cicero's, or his source's, awareness of Aristotle. Cicero nowhere (in the surviving part of our text) mentions that the paradox of the truth of future contingent statements is stated by Aristotle in *On Interpretation* 9 (cf. D. Frede [1985] 78-9; Donini [1989] 127). Deterministic views seem to be attributed to Aristotle by "Aëtius" (1.29.2) and Theodoret (*Gr. aff. cur.* 6.7 p.151.11-13 Raeder (cf. 5.47 p.136.24 Raeder) and by Antiochus of Ascalon in a Stoicizing interpretation of the Peripatetics and the Old Academy (Cicero, *Ac. Post.* 1.29); the author of the pseudo-Aristotelian *On the Cosmos,* too, adopts a deterministic position (7 401b8ff.). Karsten tried to solve the problem by emendation to "Anaxagoras" (cf. 68A66 DK), but this has not won general acceptance. Diodorus Cronus is presumably omitted from the list because our concern here is with logical, rather than physical necessity (Duhot 202).

those who thought that there were voluntary movements of minds] They are not identified. As these too are "men of old" and Chrysippus is replying to them, for them to include Carneades himself would involve anachronism. The reference could be to Arcesilaus (316-242 B.C.), the founder of the Middle Academy (von Arnim in SVF 2.974; Ioppolo; Donini [1989] 140) or Epicurus (Englert 134). Perhaps we should not look for particular candidates; Duhot 204-6 argues that the whole debate of §§39-45 is an artificial reconstruction by Cicero. It is however clear enough that Chrysippus did have to counter libertarian criticisms of his position (below, §40).

Chrysippus, like a respected arbitrator, seems to have wanted to strike a balance] In §§39-45 Chrysippus is portrayed as arguing that fate, in the guise of external causes, plays a part in causing our actions but does not necessitate them. Thus he occupies middle ground between those who claimed that fate necessitates our actions, on the one hand, and those who denied that fate had any influence on our actions at all, on the other. But since the crucial point in Cicero's account is whether our actions are necessitated by external causes or not, Cicero says that Chrysippus 'inclines to those who want the movements of the mind to be free from necessity'.

In actual fact Chrysippus held that our actions were as completely determined as is everything else, only determined through us as their primary causes, not through external factors without relevance to us. (See Introduction §§3.1.7 and 4.2.1-2, and below, Appendix (C)). Cicero or his source concentrates on the claim that external factors alone do not determine our actions, and this explains how he can claim (at the end of §44) that the differences between Chrysippus and his libertarian opponents are purely verbal - and why Yon (23f. n.4) can claim that Cicero's reconciliation of Chrysippus and his opponents is itself verbal. It is not that Cicero has actually attributed to Chrysippus views he did not hold; rather, his presentation of Chrysippus' position is selective and incomplete (so Hamelin 53 and Schmekel [1938] 269). But in fact it seems likely that the apparent reconciliation in §§39-45 is only the first part of the treatment of Chrysippus' views, and that further objections were subsequently brought against him; see below on §45 and Introduction, §4.2.2.

The arbitrator, chosen by the parties to a dispute on the basis of their mutual respect for him, seeks to settle it on the basis of equity, while a judge appointed by the praetor settles it by the letter of the law. The image is applied in a very similar way to Carneades by Cicero at *Tusculan Disputations* 5.120; it was used by Aristotle *On the Heaven* 1.10 279b8-12 (Mansfeld [1990] 3176).

seems to have wanted to] Schröder 148 points out that this hardly suggests that Cicero saw Chrysippus as succeeding. *Voluisse* depends on *videtur* at the start of the sentence; with "inclines" *(applicat)* Cicero switches to the indicative.

the movements of the mind to be free of necessity] I have accepted Davies' emendation, as do Yon and Ax. Rackham keeps to the MSS text, which would mean "want minds to be free from necessity of movement"; this gives a good enough sense but seems awkward given the frequency with which "movements of the mind" or of minds are referred to in *On Fate* (cf., with Ax, §25).

by the expressions he uses] One might well ask whether Chrysippus' actual words might not be a better guide to his position than what Cicero claims he *wanted* to argue but admits he did not argue in fact. That Chrysippus wanted to distinguish between what was and what was not necessary, even though he held that everything is predetermined, is clear enough (see Introduction §3.2.6); but his position was in fact a soft-determinist one. The suggestion of a tension within Chrysippus' views may thus be the result of Cicero or his source, from a libertarian standpoint, interpreting Chrysippus' denial of necessity in a non-determinist sense that Chrysippus himself never intended, and then criticising him for failing to establish a position he in fact never wanted to maintain.

40 in the case of "assentings"] Cicero's discussion is in general terms based on the Stoic analysis of action (for which see §42 below). When I receive an impression or "presentation" *(phantasia, visum)* through the senses, I may or may not make an assent *(adsensio, sunkatathesis)* to it, that is accept that it represents how things really are. If however I do assent to an impression that prompts me to perform a certain action, I experience an impulse *(hormê, adpetitus)* which leads to action. (This is a deliberately oversimplified statement of the general theory; for the details, see below). – I have used "assentings" here to indicate that the reference is to the many individual instances of assenting. But the simpler "assent" has sometimes been used in the commentary where the sense is clear.

the first part of my speech] or *perhaps* "my first speech"; see Introduction, §4.1.7.

Those however who disagreed with them] The argument that follows turns on the alleged incompatibility of determinism with praise and blame. Such arguments are associated with Carneades (cf. Amand, especially pp.576-8), but the connection of praise and blame with voluntary action or action for which we are responsible is already found in Epicurus (*Letter to Menoeceus* 133 = LS 20A, *On Nature* 34.21-2 = LS 20B, 34.27 = LS 20C(2), Aristotle (*Nicomachean Ethics* 3.1 1109b31, 3.5 1113b23ff., *Magna Moralia* 1.9 1487a19ff.) and Plato (*Protagoras* 323c). Amand (p.79) attributes the argument as cited in this section to Carneades; Huby, followed by Gulley 49-50, argues that it is to be attributed rather to Epicurus, and must have been formulated after the theory of assent was introduced by Zeno (Cicero, *Lucullus* 144), but before Chrysippus, who is represented as replying to the argument in §41. Pohlenz [1967] vol.1 p.355 n.30 suggested rather that the argument was Arcesilaus' reply to Zeno; so too Ioppolo, who connects "persuasively" *(probabiliter)* with Arcesilaus' taking as the criterion what was reasonable or *eulogon* (Ioppolo 422 n.80). Anachronism is in any case involved in Cicero's attribution to the "men of old", who must be the determinist "old philosophers" of §39, of a position formulated with the Stoic terminology of assent (Eisenberger 156); he may be presenting his material in a sequence that illustrates the philosophical issues rather than the chronological order of arguments (cf. Duhot, 205, and Schröder 143-4 n.17 who suggests that Cicero may present the issues in this way here because he has already dealt with them more fully in the lacuna before §5).

The terms in which the anti-determinist argument here is stated are noteworthy, for they suggest that assent results from a predisposing impulse. In orthodox – that is Chrysippean – Stoic theory impulse results from assent, or is so closely linked with it that they are as it were two aspects of a single thing (cf. especially SVF 3.171; Long [1968] 337f., Inwood 61. Eisenberger 162 n.31 points out that in the account of Chrysippus' argument in §42 below the impression *is* the proximate cause of assent, without impulse intervening.) Later Stoics did speak of an initial, unreasoning impulse or reaction which the judgement involved in assent either confirms or stops (Seneca, *On Anger* 2.4.1; cf. Epictetus, fr. 9), and LS vol.2 p.417 argue for this concept in the early Stoics as well, citing SVF 3.574. But this initial impulse is distinguished from the reasoned impulse that follows on assent. Seneca has something closer to our passage at *Moral Letters* 113.18 = SVF 3.169 (cf. Eisenberger 162 n.31; Ioppolo 407-8); LS vol. 2 p.316 however argue that this is un-Chrysippean, as does Inwood (282 n.193; cf. 179). Ioppolo 406-414 argues that impulse preceding assent was the theory of Zeno and Cleanthes, though not Chrysippus, and uses this to support her view that our argument comes from Arcesilaus replying to Zeno; she further suggests (423 n.82) that our whole passage reached Cicero through Chrysippus, reporting a debate among his predecessors. Hamelin 37 tried to resolve the problem by proposing *quae adpetitus sequuntur,* "the things on which impulses follow", for "those things which follow on impulse"; this puts assent and impulse in the correct order, but obscures the argument.

41 wanted nothing to come about without causes laid down beforehand] This could mean just that everything that comes about has *some* antecedent causes, in the sense of being related in some way to what has preceded. This much everyone would accept (see above on §23 ad fin.) even if there is room for debate about the term "cause". But it could also mean that everything is *entirely determined* by causes laid down beforehand, which Chrysippus seems in fact to have held but which Cicero's account tends to obscure (see above on §39).

so that he could both escape necessity and retain fate] See above, on §39, and the discussions in Sorabji [1980,2] 81-3 and Sharples [1981].

Some causes are perfect and primary, others auxiliary and proximate] The contrast is illustrated in §43 by the example of the cylinder; cf. also Gellius, *Noctes Atticae* 7.2, in Appendix (C). The man who pushes the cylinder starts it rolling, and it would not roll if he did not push it, but the reason for its continuing to roll, and rolling in the way it does, is not this but its shape. Similarly a sense-impression may prompt a response and indeed be a necessary precondition for it (see below on section 42); but it does not follow that it is the sense-impression rather than our own character that determines how we react. It is not in our power what impressions we receive; it is in our power (in *some* sense; see Introduction §3.1.7) how we respond. For similar arguments cf. Origen in SVF 2.988 ad fin., Plutarch *On Stoic Self-Contradictions* 47 1055F = SVF 2.994, and Augustine *City of God* 5.10 = SVF 2.995; Seneca *Letters* 87.31-4 = Posidonius F170 EK; Plotinus, 3.3 5.40ff. For the elaborate distinctions drawn by the Stoics between different types of causes, the terminology used, and the vexed questions of whether we are dealing with two or four types of cause here and of the relation of Cicero's Latin terminology to the original Greek, see the Excursus at the end of this Commentary.

we do not want this to be understood ... but as "through auxiliary and proximate causes"]. A similar view is attributed to Chrysippus by Plutarch, who argues that it is incompatible with Chrysippus' view that everything is in accordance with inexorable fate; see Appendix (D), and also Cicero in Appendix (B). The MSS' addition of *antecedentibus* seems to be an error; Yon p.lxi suggests that *causis antecedentibus* was copied by error from the text in line 4 above, that the correction *adiuvantibus* was inserted in the margin, and that both words were then incorporated in the text. Clark 361 lists this among errors which he thinks go back to an ancestor of Q written in narrow columns of 18 or 19 letters (the two occurrences of *antecedentibus* being 75 letters apart). The causes in question *are* indeed antecedent, but the point that fate is to be identified with antecedent causes has already been made; unless we are to suppose (with Hamelin 44, following Heine) that auxiliary causes are here being divided between those that are (remotely) antecedent and those that are proximate. *antecedentibus* is also retained by Pohlenz [1940] 106 and Grilli 432.

the argument which I set out a short while ago] In §40.

If all things come about by fate (he says)] Not a second quotation from Chrysippus, but a paraphrase by Cicero of what he has already quoted; so, rightly, Duhot 170 n.1.

189

If all things come about by fate] The subjunctive *fiant* is due to this being a subordinate clause in indirect speech, the following *sequi* depending on a verb of speaking understood from *occurrit;* it does not indicate doubt about the truth of what is here said, for Cicero accepts that Chrysippus *does* himself believe that all things come about by fate, even if his interpretation of this in one-sided.

it does not follow that impulse too is not in our power] The reference here is to whether *impulse* is in our power, while in §§42 and 43 the question is whether *assenting* is in our power. In the orthodox Stoic view assent preceded impulse; but in §40 above impulse was placed before assent, and that may have influenced the formulation here. Cf. Bayer, 158 n.

If we said that all things come about through perfect and primary causes] This *could* be understood from the context as meaning "if we said that it is as a perfect and primary cause that *fate* (i.e., in Cicero's presentation here, the *external* factors) brings all things about". For it is at least plausible to suppose that all things that come about do have primary causes, only that, in the case of assentings, they are not external ones. But Donini [1974-5] points out that Cicero is here concerned only to stress that the external causes are not primary; Schröder 9-10 goes further, denying that Cicero even implies that the agent's nature is either a *causa perfecta* or a *causa principalis.* (On this, however, see the Excursus below.)

42 those who introduce fate in such a way that they add necessity to it] That is, as the sequel makes clear, those who make fate a primary rather than just an auxiliary cause of our assentings.

will have to accept that conclusion] The conclusion at the end of §40 that it is not the case that all things that come about do so by fate.

(Chrysippus) thinks that he can easily explain this] This leaves open the possibility that Chrysippus is, in the view of Cicero or his source, *wrong* to think so, and so tends to support the view that criticism of the present argument followed in the lacuna after §45 (q.v.). Schröder, 149.

assenting could not occur unless aroused by a sense-presentation] The same point is made below in "it is necessary that assenting should be caused by a sense-presentation" (where the sense is, as here, that the sense-presentation is *necessary for* the assenting, not that it *necessitates* it). Sextus Empiricus *Adv. math.* 7.154 = LS 41C(8) reports Arcesilaus as objecting that assent is to *propositions* (cf., with LS vol.2 p.256, Stobaeus *Ecl.* 2.7.9b [vol.2 p.88.2-6 Wachsmuth] = SVF 3.171 = LS 33I); but the looseness of expression creates no real difficulty, since the proposition expresses the relevant aspect of the content of the sense-presentation (cf. Sandbach [1971] 12-13, Inwood 56-7). "Sense-presentation" translates Cicero's *visum,* which is the term he uses to render *phantasia.* (Cf., with Yon 39-40, Cicero *Posterior Academics* 1.40, *Lucullus* 77.) Both the Greek and the Latin term are etymologically connected with what appears to sight, but *phantasia* can apply to presentations or impressions from all the senses, and indeed to presentations which are not the immediate results of sensation at all (for example, Diogenes Laertius 7.51 = SVF 2.61 = LS 39A and 7.53 = SVF 2.87 = LS 39D. Origen in SVF 2.988 refers to the presentation of weaving that prompts a spider to weave its web; cf. Duhot 103-5). As Görler 264 n.24 points out, *videri* too can indicate what appears to the mind. The Stoic theory of action should thus not be seen as restricting human behaviour to instant responses to sensory stimuli. For the Stoics the actual contents of our minds at any moment can all be *ultimately* traced to more or less recent sense-experiences; but that is a different point. Cf. Sandbach [1971] 12; Gould [1974] 22; Sharples [1983,1]

he goes back to his cylinder and spinning-top] This suggests that the example was well-known (Schröder, 149); cf. Gellius' account in Appendix (C). It does rather suggest, too (though Schröder argues otherwise) that it had been mentioned earlier in the present treatise; see Introduction §4.1.7.

for the rest it is by their own nature that the cylinder rolls and the top moves in a curve] There are two separate points here. (I) One and the same push will cause differently-shaped objects to move in different ways, and the difference in movement is due to the shape of the objects rather than to the push. A cylinder will roll down a slope; a cone-shaped top will roll round and round, and never come to the bottom of the slope if that is far enough away. This is the point that is emphasised in Cicero's account; the example, with the addition of a sphere and a cube, is also used by pseudo-Aristotle *On the cosmos* 6 398b27, to make the rather different point that a single divine impulse can have many different results in different types of thing. But there is also the point that (II) the push is only active at the *beginning* of the process; the push may start the cylinder rolling, but it is the shape of the cylinder that causes it to continue rolling – as a cube, for example, would not. (Cf. §43 below, "it is pushed from outside but for the rest moves by its own force and nature.") Cf. M. Frede [1980] 236, and Duhot 173 and 184-6, drawing attention to the absence of an ancient belief in inertia. (II) is stressed in the account of Gellius, who only mentions the cylinder and not the cone (Appendix (C)). The primary cause of something's coming about will not *always* be internal to the thing involved; it may depend on the point of view from which one is speaking (cf. M. Frede [1980] 237). Whether the reference in (I) is to the way a cone-shaped top rolls if pushed while lying on its side, or to its movement when spun in the intended fashion, is not entirely clear; in isolation *versari turbinem* would suggest the latter, but the former gives a better contrast with the cylinder, and pseudo-Aristotle *On the Cosmos* 6 398b27 refers to throwing a cone and cylinder from a height and the ways in which they will then move. On the background of the cylinder as an example cf. G. Vollgraff, 'De lapide cylindro', *Mnemosyne* 2 ser. 52 (1924) 207-211, and the Pythagorean *Golden Verses*, 57 (ed. D. Young, *Theognis, etc.*, Leipzig, Teubner, 1961); cf. M. Dragona-Monachou, ''Ο Ύμνος στὸ Δία καὶ τὰ Χρυσᾶ ἔπη', *Φιλοσοφία* (Athens) 1 (1971) 339-378, at 361-2.

43 As he who pushes a cylinder ... so a sense-impression] The push is the initiating cause of the cylinder's rolling, but not the primary one; just so, the sense-presentation *prompts* us to assent, but it is up to us whether we do or not. There are however features of the analogy that are hardly helpful to Chrysippus' case. Once the push has occurred the cylinder's reaction is entirely predictable, and the cylinder does not show much discrimination in how it reacts to different sorts of push, either. Chrysippus held that human reactions, even if predetermined, were considerably more complex than those of inanimate objects like cylinders; indeed he argued that action in accordance with reasoned impulse was natural for human beings, just as falling straight downwards was natural for heavy bodies (Alexander, *On Fate* 13 181.13ff. = SVF 2.979 = LS 62G). But it was only too easy for libertarian critics to use these comparisons to support their claim that, if human actions were predetermined, there was no real distinction, in the respect that mattered for *them*, between human actions and the movements of inanimate objects.

and as it were stamp its appearance on the mind] Cf. Diogenes Laertius 7.45 = SVF 2.53, 7.50 = SVF 2.55 = LS 39A; Sandbach [1971] 12-13.

44 if those who deny that assentings come about by fate] This sentence is a notorious crux. Cicero distinguishes two positions, (1a) and (1b), that can be taken by those who deny that assent is fated. He compares the *second* of these ("see whether they are not saying the same thing") with the position (2) of Chrysippus, who says that assent and everything else that happens is fated, but according to Cicero means by that only to refer to auxiliary, and not to necessitating causes. (1b) and (2) thus, according to Cicero, amount to the same thing; they may disagree in their application of the *term* fate, but they are agreed that preceding sense-impressions are only *necessary for* assent and do not *necessitate* it.

The problem is that, as the text stands, (1a) and (1b) *also* seem to be saying the same thing. In both it is explicit that the assent is not fated; that the sense impression is needed is explicit in (1a), and in (1b) it is implied not only by comparison to what is asserted of Chrysippus in "For Chrysippus *too* concedes ... necessitating cause of assenting" but also - since the interpretation of that sentence too is dubious - by comparison to Chrysippus' general position. One possibility is to change the sense of (1a) to its opposite; this is the effect of the emendations of Valla, Heine and Bremi. The other is to accept that (1a) and (1b) are essentially making the same point, and that the significant difference is that (1b), unlike (1a), *makes explicit* the point that the sense-impression is not itself the sufficient cause of the assent (cf. Gercke 703; Bayer, 161-2, and Stüve cited by Hamelin 49-50). "That is another argument", perhaps to be understood in the sense of "we must argue with them in a different way", may still seem a very strong way (defended by Schröder 142 n.15) of stating what is really not much of a contrast. Kleywegt (344-6) therefore proposed to read not *ratio* but *oratio*, "that is another way of speaking". But this would most naturally be applied to a case where an apparent *conflict* of views turns out to be only a matter of terminology; here however the difference between (1a) and (1b) is not so much that they appear to be in conflict as that the latter is more fully stated than the former. Duhot 207 suggests that the lack of contrast reflects the artificial nature of the whole debate (see above, on §§39 and 40); but positions may still be clearly demarcated in an artificial debate, and should perhaps be particularly so.

because that proximate and contiguous cause does not itself bring about the assenting] The general sense must be that the sense-impression is not itself the decisive cause of the assenting; the supporters of the view stated here agree with Chrysippus on that point, but disagree in that they are not prepared to speak of assenting as the result of fate. "Proximate" has already been applied to the auxiliary cause in §41 above, and "contiguous" could be understood as indicating much the same. The word here translated by "contiguous", *continens,* has been linked with the Greek *sunektikos,* which would not naturally be applied to auxiliary causes (see the Excursus at the end of this Commentary). Yon xxxi-xxxii n.1 therefore interprets the present clause as "because that (cause) - i.e. the sense-impression - does not bring about the assent as a proximate *and continens* cause" - that is, it *is* proximate but is not *continens;* but this makes Cicero's expression very awkward, as Kleywegt 343-4 and Duhot 208 point out. See the next note.

For Chrysippus too concedes] Here too syntax and interpretation are doubtful. On any interpretation, Chrysippus must concede that all things come about by fate, while denying that they are necessitated. For, however the first part of the sentence is interpreted, it seems natural to take the last part (from "if all things come about by fate") as making this point, and if so *causis ... necessari-is* must be understood as referring to *necessitating* causes, rather than to *necessary* ones. But it is then natural to take *necessariam* earlier in the sentence as also signifying "*necessitating*".

The punctuation in the text, and the translation, follow the interpretation of

Kleywegt 346-9, adopted by Giomini and by Eisenberger (166 n.37), taking *concedet* with what *follows* it, so that it governs an *ut*-clause (for which, in the required sense of "admit" or "grant that", Kleywegt compares Cicero *On Friendship* 18 and *On Duties* 1.129). Most earlier editors took *concedet* rather with what preceded, and deleted the second *neque,* giving the sense "For neither will Chrysippus, (though) conceding (1) that the proximate and contiguous cause of the assenting is located in the sense-impression, concede (2) that this is a necessitating cause of assenting, with the result (if he *did* concede this), that, if all things come about by fate, all things would come about as a result of necessitating antecedent causes." Bayer 162 does the same by keeping the second *neque* but treating it as pleonastic. Yon, however, retained both the first and the second *neque,* taking the *second* with *concedet,* and giving the sense "For Chrysippus, not conceding (1) that the proximate and contiguous cause of the assenting is located in the sense-impression, will not concede (2) that this is a necessitating cause of assenting ..." (Yon, p.xxxii n.1; so already Hamelin 54, and similarly M. Frede [1980] 245). This builds on his interpretation of the previous sentence as claiming that the sense-impression is a proximate cause but *not* a *continens* one; but as has been seen this is difficult. Gercke's interpretation (704) is even more tortuous.

if all things come about by fate of such a sort that nothing comes about except by a cause having preceded] It would have been clearer to say 'if what is meant by "all things come about by fate" is that nothing comes about except by a cause having preceded'; once Chrysippus' opponents accept from him that *that* is what is meant by all things coming about by fate, they will have no reason to reject that claim.

45 In general there is this distinction] The distinction is between cases where things have already occurred that necessitate the outcome, so that nothing is in our power, and cases - those depending on human assent - where the antecedent causes are *necessary* but not *necessitating.*

Both sides approve this distinction] Chrysippus and his opponents, according to Cicero, agree that there is a distinction between necessary antecedent causes and necessitating ones, and accept that human assenting involves the former but not the latter; where they disagree is in that Chrysippus is prepared to describe it as fated because of the involvement of *necessary* antecedent causes, while his opponents are not, because they regard fate as *necessitating* and thus as excluding what is in our power. The last surviving part of §45, from "but the one group", explains the opponents' position. One would expect *alteri* to indicate "the first of two groups" and to be answered by a further statement of Chrysippus' position (so Yon, Bayer, and Schröder 151. The addition in the Harleian MS has no authority; Hamelin, 39).

On the question how much else has been lost before §46 and what its content might have been see the Introduction, §§4.1.9 and 4.2.2. The discussion of Chrysippus' views cannot be complete at the end of §45, because at this point we only have the account promised in §39 of how he attempted to escape the necessity of fate, and not that, also promised there, of how he failed to do so (see Introduction §4.2.2). Eisenberger 166-9 argues that Cicero does not accept §§44-5 as a satisfactory resolution of the problem; the rival views there are all described in the third person, and "this is how this case ought to be argued" at the start of §46 must refer to some positive statement of a position rather than to the claim in §45 that the difference between Chrysippus and his opponents is a matter of terminology rather than of substance. The natural candidate is a statement of Carneades' rejection of the deterministic aspect of Chrysippus' views, after which the start of §46 will state that Carneades' way of arguing against Chrysippus is superior to Epicurus', just as in §23 (Donini

Donini [1989] 140ff. suggests that Cicero went on to argue that Chrysippus' position does not in fact avoid determinism, because our characters too are shaped, according to Chrysippus, by causes which are ultimately beyond our control. This involves attributing a certain amount of disingenuousness to Carneades, whom Donini like Eisenberger regards as Cicero's source; whereas Chrysippus' original statement of the cylinder-argument, as recorded by Gellius (see Appendix (C)), makes explicit reference to the influence of external factors on our initial natural endowment, Carneades will have separated his statement of Chrysippus' position into two parts, first presenting the cylinder-argument as an attempt to avoid determinism, which it was not in fact, and then accusing Chrysippus of introducing determinism through other considerations which were in fact explicit in Chrysippus' own statement of the argument from the outset. But such tactics are not unlikely on Carneades' part. Donini further argues ([1989] 142) that the emphasis in §§41-5 on the freedom of choice from determination by *external* causes fits - up to a point - with the position attributed to Carneades in §25. Indeed, one can well imagine that in the sequel to §45 Carneades may have been presented as improving on Chrysippus' view by retaining the purely auxiliary role of sense-impressions while denying the determination of character, just as he was earlier said to improve on Epicurus' view by abandoning the atomic swerve.

Philippson 1036 placed fr.1 (see above after §4) in the lacuna between §45 and §46, suggesting that *hoc modo* at the end of fr.1 was not misplaced, but was rather a mistaken inclusion in his citation by Gellius of *hoc modo* at the start of §46; Schröder 150 n.27 rightly describes this as too bold. If fr.1 came in the lacuna between §45 and §46 the natural place for it would be not at the end of the lacuna but rather, as Schröder 151 seems to hint, at the point where Cicero moved from the superficially favourable exposition of Chrysippus' argument to overt criticism.

46 This is how this case ought to be argued] Cicero returns to his attack on the Epicurean atomic swerve, arguing in a way that has in it more of the advocate than the philosopher (see Introduction §4.1.9). He objects at length that the swerves of atoms are uncaused, failing to recognise that it is the very point of the doctrine that individual swerves *should* be uncaused at the atomic level (see above on §22). If there were a sufficient cause for a particular atom's swerving when and as it does, the indeterministic nature of the swerve, and with it its very raison d'être, would be done away with.

and from you, Epicurus, the force of weight and heaviness] Epicurus regarded both collisions and weight as among the causes of atomic movement along with the swerve (see above on §22); Cicero refers to what Epicurus added to the theory he took over. Democritus too regarded atoms as possessing weight, but did not treat this as the cause of downwards motion apart from collisions in the way Epicurus did; cf. KRS pp.421-3.

So what new cause is there in nature to make the atom swerve] With the MSS reading *quae, declinet* in this clause must be taken transitively as "cause to swerve", even though it is used intransitively in the next sentence. The admitted awkwardness does not seem unacceptable.

Or do they draw lots among themselves which will swerve and which not?] Yon compares Cicero *On Ends* 1.20, where a Roman metaphor is used to make a similar point; "this (*sc.* saying that some atoms swerve and others do not) would be like assigning provinces to the atoms, (saying) which should travel in a straight line and which obliquely."

why do they swerve by a minimum interval ...and not by two or three?] Cicero's words should probably be taken as implying that *all* swerves are by a sideways displacement of a single spatial minimum. The motive for such a doctrine is indicated by Lucretius 2.244-5; the swerve should be as small as possible if it is not to conflict with the evidence of our senses. A swerve of two or three minima would not indeed be evident to the senses either; but the argument depends on *analogy* between our perception of falling bodies and our conception of falling atoms, and if a swerve needs to be as small as possible for the former it must be for the latter as well. See above, on §22.

47 in a straight line] For *e regione* see above on §19.

48 Nor, indeed, does anyone seem to me more to confirm] The point is not that random swerve denies responsibility as much as does Stoic determinism, for the reference to confirming necessity would then be out of place; rather, Epicurus position is so implausible that it tends to lend support to the Stoic alternative. Weische 34 compares *On the Nature of the Gods* 1.69-70, where it is said that Epicurus in order to defend himself makes statements that are more shameful than having to give up his original position: this with reference not only to the atomic swerve and the denial of the truth or falsity of all future-tense statements, but also to the claim that all sensations are true, for which cf. LS 16).

For if it were granted that there are atoms (and there is no way it can be proved to me that they exist)] See above on §22.

For if it is granted to atoms by the necessity of nature] The text breaks off at the end of this sentence, and perhaps a page is lost from the end of the treatise; see Introduction, §4.1.10. It is unclear whether the present sentence is complete or not; "and that alleged swerving too is naturally necessary for some atoms, or if they like for all" may still be part of the "if" clause, but Rackham takes it as the main clause, the sentence ending with a question: "(then) is that alleged swerve also necessary for some atoms, or, if they choose, for all, in the order of nature?" On any account the *argument* cannot be complete at the point where our text breaks off.

for some atoms, or, if they like, for all] We have no direct evidence for the Epicurean view on this point; but if there can and must be no reason for a particular atom's swerving or not swerving as and when it does, there can be no reason why any given atom should not swerve at some time or other. Cicero's "for some atoms" will then be a rhetorical device intended to emphasise what is for him the implausibility of *any* swerves occurring at all. Cf. Eisenberger 169-170.

Eisenberger 170 suggests that the treatise may have concluded by Cicero pointing out that the rejection of Stoic fate - on the basis of Carneades' arguments rather than Epicurus' - does not entail the rejection of the gods or of religion; cf. *On Divination* 2.148 (above, Introduction §§2.1-2).

APPENDIX

[For the texts in the Appendix, see also Commentary on the relevant sections of Cicero *On Fate*.]

A. Origen, *Against Celsus* 2.20 (= SVF 2.957: cf. *On Fate* 28-30)

And against the Greeks] Origen's whole discussion was prompted by Celsus' claim that, if Jesus knew that Judas would betray him, Judas could not be blamed. If indeed God foreknows what will happen, the fact that a prophecy is stated in conditional form does not in itself affect the problem created for human freedom. But the conditional form of prophecy may still serve, for Origen as for Chrysippus, to emphasise that it is the human agent whose actions bring about the result. See Introduction §3.1.7.

but if he intends "certainly" in the sense of "it will happen"] Origen accepts that what God foreknows will happen, but that it will happen in such a way that it could also not happen. For Carneades as reported by Cicero in §32, on the other hand, Apollo can *only* foreknow what is necessary. See Introduction, §7.4.

B. Cicero, *Topics* 58-61 (cf. *On Fate* 34-36)

Cicero's *Topics* was written in July 44, soon after *On Fate* (Duhot 202). It is concerned with techniques of rhetorical argument, and it is in this context that the present discussion should be read. Schröder 14f. n.31 rightly points out that it should not be assumed that the whole passage is a statement of specifically Stoic doctrine.

59 some are inactive, do nothing] Schröder loc. cit. points out that the Stoics would not regard these as causes in any sense.

others however provide a certain beginning] i.e. *prokatarktika* causes (see the Excursus, below); Donini [1974-5] 189 n.3.

It is from this kind of causes ... that fate is bound together by the Stoics] This is similar to the identification of fate with initiating causes only in Cicero *On Fate* §41 and in Plutarch (Appendix (D) below). But nothing here rules it out that a *combination* of causes each of which is in itself only a necessary and not a sufficient condition may still render the result predetermined, contrary to what is asserted in the Plutarch passage and implied in Cicero *On Fate*. Cf. Schröder 14-18.

meeting had provided the cause of love] Duhot 202 points out that this example could derive from that of Medea (below).

as to whether it makes men happy on its own] The Stoics held that it did; cf. LS 61 and 63. Duhot 202 uses the fact that the point is questioned here to argue that our text does not derive from a Stoic source; but Cicero might have added his own question to a basically Stoic treatment (cf. Hamelin 41). For wisdom as the cause of being wise cf. SVF 1.89 (Duhot 148).

60 if sons cannot exist without parents] The same example is used by Alexander of Aphrodisias *On Fate* 24, but in a different context, as part of his argument against the Stoics that the unity of the universe cannot be based on antecedent causes. Cf. Sharples [1983,1] 155.

C. Aulus Gellius, *Attic Nights* 7.2 (SVF 2.1000: cf. *On Fate* 41-43)

1 Fate ... is a certain everlasting and unalterable succession] Cf. Cicero *On Fate* fr.2, above. It should be noted that Gellius says in what follows that he is quoting from memory.

3 following on and involved with another from eternity] The compound *meta-poleisthai* (not *met-apoleisthai*), not in the Liddell-Scott-Jones *Lexicon*, combines the ideas of succession and of a constant turning back and forth; cf. Gellius' *volvens*, translated "involving ... itself with itself", just above.

4 the supporters of other views and teachings] It is clear from Gellius' account that Chrysippus had to meet objections claiming that his deterministic position was incompatible with moral responsibility; but whether the formulation of the argument that follows is due to the objectors, or whether it has been devised by Chrysippus or Gellius to provide a context for Chrysippus' counter-argument, may be less certain. Compare the commentary on Cicero, *On Fate* §40, above.

6 Many acute and subtle arguments] For example those reported in Alexander *On Fate* ch. 35 = SVF 2.1003 = LS 62J and in ibid. ch.37 = SVF 2.1005.

7 through a certain necessary and primary principle] "necessary" presumably has the sense of necessitating": cf. Cicero *On Fate* §36. *principalis*, translated by "primary", could also have connotations of "beginning", "initiating"; Duhot 175 renders it by "fundamental". Cf. the reference to "types and beginnings of causes" later in the present passage, and the Excursus below.

the way in which the natures of our minds themselves are subject to fate depends on their own individual quality] Long [1971] 197 n.45 suggests that Gellius' *proprietas ... et qualitas* renders the Stoic technical term *idia poiotês* (so too LS vol.2 p.385). Gellius here suggests that, from one point of view at least, fate is the part of the causal nexus that is *external* to us; cf. also below, "that force, which assails them from outside through fate". But the difference from Cicero's account is that Gellius does not obscure the fact that our own contribution is a part of the causal nexus, not something that is contrasted with it: the natures of our minds too are initially due to causes not under our control, the eventual outcomes are described as "fated consequences" of our characters' being of a certain type, and while we can certainly influence the way in which our characters develop, there is no indication that the way in which we do so is not at every point the predetermined result of the combination of external factors and our character as it has developed so far. Cf. Donini [1974-5] 199-200.

8 If they have been fashioned by nature originally] For the two types of reaction to fate one may compare the example of the dog and the chariot; cf. Introduction §3.1.7. Since fate and universal nature are the same for Chrysippus (Stobaeus in SVF 2.913; Plutarch, *On Stoic Self-Contradictions* 34 1050ab = SVF 2.937; Philodemus in SVF 2.1076), our characters too are due to fate.

10 a fated consequence of their type itself] *fatale et consequens* form a hendiadys, *genere ipso* going with both. Schröder 152 n.30 points out that *genere* refers to the two Stoic classes of the good and wise on the one hand and the fools on the other, taking up the contrast in §8.

that bad natures should not lack crimes and errors] Cf. Marcus Aurelius 9.42, 11.18 ad fin. and 12.16, arguing that this should console us when bad people wrong us; it is natural that they should.

11 the order and rule and necessity of fate sets types and beginnings of causes in motion] Schröder 152-3 n.30 argues that "of causes" goes only with "beginnings" and not also with "types"; he takes the former to refer to types of character (cf. "a consequence of their type itself" above). Whether the "beginnings of causes" are sense-impressions as *aitia prokatarktika* (so Schröder) or whether this too refers to the responsibility of fate for our general character, there is an apparent contrast between what is governed by fate and what is not ("but the impulses of our minds ..."; cf. Görler 262 n.20). But the whole outcome is none the less the result of fate.

12 And that is why it has also been said by the Pythagoreans] The citation is from the Pythagorean *Golden Verses,* 54 (ed. D. Young, *Theognis, etc.,* Leipzig, Teubner, 1961); cf. M. Dragona-Monachou, ''Ο ῾Υμνος στὸ Δία καὶ τὰ Χρυσᾶ ἔπη', Φιλοσοφία (Athens) 1 (1971) 339-378, at 361-2.

D. Plutarch, *On Stoic Self-Contradictions* 47 1056B (= SVF 2.997: cf. *On Fate* 41)

He who says that Chrysippus made fate not a sufficient cause ... but only an initiating one] Cf. Cicero *On Fate* §41 and *Topics* §59 above. Schmekel [1938] 269-271 argued that Plutarch is here reporting an interpretation of Chrysippus by Antipater of Tarsus; however Theiler [1946] 76 n.129 drew attention to 1035E, where "if someone says that Chrysippus wrote ..." introduces a statement of Chrysippus' own doctrine. Here too we may be dealing with a hypothetical objector presented by Plutarch simply as citing passages of Chrysippean doctrine rather than as offering idiosyncratic interpretations of them. Plutarch's concern in *On Stoic Self-Contradictions* is after all with alleged inconsistencies between different statements both made by Chrysippus *himself.* (Cf. Schröder 18 n.39, and 20 n.42, defending Theiler's view against the objection of Donini [1974-5] 212 and [1988].) However, the fact that Plutarch *presents* the view that fate is only an initiating cause as Chrysippean need not mean that it is indeed so; Schröder 18-20 argues that he has distorted Chrysippus' view, illegitimately treating fate, which includes *all* the causes of events, as like the wise men, mentioned earlier by Plutarch, whose utterances are indeed only one, and not the principal one, among the causes of people assenting to what they say. The view that the existence of human responsibility means that not everything is fated is attributed to the Stoics in "Aëtius" 1.27.4 = DG p.322.13 = SVF 2.976, but this seems to be a misinterpretation.

And what we do depends on how you may be minded] Cf. Cicero, *On Fate* fr.3 above, and the Commentary there.

EXCURSUS

TERMINOLOGY FOR CAUSES

1.1. The question of the distinctions drawn by the Stoics between different types of causes, of the terminology they used for them, and of the relation of Cicero's Latin terms to the original Greek, is a vexed and controversial one which is still the subject of lively debate. Fortunately for our present purposes, these problems do not seriously hinder our interpretation of Chrysippus' position regarding determinism and of Cicero's reporting of it; as Duhot 182 points out, Gellius' report of Chrysippus' cylinder-argument (Appendix (C) above) is clear without much recourse to technical terminology, and even if Cicero is attempting to produce a Latin version of such terminology, the way in which he does so is more important for the reconstruction of technical Stoic theory than for understanding the general sense of the argument of *On Fate*. It does not seem appropriate in the present work completely to disregard issues which have prompted so much discussion; but it seems better to deal with them in an excursus which will both allow a more continuous form of discussion and avoid complicating the basic commentary.

1.2. Two initial points need to be made. First, discussion of types of cause was a major concern of medical writers concerned with the aetiology of disease; it is certain that their discussions were influenced by Stoic distinctions, and probable that there was influence in the reverse direction as well. A full treatment of ancient causal theories would take account of the medical as well as the philosophical material; but no attempt will be made to do that exhaustively here. Secondly, a major source on the topic is the last chapter (8.9) of Clement of Alexandria's *Miscellanies* or *Stromateis*. But although extensive extracts from that chapter are printed as illustrative material in von Arnim's *SVF*, it is generally agreed that it mingles material from different sources and schools.

2.1. Plutarch in Appendix (D) above refers to a claim that Chrysippus made fate only a *prokatarktikos*, "initiating", and not an *autotelês*, "self-sufficient", cause. At *On Stoic Self-Contradictions* 47 1055F = SVF 2.994 he cites Chrysippus as denying that an impression is an *autotelês* cause of assent. Clement of Alexandria, *Stromateis* 8.9 25.4 (*Griech. Christ. Schriftst.* vol. 17² p.96.2-5 Stählin-Fruchtel-Treu, Berlin 1970) = SVF 2.346 (not in fact Stoic, according to Duhot 214) describes beauty as a *prokatarktikos* cause of love because the sight of it does not *necessitate* love, contrasting it in this respect with an *autotelês* cause.

2.2. We also find references to *sunektika* causes, literally those that "hold together". Galen argues that this term was taken over from Stoicism by the Pneumatic school of medicine, and should properly be used in relation to the Stoic doctrine of breath or spirit present in all things and holding them together (for which cf. LS 47; Duhot 110ff.): Galen *Caus. Cont.* 2.1, *Corp. Med. Graec. suppl. orient.* vol.2 p.54.4-11 Lyons), *Against Julianus* 6.13, *Corp. Med. Graec.* vol. 5.10.3 p.57.15-58.1 Wenkebach and 8.22 p.70.3-6 Wenkebach = SVF 2.355, *Synopsis of the books* On types of Pulse 9 vol.9 p.458.8-14 Kühn = SVF 2.356. However, Galen himself extends the use more widely (*Against Julianus* 6.13 p.58.1-4 Wenkebach, *Caus. cont.* 8.6 p.67.10-13 Lyons. Cf. Hankinson 81-6, Duhot 151-166). In medical contexts emphasis is laid on the idea that *sunektika* causes are contemporaneous with their effects, by contrast with *prokatarktika*, the external causes that initiate diseases, and *prohêgoumena*, the internal causes that develop from these but still precede the disease itself (Galen, *Caus. cont.* 2.2-3 p.55.12-24 Lyons, [Galen], *Medical Definitions* 155-7, vol.19 p.392.10-393.10 Kühn = SVF 2.354. For *prokatarktika* and *sunektika* cf. also Clement, *Strom.* 8.9 33.1 p.101.17-19 = SVF 2.351. Grilli 432, Hankinson 87-92, Duhot 180-2). White 221 suggests rendering *sunektikos* by "maintaining cause". *sunektika* causes are sometimes identified with *autotelê* ones, as by Clement *Strom.* 8.9 25.3 p.95.31-96.2 = SVF 2.346 and 8.9 33.2 p.101.19-20 = SVF 2.351; but it is not clear how much relevance these discussions have to specifically Stoic doctrine and to Chrysippus' discussion of determinism (cf. Duhot 168, 180; Schröder 8).

2.3. We also find a contrast between *sunektika* causes and those that are *sunaitia* or *sunerga*. *Sunerga* are those which assist *sunektika* causes to achieve the results which the latter could bring about even without the aid of the *sunergon* cause; *sunaitia* are those which assist other *sunaitia*, neither on its own being capable of bringing about the result (Clement, *Strom.* 8.9 33.7-9 p.102.1-12 = SVF 2.351; cf. [Galen] *Med. def.* 159-160, vol.19 p.393.13-18 Kühn). The claim of *sunerga* to be causes at all is denied at Clement *Strom.* 8.9 p.28.3-5 p.98.5-15). But these distinctions too may not be Stoic (Duhot 232-3; cf. M. Frede [1980] 237, Hankinson 84 n.18).

3.1. Cicero *On Fate* §41 distinguishes between *causae perfectae et principales* on the one hand and *causae adiuvantes et proximae* on the other, and this distinction is subsequently illustrated by that between the push that starts a cylinder rolling and the shape that causes it to roll when pushed and to continue doing so. The questions that arise are whether Cicero is rendering Greek technical terms closely (which Schröder 153 denies); if he is, whether his two pairs of adjectives correspond to just two Greek terms, rendered in each case by means of hendiadys, or to four; and if the latter, whether both of the terms in each pair are equally appropriate to the particular example of the cylinder.

3.2. There can be little doubt that, if Cicero has particular Greek terms in mind at all, *perfectae* corresponds to *autotelês*. But there is a problem over the sense in which the shape of a cylinder is a *self-sufficient* cause for its rolling; the example makes clear that the cylinder only rolls when pushed. The difficulty has been met in various ways: by weakening the sense of *autotelês* (an "absolute" cause which nevertheless needs others to assist it, Duhot 214); by arguing that the shape is the *autotelês* cause not of the cylinder's rolling but of its *rolling when pushed* (LS vol.1 p.341); or by saying that it is the internal *pneuma* of the cylinder *as modified by the push* which sustains its motion thereafter (M. Frede [1980] 236). Or it may be that we are indeed dealing with four terms rather than two, and that it is only *principales* and not *perfectae* that is strictly relevant to the case of the cylinder (Görler 256-7; Sedley [1993]). Schröder 9-10 argues that Cicero nowhere implies that the nature of the agent is a *perfecta* or a *principalis* cause; but it seems clear both that the nature of the agent is to be compared with that of the cylinder, and that the nature of the cylinder is not an *adiuvans* or *proxima* cause, which strongly suggests that it is at least *principalis*. See also Sorabji [1980,1] 260-1.

3.3. *Adiuvantes* might render *sunerga*. Admittedly the suggestion in §2.3 above that a *sunergon* cause, as opposed to a *sunaition*, is helpful but not essential is difficult to reconcile with the fact that the push *is* needed for the cylinder to start rolling (cf. Schröder, 219f.) But the distinction between *sunaitia* and *sunerga* should perhaps not be pressed (Hamelin, 45). Alexander, *On Fate* 36 208.27, describes a stone as falling through having the particular nature it does and through having the surrounding circumstances as *sunerga*.

3.4.1. The Greek that suggests itself as a possible source for Cicero's *causae proximae* is *prosekheis* (so Stüve, Hamelin 49, Bayer 158, Grilli 432, and Turnebus ap. Bayer 159). Others have suggested that *proxima* represents not *prosekheis*, "proximate" but *prokatarktika* "initiating", or the like (M. Frede [1980] 241; LS vol.1 p.342, 2 p.384; Duhot 172). But it is difficult to see *proxima* as a translation of *prokatarktikos*, *sunaitios* or *sunergos*, even if the causes Cicero describes as *proximae* could be so described (cf. Schröder, 153-4).

3.4.2. A further complexity where *causae proximae* are concerned is the sense of Cicero's term *continens* (see above, on *On Fate* §44). It may seem natural to connect it with *sunektikos;* as Duhot 112-13 points out, *continere* is repeatedly used by Cicero in *On the Nature of the Gods* to express the Stoic doctrine of a cohesive force holding the universe together (2.19, 29, 58, 3.28). The *sunektikos* cause is regularly contrasted (above, 2.2) with the initiating or *prokatarktikos* cause, and it is explained as that which holds a thing together — as does the Stoic *pneuma* with which the shape of the cylinder, the *primary* cause, is naturally connected. Both *sunektikos* and *continens* can refer to the chief points in an argument (Cicero *Part. Or.* 103, Quintilian 3.11.9; Görler 271, Duhot 170-1). Yon notes the phrase *causae <u>cohibentes</u> in se efficientiam naturalem,* "those that contain within themselves a natural effectiveness", in Cicero *On Fate* §19 above, but, apart from the fact that *cohibentes* is a different term from *continentes,* it is not clear that *cohibentes* in §19 is being used in a technical sense or is to be linked with *sunektika;* cf. Schröder 229 n.56.

3.4.3. However, as indicated in the Commentary there are problems in interpreting *continens* in terms of *sunektikos* in §44. M. Frede [1980] 245 suggests that *continens* in §44 stands for *sunektikos*, but in a non-Stoic usage where it leaves open the possibility that the *sunektikos* cause might not have brought about the assent, taking *moveat* not just as subjunctive in reported speech, but this seems tortuous; cf. Görler 270 n.34. Others have suggested that not only *continens* but also *sunektikos* could have the sense of "proximate"; Görler argues (268-274) that Galen identifies *sunekhon, sunektikon* and *prosekhes* causes (*On the Causes of Symptoms* vol.7 p.109 Kühn; cf. *Summary of the books On types of Pulse* vol.9 p.484 Kühn, and also Hankinson 85 n.22), so that *continens* could be linked with *sunekhon* and still have the sense of "proximate", though not "auxiliary"; he suggests that there is a similar ambiguity in both the Greek and the Latin terms between what "holds together" and is decisive and what is adjacent or immediate. But Schröder 24-5 argues rightly that in the passages cited by Görler Galen is not *identifying sunektikos* and *prosekhes* causes, but rather classifying the same cause in two different ways from different points of view. So it seems that we should accept that *continens* has the sense of proximate, but not attempt to connect it with *sunektikos* (Schröder 26).

3.5.1. Most controversial of all, however, is Cicero's remaining term *causa principalis*. It has often been thought that it renders the Greek *kuria* (so Bayer 158 and Turnebus ap. Bayer 159; Hamelin 23; Pohlenz [1940] 106; M. Frede [1980] 239). But Görler 258 describes this as a "fiction", rightly pointing out that *kurios* does not appear in the Stoic classifications of causes at all. Duhot 170 suggests that *principalis* might stand for *sunektikos*.

3.5.2. *Principalis* could also have the sense of "initiating", "beginning", and Görler has suggested that Cicero's *causae principales* are actually the equivalent of the Greek *prokatarktika*, contrasted with the proximate causes, the point of Cicero's argument being that our character, like the shape of the cylinder, is already established before the stimulus which sets the process in motion but does not determine the course it takes. (The suggestion that *principalis* renders *prokatarktikos* had already been rejected by Hamelin 43; for other anticipations cf. Görler 259 n.14.) Görler's view involves a slightly awkward separation of the "initiating cause" as he sees it from the push which provides the *principium motionis* in §43; it also contrasts, as pointed out by Donini [1989] 124-5 n.1 and Schröder 211-219, with the suggestion in Plutarch (Appendix (D) above) that fate is only a *prokatarktikos* cause of our behaviour; on Görler's view fate, identified in Cicero with the external cause, will not even be that.

3.5.3. Another possibility is that *principalis* renders *prohêgoumenos*, not in the specific medical sense in §2.2 above, but in a wider application (Hamelin 42, 45, Yon xxix n.1, Greene 349 and Grilli 433-4; cf. also Donini [1989] 125 n.2). *Prohêgoumenai* may also seem to be the natural equivalent for "antecedent", *antecedentes* (so Pohlenz [1940] 106; M. Frede [1980] 241; LS vol.1 p.342; cf. Hankinson 90-91, and Görler 259 n.13, pointing out that for the Stoics *every* cause is an antecedent cause). Our sources do indeed claim that for the Stoics everything comes about in accordance with *prohêgoumenai aitiai* (cf. e.g. [Plutarch] *On Fate* 11 574d = SVF 2.912). However, *prohêgoumenos*, like *principalis*, seems to combine the senses of "earlier in time" and "primary in importance"; *kuriai* and *prohêgoumenai* causes are linked (in Peripatetic argument against the Stoics) at Alexander of Aphrodisias *On Fate* 8 174.28 and 24 194.17-19, and the term could perhaps have the sense of "preceding in a decisive way" (cf. R.W. Sharples, 'Responsibility, Chance and Not-Being', *Bulletin of the Institute of Classical Studies* 22 [1975], at 49, and Sharples [1983,1] 132-3). This would fit the reference in [Plutarch], emphasising the deterministic nature of Stoic causation. But whether this should lead us to see *prohêgoumenos* also as the source of Cicero's *principalis* is at best a matter of speculation.

Boethius, *Consolation of Philosophy*

[IV.5] 1 At this point] The Lady Philosophy has been arguing that wickedness itself makes the wrongdoer wretched, rather than his victim (a theme most eloquently developed by Plato in the *Gorgias)*. Virtue is itself happiness, and wickedness misery. But Boethius is not satisfied, and seeks an explanation of why, even so, divine providence does not assign good or bad things as commonly so regarded in accordance with men's deserving. The first part of book 4 may be influenced by Neoplatonic commentary on the *Gorgias;* Klingner [1921] 84-8, Courcelle [1967] 173-5, [1969] 307.

the actual deeds] *merita* can indicate what one deserves as a result of one's deeds; but it can also indicate the deeds through which one deserves something, and the context requires this sense here.

2 fortune as popularly understood] I.e. in contrast with Philosophy's claim that it is virtue and vice that are truly good and bad fortune.

there is a certain amount of good or evil] The Stoics had denied that external things could be good or evil; for them virtue alone was good, vice alone evil, and other things at most "preferred" or "non-preferred" (cf. LS 58). But they too had tried to show that the way in which these things were allotted was in accordance with divine providence, though it does not seem to be; LS 54Q-T.

an exile, needy and in disgrace ... rather than ... to flourish in his own city] Boethius has spoken of his present plight in such terms (I.4 §§36, 45); but Philosophy at once countered with the argument (I.5) that Boethius' real exile is his self-inflicted departure from wisdom, the true country of the wise man. The *Consolation* is itself the story of how he returns there (cf. Introduction §11).

3 the duties of wisdom] The wise man's preference for prosperity over wickedness is made to rest on the greater opportunity it gives him to perform virtuous deeds - a point that had featured in debate between the Stoics and their opponents; cf. I.G. Kidd, 'Stoic Intermediates and the End for Man', in A.A. Long (ed.), *Problems in Stoicism*, London 1971, 151-72, at 159-60. "duties" renders *officia,* Cicero's term for Stoic *kathêkonta,* actions that should be performed but are *right* actions only if performed by a perfectly virtuous man (LS 59).

prison, death, and the other tortures] Another allusion to Boethius' own situation. Most of the MSS have *lex,* "law". I have followed the recent editors in accepting *nex;* though "Death" comes oddly between prison and torture. Cf. Büchner [1940] 296; Daly. Vulpius' *nexus* would give rather "prison, bonds, and the other tortures".

why these things are turned about] There are close verbal parallels in this passage with the complaint in I m.5 28ff; Gruber, 350.

so great a design] including all that comes about in the whole world.

[IV metre 5] The poem develops the theme that it is lack of understanding that causes our perplexity; the implication being, as in the concluding section of the previous prose, that there are reasons for Providence arranging things as it does, even if we do not understand them. The metre is unique: in the odd-numbered lines the first half of a Sapphic line (- ᴗ - - -) plus an Adonean (- ᴗ ᴗ - ᴗ), in the even-numbered lines the first half of an Alcaic line (ᴗ - ᴗ - -) plus an Adonean; in each case resolutions are allowed for special effect (*celeres* in line 5, *subitis* in line 20). (I am indebted to Alan Griffiths and Malcolm Willcock for this analysis).

1 If someone does not know] The circumpolar stars never sink below the horizon; those of higher latitude spend longer above the horizon and less beneath it than those further south, rising earlier and setting later. This may not seem as surprising a phenomenon as the eclipse mentioned next; but its prominent position may be to introduce the image of rotation round a fixed point (*cardo*, pole or pivot), which will be important in the next prose section (see IV.6.15).

The stars of Arcturus ... the Ox-Driver is slow to steer his cart] Strictly Arcturus is the brightest star in the constellation Boötes, the Ox-Driver, and by extension it can stand for the whole constellation; but since the Ox-Driver is mentioned by name, "the stars of Arcturus" are here rather the Waggon or Wain itself which Boötes drives – or watches; for the Wain is also visualised as the Great Bear, whence the name Arcturus (in Greek = Bear-Watcher). (Cf. Scheible, 144). Both constellations are close to the north celestial pole; hence they seem to cover less distance in their rotation round it and to move more slowly. For the reading *regat* Sitzmann compares Seneca(?) *Octavia* 233f., *qua plaustra tardus noctis aeterna vice regit Boötes* (and for the Ox-Driver *steering* the Wain cf. Ovid *Metamorphoses* 10.447; *flexit*). The *legat* of most MSS cannot mean "unyoke" (Grüber 351; cf. Tränkle [1968] 285); Scheible 144 argues that it is being used rather in the sense of "track the steps of, follow behind" (cf. Virgil *Aeneid* 9.392, Ovid *Metamorphoses* 3.17), the Ox-Driver *following* the Wain, but in Virgil and Ovid *vestigia* are explicitly mentioned. *legat* does indeed emphasise the idea of a steady and predictable rotation round a centre. But the parallel with Seneca argues for *regat*.

4 and sinks his light late into the sea] The late setting of the Ox-Driver goes back to Homer (*Odyssey* 5.272).

7 Should the full moon's horns lose their colour] Boethius' second example: ordinary people do not understand the true cause of a lunar eclipse (known at least since Parmenides, KRS 308). "Horns" is proleptic; it is the new moon that has horns, not the full moon – until it starts to be eclipsed. "lose their colour", not "grow pale", for in an eclipse the moon is *darkened;* thus Lucan, *Pharsalia* 7.178, uses *pallere diem* when the day becomes darkened as a portent, and Statius *Thebaid* 12.406 uses the word of the stars growing dim before the dawn.

8 the cones of shadowy night] *metis* could just be the "boundary", between the part of the moon that is in shadow and the part that is still illuminated, for *meta* can mean a limit or boundary; and so Watts and O'Donnell take it here. But *meta* is also used of cone-shaped objects, the turning-posts in the Circus being cone-shaped; and the shadow of the earth which causes the lunar eclipse is indeed cone-shaped. Cf., with Gruber 351, Cicero *On Divination* 2.17, "when (the moon), in the opposite region to the sun, enters the shadow of the earth, which is the cone (*meta*) of night, so that it is necessarily darkened"; also Cicero *Republic* 1.22, Pliny *Natural History* 2.47, 2.51, Ammianus Marcellinus 20.3.8.

10 reveal the stars which she had hidden] The dimming of the moon's light makes apparent stars which could not be seen before because of the moon's greater brightness (Phoebe being a mythological name for the moon).

12 they weary bronze with frequent striking] The custom of clashing metal objects together to revive or restore the moon or sun during an eclipse is frequently attested. Cf., with Gruber 352, Tibullus 1.8.21f., Ovid *Metamorphoses* 4.333, Livy 26.5.9, Tacitus *Annals* 1.28.2, Juvenal 6.442f.

16 Phoebus] the sun, as Phoebe (above) is the moon.

17 For here ... but there] The words could be translated "in this case ... in that case"); but sea and snow are "here" in the terrestrial region, and so are familiar, while the remoteness of the heavenly bodies "there" explains our lack of understanding of their movements. (So O'Donnell).

22 would indeed ... cease to seem marvellous] The opening sentence of IV.6 takes this up by referring to the explanation of the causes of hidden things; and the idea that amazement reflects ignorance reappears at IV.6.27-8. *inscitiae* is scanned as three long syllables by synizesis of *i* and *ae* (O'Donnell).

[IV.6] it is your task to lay open the causes of hidden things] The preceding poem has emphasised the contrast between things whose causes are, and those whose causes are not, understood; the prose passage before that had ended with Philosophy's declaration that fortune as normally understood, i.e. in terms of external goods, is well ordered by divine providence even if we cannot understand how. On the whole chapter cf. the discussion of Lerer, 204-13.

concerning this] hinc: a late Latin usage, cf. Gruber 353.

3. like the heads of the Hydra] When Hercules tried to slay the many-headed monstrous Hydra (below, IV m.7), two heads sprang up in the place of every one he cut off, and he solved the problem by burning the stumps (IV m.7.22 below). Hence "to check them with the most lively *fire* of the mind".

4 the singleness of providence, the sequence of fate] see below on §§8-17. For the "sequence" of fate, cf. above on Cicero *On Fate* §27, and cf. Calcidius, *On the* Timaeus 145, p.183.8-9 Waszink, with Sulowski [1957] 83.

5 part of your treatment] In I.5 Philosophy describes her whole exposition as a restoration of Boethius to right understanding. Throughout this chapter emphasis is laid on the limitations of human understanding; cf. Lerer 204-13 and Introduction §11.5.

6 the delights of musical song] see §58 below, and Introduction §11.2.

while I weave arguments bound together in sequence] Lerer 207 points out how the imagery links Philosophy's exposition with the ordering of fate itself.

8 when this rule is considered ... it has been called fate by the ancients] Fate is here presented as the working-out in extended time of the providential plan which exists all at once and all together on the level of divine intellect. The distinction has a long history; see Introduction, §8.

10 this whole temporal unfolding, when united in the view of the divine mind] These words already contain the germ of the solution to the problem of reconciling free will and divine foreknowledge that will be advanced in book V.

12 just as the craftsman] That the craftsman realises in his materials the form already present in his mind is the doctrine of Aristotle *(Metaph.* Z 7 1032a32ff.); here it is coupled with the observation that, while the form can be understood in a single moment, its realisation in the material takes time - this providing an analogy to the contrast between timeless providence and fate unfolding in time.

13 whether fate is carried on] Boethius gives a list of alternatives, stressing the basic point that fate is subordinate to providence. Plotinus *Ennead* 3.1 considers alternative explanations of fate in terms of atomic movements, a world-soul, the movement of the heavens and the chain of causes, ending by emphasising that the righteous soul can rise above fate; cf. Introduction §8.3. Chadwick 242 also compares Augustine *City of God* 5.9 and *On the Trinity* 3.4.9. For the *world-soul* cf. Plato *Timaeus* 34a ff. and *Philebus* 30a (Gruber 357); for its identification with fate cf. Introduction §8.3. The identification of fate and *nature* is Stoic; cf. LS 55MN. The connection between fate and the *heavenly bodies* might naturally be interpreted in astrological terms; but Aristotle had linked sublunary changes to the motion of the heavenly bodies and especially to the annual motion of the sun along the ecliptic (*On Coming-to-be and Passing-away* 2.10-11), and Alexander of Aphrodisias (c.200 A.D.) had used this idea in his account of a divine providence which he identified also with fate (cf. Sharples [1983,1] 25-7). Destiny is linked with the stars by Boethius *On* On Interpretation[2] 231.3ff. (Chadwick 162, 242). *daemones,* inferior deities, are linked with providence by the Stoics (cf. Introduction §9.4) and by Platonists ([Plutarch] *On Fate* 574B, Proclus *On the Republic* vol.2 p.255.19 Kroll, explicitly claiming "angels" as a "Greek", i.e. pagan, term; id. *Ten problems* 62). Courcelle [1967] 205f. rightly argues that for Boethius too the suggestion (for it is no more than that) must relate to Neoplatonic is Neoplatonic *daemones,* for the servants of providence cannot be Christian *devils.* See also Introduction, §13.2.

14 the first divinity] The terminology is scarcely Christian (Gruber 357).

firmly fixed] The reference is to the Platonic forms (de Vogel [1972] 29-30).

15 when circles turn around the same pivot] Boethius illustrates the relation of fate to providence by that of the moving circumference of a circle to its still centre; the closer things are to the divine mind - and in particular, the more our souls turn towards it - the more they are free from fate and the physical movements it produces. The sources of this analogy have provoked much controversy. Plotinus speaks of the universe as a sphere caused by soul to rotate round its centre (2.2.1-2, 3.2.3), of the Good being to the whole as the centre to a circle and the sun to its light (1.7.1), of the One being to Intellect as centre to circle (6.8.18) and of soul circling round the One (6.9.8-9). Patch [1929] suggested that Boethius used Plotinus to supplement ideas which he found in Proclus' illustration of the relation of fate to providence in *On Providence* 5-9 (already suggested as a source for Boethius by Klingner [1921] 88 n.5 and others); in particular Patch argued that the idea of *drawing closer to the centre* is absent from the Proclus passage. Courcelle [1967] 206-7, [1969] 305-6 pointed out that Proclus in *On Providence* 5 speaks of a circle while Plotinus in some of the passages cited by Patch speaks rather of a sphere. De Vogel [1971] 56 and Obertello [1974] 516-17 argue that Boethius is combining ideas from both authors; Scheible 185-8 n.8 however points out that, though the notion of *several concentric* circles is not explicit in either Plotinus or Proclus, it is implied in Plotinus 6.8.18 (above), and argues that Boethius is building on this. Chadwick 242 notes that Augustine *On the Trinity* 3.9.16 (CCSL vol. 50 p.143) speaks of God as the supreme pivot *(cardo)* of causes.

17 as reasoning is to understanding] That is, as human discursive reasoning is to divine intuition; cf. below on V.4.30. On time and eternity cf. V.6.4.

19 by an indissoluble connecting of causes] the language is Stoic (cf. Cicero *On Fate* fr.2 above, and "by an undeviating sequence of causes" in §20 below; also Cicero *On Divination* 1.125 = LS 55L); the thought too is Stoic and Neoplatonist rather than Aristotelian - *everything* in the physical world is the product of a single inexorable ordering, while for some Peripatetics at least, and notably Alexander, fate or providence was only concerned with what *generally* happens, and left room for chance occurrences and the free choices of individuals. As Patch [1929] 63 points out, Boethius draws no distinction here between fortune and fate. See further below on V.1.

21 by their own rule] The use of *suus* for "one's own" even where the possessor is not (in the Latin, as opposed to the translation) the grammatical subject of the sentence, and has not even been explicitly mentioned yet, is particularly characteristic of later Latin: Hofmann-Szantyr 175, Gruber 359.

22 as has been most amply shown] In IV.2. Compare Plato, *Gorgias* 467-8, and see above on IV.5.1.

that starts from the supreme good] *proficiens* is used in the sense of *proficiscens*; Prinz 172, Gruber 359.

23 But, you will say, what confusion] This was Boethius' question; how can the prosperity of the wicked and the sufferings of the righteous - like Boethius himself - be justified? The use of both *quae* and *ulla* is a redundancy characteristic of late Latin: Hofmann-Szantyr 801, Gruber 359.

24 human beings do not enjoy such sureness of judgement] The first reply; who are we to judge who *is* righteous or unrighteous?

26 But let us grant] The second reply; virtue and wickedness are like health and disease, and good and bad fortune are allotted by God with a view to their effects on the souls of the people concerned. The analogy between health or sickness of the body and virtue or wickedness of the soul is characteristic of Plato's Socrates (e.g. *Protagoras* 313, and *Gorgias* 477-8 on which *Consolation* IV.4.38-42 are based); characteristic of Plato too is the thought that punishment should be aimed at curing the offender if possible, rather than being retributive - which is what those who are concerned about just rewards, in the way Boethius was in posing his question, are actually asking it should be; and concern with the improvement of the offender leads Plato himself into an approach to punishment which may well be found wanting if considered by the strict standard of what people *deserve* (cf. A.W.H. Adkins, *Merit and Responsibility,* Oxford 1960, 304-311). "Temperament" is a medical term; on its use also as a musical image, cf. Chamberlain 93.

27 sweet things ... and bitter things] Gruber compares Cicero *On Fate* §8 above.

30 the lofty-observation-post of providence] Cf. Plato, *Statesman* 272e (where however it is linked with the temporary *withdrawal* of divine involvement in the world), and below on V.6.17.

32 most just and most observant of what is right] an echo of Virgil, *Aeneid* 2.426-7, "Rhipeus too fell, the single most just person among the Trojans and the most observant of what is right" *(cadit et Rhipeus, iustissimus unus/qui fuit in Teucris et servantissimus aequi).* Virgil continues "but it seemed otherwise to the gods" *(dis aliter visum);* cf. §33 here.

33 our Lucan] because of his devotion - like that of the younger Cato to whom he here refers - to (Stoic) philosophy. The allusion is to Lucan, *Pharsalia* 1.128, *victrix causa deis placuit, sed victa Catoni;* Cato chose the losing, republican side in the civil war against Julius Caesar. H. Friedrich, 'Cato, Caesar und Fortuna bei Lukan', *Hermes* 73 (1938) 391-423, at 410 argued that Lucan's observation has an ironical intent which Boethius misses; Lucan does not mean us to accept without question that the gods' decision was the right one. (So too O'Donnell and Gruber). But it seems much more likely that here, as with Virgil in §32, Boethius is not misunderstanding but consciously adapting; for Philosophy, who has true understanding, God *does* judge best, even if Lucan thought otherwise and Virgil left the question unanswered. So Mueller-Goldingen, 385-6.

34 falling short of your hope] After O'Donnell; literally, as he points out, "on this side of hope". The usage is post-classical and appears only here in the *Consolation* (Gruber 361).

it is in your opinion that there is distortion and confusion] see above, §21. Nemesius, *On the Nature of Man* 44 (133.21-2 Morani) similarly argues that we should not deny providence on account of our own ignorance.

35 Suppose that there should be] The second reply (above, on §26) is developed by a series of examples where the apparently just treatment is *not* in fact the one that will have the best results. His discussion is throughout informed by application on a cosmic scale of the Platonic notion that what matters is not so much that people should suffer for their past misdeeds, as that they should be treated in a way that will improve them for the future; see above on §26.

In Boethius' discussion we may distinguish:
[A] *The prosperity of the good:*
    (i)   (35-6) a good man who is spared from suffering because he could not in fact stand up to it;
    (ii)   (37-8) a man so good it would be wrong for him to suffer;
    (iii) (39) good men whose power and prosperity serves to punish the wicked.
[B] *The misfortunes* (of the good, it is implied; cf. 43):
    (iv) (40-1) misfortune intended to restrain self-indulgence, strengthen the weak, or test the over- or under-confident;
    (v)   (42) misfortune that brings glory or serves as an example to others.
[C] *The misfortunes of the wicked,* which create no problem (44).
[D] *The prosperity of the wicked:*
    (vi) (44) The prosperity of the wicked shows how worthless such happiness is.
    (vii) (45) Providence allows some wicked people to prosper because they would commit worse crimes if it did not.
    (viii) (46) In other cases a wicked man's realisation that his good fortune is undeserved may itself lead him to repent.
    (ix) (47) Good fortune badly used may bring ruin.
    (x)   (47-52) Some evil people are given the power to punish others because this will exercise the good and punish the wicked.

38 as someone better than me said] The Neoplatonist Thomas Taylor (1758-1835) pointed out that the quotation is attributed by Philosophy to someone even higher than herself, and on this basis argued that the text comes from the Chaldaean Oracles, used by the Neoplatonists as a sacred text. It is accepted as fr.98 of the Oracles by des Places; so too Chadwick, 243. Courcelle [1967] 167 and [1969] 304 compares the Chaldaean oracle at Proclus *On the Timaeus* 3.266.19, and describes our quotation as Chaldaean or Orphic, derived by Boethius from Proclus. Shanzer [1983] argues that the quotation comes rather from the corpus of writings attributed to Thrice-Greatest Hermes.

The heavens have built the body of a holy man] which is therefore immune to ordinary ills. The text in the MSS is garbled due to the Latin scribes' ignorance of Greek. Shanzer [1983] accepts that the generally printed text represents what was in the archetype of the extant versions, but argues that the archetype had already been corrupted, and restores "The Powers have made the body of a holy man" on the basis of the translation of the *Consolation* into Greek by Maximus Planudes (14th century) and early Latin glosses. (See also Tester's note on the passage.) Shanzer points to a parallel in *Corpus Hermeti-*

cum 13, where ten virtues or powers, linked with the heavenly bodies, regener-
ate the spiritual body of a virtuous man. But her reading requires a familiarity
with esoteric doctrine in the reader in a way that a reference to the heavens
would not; and such presupposition of esoteric knowledge if a point is to be
understood *at all* is not characteristic of the *Consolation*.

40 some it vexes] The idea of providence exercising the good by misfortune is
found in Seneca, *On Providence* 4.5ff.; cf. also Plutarch *On Stoic Self-Contradictions* 1057AB = SVF 3.177.

43 that the wicked ... the same causes] Courcelle [1967] 208 compares Proclus
Ten Problems 32-42; Klingner [1921] 89 suggests a Stoic source.

44 indeed their punishments] Again, the approach to punishment is Platonic; it
corrects the wrong-doers themselves or serves as a warning to others – the
motive is *not* revenge.

47 Some are allowed the right to punish] The thought is; even if I am good,
divine providence may allow someone who is evil to punish me – undeservedly,
clearly – for the good of my soul. (On the notion of providence exercising the
good by means of adversity see above, §40). And good may also be achieved
when the wicked punish the wicked.

49 They are each at variance with themselves] That the wicked are at variance
with themselves and therefore weak is argued at Plato *Republic* 1 351-2, and
indeeed underlies the whole of Plato's argument that the virtuous soul is in a
properly ordered condition and hence happier (cf. *Republic* IV 444).

52 To the divine power alone evil things too are good] This had been asserted
in typically cryptic form by Heraclitus (fr.102 = KRS 206); for the idea that
divine providence can turn the actions of evil men to its own purposes cf. the
Stoic Cleanthes (LS 54I) and Plotinus, *Ennead* 3.3.5.

53 admittedly a different one] At first sight the reference to a *different* order
may seem to conflict with the idea of an *inexorable* outworking of providence
put forward at §20 above; but this conflict is really an aspect of that between
universal determinism and human freedom, and the solution to the particular
problem will appear in V.6.40-2 in the course of the solution to the general one.
Your free actions do not change what God foresees, for he already foresees how
you will act – and, we may add, he plans to suit this, while if you were going
to act differently his plan would be different.

54 It is difficult for me to utter all these things like a god] Homer, *Iliad* 12.176.

55 Nor is it right for a human being] For the emphasis on the limitations of
human understanding, and especially of Boethius' until Philosophy's cure is
complete, Lerer 212 compares II.8.2, III.1.7.

56 just to have seen this, that] *perspexisse* is followed by a *quod*-clause rather
than the classical accusative and infinitive. *proditor* is used in the non-classical
sense of "producer"; in classical Latin it would have meant "betrayer" (hence
Tränkle's emendation, [1968] 286, cf. [1977] 155; but cf. Gruber 363-4).

in his own likeness] The notion of God producing in his own image is pagan and
Platonic, as well as biblical (*Genesis* 1.27); cf. Plato *Timaeus* 29e, Plotinus
2.9.4.26, and Hierocles *On the Golden Verses* 1.14 p.11-12 Koehler; Gruber 281.

57 wearied by the length of the reasoning] IV.6 is in fact the longest prose chapter in the entire work. Orth's *orationis* ("the length of my speech"; E. Orth, *Helmantica* 4 (1953) 279-283) is rejected by Bieler and by Gruber 364, the latter comparing, for "reasoning", III.10.10.

58 waiting for the sweetness of song] cf. above, §6; Crabbe 260.

accept a draught] with medicinal overtones, as O'Donnell points out.

[IV metre 6] This poem develops the theme of order and harmony, first of all in the heavens where it is most obvious, but extending from there to the earth, indicated in §18 of the preceding prose passage. The concluding part of the poem is a Neoplatonic account of the relation of things to their first cause. Patch [1933] 41 argues that this poem forms part of a series concerned with cosmic order (I m.5, II m.8, III m.9, IV m.6, V m.3). In particular it forms a counterpart to I m.5, which shares the same metre but emphasises what at that stage seems to Boethius the *lack* of divine order on earth, as opposed to that in heaven. (Cf. also Klingner [1921] 89-90; Mueller-Goldingen 379; Gruber 134, 364; Curley 360.) Curley 349 points out how the emphasis on the heavenly order in several of these poems contrasts with Boethius' situation in the prison cell. The theme of concord between the elements in the world also appears in Boethius' *On Musical Education;* cf. Chadwick 101 and n.59, and Chamberlain, especially 89. There is a verse translation of lines 1-18 in Waddell 64. The metre is anapaestic dimeters; four anapaests (⌣ ⌣ -), each of which may be replaced by a spondee (- -) or a dactyl (- ⌣ ⌣).

1 the Thunderer] Jupiter.

9 the Bear ... never bathed in the western deep] See above on IV m.5, and cf., with Gruber 365, Homer *Iliad* 18.489, Virgil *Georgic* 1.246: Gruber 365.

12 moisten its flames in the Ocean] Virgil *Georgic* 2.481 = *Aeneid* 1.745; Gruber 366.

14 the Evening Star ... and the Morning Star] They are in fact the same (as Parmenides, we are told, already knew in the fifth century B.C.; Diogenes Laertius 9.23), i.e. the planet Venus.

34 the Founder is seated on high] Cf. [Aristotle] *On the Cosmos* 6 397b25, 400a5.

40 if he did not call them back from their straight course] The reference is first of all to the circular movement of the heavens, and also perhaps to the "circular" interchanges of the elements and cycling of the seasons. But Boethius transforms this into a description of the Neoplatonic triad of progression, return and repose (Theiler [1964] 319-321); lower levels of being proceed from higher ones and are given form when they turn back to contemplate their sources. The *Consolation* itself describes the turning back of Boethius' own soul; see below on V.1.4 and Introduction §11.1. But there are also features in Boethius' description which appear distinctively Christian. The pagan Neoplatonists would not describe the highest principle as Founder. There has already been a non-Platonic identification of the supreme good with the creator in III m.9 (De Vogel [1973] 358).

43 would be separated from their source and fall to pieces] The language is Neoplatonic; Courcelle [1967] 191 n.1. For the doctrine cf., with Theiler [1964] 319-321, Proclus *Elements of Theology* 144.

47 turning back with love returned] Watts, interprets this in terms of the creatures *returning* the love which the creator feels for them; but the words are more naturally taken simply as indicating that the love of the creatures is now turned back towards the Creator rather than the material world. The notion of love felt by a higher principle for a lower is un-Platonic. C.J. De Vogel, 'Amor quo caelum regitur', *Vivarium* 1 (1963) 2–34, indeed interprets II m.8 in terms of the providential love of God, and finds the idea of the providential love of the higher for the lower not only in the Christian Neoplatonism of pseudo-Dionysius (*On the Divine Names* 11.1, PG 3.948ff.; Klingner [1921] 91), but also (30) in Proclus, *On Plato's* First Alcibiades 55.10–56.4 Westerink. However, it is there a matter of the love of higher gods for lower *gods*. Cf. E.R. Dodds (ed.), *Proclus: Elements of Theology*, Oxford [2]1963, xxviii; Reiss 152–3.

[IV.7] 1 Then do you now see what follows] Philosophy's lengthy exposition in the preceding prose section is now followed by a lively exchange of dialogue between Boethius and herself. Cf. Introduction, §11.

2 all fortune is surely good] Philosophy had argued in IV.3–4 that no ill fortune could come to a good man because virtue is its own reward, vice its own punishment. Boethius had responded in IV.5 that this did not explain the apparent afflictions of the virtuous; Philosophy had replied in IV.6 that everything that happens is designed by providence, and that the aims of providence are to reform the wicked and exercise the good; therefore, she now argues, all fortune is good because it is either just or useful. Courcelle [1967] 219 compares Simplicius *On the Physics* 361.1ff. (cf. Cioffari 89); Chadwick 244, Hierocles *On The Golden Verses*, ch.11.244.

7 would you like us ... to approach the way of speaking of ordinary people] Philosophy will take up the same possibilities that were mentioned in §3 above, rewarding or exercising the good or punishing or correcting the wicked; exercising and correcting are discussed at §§9–10, reward at §11, and punishment at §§ 12ff. But in deference to popular opinion, she now allows that the bad fortune of those who are only punished but not improved by it is indeed bad. This however will again lead to the conclusion, at §15, that only bad people endure truly *bad* fortune. In effect Philosophy abandons her claim that the punishment of the wicked is good because it is *just* (cf. section 3 above) and confines goodness to what is beneficial.

8 do you not judge that to be good which is beneficial] cf. Plato, *Gorgias* 474e–475a; Xenophon, *Memorabilia* 4.6.8.

17 whenever he is brought into a trial of fortune] Cf. above on IV.6.40.

19 This is why virtue is so called ... resting on its own strength] Boethius is deriving *virtus*, virtue, from *vires*, strength. *virtus* is applied in particular to courage; this fits with the imagery here.

21 Hold the middle ground] The Aristotelian notion of virtue as a mean between extremes.

Whatever stops too soon or goes beyond involves contempt of happiness] The point is that if you do not follow the proper path, and deviate from it in *either* direction, you will lose your happiness and gain no reward.

22 It rests with you what sort of fortune] If you are good or trying to be, adverse circumstances will be intended by providence as exercise or correction, and so be good; if you are wicked, adverse circumstances will be punishment and therefore – at least by the popular argument of this chapter – bad.

[IV metr. 7] The last poem of book 4 uses mythological examples to develop the theme of punishment of wickedness and reward for virtue. The greater part of the poem is devoted to an account of the labours of Hercules, taking up the theme of striving for virtue at the end of the preceding prose passage. Lerer 180-202 discusses the poem at length, arguing that it forms a triad with the earlier poems on Orpheus (III m.12) and Ulysses' men transformed by Circe (IV m.3), linked both by the references to animals and by the adaptation of themes from Seneca's tragedies (see below). Orpheus could charm animals but could not console himself or regain Eurydice; Ulysses' men were turned into animals; Hercules *overcomes* monstrous animals.

The metre of the poem is a series of repeated Sapphic lines, as in the first three lines of a Sapphic stanza, (- ◡ - - - | ◡ ◡ - ◡- ◡), the whole sequence ending, as does a Sapphic stanza, with an Adonean (- ◡ ◡ - ◡). The pattern is particularly characteristic of Seneca (cf. D.S. Raven, *Latin Metre*, London 1969, 144-5). Medieval MSS illustrations to the poem are discussed at Courcelle [1967] 233-5 and plates 112-118, and a musical setting of the poem in a MS of c.1000 is described at C. Page, 'The Boethian Metrum "Bella bis quinis": a new song from Saxon Canterbury', in Gibson 306-11. Other poems from the *Consolation* were also set to music as early as the eighth century; ibid. 307 and n.6.

1 Having waged war for ten years] Agamemnon (*Atrides*, son of Atreus) attacked Troy in retaliation for the elopement with Paris of Helen, the wife of Agamemnon's brother Menelaus. When adverse winds prevented the fleet from sailing to Troy from Aulis, Agamemnon was advised that he must sacrifice his daughter Iphigenia to Artemis. Boethius' version is based on Seneca, *Agamemnon* 162-175 (Lerer 191).

6 put off the role of father] so, of Brutus, the founder of the Roman Republic, who executed his own sons for treason, at Valerius Maximus 5.8.1: Gruber 373, who also points out that *foederat* is used here in place of *foedat*.

8 The man from Ithaca wept for his lost comrades] The story is told in Homer, *Odyssey* 9; the Cyclops Polyphemus confined Odysseus and his comrades in his cave and ate six of them, but Odysseus retaliated by blinding the Cyclops in his single eye, and then escaped with the survivors.

13 Hercules is made famous by his hard labours] The following list is unusual both in its order and in not including several of the normally recognised Labours, for which other episodes in the story of Hercules are substituted. Those omitted include the capture of the Ceryneian hind, the cleaning of the Augean stables, the capture of the Cretan bull and the seizing of the girdle of the Amazon Hippolyte. Lerer 196 argues that Boethius' account (though not the order) is based on that in the chorus at Seneca, *Agamemnon* 808-866, taking up the reference to Agamemnon at the start of this poem.

14 He tamed the proud Centaurs] A story treated by Apollodorus (2.5.4) not as a separate Labour but as an incident in the capture of the Erymanthian boar (below).

15 He took his trophy] the second labour, the killing of the Nemean lion whose skin Hercules thereafter wore as a trophy.

16 He pierced the birds] The third labour: the slaying of the Stymphalian birds.

17 He stole the apples] The fourth labour, the gathering of the golden apples of the Hesperides, guarded by a never-sleeping dragon.

211

19 He dragged up Cerberus] The fifth labour, the bringing up from the Under-world of the three-headed guard-dog Cerberus.

20 It is said that as victor] The sixth labour, the overcoming of the Thracian king Diomedes and feeding of him to his own man-eating horses.

22 The Hydra perished] The seventh labour, the slaying of the Lernaean Hydra. See above on IV.6.3.

23 The river Achelous] Hercules wrestled with the river-god, his rival for his bride Deianeira, and tore off the horn on Achelous' forehead when the god took the form of a bull (Ovid, *Metamorphoses* 9.80–88); the horn was dedicated as the Horn of Plenty (cornucopia). This is not normally counted as one of the La-bours.

25 Hercules laid Antaeus out on the Libyan sands] The giant Antaeus regained his strength every time he touched his mother the Earth; Heracles defeated him by crushing him while holding him in mid-air. This again is sometimes treated as an episode on Hercules' return from collecting the apples of the Hesperides, rather than as a separate Labour. Lerer 200 n.81 derives the reference to the Libyan sands from Seneca, *Medea* 653; see below.

26 Evander's anger at Cacus] The ogre Cacus, who lived in a cave on the Aventine hill in Rome, had terrorised Evander's people; Hercules slew him after he stole the cattle of Geryon, which Hercules had seized and was driving back to Greece. The tale was naturally popular with Roman poets; cf. Virgil *Aeneid* 8.200ff., where the story is told to Aeneas by Evander, and Propertius IV.9. Again it is not normally counted as one of the Labours, but as an episode on the return from taking the cattle of Geryon.

28 The bristling boar] The Erymanthian boar is one of the canonical labours.

The shoulders on which the lofty sphere would press] In order to obtain the apples of the Hesperides Hercules for a time took the burden of the sky from Atlas, the giant who normally supported it, so that Atlas could take the apples for him. This episode is normally regarded as part of the collection of the apples of the Hesperides, but here it is treated as a separate Labour, developed in the next sentence "As his last labour ...", to make up the total of twelve. As Gruber 376 points out, by making the holding up of heaven (rather than, as usual, the capture of Cerberus) the last of the Labours Boethius is able to effect a transition to Hercules' own ascent to heaven, which is the climax of the poem.

30 and conversely earned heaven] When Heracles' mortal part was consumed by the funeral pyre because he could no longer endure the torment of the poison placed on his tunic through a trick of the Centaur Nessus, his divine part was taken up to heaven and he was made consort of the goddess Hebe. Cf. Sopho-cles' *Trachiniae* (where the apotheosis is not explicit) and Ovid, *Metamorphoses* 9.239ff. In Homer's *Odyssey* (11.602) the ghost of his mortal part is in the underworld. Heracles was described as striving for virtue, rather than succumb-ing to the enticements of pleasure, by the Sophist Prodicus in his story of Heracles' choice at the crossroads (Xenophon, *Memorabilia* 2.1.21–34), and was adopted as an exemplar of virtue by the Cynics and Stoics. Cf. G. Karl Galinsky, *The Herakles Theme*, Oxford, Blackwell, 1972, especially 101–7.

32 Go now, brave ones] This echoes Seneca *Hercules Furens* 89–91 (Lerer, 199–200, also comparing Seneca *Medea* 650–1 and 1007–8); after Hercules has complet-ed the Labours Juno, about to drive him mad, taunts him thus: "Go now, proud one, seek the abodes of the heavenly ones and despise human affairs: do you believe you have escaped the Styx and the cruel spirits of the dead?". The bitter words of Seneca's Juno are adapted to Philosophy's inspirational challenge; Boethius is indeed to seek heaven and despise human affairs (cf. V.5.12 below).

33 Why do you hesitate and turn your backs] Literally "bare your backs" in flight; so Scheible 156, comparing Virgil, *Aeneid* 5.586, Tester and O'Donnell. Gruber 376 interprets as "with bare backs, rather than taking up your burdens"; but the verb *nudatis* is better taken as indicating an action (a point I owe to Alan Griffiths).

Book V

[V.1] 1. The Lady Philosophy had spoken] In IV.6 Philosophy has outlined the distinction between Providence and Fate, and has argued that all things are in fact well ordered by the divine plan. In IV.7 she drew the conclusion that there is no such thing as truly bad fortune. Book V will be concerned with divine foreknowledge and human freedom; but first Boethius raises the question whether chance exists and what it is.

certain other matters] Probably, as Klingner [1921] 93 argues, the discussion of divine foreknowledge and human freedom in V.3 ff.; though Tränkle [1977] 153-4, arguing that the *Consolation* is unfinished, claims that this does not amount to a new topic and that the present reference is never picked up. See below, on V.6.48.

2 Your exhortation] At the conclusion of IV m.7.

what you said some time ago] At IV.6.2-4.

3. what you think it is] *arbitrere* is the short form for *arbitreris,* second singular present subjunctive in an indirect question.

4. your fatherland] That is, the understanding of the true nature of things brought by philosophical understanding, from which Boethius at the start of the *Consolation* had wandered and hence was in despair. Cf. especially I.5 and the promise to bring Boethius home in IV.1; and see above on IV m.6. For Stoics the whole world (but still, characteristically, *this* world) is the country of the wise; more relevant here is Plato's image of the soul being truly at home in the world of intellect rather than that of sense *(Phaedo* 67e; cf. 109e, and the image of the world of sense as the Cave in Plato, *Republic* VII.)

6 will have been like rest for me] Literally, "will be in place of rest for me."

7. When every aspect of your argument has been established] *constiterit* is future perfect indicative *ambigatur* is present subjunctive, apparently used instead of the future indicative to make the assertion "there will be no doubt" rather less positive in its form; but this is a matter of expression rather than of any real hesitation. The passage serves to justify the digression.

8. I will do what you want] *morem gerere* is to gratify somebody's wishes, go along with them, humour them.

If someone defined chance as an outcome produced by random motion and by no connection with causes] As for example in the case of the Epicurean atomic swerve; see Introduction, §3.1.

without indicating any subject] *praeter* in this sense is a late Latin usage; Gruber 379, Hofmann-Szantyr 244.

9. nothing comes from nothing] This was argued by Parmenides (fr. 8.7 = KRS 296), but assumed even by earlier Presocratic philosophers, and appears as a saying first in Alcaeus fr. 23 Diehl (Gruber 380). It is said (Sextus Empiricus, *adv. math.* 10.18-19; Diogenes Laertius 10.2) that Epicurus became a philosopher because his schoolteacher could not answer his question where Hesiod's Chaos came from ("First of all Chaos came to be", *Theogony* 116); and the theme is developed by Lucretius (1.159ff.). Boethius is right in saying that the Presocratics applied the dictum to the material, rather than the efficient cause; though Lucretius (1.159ff. = LS 4B), Epicurus *(Letter to Herodotus* 38) and probably Democritus too (to judge from Aristotle, *Physics* 2.4 196a28-30; cf. W.D. Ross, *Aristotle's Physics,* Oxford 1936, 515 ad loc.) had it seems used it to explain not only the conservation of matter but also regularity and order in the universe. (Cf. Long [1977] 64 and n.4). Epicurus' atomic swerve is however a (partial) contravention of the principle. Boethius' phrasing does not absolutely exclude the possibility of a creation of the world from nothing as far as its matter is concerned; for it is not to matter but to efficient cause that he applies the principle (see below on V.6.9, and Sulowski [1961] 84 n.87; Obertello [1974] 671-2 and 706 n.33). For the use of *quamquam* with a subjunctive rather than an indicative cf. Hofmann-Szantyr 603.

11. either chance or fortuitous] Boethius' *casus* and *fortuitum* represent Aristotle's *tuche* and *automaton,* which are distinguished in that *tuche* applies in cases where chance produces a result that might have been intended *by a human agent, automaton* rather to things that happen by coincidence to animals or inanimate objects. *Automaton* is also used as the generic term covering both of these (Aristotle, *Physics* 2.6 197a36ff.).

even if it is generally unknown] *vulgus* is the direct object of *lateat* in the sense of "to escape the notice of" (= Greek *lanthanein*); this use of *latere* in prose is post-Augustan.

12. My Aristotle] This account of chance is ultimately based on Aristotle, *Physics* 2.5-6; a similar account is also given by Aristotle in *Metaphysics* Δ 30. For Aristotle, chance is essentially the mimicking by coincidence of a result that could have been deliberately intended. His account, and the example of finding buried treasure (from *Metaphysics* Δ 30 1025a15-19), became standard in later ancient philosophy. Cf. Alexander of Aphrodisias, *On Fate* ch.8 and *mantissa* pp.176-9 Bruns; [Plutarch] *On Fate* 572a; Nemesius *On the Nature of Man* 39 p.112.19-24 Morani; Calcidius *On the* Timaeus 159 192.17-193.13; Ammonius *On On* Interpretation 142.3ff.; Philoponus *On the* Prior Analytics 152.4ff., *On the* Physics 276.18; Simplicius *On the* Physics 337.25; Boethius *On On* Interpretation[2] 193.26ff. Meiser, and *On Cicero's* Topics, PL 64 1152c ff. Illustrations of the finding of treasure in medieval MSS of the *Consolation* are discussed at Courcelle [1967] 235-6 and plates 127-131; the illustration on Courcelle [1967] pl.130 is also reproduced as the frontispiece to Sorabji [1980,2]. See further above, on Cicero *On Fate* §19.

Boethius' combining of the example from the *Metaphysics* with the account from the *Physics* has prompted considerable discussion. Courcelle [1967] 218-19 and [1969] 311-12, noting the similar combination in Simplicius and Philoponus, uses it to argue that the present discussion derives from Ammonius' lost commentary on the *Physics;* but as Obertello [1974] 539-40 points out, this is hardly conclusive, especially as the use of the example was commonplace. See further Introduction, §12.2.2. More importantly are the subtle differences between Boethius'

account and Aristotle's. Where Aristotle speaks of an unintended result attach-
ing to an action with some other primary purpose, Boethius speaks explicitly of
the meeting of two separate causal chains. This is characteristic of the Platonic
tradition in particular ([Plutarch] *On Fate* 572c, Nemesius *On the Nature of Man*
39 p.112.19-20 Morani, and Calcidius *On the* Timaeus 159 p.192.17ff. Waszink. Cf.
Courcelle [1967] 110, 212-13.) And Boethius' account takes on a different aspect
through being introduced in the context of a theory of universal divine providence (see further below on V.1.19).

16 **causes which meet each other and come together**] Boethius' word here for
"come together" is *confluere*, literally "flow together" - which suits the imagery
of the following poem.

17 **where the other had buried it**] *quo* is used for *ubi*; cf. Hofmann-Szantyr 277
and V m.3 below.

18. **So chance may be defined**] With this formal definition cf. Aristotle *Physics*
2.5 197a5-6; "*tuche* is "an accidental cause in those, of things that are for the
sake of something, that are consciously chosen".

things that are being done for the sake of something] This requirement comes
from Aristotle, though there is some obscurity in his account as to whether the
point is (i) that the action to which the chance result attaches, in our example
the digging, must be done for a purpose, or (ii) that the chance result is the
sort of thing that could have been done for a purpose - whether by the con-
scious intention of a human agent or by what for Aristotle is the unreflecting
purposefulness of natural processes. (ii) is more to the point; chance, for Aristotle, mimics purpose, producing what could have been produced purposefully.
Cf. Aristotle *Physics* 2.6 197b20-22.

19. **But the coincidence and coming together of causes is brought about**] A
chance combination of causes may have no explanation over and above the
explanations or causes of the individual components of the coincidence (see
above, on Cicero *On Fate* §19); and this is so even if everything is predetermined, provided that the deterministic causal nexus is one that proceeds blindly
with no overall plan or pattern. Boethius however has already argued, in book
IV chapter 6, that everything is ultimately controlled by providence; and if so
nothing that happens will really be a coincidence with no explanation, even if it
seems so from our perspective. Philosophy has now raised Boethius to a level
where Fortune can be seen for what it really is. Boethius does not explicitly
suggest here that Providence may have arranged the finding of the treasure
for some purpose of her own; but compare IV.6, especially §45. His consequent
modification of the Aristotelian view (only here, and not in the commentary on
On Interpretation) is noted by Cioffari 128 n.103. Obertello [1974] 706-7 and n.35
suggests that it is ironic that Boethius, who is in effect denying the independ-
ent reality of Fortune, influenced the medieval conception of Fortune and her
wheel *(Consolation* II.2); but Reiss 152 points out that it was precisely by trans-
forming Fortune in the way he does here that Boethius gave the Western world
a way of regarding it that was compatible with Christianity. For the idea that
chance is really divine providence Mauro 364 compares Aquinas' short *Compen-
dium of Theology*, 137.

that order, advancing by unavoidable connections] i.e. Fate. For the relation
between Providence and Fate see above, IV.6. The language is close to Stoic
definitions of fate; cf. IV.6.19-20 above and Commentary there.

[V metre 1] In this short poem (metre: elegiac couplets) Boethius uses an elaborate image to illustrate the theory of chance set out in the preceding prose

section. The two rivers represent two separate chains of causation; they both proceed from a single source, divine providence; if they should meet, their meeting would represent the concurrence of causes that constitutes chance, but the fact of the chance meeting would in no way imply that the course of each river *individually* was not entirely governed and regulated by natural laws (cf. Cioffari 87). What the image cannot directly represent is the idea that Providence itself plans the coincidence (though the last line may hint at this). The fountain can hardly be seen as directing the lie of the land through which the rivers flow. But this simply reflects the fact that the picture of fate as a causal nexus which is itself subject to governance by Providence is not a picture that can easily be accommodated without multiple levels of reality; see Introduction, §8.

The Tigris and Euphrates do not and did not rise from a single source, though their sources are close together in Eastern Turkey. (Gruber 382 may be wrong to interpret Lucan, *Pharsalia* 3.256ff. as asserting that they do have a single source, for his *non diversis fontibus* can be interpreted, with the Loeb, as "not far apart".) Pliny *Natural History* 6.130 (cf. 126) indicates that, while their mouths had originally been separate, irrigation work had already in his time diverted the Euphrates so that it met the Tigris before the latter entered the sea. Since then silting has advanced the coastline considerably; the two rivers now unite and flow together into the Persian Gulf through the Shatt al-'Arab. But Boethius' reference is probably more general; what he has in mind is not the positions of the mouths, but the implications if the rivers were to meet at some point in their courses, which certainly were and are separate for the great part of their length.

2 where the fleeing warriors] Persian archers mounted on horseback would shoot back at their pursuers even while they were retreating. The image is a common one in Latin poetry; Bieler compares Virgil *Georgics* 3.31 and Propertius 2.13.1-2, which does not have the point about turning in flight but of which there are several verbal echoes in our passage: *Achaemeniis ... sagittis spicula ... pectore fixit*. Cf. also Horace *Odes* 1.19.11. *versa* is accusative plural, agreeing with *spicula*.

9 with reins slackened] i.e. not being firmly controlled.

[V.2] 2 is there any freedom for our choice] Philosophy's account of chance has been given; now Boethius asks her about human choice. See above, IV.6.4.

the chain of fate] Cf., with Rand cited by Patch [1929], Gellius in Appendix (C) §1 above.

3 There could not be any rational nature that did not have freedom of choice] Reason is used in choosing between what we should pursue and what we should avoid. The argument appears in Alexander of Aphrodisias *On Fate* 11, linked with the point, going back to Aristotle, that deliberation is only relevant where there is a possibility of things being otherwise (Aristotle, *Nicomachean Ethics* 3.3 1112b2, 6.5 1140a31ff.); it is adopted by Boethius in *On* On Interpretation[2] 220.8ff. The terminology of pursuit and avoidance also goes back to Aristotle (*On the Soul* 3.7 431a9-10, *Nicomachean Ethics* 2.2 1104b22). Alexander and Boethius there add explicitly the point that nature does nothing in vain (cf. Aristotle *On the Heaven* 1.4 271a33, *Politics* 1.2 1253a9, 1.8 1256b20); human beings would not have the power of deliberation if there was no possibility of their using it. (So too Ammonius, *On* On Interpretation 148.11ff.) This must be assumed here too, unless it is supposed that being able to make choices is actually part of the definition of being rational. *fuerit* is a perfect subjunctive used potentially.

6 this is not equal in all of them] Alexander (cited in connection with §3 above) is concerned to establish human freedom as the possibility of making alternative choices. But for the Platonic tradition that Boethius is following freedom is not the neutral possibility of choosing in either of two ways; rather, it is freedom from error and the freedom to choose aright. Error and ignorance are linked with the body; so true freedom consists in rising above the body, and above fate which is linked with it. See above on IV.6.13, and Introduction §8.3.

7. The divine beings above] Probably, in view of the next section (q.v.), not the physical heavenly bodies (the constancy of whose motions shows that their will does not deviate), but souls that are altogether free from bodies (Gruber, 384). The expression is not Christian.

8 less so when they descend to bodies] These are ethereal or "astral" bodies, by contrast with the "earthly limbs" that follow (Gruber 384, citing Macrobius *On the Dream of Scipio* 1.11.12). The implication here and elsewhere in the *Consolation* (Sulowski [1961] 77 n.44 compares III m.6.5 and III.12.1) that human souls exist before they enter human bodies caused problems for Christian interpreters; Courcelle [1967] 287, 290, 294, 329, 331-2.

9 fall from possession of the reason that is theirs] At *Consolation* IV.3.16 wicked people are described as becoming animals, only their outward bodily form still being human.

are in a certain way prisoners through their own freedom] It is our freedom to choose that enables us to devote ourselves to the body, and our being attracted by bodily desires that keeps us enslaved to it.

11 providence ... arranges what is predestined according to what each individual deserves] See above, on IV.6.53. This need only imply that providence foresees our actions and predestines what we deserve as a consequence of them, not that our actions themselves are predestined. But see below on V.6.42.

[V metr. 2] This poem picks up the theme of the timeless gaze of divine providence from the last sentence of the preceding prose passage, but serves chiefly to introduce the part this will play in the discussion of the relation between divine foreknowledge and human freedom which occupies the rest of the book; the problem is stated in the next prose section, but the timelessness of providence, already introduced in IV.6.10 and 17 and indicated here in lines 10-11, is not brought in as part of the solution in the prose discussion until V.6.15. Metre: dactylic tetrameter (- ◡ ◡ - ◡ ◡ - ◡ ◡ - ◡ , with substitution of - for ◡ ◡).

2 Phoebus] The Sun.

3 so sings Homer] Cf. *Iliad* 3.277 and *Odyssey* 11.109 = 12.323; Homer's words are adapted to fit the syntax here. The sweetness attributed to Homer was seen more negatively in I.1.11, where it typified the attractions of the Muses, likened to Sirens keeping Boethius from the true consolations of philosophy; Mueller-Goldingen 383. This line of Homer is a favourite with Neoplatonic writers, among them Proclus *On the Cratylus* 37.8 Pasquali and *On the Timaeus* 2.82.8, Hermias *On the Phaedrus* p.68.9 Couvreur, Olympiodorus *On the Phaedo* 26.28 Norvin = 49.5, p.85 Westerink (Courcelle [1967] 166-7, [1969] 303-4 n.58, Gruber 385-6, Shanzer [1983] 277, Mueller-Goldingen 383 n.41). Courcelle suggests that Boethius is here following Proclus' *Timaeus* commentary.

6 he who established] see IV m.6.34.

8 the earth does not resist him] Boethius first indicates that the divine vision is not, like the sun's rays, hindered by the solidity of the earth, then that it is not impeded by darkness, and finally moves on to the real point as far as the argument is concerned, that it is not limited by time.

10 what has been, what is, what is to come] Cf., with Gruber 387 and Chadwick 245, Homer, *Iliad* 1.70, Hesiod *Theogony* 38, and Virgil *Georgic* 4.392.

13 you could call him the true Sun] Boethius is playing on the words *solus*, alone or "in his solitude", and *Sol*, the Sun; so too Varro *On the Latin Language* 5.68 (Gruber 387). For the Neoplatonists the One was the true Sun, and the sun that shines in the sky only a semblance of this; the idea goes back to Plato's analogy of the Sun for the Form of the Good in *Republic* 6.508-9 (cf. also 7.516b). Cf. Plotinus 1.7.1 and (with Courcelle [1967] 215) Ammonius *On On Interpretation* 132.25ff., and, in particular, with Scheible 161, Proclus' *Hymn to the Sun*, 1.34 (ed. E. Vogt, Wiesbaden 1957), where the visible sun is the 'image of the god who is father of all', and the elaboration of the doctrine in the *Hymn to the Sun* of the emperor Julian the Apostate (= Julian, *Oration* 4).

[V.3] Boethius states the problem he sees in reconciling free will and divine foreknowledge, and indicates why he finds one attempted solution inadequate. This is his last major contribution as a speaker in the dialogue; Lerer 218 points out that it is his one chance to contribute on the philosophical level. It is also one of only two places in the work where a long speech from Boethius is followed by a poem also uttered by Boethius rather than by Philosophy; the other is I.4, and De Vogel [1972] 39 and Crabbe 261 point to the deliberate contrast between the serious philosophical argument here and the self-pitying narrative there of the events that had led to Boethius' plight, De Vogel further emphasising the specifically Christian tone (as she sees it; see below) of the conclusion of the present chapter, absent in I.4. See Introduction §§11.1,5.

3 there is a complete opposition and inconsistency between God's foreknowing everything and there being free choice] The question which will concern us from here to the end of the work. See Introduction, §7 and §12.2.3-5.

6 from that in which they were foreseen] The feminine *provisae* (if this rather than the neuter is correct - see the apparatus) agrees with "wishes", *voluntates,* taking up the preceding mention of *voluntas* in the singular.

but rather an uncertain opinion] If we have free choice, God cannot be *certain* that we will choose in one way rather than another, even if he has strong grounds for supposing that we will; he will then have not knowledge but opinion, and it is impious to suppose this of God. As Pike 42 points out, it is crucial to Boethius' difficulty that God not only *is* not wrong but *cannot* be.

7 I do not approve that argument, either] The claim is that what providence foresees depends on what actually happens when the time comes, and not vice versa. (For a similar point relating to the truth of future-tense statements, rather than to divine foreknowledge, see above on Cicero, *On Fate* §17.) Boethius responds (in §§9-14) that this is beside the point; whichever causes the other, the fact that the event occurs or the fact that God foreknows it, it is still the case that the truth of one implies that of the other, and that is what creates the difficulty. God cannot know that you will do X unless you do in the event do X; but if God knows that you will do X, you cannot not do X.

certain people]: Courcelle [1967] 216 and [1969] 309 points to the occurrence of a similar argument to this in Ammonius *On On Interpretation* 136.25ff., and uses it to support his general thesis of Boethius' dependence on Ammonius. So too

Obertello [1974] 537 and n.75, who argues that, while Boethius criticises this particular argument in Ammonius, he then proceeds to argue in a similar way to Ammonius in stating his own position in V.4-6. However, Boethius' argument there goes beyond Ammonius' (Introduction, §12.2.4). Klingner [1921] 97-8 and 108 had drawn attention rather to parallels in Christian writers: Origen cited by Eusebius, *Preparation for the Gospel* 6.11.36-7, John Chrysostom, *Homilies on Matthew* 60.1 (PG 58 p.574), and Jerome *On* Ezekiel 1.2.5 (CCSL vol.75 p.28.738-41); but Huber 30-4 argues against Klingner that the Christian authors depend on the philosophical tradition rather than vice versa.

10 For indeed if anyone should be sitting] The example had been used in discussion of the paradox of future truth by Boethius and others; Ammonius *On* On Interpretation 153.24; Philoponus *On the* Prior Analytics 151.27ff.; Boethius *On* On Interpretation[1] 122.1ff., *On* On Interpretation[2] 241.8ff. (Cf. also Aristotle *On Sophistical Refutations* 4 166a24, and above on Cicero, *On Fate* fragment 4.) It had been used to make a distinction which Boethius passes over for the present but will introduce in V.6.27. While it necessarily follows from the fact that you are sitting that the opinion "you are sitting" is true, it does not follow from the fact that you are sitting that the opinion "it is *necessary* that you are sitting" is true - at least not if *necessary* is taken unconditionally; what does follow is the truth of the opinion "*if you are sitting,* it is necessary that you are sitting" (or "necessarily: if you are sitting, you are sitting").

if, concerning anyone, the opinion that he is sitting is true] *quoniam* for "that" is common in later Latin; Hofmann-Szantyr 628, Prinz 172. Its use here avoids the awkwardness of two successive accusative-and-infinitives (Gruber 389-390).

12 the opinion is true, because the person's sitting ... came first] Similarly, in the context of the paradox of future truth rather than of divine foreknowledge, Boethius *On* On Interpretation[2] 206.9-23: Huber, 35 n.22.

15 But how back-to-front this is] A new point; not only does the claim that the event causes the foreknowledge, rather than vice versa, not solve the problem of free will, it also makes God's knowledge depended on temporal things when temporal things should be dependent on God. And indeed it might be supposed that God at least *should* be the cause of things he foreknows, being the cause of everything: cf. Introduction §7.4. The solution to the problem will appear at V.6.42. Cf. Huber 35-6.

16 than to think that things which have happened in the past] God could not have foreseen past things if they had not come about; and, we may add, could not know now that they did come about if they had not in fact done so. This much Boethius will in a sense accept, while rejecting the claim that the events cause God's knowledge; but "foreknow" and "know now" will turn out to be inappropriate language to use of God (see below, V.6). The reference to the past here serves to indicate that from the point of view of this argument past, present and future are alike (Gruber 390).

18 that is not only not knowledge, but false opinion] A third difficulty, not fully developed until §22. If future events, such as our free choices, are in fact contingent but God foresees them as necessary, he does not foresee them accurately and does not have foreknowledge. But if he foresees them as they actually are, i.e. contingent, what does this foreseeing of his amount to?

24 If he judges these things are going to be in the way they actually are going to be] This formulation is ambiguous. [I] It may mean that God knows what will in fact occur, but is also aware that, though it will occur, it might not have. Or [II] It may mean only that God knows what the possible outcomes are on a given occasion, without knowing which of them will in fact (contingently) occur. The claim that God's foreknowledge of the contingent must be of the contingent *as contingent* had been interpreted in sense [II] by Alexander and Porphyry, but in sense [I] by Proclus (cf. Introduction, §7.4). Boethius' objections appear to interpret what is claimed here in sense [II] (see below); and this is natural enough, for nothing has *yet* been said to show how [I] could be possible.

25 how does this differ from that ridiculous prophecy of Tiresias] The prophecy attributed to Tiresias (Horace, *Satires* 2.5.59) is a truism; what he says either will happen or won't, but there is no indication which. This suggests that God's foreknowledge is being interpreted in sense [II] rather than in sense [I]. Boethius' use here of *refert* with the ablative in the sense of "differ from" is a development of the use of *refert* with *inter*, "what difference does it make, what does it matter, as between ...", by analogy with the ablative of separation after words like *differt;* the use of the ablative with *refert* in the sense of "differ from" cannot however be parallelled before the medieval period (Prinz 172).

26 how would divine providence be superior to human opinion] Again it must be sense [II] that is meant; for to know what the outcome would be, as in [I], even while knowing that it did not have to be so, would certainly be an advance over our normal human state.

30 in vain will rewards or punishments] A standard argument against determinism; cf. Cicero *On Fate* §40 above and comments there.

32 it comes about] vivid indicative after the potential subjunctives (O'Donnell).

33 there is no reason to hope for anything or pray for anything] This is used as an argument against determinism by [Plutarch] *On Fate* 574de, Alexander, *On Fate* 20 190.27; Gruber 392, Sharples [1983,1] 151. These passages make questionable De Vogel's argument ([1973] 363) that the reference to prayers here belongs to the Christian rather than to the pagan Greek philosophical tradition, because in the latter God already arranges things for the best without our asking him (cf. Seneca, *Questions on Nature* 2.35.2). On how far the last section of this chapter is distinctively Christian cf. de Vogel [1972] 4–7, and above, Introduction §13.2. For *deprecari* in the sense of "pray for" rather than "pray to avert" see Mohrmann 56, comparing V.6.46 below.

34 that single sort of commerce between gods and men] The phrase goes back to Plato, *Euthyphro* 14e. Mohrmann 55–9 points to the influence of Christian liturgical language on this whole passage; in particular (57–8) *commercium*, though used of any exchange, is used especially of gifts and, in Christian contexts, of the Incarnation, and of offerings at the Eucharist.

purchases for us] Literally, "by the price of humility we earn" *(pro-mereri)*.

the inestimable reward of divine grace] Klingner [1921] 101 and de Vogel [1973] 362 argue that the references to humility and grace here are distinctively Christian. Gruber points out with Theiler [1964] 324–5 that Porphyry spoke of "grace", according to Augustine *City of God* 10.29 (p.448.10-15 Dombart), and that humility is commended by Plato at *Laws* 4.716a; so Boethius' thought here, even if inspired by Christianity, would not be unacceptable to pagans.

this is the only way] *qui* refers to *commercium*, but is attracted into the gender of *modus.*

that inaccessible light] That this is biblical, deriving from *I Timothy* 6.16, is asserted by Klingner [1921] 101, de Vogel [1972] 6, and, more tentatively, by

Chadwick 238. Boethius uses the classical *inacessus* rather than the Vulgate *inacessibilis*. The reference to light is in itself appropriate in Neoplatonic terms too (Theiler [1964] 324-5).

before they obtain it] i.e., while they are still in this earthly life (O'Donnell).

35 in what way could we be united to and cleave to that highest Prince of all things] The incompatibility of prayer with the determinism that seems to be implied by divine foreknowledge threatens the connection between men and God. "Prince" is used here because it is the personal form of the abstract philosophical "principle" *(principium)*; Mohrmann 58-9. Klinger [1921] 101-2 suggests that "cleave to" *(adhaerere)* is distinctively Christian language; but prayer is described as union with God by Proclus *in Tim.* 1.208.7, 1.211.3-4 (Mueller-Goldingen 377f. n.26).

as you sang a short while ago] in IV m.6.43. Boethius is taking Philosophy's poem as an authoritative text to interpret (Lerer 219-20; cf. Introduction §11.5.)

[V metr. 3] This poem takes its start from the conflict between free will and divine foreknowledge set out in the previous prose section, and develops an account of the Platonic theory of recollection as outlined in the *Meno, Phaedo* and *Phaedrus*. That theory presents the recovery of truths as a remembering of the world of Forms seen before our birth. And the solution of the present problem will mark the completion of the return of Boethius to true philosophical understanding that is the theme of the whole *Consolation of Philosophy*. The metre is anapaestic dimeters (ending with a single *metrum)* and this links the poem with I m.5 (see above, on IV m.6). Curley 361, 364-5 notes that V m.3 is the only poem spoken by Boethius in the whole of books II-V, and contains what are almost Boethius' last words in the whole work; it poses its question in intellectual terms rather than the emotional ones of I m.5, and Boethius himself suggests the answer. Poetry has thus been transformed from the temptation to emotion, rather than philosophical thought, which it appeared as in book I, and Boethius is shown to be cured (cf. Lerer 220-4). The abstract quality of the present poem, apart from its light-imagery, is noted by Gruber 393. Cf. Introduction §11.4. There is a verse translation in Waddell, 58-61.

3 two truths] Free will and divine foreknowledge.

8 our mind, overwhelmed by the blindness of our body] A central theme of Plato's *Phaedo*. The limitations of human knowledge have been a recurrent theme since IV.6; they will be emphasised in V.4.

11 But why then does our mind burn with such desire] The effect of the body on the mind has been invoked to explain our inability to see the explanation that there must be for the apparent incompatibility; why then is our desire for understanding not diminished along with our understanding itself?

15 If however it does not know, what is it seeking] The paradox goes back to Plato, *Meno* 80de, where it prompts the first statement of the Platonic theory of recollection.

18 where would he find it] *quo* is used for *ubi:* see above on V.1.17.

Or who ... when he found it] *quisve* restores the metre, if the first syllable of *repertam* is taken as short; alternatively *quis* may be retained if the first syllable of *repertam* is treated as long. Prinz 173 argues for doing this while retaining the MSS spelling, as against Weinberger's *reppertam*. However, *reperire* in line 12 must have a short first syllable (for the non-classical spelling of the

MSS cf. V.1.16); and there seems no particular reason to link *quo inveniet* with the preceding clause by a conjunction but not to do this for *quis ... queat.*

20 when our soul beheld the Mind on high] In Neoplatonism the totality of the Platonic Forms is identified with the Mind or Intellect whose thoughts they are, in accordance with the Aristotelian principle that in immaterial things there is no distinction between thinker and thought; Mind *is* what is thought.

21 the whole and its parts alike] For the Neoplatonists the level of Mind is characterised by unity-in-diversity; mind is identical with its objects where immaterial objects are concerned, and the many Forms which are also minds are in a way identical with Mind as a whole and with each other, since each is thinking of itself and all the others.

24 keeps hold of the whole while losing the parts] That is, presumably: we are aware in general terms of the 'truth we are seeking, but have forgotten the particular truths that go to make it up. Plato's picture is different and suggests rather a movement from part to whole; because all nature is akin, he who has recollected one thing can go on to remember all things (Plato, *Meno* 81d). But compare the last lines of Boethius' poem: "so that he can add the forgotten parts to those that are retained".

[V.4] 1. Marcus Tullius, when he did away with divination] The MSS have "when he distinguished types of divination"; but the difficulty of finding a precise parallel in Cicero's *On Divination* (Bieler suggests 2.8; Courcelle [1967] 210 n.5 and [1969] 308 n.86, 1.125) prompted Klingner [1921] 1034 to suggest that Boethius is here citing Cicero not directly but on the basis of Augustine's report in *City of God* 5.9 (for which see above on Cicero, *On Fate* fragment 4). However, Augustine's report begins "Cicero strives to refute those (the Stoics), but thinks that he cannot achieve anything against them unless he does away with *(auferat)* divination, which he tries to do away with *(auferre)* in the following way ..." (p.202.21ff. Dombart), and Theiler [1946] 64 n.78, noting that *destruant* occurs at 203.2 Dombart, emended *distribuit* "distinguished" here to *destruit* "did away with". Cf. Gegenschatz [1966] 52.

investigated extensively by you yourself] The reference is to Boethius' earlier works; cf. especially *On On Interpretation²* 225.9ff.

any of you] This could mean "no *Roman* philosopher" (Klingner [1921] 105, Gegenschatz [1966] 521); but given that Boethius will here be putting forward a *new* solution (cf. Introduction §12.2.4), it is more likely to mean "no philosopher" in general (Huber 4 and n.5; Reiss 126).

2 the movement of human reasoning ... the simplicity of divine foreknowledge] See above, IV.6.17; but more has yet to be said about the latter.

4 that method of solving the problem (more literally, "of those who solve the problem")] The argument that divine foreknowledge is not the *cause* of the necessity of the events it foresees; above, V.3.7-9.

5 Surely you do not yourself base your argument] Literally, "you do not draw your proof ... from anywhere else than from the fact ...". Cf. V.3.4 (Gruber 397). Philosophy first considers what would happen if there were no foreknowledge at all (§§7-8) and then what would happen if there is, but it does not impart necessity to things (§9). It is only at §10 that she takes up Boethius' point at V.3.9-14 that the problem is not solved by arguing that foreknowledge does not *cause* the events it foresees to be necessary, if it still follows logically that events must *be* necessary to be foreseen.

6 A short while ago] At V.3.9.

10 nevertheless it is a sign that they will necessarily come about] Philosophy has dismissed the claim that
[A] Foreknowledge of an event causes the event to be necessary.
She now considers the claim that
[B] Although the foreknowledge does not itself cause the event to be necessary, if an event is foreknown then it will necessarily occur.
That claim is ambiguous, for there is a distinction between [B1] the claim that the foreknowledge of an event is a sign that the event is necessary *in itself* and [B2] the claim that what is foreknown is necessary conditionally, that is that it is necessary that *if* it is foreknown *then* it will happen (see above on V.3.10). Philosophy will first argue (§§11-14) that the foreknowledge could only be a sign that an event was necessary if there were other grounds for supposing the event to be necessary in this way. The distinction between [B1] and [B2] is still not explicit - we have to wait till V.6 for that - but it is clearly [B1] that is being denied; cf. "in their own nature" at §14 below. So Huber, 53.

11 for every sign only shows what is the case] Signs by their nature show what is the case, rather than causing it to be the case; so foreknowledge could not show that events were necessary unless there were grounds for supposing them to be necessary quite apart from the foreknowledge.

12 So it must first be shown that nothing comes about except from necessity] Alexander of Aphrodisias (*On Fate* 30 201.24ff.) had argued that, rather than using foreknowledge as an argument for determinism, the Stoics should consider the question the other way round, the implication being that, if they could not establish determinism, they should concede that they could not establish universal divine foreknowledge either. Alexander agreed with the Stoics that determinism and foreknowledge stood or fell together; Boethius will argue differently.

14 how can it happen that those things do not come about which are foreseen] Indeed this cannot happen; what is foreseen as true *does* come about, but that does not mean that it must in itself be necessary rather than contingent.

As if we believed that those things, which providence foreknows ... are not going to come about] The issue is not whether what is foreknown comes about or not; of course it does. The question is rather whether it must, not just come about, but come about through necessity; and this Boethius denies, using *present*-tense examples to prove the point. The use of *sui* rather than *sua* is late Latin; cf. Hofmann-Szantyr 61. So too at §25 below.

15 There are many things which we see before our eyes] If we see something happening, it must be happening, but that does not mean it could not have not happened.

17 before they happen The use of the subjunctive with *prius quam* here is late Latin: Hofmann-Szantyr 600, Gruber 398.

19 For I do not think that anyone will say that the things which are now happening were, before they happened, not going to come about] People - and notably Epicurus - *had* however said that it was not *true* before certain events came about that they were going to come about. See Introduction, §3.2.2 and §7.6. *nullum* is used for *neminem,* as in §36 below; cf. Hofmann-Szantyr 205.

21 But it is this very thing, you say, that is in doubt] Philosophy has argued that the fact that an event is foreknown does not mean that it is necessary (in itself), rather than contingent. But that still leaves the question how a contingent event *can* be foreknown; and it is the answer to this, in terms of the difference in nature between divine and human knowledge, that will provide the second main theme of the present chapter. See above, on Cicero, *On Fate* §§32-3, and Introduction §7.

23 those things whose outcome is uncertain] Literally, "those things that are of uncertain outcome".

25 Everything which is grasped is grasped not according to its own power but rather according to the capacity of those who know it] The theory adopted by Proclus and attributed by Ammonius to Iamblichus; cf. Introduction §7.2.

26 the same roundness of a body] Shape is mentioned among the "common sensibles" perceived by more than one sense at Aristotle, *On Sensation* 1 437a9, 4 442b4.

26 by casting its rays] the common ancient belief that sight functions by rays travelling *from* the eyes rather than, or as well as, those from the object seen; cf. Theophrastus, *De sensu* 50 (= KRS 589) for Democritus; Plato, *Timaeus* 45be.

27 sensation, imagination, reasoning, understanding] For the contrast between reasoning and understanding cf. IV.6.17 above. As Ralfs 360ff. points out they correspond, in terminology at least, to the two highest stages, *dianoia* and *noêsis*, of the Divided Line of Plato, *Republic* 6.511de, but the lower stages of *pistis* and *eikasia* are here replaced by imagination and sensation; Ralfs derives from Aristotle both this and the connection in V.5 below with the faculties of different creatures. Similar classifications of modes of apprehension to that here are implied in Proclus (*Ten Problems* 3, *On Providence* 31, *On the* Timaeus 1.351.16-18); cf. Courcelle [1967] 220, Obertello [1974] 513-15, Gruber 399.

30 The eye of understanding rises still higher] Reasoning considers the form *in* the individuals, the immanent Aristotelian form; understanding rises to the level of Neoplatonic intellect (cf. V. m.3.20) and contemplates the transcendent Platonic form. The combination of the two types of form in a single account goes back at least as far as the time of Seneca, *Letter* 65.7, and is common in Neoplatonism. Cf. Ralfs 366-8. "rises" renders *exsistit* in the sense of "emerges"; but it may be no more than an equivalent for *est* (so Gruber 400; and cf. §39 below).

30 for passing above the circumference of the universe] So Watts, O'Donnell and Gruber; and for the Platonic Forms being pictured as beyond the heavens cf. *Phaedrus* 247bc. But reasoning has just been contrasted with understanding, reasoning is said to consider the enmattered form in universal terms, and the transcendent Platonic form observed by understanding is contrasted with the particulars rather than present in them like the enmattered form; it therefore seems natural to interpret Boethius' words *also* as "passing above the sphere of universality", suggesting that understanding is no longer concerned with the one-in-many, the universal, in the way that reasoning is. A similar contrast is drawn in the next paragraph: "nor does imagination observe the universal forms, nor does reasoning grasp the simple form".

33 if I may put it that way] *formaliter* is a new coinage (Gruber 401).

34 Reasoning too ... grasps the objects of imagination and the senses] Huber 43-4 compares Ammonius *On* On Interpretation 135.19-25, while pointing out that Boethius will link this point directly to the problem of divine foreknowledge in a way that Ammonius does not; cf. Introduction §12.2.4. Stephanus *On* On Interpretation 35.23, too, describes reason as knowing the sensible individual in a way superior to the individual itself, by apprehending its imperishable essence.

224

35 Man is a rational biped animal] Lerer 228 notes that in I.6.15 Boethius defined man, when asked to do so by Philosophy, as "rational mortal animal", and Philosophy observed that his inability to say what more man is than that showed his loss of understanding. The present definition, Lerer argues, has more significance than the stock answer there (see also Lerer 108-110); for Boethius has now recovered his philosophical understanding, and the *upright* nature of man's posture as a *biped* will be emphasised (see V m.5 below).

36 Although this is a universal notion] Gruber 401 compares Hofmann-Szantyr 625 for *cum* in the sense of "although" followed by *tum*, arguing that Bieler's emendation is thus unnecessary.

[V metr.4] The preceding prose passage ended with an account of how higher mental faculties comprehend the objects of lower ones, but not vice versa. The Stoics (like the Epicureans) adopted an empiricist position, arguing that the human mind was a blank at birth and that our understanding resulted from sensory experience. (Cf. LS 39-40, especially 39E). Philosophy argues against this that the mind has powers of its own and that sense-experience serves only to arouse these; she puts the point in terms of the Platonic theory of recollection, thus carrying on the theme of V m.3, but the general analogy to Chomsky will strike many readers. The Stoics are similarly criticised at Augustine *City of God* 8.7 (Gruber 401; see also Ralfs 364-5). Lerer 226-7 notes that the poem fits with the general movement in the concluding part of the *Consolation* away from experience of this world to inward philosophical contemplation. Metre: glyconic (- - - ∪ ∪ - ∪ ⌣).

1 the Porch] Greek *Stoa;* the *Stoa Poikile*, "Painted Porch", in the Athenian *agora*, where the Stoics taught and from which they took their name. (Cf. LS pp.2-5).

4 imprinted on minds from external bodies] The extent to which the Stoics were committed to pure empiricism is debated; the Stoic account of concept formation in LS 39D includes the claim that "the idea of something just and good is acquired naturally". It *may* be that this simply relates to the tendency of our environment to stimulate us to form these concepts, the mind itself being a complete blank to begin with and not having any inbuilt tendencies to form concepts in particular ways. Cf. F.H. Sandbach, '*Ennoia* and *Prolepsis*', in A.A. Long (ed.), *Problems in Stoicism*, London 1971, 22-37, at 27-30 and 33-4. The second syllable of *corporibus* is here scanned as long (O'Donnell).

6 with a swift stylus ... on the smooth surface of a page] The page is a page of a wax tablet; the image of the wax tablet for the mind goes back to Plato, *Theaetetus* 191c.

22 now raises its head to the highest point, now goes down again to the lowest parts] The picture of a single power moving through all levels of reality is particularly Neoplatonic. It also recalls the way in which Philosophy appeared to Boethius sometimes of human and sometimes of superhuman stature in I.1.

26 These things are produced more by a cause] Taking *magis* with *efficiens* rather than with *potentior,* to avoid redundancy; Gruber 403.

30 awakes and sets in motion the powers of the mind] The beginning of the process of recollection of the Forms.

39 and mingles the impressions with the forms stored within itself] The empiricists would agree with this as a description of what happens in sense-perception *after the concepts have been formed;* but Boethius insists that forms in the mind have a part to play in the process from the outset.

[V.5] 1 In the case of perceptible bodies] Philosophy develops further the themes of the preceding prose passage, which distinguished the different faculties of apprehension, and the subsequent verse passage, which emphasised that our apprehension is not purely passive but that sense-impressions prompt the mind to action. Now the point is made that different creatures will perceive in different ways, and that God will perceive by his own understanding alone.

the effect upon the body precedes the activity of the mind] Rendering *passio:* "what the body experiences". Similarly in "the mind is not marked by some effect on it" below.

calling the mind to activity within itself] i.e. within the body, Gruber 404.

how much more will those things which are free from all bodily feelings] or "bodily affects", *corporum affectionibus.* One might have expected a reference to incorporeal *objects* of apprehension, i.e. Platonic Forms; instead we get a reference to incorporeal *subjects* - i.e. God (and perhaps, as O'Donnell notes Chaucer's translation indicates, his angels as well). But in Neoplatonism incorporeal intelligible form *is* incorporeal intellect.

3 Sensation alone] According to Aristotle, creatures that cannot move (but need to react in one way to pleasurable stimuli such as food, in another to unpleasant and harmful stimuli) have the senses of touch and taste, but not imagination, or have both movement and imagination only in a vague and indefinite way; creatures other than man that can move (and so need to form some image of the goal to which their movement is directed) have imagination but not reason. Cf. Aristotle, *On the Soul* 3.10 433a12, 3.11 434a4, *Metaphysics* 1.1 980b25, *Parts of Animals* 1.1 641b8. Gruber 404; Ralfs 366.

some response of avoidance or pursuit] "response" translates *affectus*. For pursuit and avoidance as fundamental to the explanation of animal movement cf. Aristotle *On the Soul* 3.9 432b28. See also above on V.2.3.

4 Reasoning however belongs to the human race alone, as understanding alone does to the divine] Human beings are similarly placed between gods and irrational animals in the discussion of the nature of divine foreknowledge by Ammonius, *On* On Interpretation 133.33-134.3.

those to which the other ways of apprehending apply] above, V.4.31ff.

6 they might say that what can be sensed or imagined cannot be universal] Sensation and imagination cannot themselves conceive of things as universal; they therefore assume that, since human beings, for example, *can* be perceived by the senses, reasoning is wrong to regard the nature of human beings as something universal. They fail to recognise that the same thing can be grasped in different ways by different faculties.

8 Similarly with the fact that human reasoning] The argument is now applied to the problem at issue; just as sensation cannot judge what is possible for reasoning, so the fact that we cannot know in advance things whose outcome is undetermined does not mean that divine understanding cannot do so.

9 For what you are saying is as follows] Referring back to V.3.19. (Gruber 405).

11 so to have judgement of the divine mind] The Latin is ambiguous; it could mean either "to share in the judgement that the divine mind has" ("possess the judgement belonging to the divine mind", in the revised Loeb edition) or "to judge how the divine mind operates" ("judge of the mind of God", Watts). But one cannot do the latter without to some extent doing the former; and indeed the ambiguity may be intentional.

12 So let us rise up to that highest summit of understanding] This looks forward to the concluding argument of V.6. For the idea that we can move between different levels of understanding cf. V m.4 21ff. above, and for a connection with the mysticism of Meister Eckhart cf. Ralfs 371-3.

the simplicity of the highest knowledge] For the simplicity of Intellect and providence, as opposed to the complexity of the perceptible world and fate, cf. IV.6.17, V.4.30.

not confined within any limits] but certainly not *indefinite;* cf. Introduction §7.2.

[V metr.5] The last verse passage develops the theme of the preceding prose passage, which alluded to the different faculties of perception of different types of creature (V.5.2-4). The various kinds of creature are here described in the form of a *Priamel* (Gruber 406), leading to an exhortation to Boethius, and to the reader, to realise his true inheritance. This introduces the final stage of the argument in V.6, and taking up the theme of the whole work, Boethius' return to reason and his true home. Lerer points to the way in which the contrast between man and the lower animals picks up the theme of the mythological poems (see above on IV m.7); man's upward gaze here contrasts with Orpheus' longing for Eurydice in the underworld (3 m.12) and, as Reiss 136 points out, with the downwards gaze of the shackled prisoner in I m.2. The metre is Archilochean ($- \cup \cup - \cup \cup - | \cup \cup - \cup \cup | - \cup - \cup - \times$, with substitution of - for $\cup \cup$), as in alternate lines of Horace *Ode* I.4 (on human mortality). For illustrations in medieval MSS of the *Consolation* illustrating the variety of creatures cf. Courcelle [1967] 237-8 and plates 125-6.

7 cross green plains] *transmittere* is used thus by Virgil, *Aeneid* 4.154.

10 Only the race of man lifts its head up higher] The ideas that man's upright posture shows his superiority, and in particular that man alone can look up at the sky, were widespread; cf. Xenophon *Memorabilia* 1.4.11, Plato *Timaeus* 90a, 91e, Aristotle *Parts of Animals* 4.10 686a27, Cicero *On the Nature of the Gods* 2.140, Ovid *Metamorphoses* 1.84ff. (Gruber 406-7).

14 raise your thoughts on high too] The emphatic word is *too.* Boethius gives the old image a new turn; the fact that men stand upright physically is no guarantee that their thoughts are directed above rather than towards the earth.

14 sink to ruin] *pessum* has the double sense of "physically downwards" (the word is cognate with *pes,* foot), and metaphorically "to ruin".

[V.6] In this final chapter Boethius will combine the two elements of his solution to the problem of reconciling divine foreknowledge and human freedom; knowledge depends on the nature of the knower not of the thing known (as argued in V.4.25), and, since God's eternity is like a perpetual present, he sees even future events as present. But this means that his knowledge of future things no more conflicts with their freely occurring or not than does our knowledge of present things; cf. V.4.15-16.

in so far as it is right to do so] Cf. V.5.12.

4 this is made clearer by comparison with temporal things] The contrast between everlasting temporal duration and eternity goes back arguably to Parmenides (fr.8.5 = KRS 296) and certainly to Plato, *Timaeus* 37d-38b. Cf. also Plotinus 3.7.3; Calcidius *On the Timaeus* 25 75.16ff. and 201 221.15-16 Waszink, Proclus *Elements of Theology* 55, *On the* Timaeus 1.239.3 and 1.278.3-279.29, *On the* Parmenides 1213.17ff.; Simplicius *On the* Physics 1154.29-1155.18; Boethius *On the Trinity* 4. Courcelle [1967] 225-6; [1969] 313 n.113; Sulowski [1957] 84, [1961] 91-2; Merlan 198; Scheible 175-7; Gruber 409-10; Chadwick 217-8. On the general question of the eternity of God in Boethius' works cf. Obertello [1974] 673-99. See also below on §15.

6 as Aristotle supposed about the world] Aristotle *On the Heaven* 1.12. It may be no accident that Plato and Aristotle, whose doctrines Boethius had intended in his programme of philosophical writing to present as a unified and harmonised whole, both appear by name in the last chapter of the *Consolation* (Lerer 230).

9 certain people are wrong who, when they hear that in Plato's opinion this world neither had a beginning of time nor will have an ending] In the *Timaeus* Plato speaks of the world as having a beginning in time (28b); what is created is in principle perishable, but the creations of the supreme divine Craftsman are preserved everlastingly through his will (cf. 32c, 41ab), so that the world had a beginning but will have no end (so Plato is interpreted by Aristotle, *On the Heaven* 1.10 280a30). But already in the time of Aristotle Plato's successors as heads of the Academy, Speusippus (fr.61 Tarán) and Xenocrates (fr. 54 Heinze), had interpreted Plato in the *Timaeus* as giving a mythological account "for the purpose of instruction" of a world that was in fact without beginning or end in time; and although the question continued to be disputed, it was the general interpretation of the Neoplatonists that Plato intended the world to be without a literal beginning or end in time. For example Simplicius, *in phys.* 1154.3-1156.3, argues that Aristotle and Plato were in fact agreed that the world is everlasting. (Obertello [1974], 542 and n.100.)

However, even if the world had no beginning in time, that does not mean that there ceases to be a distinction between God's eternity and the everlastingness of the world in time (cf., with Sulowski [1961] 91, Calcidius *On the* Timaeus 26 77.1-8). And Philosophy is here criticising certain people who misinterpret the claim that the world is everlasting as a claim that it is *co-eternal* with God in a sense that would remove the distinction between eternity and time, between the creator and what is dependent on him even if it had no *temporal* beginning. Courcelle [1967] 226-8 and [1969] 313-318 argued that Boethius is here opposing the Christian Zacharias of Mytilene who in his *Ammonius* (PG vol. 85), arguing for the world having a beginning in time, wrongly attributed to Ammonius the view that the world was not just everlasting without beginning or end, but *co-*eternal with God. (The Christian Philoponus would later misrepresent Proclus similarly; Philoponus *On the eternity of the universe, against Proclus* 14.10ff. Courcelle [1967] 314, [1969] 227). Cf. Obertello [1974] 540-3, 673-9.

Boethius, it should be stressed, is *not* attacking the interpretation of Plato as supposing that the world had no beginning in time; indeed his apparent acceptance, both here and in III m.9, of the view that the world had no beginning in time and has always existed has caused problems for both medieval and modern commentators, because of its incompatibility with orthodox Christian doctrine. On the medieval discussions cf. Courcelle [1967] 276, 312-13; he points out, at [1967] 318 and 343 and [1969] 322, that no less orthodox a Christian than Aquinas, in his short work *On the eternity of the world, against those who grumble*, could use Boethius to defend Aristotle against the criticisms of Augustine – reason shows that the world is *dependent on a creator,* but whether or not it had a *beginning in time* is a matter for revelation and faith.

11 Nor is it through length of time that God should seem prior] That is, God's seniority is a matter of ontological status, not of temporal duration. *Antiquior* is often used for what is superior in rank or value, rather than earlier in time.

12 it descends from changelessness to change] For time is the life of the soul, which descends from the eternal Intellect; the language ("descends" and "is reduced") is Neoplatonic, as Gruber points out.

it seems up to a point to imitate that which it cannot fully express] The idea of time as a moving image of eternity is expressed by Plato in the *Timaeus* (37d).

15 considers all things as if they were happening now] For this description of God's knowledge Courcelle [1967] 217 compares Ammonius *On* On Interpretation 136.1ff.; Klingner [1921] 111 and Liebeschütz 549–50 trace it rather to such passages in Augustine as *Confessions* 11.31 and *City of God* 11.21. Sorabji [1983] 256 and 264 sees even earlier antecedents in Philo *That God is unchanging* 6.29–32 (above, Introduction §7.2) and Plotinus 4.4.15–16; cf. also Plotinus 3.7.3 and 6.7.1 with Huber 48 nn.45-6 and Patch [1935,1] 399. But for Plotinus the idea that for the divine everything is in the present does not include awareness of changeable things (Introduction §7.1). Cf. also Nemesius *On the Nature of Man* 44 129.28ff. Morani; Simplicius, *On Epictetus'* Manual, p.104 Dübner, and, with Mignucci [1985] 239, Proclus *Platonic Theology* 1.21.

17 not *praevidentia* ... but *providentia*] Sulowski [1957] 84 compares Calcidius *On the* Timaeus 176 205.3-8. However *providentia* is there derived not from *pro-* "forth" but from *proprium*, as the vision that is proper to God.

it looks forth on all things as if from a high peak among things] Aquinas, adopting the essentials of Boethius' solution, developed this point further: as we travel along a road we cannot see those who come after us, but God, watching from a height, sees at once the whole road and all those travelling along it (*Summa Theologiae* 1 q.14 art.13 ad 3; cf. Sorabji [1980,2] 125). Courcelle [1967], 236-7 and plate 132, reproduces an illumination in a 15th-century manuscript of Boethius in which Providence, seated in a high tower, watches Philosophy and Boethius who have come to a road-junction (cf. Prodicus' choice of Heracles; above on IV m.7) where Boethius must turn one way or the other. But precisely at this point the analogy breaks down; even a watcher in a high place cannot see which way someone is going to turn at a junction they have not yet reached, though even we, the travellers on the road, have some possibility of observing the choices made by those who have gone before us. The attempt to represent God's timeless knowledge by an analogy in terms of space and time breaks down, as it must; and it breaks down when an attempt is made to introduce the notion of free human choice. If God's timeless knowledge makes any sense at all, it must be unlike anything that we can express in terms familiar to us from our ordinary experience in time.

19 Surely, when you see present things, your gazing does not impart any necessity to them] See above, V.4.15-16.

Certainly not] Bieler gives this to Philosophy, answering her own question, and compares §40 below. Admittedly, in section 40 Philosophy is herself answering an open question which she has explicitly put into Boethius' mouth; while here the question is one ostensibly addressed *to* Boethius, and is not an open question but one inviting a negative response. But Lerer 229-30 points out that there is nothing in the MSS to suggest that the remark is Boethius', and that giving it to Philosophy fits Boethius' silence in this last part of the work; if it were given to Boethius it would constitute his last contribution to the dialogue, and it hardly seems a very significant note on which to conclude his contribution.

22 he does not make confused judgements about things] That is, he does not mistakenly regard as necessary what is in fact contingent; cf. above, V.3.23.

a man walking on the earth and the sun rising in the sky] For walking as an example of a contingent action see above, on Cicero *On Fate* fr.4. For the rising or more generally the movement of the sun as something necessary (at least in an everlasting Platonic or Aristotelian universe) cf. Ammonius *On* On Interpretation 153.13ff., Boethius *On* On Interpretation[2] 241.4 and *On Cicero's* Topics, PL 64 1152c. Cf. Patch [1935,1] 401-2, and below on §25.

24 this is not opinion, but rather knowledge] Answering the point of V.3.18 above (Gruber 412). *quid* is the antecedent of *quod idem,* as O'Donnell notes.

25 Here you may say] As at V.3.4; Gruber 412.

If you tie me to this term of "necessity"] Philosophy now introduces the contrast between absolute and conditional necessity that remained tacit at V.3.10-14 and V.4.14-16. The fact that it is necessary that you are walking, when you are seen to be walking (whether by a human being at the time or by God beforehand), is not the same as saying that your walking is necessary, rather than contingent, in itself. The distinction drawn here has its basis in Aristotle, *On Interpretation* 9 19a23; it appears at Ammonius *On* On Interpretation 153.13ff., Boethius *On* On Interpretation[1] 121.20ff. and *On* On Interpretation[2] 241.1ff. In these texts, however, what is at issue is the necessity of something being so when it is so, which is not quite the same as the necessity of what is *known* here; that introduces a condition *different* from the occurrence of the thing itself. (Walking and moving forward, in §29, constitute a type of example intermediate between these two; the moving forward is not distinct from the walking in the way that your seeing someone's doing something is different from his or her doing it.) See also Aristotle *On Coming-to-Be and Passing-Away* 2.11 337b14ff. and *Physics* 2.9 199b34ff., and Alexander of Aphrodisias *On the Prior Analytics* 141.1ff., with the comments of Patch [1935], De Vogel [1971] 65 n.31, Chadwick 162 and Huber 54ff.

27 its being necessary that all men are mortal] For the example see above on Cicero *On Fate* §17; also Calcidius *On the* Timaeus 155 189.13ff. Waszink and Boethius *On* On Interpretation[1] 122.15.

29 it is necessary that he move forward at the time he walks] Necessarily, walking involves moving forward (or "*if* you walk, you necessarily move forward"); but that does not mean that a person has no choice about moving forward, that his or her doing so is necessary in itself or absolutely.

31 but considered in themselves they do not cease from the complete freedom of their own nature] Cf. Ammonius *On* On Interpretation 136.30 and Aquinas *Summa Theologiae* 1 q.14 art.13 ad 2 and ad 3.

33 What difference does it make, then] It is still the case that whatever God foresees must (by conditional necessity) come about; but this does not remove the difference between things that are necessary *in their own nature* and those that are not. The use of the indicative with *cum* in a causal sense is a late Latin one; cf. Hofmann-Szantyr 625. So in §48 below, and in §46 below with *cum* in a conditional sense.

34 the things that I mentioned a short while ago] At V.6.22.

37 If it rests in my power to change my intention, I will make providence empty] By not doing what providence had foreseen I would do; but, as Philosophy immediately points out, providence which foresees everything will also foresee your change of intention. All your twists and turns, as it were, are anticipated; and (though Boethius does not make this point absolutely explicit) there may well be situations where you are *genuinely undecided* what course to follow but Providence knows better than you which option you will eventually adopt. See above on IV.6.53.

39 will divine knowledge be changed] The answer is no, just because it foresees simultaneously all the changes that a human agent may make in his plans over time; and indeed, providence being outside time *could not* change.

42 the point you made a little earlier] At V.3.15. But there is an unresolved problem. Boethius' words seem to require that God determines our actions (so Gegenschatz [1958] 128-9), for otherwise it seems that it *would* be on our actions that God's knowledge depends, and even if they are not *future* actions as far as God is concerned, that does nothing to answer the objection of V.3.15. But if God does determine our actions, there is a problem of predestination which is not answered in the *Consolation,* as well as the problem of foreknowledge which Boethius has attempted to resolve. See Introduction, §7.4 and §12.2.5.

44 rewards and punishments] cf. above, V.3.30.

45 concurs with the future quality of our actions] God can foresee what we will do, and allocate our fortune to us accordingly (cf. IV.6, and V.2.11).

distributing rewards to the good and punishments to the bad] but not always, as there is sometimes advantage in doing otherwise; above, IV.6.

46 Nor are hopes placed in God and prayers ... in vain] See above, V.3.33-5.

47 lift up your mind to righteous hopes] Cf. the end of V m.5, above. Lerer 231 argues that Boethius the character has by this point dropped out of the work together, and Philosophy is addressing the reader directly. De Vogel [1973] 364 and Mohrmann comment on the liturgical language and Christian tone of the exhortation, Mohrmann (60-1) noting especially the reference to *humble* prayers; but see above on V.3.34.

48 A great necessity to be good is laid upon you] With this final exhortation compare the end of IV m.7. There is an irony, perhaps intentional; Boethius has been distinguishing types of necessity precisely to show that divine foreknowledge is not in itself incompatible with human freedom. But that does not mean that there is not another type of necessity that constrains us, the necessity of moral obligation.

Is the *Consolation* complete? Tränkle [1977] 150 argued that the absence of a poem at the end can hardly be intentional, when all the other books end with a poem; he further claimed (152-3) that no answer is given to the question in I.6.15-17 of what a human being is (but see above on V.4.35), and also (153-5) that Boethius fails to take up references forward in V.1.1 (where see Commentary) and to punishments after death in IV.4.22ff. In the latter passage however it is nor clear that the topic is to be taken up again at all. More convincing is the explanation of Lerer (231): there is no further poem because poetry has been replaced by argument, and the argument in its turn is complete; what is needed is action and specifically prayer. The structure of the sequence of poems, with III m.9 as the centrepiece and the other poems grouped round it, suggests the work is complete (Gruber 23, Chadwick 234, 247). See further Introduction, §§11 and 13.

Bibliography

This bibliography is selective; it does not include all modern discussions of the texts, but only those which will be found most useful. Where Boethius is concerned it is directed towards the particular concerns of the present volume; see the Preface.

Amand, D.   (E. Amand de Mendieta), *Fatalisme et liberté dans l'antiquité grecque,* [1]Louvain 1945; [2] Amsterdam 1973.

Asmis, E.   'Free Action and the Swerve', *Oxford Studies in Ancient Philosophy* 8 (1990) 275-291.

Ax, W.   *Cicero: De divinatione, De fato, Timaeus,* Stuttgart, Teubner, 1965.

Balme, D.M. [1939] 'Greek Science and Mechanism: I, Aristotle on Nature and Chance', *Class. Quart.* 33 (1939) 129-138.

Balme, D.M. [1941] 'Greek Science and Mechanism: II, The Atomists', *Class. Quart.* 35 (1941) 23-8.

Bark, W.   'Theodoric vs. Boethius: Vindication and Apology', *American Historical Review* 49 (1943-44) 410-426, reprinted in Fuhrmann-Gruber 11-32.

Barnes, J. [1981] 'Boethius and the Study of Logic', in Gibson (q.v.) 73-89.

Barnes, J. [1982] 'Medicine, Experience and Logic', in J. Barnes et al., eds., *Science and Speculation,* Cambridge and Paris, 1982.

Barnes, J. [1985,1] 'Cicero's *De fato* and a Greek source', in J. Brunschwig et al., eds., *Histoire et Structure: à la mémoire de Victor Goldschmidt,* Paris, 1985, 229-239.

Barnes, J. [1985,2] 'Pithana sunnemena', *Elenchos* 6 (1985) 453-468.

Bases, S.   'De locis quibusdam Boetii librorum', *AQHNA* 4 (1892) 341-63.

Bayer, K.   (ed.) *Cicero: De fato,* Munich 1963.

Botros, S.   'Freedom, Causality, Fatalism and Early Stoic Philosophy', *Phronesis* 30 (1985) 274-304.

Bieler, L.   (ed.) *Boethii Philosophiae Consolatio,* Turnhout 1957 (CCSL 94).

Büchner, K. [1940] 'Bemerkungen zum Text der Consolatio Philosophiae des Boethius', 75 (1940) 279-297.

Büchner, K. [1964] *Cicero. Bestand und Wandel seiner geistigen Welt,* Heidelberg 1964.

Büchner, K. [1977] (ed.) *Boethius: Philosophiae Consolationis libri quinque,* Heidelberg [3]1977. (*Editiones Heidelbergenses,* 11).

Chadwick, H.   *Boethius: the consolations of music, logic, theology and philosophy,* Oxford 1981.

Chamberlain, D.S. 'Philosophy of music in the *Consolatio* of Boethius', *Speculum* 45 (1970) 80-97, reprinted in Fuhrmann-Gruber 377-403.

Cioffari, V.   *Fate and Fortune from Democritus to St. Thomas Aquinas,* New York 1935.

Clark, A.C.   *The Descent of Manuscripts,* Oxford 1918.

Coster, C.H.   'The fall of Boethius: his character', *Annuaire de l'Inst. de Philologie et d'Histoire orientales et slaves* (Brussels) 12 (1952) 45-81 (= *Mélanges H. Grégoire*), reprinted with a Postscript in Coster, *Late Roman Studies,* Cambridge, Mass. 1968, 54-103. (References are to the reprint.)

Courcelle, P. [1967]	*La Consolation de Philosophie dans la tradition littéraire*, Paris 1967.
Courcelle, P. [1969]	(tr. H.E. Wedeck), *Late Latin Writers and their Greek Sources*, Cambridge, Mass. 1969.
Crabbe, A.	'Literary design in the *De Consolatione Philosophiae*', in Gibson (q.v.) 237-274.
Crouse, R.	'Semina rationum: St. Augustine & Boethius', *Dionysius* 4 (1980) 75-85.
Curley, T.F., III	'The *Consolation of Philosophy* as a work of literature', *American Journal of Philology* 108 (1987) 343-67.
Daly, E.J.	'An early 9th century MS of Boethius', *Scriptorium* 4 (1950) 205-19.
de Vogel, C.J. [1971]	'Boethiana I', *Vivarium* 9 (1971) 49-66.
de Vogel, C.J. [1972]	'Boethiana II', *Vivarium* 10 (1972) 1-40.
de Vogel, C.J. [1973]	'The problem of philosophy and Christian faith in Boethius' *Consolatio*', in W. den Boer et al., eds., *Romanitas et Christianitas: studia J.H. Waszink ... oblata*, Amsterdam 1973, 357-70, reprinted in Fuhrmann-Gruber, 286-301.
den Boeft, J.	*Calcidius on Fate: his doctrine and sources*, Leiden 1970.
Donini, P.L. [1973]	'Crisippo e la nozione del possibile', *Rivista di filologia* 101 (1973) 333-351.
Donini, P.L. [1974-5]	'Fato e volontà umana in Crisippo', *Atti dell'Accademia delle Scienze di Torino* 109 (1974-5) 187-230.
Donini, P.L. [1988]	'Plutarco e il determinismo di Crisippo', in I. Gallo (ed.), *Aspetti dello Stoicismo e dell'Epicureismo in Plutarco*, Ferrara 1988 (*Quaderni del Giornale Filologico Ferrarese* 9) 21-32.
Donini, P.L. [1989]	*Ethos: Aristotele e il determinismo*, Alessandria (Torino) 1989.
Dorey, T.H.	(ed.) *Cicero* (in the series *Studies in Latin Literature and its Influence)*: London 1964.
Douglas, A.E. [1964]	'Cicero the Philosopher', in Dorey (q.v.) 135-170.
Douglas, A.E. [1968]	*Cicero* (Greece and Rome New Surveys in the Classics 12), 1968.
Dronke, P.	Review of Courcelle [1967], in *Speculum* 44 [1969] 123-8, reprinted in Fuhrmann-Gruber 436-443.
Duhot, J.J.	*La conception stoïcienne de la causalité*, Paris 1989.
Ebbesen, S.	'Boethius as an Aristotelian commentator', in J. Wiesner (ed.), *Aristoteles: Werk und Wirkung, Paul Moraux gewidmet*, vol.2 (Berlin 1987); reprinted in R. Sorabji (ed.), *Aristotle Transformed*, London 1990, 373-392 (references to the reprint).
Eisenberger, H.	'Zur Frage der ursprünglichen Gestalt von Ciceros Schrift *De fato*', *Grazer Beiträge* 8 (1979) 153-172.
Englert, W.C.	*Epicurus on the Swerve and Voluntary Action*, Atlanta 1987 (*American Classical Studies*, 16).
Fine, G.	'Aristotle on Determinism: a review of Richard Sorabji's *Necessity, Cause and Blame*', *Philosophical Review* 90 (1981) 561-80.
Fontenrose, J.	*The Delphic Oracle*, Berkeley 1978.
Frede, D. [1982]	'The Dramatisation of Determinism: Alexander of Aphrodisias' "De fato"', *Phronesis* 27 (1982) 276-298.
Frede, D. [1985]	'The Sea-Battle reconsidered: a defence of the traditional interpretation', *Oxford Studies in Ancient Philosophy* 3 (1985) 31-88.
Frede, M. [1974]	*Die stoische Logik*, Göttingen 1974 (*Abh. Göttingen*, phil.-hist. Kl. 3.88).

Frede, M. [1980]   'The Original Notion of Cause,' in M. Schofield etc. (eds.), *Doubt and Dogmatism*, 217-249: reprinted in M. Frede, *Essays in Ancient Philosophy*, Minneapolis 1987, 125-150. (References are to the pages of the original article.)

Fuhrmann, M. and Gruber, J. (eds.), *Boethius*, Darmstadt 1984 *(Wege der Forschung* vol. 483).

Furley, D.J.   *Two Studies in the Greek Atomists*, Princeton 1967.

Gegenschatz, E. [1958]   'Die Freiheit der Entscheidung in der *Consolatio Philosophiae* des Boethius', *Museum Helveticum* 15 (1958) 110-29, reprinted in Fuhrmann-Gruber, 323-349.

Gegenschatz, E. [1966]   'Die Gefährdung des Möglichen durch das Vorauswissen Gottes', *Wiener Studien* 79 (1966) 517-530.

Gercke, A.   'Chrysippea' *Jahrb. für klass. Phil.* Supplbd. 14 (1885) 689-781.

Gibson, M. (ed.)   *Boethius: his life, thought and influence*, Oxford, Basil Blackwell, 1981.

Giomini, R.   (ed.) *Cicero: De divinatione, De fato, Timaeus*, Leipzig, Teubner, 1975.

Görler, W.   '"Hauptursachen" bei Chrysipp und Cicero?', *Rheinisches Museum* 130 (1987) 254-274.

Gould, J.B. [1970]   *The Philosophy of Chrysippus*, Leiden 1970.

Gould, J.B. [1974]   'The Stoic conception of fate', *Journal of the History of Ideas* 35 (1974) 17-32.

Greene, W.C.   *Moira: Fate, Good and Evil in Greek Thought*, Cambridge, Mass., 1944, repr. New York 1963.

Grilli, A.   'Contributo alla storia di προηγούμενος', in *Studi linguistici in onore di V. Pisani*, Brescia 1969, 409-500.

Gruber, J.   *Kommentar zu Boethius De Consolatione Philosophiae*, Berlin 1978 *(Texte und Kommentare, 9)*.

Gulley, N.   'Lucretius on Free Will,' *Symbolae Osloenses* 65 (1990) 37-52.

Hagendahl, H.   *Augustine and the Latin Classics*, Göteborg 1967.

Hager, F.P.   'Proklos und Alexander von Aphrodisias über ein Problem der Vorsehung', in J. Mansfeld et al. (eds.), *Kephalaion: Studies in Greek Philosophy and its Continuation presented to C.J. de Vogel*, Assen 1975, 171-182.

Hamelin, O.   *Sur le de fato,* publié et annoté par M. Conche, 1978 (references are to the pages of the published version, not to the pages of Hamelin's MSS).

Henkinson, R.J.   'Evidence, Externality and Antecedence: inquiries into later Greek causal concepts', *Phronesis* 32 (1987) 80-100.

Henry, M.Y.   'Cicero's treatment of the free will problem', *Transactions of the American Philological Association* 58 (1927) 32-42.

Hintikka, J.   *Time and Necessity*, Oxford 1973.

Hofmann-Szantyr   J.B. Hofmann, rev. A. Szantyr, *Lateinische Syntax und Stilistik*, Munich 1965 *(Handbuch der Altertumswissenschaft, 2.2.2)*.

Huber, P.   *Die Vereinbarkeit von göttlicher Vorsehung und menschlicher Freiheit in der Consolatio Philosophiae des Boethius*, Zurich 1976.

Huby, P.M.   'An Epicurean Argument in Cicero, *De Fato* XVII-40', *Phronesis* 15 (1970) 83-5.

Inwood, B.   *Ethics and Human Action in Early Stoicism*, Oxford 1985.

Ioppolo, A.M. 'Le cause antecedenti in Cic. De Fato 40', in J.Barnes and M. Mignucci, *Matter and Metaphysics*, Naples 1989, 399-424.

Johanson, C. and Londey, D. 'Cicero on Propositions: *Academica* 2.95', *Mnemosyne* 4.41 (1988) 325-332.

Kleywegt, A.J. 'Fate, Free Will, and the Text of Cicero', *Mnemosyne* 26 (1973) 342-9.

Klingner, F. [1921] *De Boethii consolatione philosophiae*, Berlin 1921.

Klingner, F. [1940] Review of Weinberger, *Gnomon* 16 (1940)26-32.

Kretzmann, N. 'Boethius and the truth about tomorrow's sea battle', in *Logos and Pragma: Essays on the Philosophy of Language in Honour of Professor Gabriel Nuchelmans*, Nijmegen 1987 (*Aristarium* suppl. 3), 63-97.

Lerer, S. *Boethius and Dialogue: Literary Method in the Consolation of Philosophy*, Princeton 1986.

Liebeschütz, H. 'Boethius and the legacy of antiquity', in A.H. Armstrong (ed.), *The Cambridge History of Later Greek and Early Medieval Philosophy*, [2]Cambridge 1970, 538-564.

Loeb edition (of Boethius): see Stewart, H.F.

Lörcher, A. *De compositione et fonte libri Ciceronis qui est De fato*, diss. Halle 1907. (Not seen by me.)

Long, A.A. [1968] 'The Stoic Concept of Evil', *Philos. Quart.* 18 (1968) 329-343.

Long, A.A. [1971] 'Freedom and Determinism in the Stoic Theory of Human Action', in A.A. Long (ed.), *Problems in Stoicism*, London 1971, 173-199.

Long, A.A. [1974] *Hellenistic Philosophy*, London 1974.

Long, A.A. [1977] 'Chance and Natural Law in Epicureanism', *Phronesis* 22 (1977) 63-88.

Long, A.A. and Sedley, D.N. *The Hellenistic Philosophers*, Cambridge 1987 (= LS).

Luck, G. 'On Cicero *De fato* 5 and related problems', *American Journal of Philology* 99 (1978) 155-8.

Machan, T.W. 'A note on *De consolatione philosophiae*', *Classical Philology* 81 (1986) 328-9.

Mansfeld, J. [1988] '*Diaphonia:* the argument of Alexander *De fato* chs. 1-2', *Phronesis* 33 (1988) 181-207.

Mansfeld, J. [1990] 'Doxography and Dialectic. The *Sitz im Leben* of the "Placita" ', *Aufstieg und Niedergang der römischen Welt* II.36.4, Berlin 1990, 3056-3229.

Matthews, J. 'Anicius Manlius Severinus Boethius', in Gibson (q.v.) 15-43.

Mauro, L. 'Il Problema del Fato in Boezio e Tommaso d'Aquino', in Obertello [1981,2] 355-365.

Merkelbach, R. *Kritische Beiträge zu antiken Autoren*, Meisenheim am Glan 1974.

Merlan, P. 'Ammonius Hermiae, Zacharias Scholasticus and Boethius', *Greek, Roman and Byzantine Studies* 9 (1968) 193-203.

Mignucci, M. [1978] 'Sur la logique modale des Stoïciens', in *Les Stoïciens et leur logique, Actes du colloque de Chantilly*, Paris 1978, 317-346.

Mignucci, M. [1985] 'Logic and Omniscience: Alexander of Aphrodisias and Proclus', *Oxford Studies in Ancient Philosophy* 3 (1985) 219-246.

Mitsis, P. *Epicurus' Ethical Theory*, Ithaca 1988.

Mohrmann, C.	'Some remarks on the language of Boethius, *Consolatio Philosophiae*', in J.J. O'Meara and B. Naumann (eds.), *Latin Script and Letters A.D. 400-900: Festschrift presented to L. Bieler*, etc., Leiden 1976, 54-61, reprinted in Fuhrmann-Gruber, 302-10.
Montanari Caldini, R.	'Nota testuale ed esegetica al *De fato* ciceroniano', *Quaderni Urbinati di Cultura classica* n.s. 4 (1980) 83-92.
Morton, C.	'Boethius in Pavia: the tradition and the scholars', in Obertello [1981,2] 27-38.
Mueller-Goldingen, C.	'Die Stellung der Dichtung in Boethius' *Consolatio Philosophiae*', *Rh. Mus.* n.f. 132 (1989) 369-395.
Obertello, L. [1974]	*Severino Boezio*, Genoa 1974.
Obertello, L. [1981,1]	'Proclus, Ammonius and Boethius on divine foreknowledge', *Dionysius* 5 (1981) 127-164.
Obertello, L. [1981,2]	(ed.) *Atti del congresso internazionale di studi boeziani, Pavia 5-8 Ottobre 1980*, Rome 1981.
O'Connor, D.J.	*Free Will*, Garden City 1971/London 1972.
O'Daly, G.J.P.	*The Poetry of Boethius*, London 1991. (This book was published too recently for me to take it into account in writing the present one.)
O'Donnell, J.J. (ed.)	*Boethius: Consolatio Philosophiae*, Bryn Mawr 1984 (text reprinted from ed. of W. Weinberger in *Corpus Scriptorum Ecclesiasticorum Latinorum*, Vienna and Leipzig, 1934).
Paolillo, M.	*De fato* (Florence 1966). Not seen by me.
Patch, H.R. [1929]	'Fate in Boethius and the Neoplatonists', *Speculum* 4 (1929) 62-72.
Patch, H.R. [1933]	'*Consolatio Philosophiae* 4 m.6.23-4', *Speculum* 8 (1933) 41-51.
Patch, H.R. [1935,1]	'Necessity in Boethius and the Neoplatonists', *Speculum* 10 (1935) 393-404.
Patch, H.R. [1935,2]	*The Tradition of Boethius*, New York 1935.
Philippson, R.	review of Yon, *Phil. Wochenschr.* 54 (1934) 1030-9.
Pike, N.	'Divine Omniscience and Voluntary Action', *Philosophical Review* 74 (1965) 27-46.
Pohlenz, M. [1940]	*Grundfragen der Stoischen Philosophie*, *Abh. Göttingen*, phil.-hist. Kl. 3.26, 1940.
Pohlenz, M. [1967]	*La Stoa: storia di un movimento spirituale*, rev.and tr.V.E. Alfieri et al., Florence 1967.
Prinz, K.	'Bemerkungen zur *Philosophiae Consolatio* des Boethius', *Wiener Studien* 53 (1935) 171-5.
Rackham, H. (ed.)	*Cicero: De Oratore book III, De Fato*, etc. London and Cambridge, Mass. (Loeb Classical Library), 1942.
Ralfs, G.	'Die Erkenntnislehre des Boethius', in Fuhrmann-Gruber 350-372.
Rand, E.K. [1904]	'On the composition of Boethius' *Consolatio Philosophiae*', *Harvard Studies in Classical Philology* 15 (1904) 1-28, reprinted in Fuhrmann-Gruber 249-277. (References are to the reprint).
Rand, E.K. [1918]	see Stewart.
Rawson, E.D.	*Cicero: a portrait*, London 1975.
Reiss, E.	*Boethius*, Boston 1982.
Rist, J.M.	*Stoic Philosophy*, Cambridge 1969.
Ryle, G.	*Dilemmas*, Cambridge 1954.
Sambursky, S.	*Physics of the Stoics*, London 1959.
Sandbach, F.H. [1971]	'Phantasia Kataleptike' in A.A. Long (ed.), *Problems in Stoicism*, London 1971, 1-21.

Sandbach, F.H. [1975]   *The Stoics*, London 1975.

Saunders, T.J.   'Free Will and the Atomic Swerve in Lucretius', *Symbolae Osloenses* 59 (1984) 37-59.

Scheible, H.   *Die Gedichte in der Consolatio Philosophiae des Boethius*, Heidelberg 1972.

Schmekel, A. [1892]   *Die Philosophie der mittleren Stoa*, Berlin 1892, at 155-184.

Schmekel, A. [1938]   *Forschungen zur Philosophie des Hellenismus*, Berlin 1938 (= *Die positive Philosophie in ihrer geschichtlichen Entwicklung*, vol.1), at 258-271.

Schofield, M.   'Cicero for and against divination', *Journal of Roman Studies* 76 (1986) 47-65.

Schröder, S.   'Philosophische und Medizinische Ursachensystematik und der stoische Determinismus', *Prometheus* 15 (1989) 209-239; 16 (1990) 5-26; 16 (1990) 136-154.

Sedley, D.N. [1977]   'Diodorus Cronus and Hellenistic Philosophy', *Proc. Camb. Phil. Soc.* n.s. 23 (1977) 74-120.

Sedley, D.N. [1982]   'On Signs' in J. Barnes et al. (eds.), *Science and Speculation*, Cambridge and Paris, 1982, 239-272.

Sedley, D.N. [1983]   'Epicurus' Refutation of Determinism', *Syzetesis* (Festschrift Gigante), 1983, 11-51.

Sedley, D.N. [1989]   'Epicurean anti-reductionism', in J. Barnes and M. Mignucci (eds.), *Matter and Metaphysics*, Naples 1989, 297-327.

Sedley, D.N. [1993]   'Chrysippus on psycho-physical causality', in M. Nussbaum, ed., *Passions & Perceptions*, Cambridge 1993, 313-331.

Shackleton Bailey, D.R.   *Cicero's Letters to Atticus*, vol. 6, Cambridge 1967.

Shanzer, D. [1983]   'Me quoque excellentior: Boethius *De Consolatione Philosophiae* 4.6.38', *Class. Quart.* 33 (1983) 277-283.

Shanzer, D. [1984]   'The death of Boethius and the *Consolation of Philosophy*', *Hermes* 112 (1984) 352-366.

Sharples, R.W. [1981]   'Necessity in the Stoic doctrine of fate', *Symbolae Osloenses* 56 (1981) 81-97.

Sharples, R.W. [1983,1]   *Alexander of Aphrodisias On Fate*, London 1983.

Sharples, R.W. [1983,2]   'Nemesius of Emesa and some theories of divine providence', *Vigiliae Christianae* 37 (1983) 141-156.

Sharples, R.W. [1986]   'Soft determinism and freedom in early Stoicism', a reply to Botros, *Phronesis* 31 (1986) 266-279.

Sharples, R.W. [1987,1]   'Alexander of Aphrodisias: Scholasticism and Innovation', *Aufstieg und Niedergang der römischen Welt*, vol. II.36.1 (1987) 1176-1243.

Sharples, R.W. [1987,2]   'Could Alexander (follower of Aristotle) have done better? A response to Professor Frede and others, *Oxford Studies in Ancient Philosophy* 5 (1987) 197-216.

Sharples, R.W. [1995]   'Causes and Necessary Conditions in the *De Fato*', in J.G.F. Powell (ed.), *Cicero the Philosopher*, Oxford 1995, 247-271.

Shiel, J.   'Boethius' Commentaries on Aristotle', in R. Hunt, R. Klibansky, L. Labowsky (eds.), *Medieval and Renaissance Studies* 4 (1958) 217-244; reprinted in Fuhrmann-Gruber 155-183 and in R. Sorabji (ed.), *Aristotle Transformed*, London 1990, 373-392. (References to the latter reprint.)

Silk, E.T.   'Boethius' *Consolatio Philosophiae* as a sequel to Augustine's dialogues and *soliloquia*', *Harvard Theological Review* 32 (1939) 19-39.

238

Sorabji, R.[1980,1]   'Causation, Laws and Necessity', in M. Schofield etc.
                         (eds.) *Doubt and Dogmatism*, Oxford 1980, 250-282 (or
                         in Sorabji [1980,2] ch.4).
Sorabji, R.[1980,2]   *Necessity, Cause and Blame*, London 1980.
Sorabji, R. [1983]   *Time, Creation and the Continuum*, London 1983.
Starnes, C.J.   'Boethius and the development of Christian humanism;
                         the theology of the *Consolatio*', in Obertello [1981,2]
                         27-38.
Stewart, H.F. and Rand, E.K. *Boethius: Theological Tractates, Consolation of
                         Philosophy*, Loeb Classical Library, 1918. (The text of
                         the *Consolation* is by Rand, the translation by "I.T."
                         revised by Stewart.) A later edition with a new trans-
                         lation by S.J. Tester, 1973.
Stough, C.   'Stoic Determinism and Moral Responsibility', in J.M. Rist
                         (ed.), *The Stoics*, Berkeley 1978, 203-232.
Sulowski, F.J. [1957]   'Les sources du *De consolatio Philosophiae* de Boèce',
                         Sophia 25 (1957) 76-85.
Sulowski, F.J. [1961]   'The Sources of Boethius' *De consolatione Philosophiae*',
                         Sophia 29 (1961) 67-94.
Szymánski, M.   'De fato 8.15', *Hermes* 113 (1985) 383ff.
Talanga, J.   *Zukunftsurteile und Fatum*, Bonn 1986.
Tester, S.J.   See Stewart, H.F.
Theiler, W. [1946]   'Tacitus und die antike Schiksalslehre', in *Phyllobolia
                         für P. von der Mühll* (Basel 1946) 35-90, reprinted in
                         Theiler, *Forschungen zum Neuplatonismus*, Berlin 1966,
                         ch.2 (references are to the reprint).
Theiler, W. [1964]   'Antike und christliche Rückkehr zu Gott', *Mullus:
                         Festschrift Theodor Klauser (Jahrb. f. Antik. und
                         Christentum suppl.1)*, 1964, 352-361, reprinted in
                         Theiler, *Forschungen zum Neuplatonismus*, Berlin 1966,
                         ch.9 (references are to the reprint).
Tränkle, H. [1968]   'Textkritische Bemerkungen zur Philosophiae Consolatio
                         des Boethius', *Vigiliae Christianae* 22 (1968) 272-283.
Tränkle, H. [1977]   'Ist die Philosophiae Consolatio des Boethius zum vorge-
                         sehenen Abschluss gelengt?', *Vigiliae Christianae* 31
                         (1977) 148-156, reprinted in Fuhrmann-Gruber, 311-
                         319.
Troncarelli, F.   'Una nuova edizione della *Consolatio Philosophiae* di
                         Boezio nel Corpus Christianorum', *Scriptorium* 41
                         (1987) 133-50.
Turnebus, A.   Commentary on Cicero *De fato*, Paris 1552; extensively
                         cited in Bayer, q.v.
Verrycken, K.   'The metaphysics of Ammonius son of Hermias', in R.
                         Sorabji (ed.), *Aristotle Transformed*, London 1990,
                         199-231.
Waddell, H.   *Medieval Latin Lyrics*, Harmondsworth 1952.
Wallis, R.T.   *Neoplatonism*, London 1972.
Watts, V.E.   *Boethius: The Consolation of Philosophy*, Harmondsworth
                         1969.
Weinberger, W.   (ed.) *Boethii Philosophiae Consolationis libri quinque*,
                         Vienna 1934 (*Corpus Scriptorum Ecclesiasticorum
                         Latinorum*, 67).
Weische, A.   *Cicero und die neue Akademie*, Münster/ Westf. 1961.
White, M.J.   *Agency and Integrality*, Dordrecht 1985.
Yon, A. (ed.)   *Cicéron: Traité du Destin*, Paris (Budé) 1933, reprinted
                         1944 and 1950.

Additional Bibliography since the first impression

Gaskin, R.　　　　　　　*The Sea Battle and the Master Argument,* Berlin 1995, 221–235, 306–318.

Lévy, C.　　　　　　　　*Cicero Academicus,* Rome 1992, 589–617.

Powell, J.G.F. (ed.)　　*Cicero the Philosopher,* Oxford 1995.

INDEX

This index is selective and should be regarded as complementary to the Table of Contents and (for the names of modern scholars) the Bibliography. No attempt has been made to provide an *index locorum* of all citations to ancient sources. All references are to pages of this book; those in brackets are implicit only.

pre-existence of souls, 47 n.3
predestination 45 n.4, 105, 121, 217, 231
present: all time as present to God, 27, 42, 44-5, 153, 227, 229
presentation see sense-presentation
Priam 180, 183
Proclus 26-7, 43-4, 45 n.2, 205, 207, 209-10, 218, 220
Prodicus 212, 229
propositions 53, 159
providence 4, 8, 11, 29-33, 43-4, 105-11, 115-17, 125, 129, 131-5, 139-41, 153-7, 202, 204-8, 210, 215-18, 220, 227, 229-231
pseudo-Plutarch, *On Fate,* 31
punishment and reward 85, 97, 103, 111-15, 119-23, 135, 157, 206-8, 210-11, 220, 231
pursuit and avoidance 129, 147, 216, 226
Pythagoreans 99, 198

reason, reasoning 108, 129, 143, 147-9, 157, 205, 216-17, 224, 226
recollection 139, 221, 225
reductionism 7-8
reservation 9
responsibility (depending on: *and see* power, in one's) 9, 15, 57, 97-101, 188, 197
revelation, and reason, 47
reward (*and see* punishment), 123-5
rhetoric 53-5, 160, 174-5, 184, 195-6
Ryle, Gilbert 12

scepticism (*and see* Academy) 10-11
Scipio the younger 55-7, 69, 75, 161, 168, 172, 178
sea-battle paradox, *see* future truth
seasons, four 117
Seneca 30 n.3, 43, 188, 208, 211-13, 224
sensation, sense-perception 143-7, 157, 223, 225-6
sense-impression 87-9, 188, 190-3
Servius 24
signs (*and see* divination) 223
skill 141
Socrates iv, 2 n.2, 3, 38, 63, 77, 166, 180, 206
soul, world-soul (*and see* pre-existence) 30 n.3, 31, 107, 129, 135, 205, 229
Speusippus 228
Spinoza 18 n.2
spirits 107
stars *see* heavens

Stephanus 27, 223
Stilpo 63, 166
Stoics (*and see* Chrysippus) 4, 6, 7 n.2, 8-15, 25, 26 n.2, 27, 29-30, 31-2, 57, 67, 81, 145, 159, 161-71, 173, 176, 179, 183-4, 186, 188, 190, 195-6, 198-202, 205-6, 208, 212-13, 215, 223, 225
sun 105, 117, 131, 217-18
swerve, atomic 7-8, 22, 69-73, 91, 172-3, 175-6, 194-5
Symmachus 34, 37
sympathy (natural connection) 4, 9, 20, 22, 59-61, 79, 163

tempering 117
Thebes 61, 165
Theodoric 34-7
Theophrastus 61, 165
Thomas Aquinas *see* Aquinas
Tigris 129, 216
time, timelessness, *see* eternity
Tiresias 135
Troy, Trojans 81, 123, 211
Tyndareus 81

Ulysses (123), 211
uncaused events, uncaused motions 8, 18, 23, 69-75, 127, 175-8, 214
understanding 108, 143, 147, 149, 205, 224, 226-7
universal 143, 147-9, 224

Varro 1 n.6
vice *see* evil
Virgil 206
virtue, virtuous *see* good
void (*and see* emptiness) 91
voluntary *see* will

Wain *see* Bear, the Great
weight 71-5, 91, 175, 177, 194
wicked *see* evil
will, wish (voluntary: *and see* freedom) 61-3, 73-5, 85, 91, 97-9, 129, 131, 139, 157, 175-7
wisdom, wise man 9, 95, 202
world, whether has always existed 47, 151-3, 214, 228
world-soul *see* soul

Xenocrates 228

Zacharias of Mytilene 228
Zeno (of Citium, the Stoic) 61, 165, 188
Zeus *see* Jupiter
Zopyrus 63, 166

9780856684760